RUSSIANS ON TRUMP

PRESS COVERAGE AND COMMENTARY

RUSSIANS ON TRUMP

PRESS COVERAGE AND COMMENTARY

FOREWORD BY MARK GALEOTTI

EDITED BY LAURENCE BOGOSLAW

RUSSIANS ON TRUMP: PRESS COVERAGE AND COMMENTARY

Foreword by Mark Galeotti
Edited by Laurence Bogoslaw

Copyright © 2018 by East View Information Services

All rights reserved. No part of this book may be reproduced or transmitted in any form or by any means, electronic or mechanical, including photocopying, recording, or by any information storage and retrieval system, or conveyed via the Internet or a website without written permission of the publisher, except in the case of brief quotations embedded in critical articles and reviews.

Published by East View Press, an imprint of East View Information Services, Inc.
10601 Wayzata Blvd
Minneapolis, MN 55305 USA
www.eastviewpress.com

Cover and layout designed by Carol A. Dungan

Printed in the United States of America

ISBN: 978-1-879944-89-3

First Edition, 2018
3 5 7 9 10 8 6 4 2

FOREWORD

By Mark Galeotti

As I write this, the first set of indictments against specific Russians has emerged from the deliberations of the investigatory team assembled by former FBI director Robert Mueller into the whole issue of Moscow's interference in the 2016 presidential election. As with so many developments in the convoluted tale, this has to a considerable degree simply become a vessel for the hopes and fears, expectations and suspicions of the reader. Does this demonstrate collusion between Donald Trump's team and the Kremlin, or prove its absence? Is this an explosive development or a damp squib? Is this the start of a process or its end? The truth of the matter is that we do not know, not yet, but the whole debate about Trump himself—genius or imbecile, elitist or everyman, entrepreneur or amateur?—illustrates one of the uncomfortable facts of the modern world. This is that truth is increasingly not something decreed by authority figures, whether newspaper editors, scholars or politicians, but a subjective commodity traded, haggled over and asserted by everyone who wants to get in on the act.

If Americans seem so divided about Trump, should it surprise us that Russians likewise have little sense of who this most protean of presidents might be? When Trump was elected, whether or not with Russian help, the ultra-nationalist court jester of Russian politics, Vladimir Zhirinovsky, was opening champagne in the State Duma. Meanwhile, sober-minded professionals, like the Ministry of Foreign Affairs desk officer who had airily assured me a couple of months earlier that "the American establishment will never let a Trump be elected," were desperately scrambling to try and understand what this meant. On the one hand, he was full of warm words for Putin; on the other, he was impossible to read or predict. For what did he stand, other than Donald Trump? Was he an ally, a clown, or a potential threat? Simply on the basis of seven and a half years spent as a professor at New York University, even I—a Briton, a Russia specialist—found myself being pressed by Russians for my (nonexistent) insights. Meetings at which I had hoped to learn became ad hoc brainstorming sessions at which we all pooled our minimal information and, generally, ended up realizing how little we knew about the man and what his presidency portended.

However, it is not as if Trump was unknown to the Russians. He had visited several times, pushing business, partying hard. He had been, as this book demonstrates, a staple in the media for decades. But information is not understanding, and Moscow was hungry for the latter, and time and again getting wrong-footed by what was happening in his White House.

For example, I was back in Moscow in April 2017, when a Syrian government chemical weapons attack on the town of Khan Sheikhoun triggered a US cruise missile strike on Shayrat Air Base, regarded as its source. That same foreign service officer was downbeat, and nervous. To him, "this is exactly our worst nightmare": a US president who changes his mind literally overnight based on what he sees on TV, who feels no need to telegraph changing policies to allies, let alone adversaries, and who has a relatively low threshold for the use of force. No wonder people in Moscow were grudgingly admitting that they might have done better with a Hillary Clinton presidency.

So what this fascinating and far-ranging collection of articles demonstrates is that this tendency for Trump to be a vessel for the hopes, prejudices and fantasies of his audience predates his presidency and appears to be one of his most abiding characteristics. This may be why he has been so much more effective in building a personal brand, and leveraging it in television, than managing his real estate businesses. So as much as anything else, tracking the changing perceptions of Trump tells us something about how Russia views itself and the United States.

In the 1990s, the "super-rich" Trump, the "celebrated wheeler-dealer," represented the raw capitalism that was reshaping Moscow and, many felt, devouring the rest of Russia. In the midst of the anarchic era of Boris Yeltsin, when fortunes were being made by a microscopic few, at the expense of the rest, there was little real time for Trump, or the rest of the Western entrepreneurs who promised much and delivered little as they picked over the opportunities to be had in Russia.

In the 2000s, though, Trump becomes a more recurring character in the Russian media. Even in 2002, in a process which would become central to today's claims of corruption and collusion, he was promoting his glitzy American apartments to Russia's dirty new rich. More to the point, he was forever promising great things tomorrow, a Trump Tower here, a joint project there. The compulsive storyteller, whose business model was rooted in bright futures and over-the-top rhetoric, was in some ways honing the skills that would eventually get him to the White House. Nonetheless, this was a different Russia, an increasingly stable and self-confident one, where more people had learned to read balance sheets and look behind the brochure. The Russian media, while still often entranced by Trump's infinite self-confidence and glittering promises, were also more searching, more critical. This was Russia in that all-too-brief time between failing state and geopolitical adversary, which was looking West with interest, but not uncritical awe.

By the 2010s, Putin's Russia (let's not pretend it was ever anything but, even during the 2008–12 interregnum of President Dmitry Medvedev) was in a different place. A decade of strong rule and stronger oil and gas prices had reversed the decay of the 1990s, breeding a degree of self-confidence that had also created a more complex relationship with the West. It offered the quality of life to which Russians still aspired, but also a challenge to Putin's new geopolitical assertiveness. By his return to the presidency in 2012–13, Putin not only saw the West as a rival—something which had been brewing since his infamous confrontational Munich speech of 2007—but also as something degenerate, corrupting and self-indulgent.

What, then, to make of Donald Trump, at once an exemplar of those Western vices and yet also the disruptive and populist figure promising to "drain the swamp" in Washington of the old political elite and usher in a new, pragmatic era, in which it would be possible to deal with Russia on a pragmatic basis? The way the Russian perception of Trump spun in multiple directions, sometimes at the same time, also says much about the state of the media. This is not a totalitarian country in which the media all speak with a single voice, but nor is it wholly free. Television, the great engine of modern socialisation, is very much under the Kremlin's direct and indirect control. Dmitry Kiselyov, head of the massive Rossia segodnya news agency and deputy director of state TV holding company VGTRK, may only have a single quote in this book, but his voice echoes through much of the official coverage. Trump is first a symptom of US decline and division; then an outsider speaking for disenfranchised masses; then a potential ally in the Oval Office, stymied by a conspiratorial American "deep state"; and finally a disappointment, even if one whose failings open up opportunities for Moscow.

However, just as, in the Russian saying, "the Kremlin has many cupolas," so too even media close to the state express a variety of views of Trump, and this is doubly so for all those outlets which remain much more free. The Russian print and online media are still refreshingly pluralistic, and here one can find every kind of take. Trump is at once a weakling and a fool, and a titan seeking to break the shackles of Congress and bureaucracy; he is a masterful communicator, and an inarticulate dullard. In other words, even as we seem to slip deeper into Cold War 2.0, it is worth noting that in this respect, this inability to quite grasp and agree on what Donald Trump really is, there seems far more that unites Russians and Westerners than divides us.

Prague, February 2018

Prof. Mark Galeotti is a senior researcher at the Institute of International Relations Prague.

EDITOR'S PREFACE

Russians on Trump: Press Coverage and Commentary

By Laurence Bogoslaw

More than two years since the 45th US presidential race began, and well over a year since the election itself, the name "Trump" still explodes like a firecracker in the American public space—again and again. Every day, our nation's news media print and play the president's sound bites. His tweets are viewed and reposted thousands of times. His decisions move people to build public movements and break private friendships. His remarks spark heated diatribes and debates in every imaginable forum, from articles and essays to blogs and social media, from boardrooms to living rooms. Of all the words that come to mind when Americans think of Donald Trump, one of the most frequent these days is "Russia." The two concepts have become as inextricably linked as Nixon and China, or Bush and Iraq.

This increasing focus on Russia in connection with Trump prompted the compilation of this book. As you read this preface, you may be wondering whether Trump has generated as intense a buzz in Russia as in the US. The short answer is: Yes, but for different reasons. Many details about Trump and his associates that have galvanized American public opinion are virtually ignored in the Russian press: the "alternative facts" presented at the 2016 pre-election debates; Trump's refusal to disclose his tax information; mounting evidence of sexual misconduct, including harassment, against Trump and other Republican officials; nationwide rallies around the January 2017 inauguration; and continual domestic protests since then over Trump's presidential decisions, such as the ban on travelers from several predominantly Muslim countries, the Mexican border wall, and the immigration policy on "dreamers."

What does concern and fascinate Russian journalists, analysts and public officials is Trump as an actor on the geopolitical stage. At first, they found him merely entertaining as a celebrity, but once his presidential campaign gained traction, they began seriously considering the possibility of political friendship between the two countries, as well as personal friendship between Trump and Russian President Vladimir Putin. Arguably, Russian experts started contemplating Trump as presidential material even earlier than their American counterparts. On the other hand, since the election there has been a great deal of controversy over whether Trump is good for Russia or not. This is reflected not only in the range of emotional reactions to the billionaire's surprise victory (ranging from euphoria to despair), but also in analyses of the implications of Trump's foreign policy: Will his promises to reduce NATO funding strengthen or weaken Russia's security? Will his assertiveness in the Middle East help Russia and its allies defeat ISIS, or will it threaten Moscow's economic interests? Will his saber-rattling against North Korea hasten nuclear disaster or open up an opportunity for Russia to play peacemaker?

One area where you might expect the Russian media to be tight-lipped is the issue of Moscow's interference in the US election. After all, months of investigations by the FBI and the Justice Department have identified Russians (individual ones) as agents of influence in Trump's campaign—allegations that are bound to make officials in the Putin government resentful and defensive. However, reactions in the Russian media are more nuanced than that. Although Russian officials have repeatedly denied (in some cases, even ridiculed) the idea that efforts by their country could have made any difference in the outcome of the US election, they have not denied that certain media companies and individuals attempted to influence American public opinion—at the very least, by exploiting existing divisions (class, wealth, race, etc.) to sow discord and confusion. Moreover, experts acknowledge openly that the state itself engages in cyber espionage as standard practice, including hacking and wiretapping. As Vladimir Frolov explains matter-of-factly in an October 2016 article: "Cyber operations to collect intelligence are normal spycraft.... You get intelligence by eavesdropping on people with access to real secrets." What seems to dismay Russian officials and experts the most is that the hype about "Russian meddling" in the American media is further damaging relations between Washington and Moscow.

As Mark Galeotti writes in the Foreword to this book, the Russian media are more pluralistic than most Westerners think. Yes, the outlets with the broadest audiences are either owned by or sympathetic to the state, but there is room for dissent—and you will find plenty of it in this collection, alongside official statements and interviews. Another way in which most Russian journalists uphold their independence is by quoting Trump directly, without relying on official Moscow news channels. Pavel Palazhchenko, a professor of linguistics who served as Mikhail Gorbachev's personal interpreter, has shown that sources like Tass and Interfax "embellish" Trump's tweets and sound bites when rendering them in Russian, eliminating repetitious phrasing and upgrading lowbrow words like "dumb." However, the publications included here translate Trump into Russian completely and accurately, by and large. For this reason, my colleagues and I have chosen not to back-translate the Russian versions into English, but to quote the original wording whenever possible. In the rare cases where a mistranslation or significant omission occurred, we have provided explanatory notes.

While matching the tone of the "Russian Trump" to the "American Trump" presented some challenges, choosing material for this book was definitely a greater challenge. This controversial political figure has generated so much coverage in the Russian press, especially since 2016, that we could easily have published a collection twice this size. This book seeks to do justice to the many viewpoints Russian sources present on a broad range of topics without inordinate repetition of argumentation or narratives of events. The parts are laid out in roughly chronological order: After a short prologue that runs through the precampaign years (highlighting the themes of business, buildings and beauty pageants), the major parts of the book cover the primaries and the run-up to the election; the election itself and Russian reactions to Trump's victory; and the first months of Trump's actual presidency.

The theme of "Russian meddling" posed a problem in that important events (such as Russia-based media posts, as well as meetings between the Trump team and powerful Russian individuals) took place before the election, whereas many crucial details about them did not come to light until afterward. We decided that the most logical place to present this material was in Part Three, just after the election, since it reflects on the Trump team's campaign strategy and discusses contacts among key figures like Paul Manafort, Jared Kushner, Michael Flynn and Sergei Kislyak that took place both before and after Trump's victory. Part Four does not follow strict chronological order, either, but is divided into thematic areas of Trump's foreign policy. To counteract any cognitive dissonance that these editorial decisions may cause, we have included a timeline of key events as an appendix.

This book does not purport to be an antidote to the "fake news" and "trolling" of which Americans seem to have become so painfully, and suddenly, aware. The articles, analyses, opinions and interviews collected here are not necessarily any more "real" than those presented in the US media. However, this content offers perspectives that most American media do not: the personal image that Trump projects in Russia, the inferences that Russian analysts make from his statements, and the unforeseen reverberations of his policies.

ACKNOWLEDGMENTS

Most books are team efforts, and this book is no exception.

We wish to thank the following Russian publications for granting their express permission to have material translated and/or republished for this collection:

- Ekspert
- Gazeta.ru
- Itar-Tass Daily
- International Affairs (Mezhdunarodnaya zhizn)
- Izvestia
- Kommersant
- Meduza
- The Moscow Times
- Nezavisimaya gazeta
- Novaya gazeta
- RBC Daily
- Rossiiskaya gazeta
- Russia in Global Affairs
- Republic.ru (formerly Slon.ru)
- Sovetskaya Rossia
- Strategic Culture Foundation Online Journal
- Vedomosti
- Zavtra

We also wish to thank Natalia Smirnova for contacting the above sources to secure publication rights.

All articles in this collection are translated from Russian, except those originally published in *Itar-Tass Daily*, *The Moscow Times* and *Strategic Culture Foundation Online Journal*, which appeared in English. In the latter cases, some phrasing has been edited for stylistic purposes. Most of the above material was previously published in East View Press's weekly periodical *The Current Digest of the Russian Press*, but a number of articles have been selected and translated exclusively for this collection. Some of these (both new material and reprints) have been condensed for brevity. Text omitted by East View Press editorial staff is designated with an ellipsis (…). In other cases, the staff of the original publication chose to condense certain text (for example, a quotation from a public speech); such omissions are indicated by asterisks (* * *).

Some additional information that may be helpful to the general English-speaking audience can be found in annotations within the articles. All such additions are indicated in brackets, and some longer annotations are attributed to *Trans*. Supplemental information provided by the editors of the original publication is included in parentheses with the attribution *Ed*. More detailed and extensive clarifications, as well as other background information, are provided in endnotes following the main text.

For supplying the above editorial material, as well as doing internal proofreading, we thank Laurence Bogoslaw, Matthew Larson and Xenia Grushetsky. We'd also like to thank Carol Dungan for her inspired work on the cover design and layout, and Ana K. Niedermaier for doing comprehensive proofreading.

Finally, we'd like to thank Mark Galeotti for writing the Foreword and Laurence Bogoslaw for his great work in putting together this book. We hope that *Russians on Trump* serves as a relevant and timely addition to the growing body of writings on our 45th president.

James Cahoy

Director, East View Press

TABLE OF CONTENTS

Foreword... i
Editor's Preface.. v
Acknowledgments ix

PROLOGUE: Business, Buildings and Beauty 1
    One Visit, Then Another: General Lebed
    Tries to Make His Way into Kremlin Through the US 2
    Patrick Buchanan: Scandalous Strategist 4
    Trump Brings NY to Moscow.................................... 5
    Billionaire Donald Trump on Brink of Bankruptcy Again 7
    Marketing Florida Condos to Moscow's Elite 9
    Donald Trump to Sell His Name 11
    Georgia Getting Its Own Trump Tower 13
    Universe of Billionaires...................................... 14
    Crocus Group Owner Aras Agalarov: A Beauty Pageant
    Is More Profitable Than State Construction Projects 15
    Donald Trump Plans to Build Office Center in Russia
    Similar to NY Trump Tower 17
    Donald Trump in New Emin Video 18

PART ONE: The Trump Campaign (2015–2016) 21

1.1 Chemistry and Spin: Putin, Trump and Other US Candidates ... 23
    US Presidential Hopeful Trump Says He and Putin
    Would Be Pals 24
    What President Trump Would Mean for Russia 25
    Trump Slams Obama, Gives Putin an 'A' for Leadership 27
    Odd Checks, Asymmetrical Balances 28
    Losing the Trump Card 31

From Hillary to Trump: What the Kremlin Can Expect
From the Candidates 33
Who's Afraid of Donald Trump? 36
(Editorial)—Antidemocracy 38
White House and Television: Who Invented Donald Trump? 40
Exceptional Case 43
Through the Looking Glass 46
Trump as a Mirror 48
Hillary or Donald, It's All Nuts 51

1.2 **Forecasts and Analyses** 55
Is Mr. Trump the Next US President? 56
Breaking Democracy's Morals: The Trump Phenomenon
Makes US Politics Look More Like Those of Europe 59
The America Watchers 62
Russia-US Relations After the Election: 'We Will Be
Ready for a New Start' 66
US Gives Another Reason to Believe Its Democracy
Is Deeply Flawed 71
Good-Bye Familiar America? US Foreign Policy:
A Forecast Until 2024 74

PART TWO: 'Black Swan': Responses to Trump's Victory 81

2.1 **How Did This Happen?** 83
Trump Card: A Donald Trump Fan Club Watched
the Unthinkable Unfold in Moscow 85
Hey Trump, Come on Over! 87
Actor's Triumph: What to Expect From the US President-Elect 89
Four Years for White Men 94
Transatlantic Backlash 97
The US Has Sneezed and Now Russia Will Catch a Cold 100
In Search of a Russian Trump 102
Sergei Glazyev: 'Trump Needs Help!' 104

2.2 **What Next? Forecasts of a New World Order** 107
    The Shape of Things to Come 109
    Will Donald Trump Abolish NATO? 114
    Two Faces of American Capitalism 117
    Will Trump Tear Up the Nuclear Deal With Iran? 122
    How Will Russia Respond to Trump? 124
    What Will the Middle East Look Like Under
    Putin and Trump? 128
    Europe Turns Toward Russia in Major
    Foreign Policy Change 132
    What Are the Implications of Israeli-US Conflict
    Over UN Resolution? 134
    Battle of Ideas in Washington 137
    'There's No Reset Button. We're Either Going to
    Get Along or We're Not' 139

PART THREE: **The Story of Trump's 'Russia Ties'** 143

3.1 **Contacts With Russia and Ukraine** 145
    Trump Changes Horses 147
    Republican Party of Regions 149
    Why Donald Trump Is Not a Putin Agent 154
    The Crimea for Lease: A Russian Trail in Settlement
    Plans for Ukraine 160
    Russian Lawyer Tells State TV She Met Trump Jr. to
    Ask for 'Help' 163
    Kremlin Not Surprised by Media Reports on
    Eavesdropping on Russian Ambassador to US 165
    Senator Blasts Resignation of Trump's National Security
    Adviser Over Russia Contacts 166
    Rendezvous Without Hope for a Reset 167
    Dancing With Washington 168
    Russian Ambassador Kislyak on Meeting With Trump
    Adviser Flynn: 'There Were No Secrets' 170

3.2 Spying on the Competition: The Hacking Scandal 173
Spying on Uncle Sam 175
One Hack Too Far 178
Attacks From Moscow: Did the US Believe
in Russian Hackers? 181
America Comes Out on Different Sides of Russia 185
Five-Fake Report 189
Watergate for Trump 192
A World Without Illusions, Myths 195
'Dangerous but Predictable': How Russia Spooked the
World With Hackers and Prostitutes 198

PART FOUR: President Trump: The First 200 Days of Foreign Policy 203

4.1 'Paying Their Fair Share': Europe and NATO 205
Munich: Cold Talk 206
Seducing Europe 209
Munich Shows Western Elite's Total Discombobulation 213
NATO: Trump's Burden 215
The Foundation of the West Is Shaken, Its Future Uncertain ... 224
The Whole Earth Minus the US: The Consequences
of America Exiting the Climate Agreement 227
How Trump Is Stealing Eastern Europe Right From
Under Russia's Nose 230
The World Comes to Those Who Wait 233
Macron Displaces Merkel 235

4.2 Let's Crush ISIS Together: Terrorism and the Middle East ... 237
Moscow Proposes Trump Take a Different View of Iran 239
Will Tomorrow Come? 241
Trump to Halt Plan to Fight Islamic State With Russia 243
US Strikes Syria: Trump Is a President Who
No Longer Calls the Shots 245
Uncle Donald's Show 247
We Have Contact 254

     President Trump Pushes for 'Arab NATO'
     in the Middle East 256
     Trump Appears in the East 260
     Top Salesman 263
     Trial Agreement 264

4.3 Loose Cannons: Nuclear Policy and North Korea 267
     Second Nuclear Century? 269
     Donald Trump's Nuclear Policy: First Outlines 272
     We Need an Iran Deal With North Korea 277
     False Calm: Why Russia Prefers Not to Notice the
     Nuclear Crisis at Its Borders 280
     Short Victorious War: US President's Magic Wand to
     Wave in a Pinch 283
     Mutually Assured Distraction 286
     Nuclear Deterrence: An Eternal Guarantee 288
     North Korea Nuclear Crisis: Why Russia's Attempt to
     Get Involved in the Big Game Is a Bad Idea 293

4.4 Can We Be Friends? Russian-American Relations 297
     Trumponomics 299
     No Golden Opportunity 302
     Russian Matryoshka: How Many Demands for Trump
     Can Hide Inside Putin? 305
     Sergei Lavrov: 'We Are Willing to Work With the
     Donald Trump Administration on the Entire Agenda' 308
     Honeymoon 310
     Kremlin and White House Intent on Eliminating
     Negative Balance 312
     'They Tricked Us': White House Didn't Expect
     TASS Photographer to Cover Trump-Lavrov Meeting 314
     Lavrov Briefed Putin on His Meeting With Trump 316
     Opponents Shake Hands: Results of the First Meeting
     Between Putin and Trump 317
     Worse Than Under Obama: Why New US Sanctions
     Have Caused Panic in Moscow 320
     Statement From the Russian Foreign Ministry 322

How Putin Expelled Diplomats and Hinted at
Cooperation With the US 324
After Sanctions, There's No Way Back 328
Sanctions 330
'Trump Is His Own Person' 333

EPILOGUE: Where Things Stand in
Russian-American Relations 337
A Generation Raised on Meddling 339
How the New Cold War Is Getting Out of Control 342
Head in the Sand 345
The 'Russian Trail' Saga: How Trump's Hopes
Were Lifted and Then Dashed Again 351
Cold Peace and Hybrid War: How Russia Will
Respond to New Sanctions 354
Why Trump, Putin Only Chatted on the Sidelines 357

Timeline of Relevant Events During Trump's
Candidacy and Presidency 361
Endnotes 369
Subject Index 379
Publication and Author Index 401

RUSSIANS ON TRUMP
PRESS COVERAGE AND COMMENTARY

PROLOGUE
Business, Buildings and Beauty

Introduction

Before Donald Trump announced his presidential candidacy in 2015, the Russian press paid him only sporadic attention. In the political arena, he was first mentioned as a potentially promising contact for Russian presidential hopeful Gen. Aleksandr Lebed in 1997. Two years later, his brief rivalry with Pat Buchanan (who, coincidentally, was called an "American Lebed" by the newspaper *Sevodnya*), garnered some colorful coverage as the two vied for the presidential nomination from Ross Perot's Reform Party.

Articles from the 2000s chiefly cover Trump's various business negotiations with Russian companies and individuals. Commentators report on deals such as trademarking the Trump brand for vodka and perfume, selling US luxury real estate to rich Russians, and a groundbreaking ceremony for a Trump Tower in Georgia. (The latter has never been built; recent research[1] published in *The New Yorker* suggests that the project was meant only to bolster the flagging image of then-Georgian president Mikhail Saakashvili.)

Trump's Russian connections become more personal in 2013, when fellow developer Aras Agalarov makes contact with him through son Emin Agalarov, an aspiring music star. The immediate outcomes of these contacts may not seem relevant to Trump's later career in politics, since they are decidedly in the realm of pop culture: Trump, as owner of the rights to the Miss Universe pageant, gives the green light for the international competition to be held in Moscow for the first time (at Aras Agalarov's Crocus City Hall auditorium); and shortly after the event, the American billionaire appears in one of Emin's music videos.

However, the Agalarovs become highly relevant to Trump the politician a few years later: Through their prior acquaintance with the Trump family, they arrange a meeting in New York between Donald Trump, Jr., Jared Kushner and Russian attorney Natalya Veselnitskaya. This June 2016 meeting, ostensibly for the purpose of providing the Trump campaign team with compromising material on rival Hillary Clinton, would later become the focus of far-reaching investigations by the US Congress and Justice Department into Trump's collusion with Russia (see Section 3.1, below).

One Visit, Then Another: General Lebed Tries to Make His Way into Kremlin Through the US

By staff correspondent Vladimir Nadein. *Izvestia*, Jan. 25, 1997, p. 3.

Washington—Lebed went to America all but uninvited, but the trip was successful, building on the success of his visit one month earlier.

After quiet, heart-to-heart talks in Wilmington [Delaware, where he met with Dupont executives, Chamber of Commerce members and politicians—*Trans.*] and a meeting with New York's super-rich Donald Trump, something very much resembling mutual liking emerged between the general who recently emerged from Russia's provincial barracks and the polished American business world....

Lebed wants the Kremlin. He will not settle for less. He said so in America, to anyone and everyone. He charmed some and angered others, but he said so nonetheless.

The brief interlude between the two visits to the US showed how easy it is for Lebed to give up his prejudices. In contrast to other, more experienced colleagues, it did not take much at all for him to grasp the simple truth that he who turns the West against himself has no chance of becoming president of a democratic, market-oriented Russia.

From all indications, an analysis of his first trip convinced Lebed of the need for new efforts. On his earlier visit, he was unable to completely destroy his established image. Politicians and investors in the US were scared off by his attacks on democracy and his crude populist antics. Therefore, he repeated his favorite saying: Russia has completely exhausted its capacity for violence for a century to come.

Lebed took into account the mistakes he had made on his previous trip, when he portrayed himself as the country's only politician with a serious future....

This time, G[rigory] Yavlinsky and S[vyatoslav] Fyodorov were favored with flattering remarks describing them as politicians who not only were suitable for an alliance but also were ready to forge one.

The meeting with billionaire Trump was the crowning event of the New York leg of the visit. "He invited me to Russia. I accepted the invitation," Trump said. The celebrated wheeler-dealer, who has taken the risk of investing enormous sums of money in the construction of very costly skyscrapers in various parts of America, gave the general a crystal apple. (Here, that's a symbol of New York, not of Yavlinsky [Yabloko, the name of Yavlinsky's party, is the Russian word for "apple"—*Trans.*].) In addition, Trump promised to build "something very substantial" in Moscow: a high-rise hotel or a luxury apartment building.

Build whatever you like, with one exception, Lebed replied. "The highest skyscraper in the world cannot be built next to the Kremlin. We cannot allow anyone to spit on our Kremlin from a skyscraper roof." ...

The Lebeds have left New York and flown home, but the trip was undoubtedly not their last visit to America: In the eyes of Americans, it is still hard to put Aleksandr Lebed on the same level as Yeltsin. And understandably so. Take, for example, his remarks on freedom of the press, which he said should not extend to the publication of personal attacks on a country's leaders. This opinion immediately draws a great many questions from any American: First of all, where do you draw the line between attacks and criticism? ...

"I widened my circle of friends," Lebed said, summing up his trip. But two centuries of democracy have taught Americans that, no matter how amusing caustic language might be, the ability to find a common language is more important....

Patrick Buchanan: Scandalous Strategist

By Vladislav Dunayev, US correspondent for *RIA Novosti*. *Nezavisimaya gazeta*, Oct. 26, 1999, www.ng.ru/world/1999-10-26/bewkenen.html.

Patrick (Pat) Buchanan—political commentator, columnist for some of the largest US media corporations, creator of popular TV programs for CNN and NBC, [former] senior political adviser to presidents Nixon, Ford and Reagan, as well as White House communications director [under Reagan]... —announced on Monday [Oct. 25] that he was leaving the Republican Party and switching to billionaire Ross Perot's Reform Party. He is doing so in order to become that party's nominee for president and to win [the 2000 election].

This is undoubtedly the most significant and controversial event of the whole election campaign so far. First, it may well lead to the emergence of a three-party system for the first time in US history. Second, in terms of the tonnage of mud slung at [campaign] rivals, the US may be a match for Russia this time around. There's a brawl ahead for the Reform Party nomination. Another prominent Republican—billionaire Donald Trump, known to Russians as a character from the movie "Pretty Woman"—also announced yesterday that he was leaving [the Republicans] for Perot's party. But this candidate can't stand Buchanan and has already branded him a "Hitler lover." Meanwhile, one of Trump's ex-wives has promised to tell things about him that America has never heard. Obviously, there's more at the root of all this than the contentiousness of many of Buchanan's opinions: The US is also seeing the unprecedented escalation of a battle of ideas, not just candidates....

[Before Buchanan switched parties,] Gov. Jesse Ventura of Minnesota stated that Buchanan's views went against the platform of the third party (i.e., the Reform Party, created by Perot in 1992), so nominating him as a candidate of that party would be out of the question if he decided to leave the ranks of the Republicans. Apparently, given Buchanan's tacit support from the authoritative Perot, Ventura decided to "bring out the heavy artillery" by rushing to nominate a new candidate from the Reform Party: the rather odious figure of Donald Trump....

Trump Brings NY to Moscow

By Simon Ostrovsky, staff writer. *The Moscow Times,* Sept. 26, 2002, p. 5, https://dlib.eastview.com/browse/doc/4377915

Famed developer Donald Trump wants life to be a bit easier for well-heeled Russians by selling his New York real estate in Moscow, making it simpler to buy one of his luxury Manhattan apartments without even leaving the country.

Trump's real estate agent Sotheby's International Realty, together with Russian partner Kirsanova Realty, held a reception Tuesday night at Moscow's Baltshug Kempinski Hotel in a quest to bring their business to Russians, who are increasingly shopping abroad.

On offer were three elite New York projects: Trump World Tower at United Nations Plaza, Trump Palace on Riverside Boulevard, and the AOL Time Warner building on Columbus Circle. Buying into the Trump empire doesn't come cheap—apartments range in price from just under $1 million to $30 million, with property taxes correspondingly stratospheric, climbing as high as $15,000 per month. But with steep prices come world class perks: Hollywood stars as neighbors, hotel service at home, valet parking and nice views.

It was only recently that Sotheby's took notice of the growing number of Russians snapping up real estate in the US. "I proposed to find a partner to work with our Russian clients one year ago," said Mika Sakamoto, SIR senior vice-president.

Company president Stuart Siegel said Sotheby's came to Russia to test the market and get exposure. "We've found there is a very well-defined buying public of Russians interested in US property," he said, adding that the presentation in Moscow was also a way of getting to know clients they have worked with indirectly in the past.

When asked about the prospect of acquiring property through Sotheby's and Kirsanova Realty, guests at Tuesday's reception shied away from saying directly whether they were interested in the super expensive apartments. One guest said most were there to see "how the other half lives."

"I'm not in New York enough to buy an apartment there," said Natalia Sergeyeva, a bank employee. "But it's interesting to see what's on offer there so that there is something to compare housing here with."

In the past decade, Russians have gained a reputation for buying up prime property in Europe, mainly on France's Côte d'Azur, southern Spain and Cyprus, according to Natalia Krol, a real estate expert with Mir i Dom [World and Home] magazine. Now American realtors are seeing more Russians on the US market.

How much capital actually escapes Russia for real estate purchases is impossible to calculate, as neither Russian nor Western real estate companies keep those kinds of statistics. Foreign embassies in Moscow said they also had no access to that information.

"People are reluctant to show how much they spend," said a source in the real estate business.

However much it is, though, Sotheby's partner Kirsanova Realty is keen to get a slice of the action.

"Lots of Russians are buying up property in the States, why shouldn't I get a piece of that?" said Filipp Bogdanov, a manager at Kirsanova. "Sotheby's approached us to be their affiliate in Russia. They looked around and saw that we were the best."

Kirsanova Realty will get a "small percentage" from every sale made through their office, Bogdanov said.

Billionaire Donald Trump on Brink of Bankruptcy Again

By Lev Sinebryukhov. *Izvestia*, Jan. 28, 2005, p. 15.

Next week, a US court may put the casino network of one of America's most controversial billionaires, Donald Trump, on the auction block. Trump's first major bankruptcy almost sank him 14 years ago, when he frittered away $10 billion he had borrowed from banks. But then he managed to borrow even more, and saved his business. Trump now owns skyscrapers in New York and a fleet of casinos, as well as the Miss America [*sic*; Miss USA—*Trans.*] and Miss Universe contests. A great admirer of beautiful women, as well as a failed presidential candidate, he became the author of the bestseller "How to Get Rich."

Skyscraper of blocks.

His reality show, "The Apprentice," was the [biggest new] hit on American TV last week. Contestants vied for a $250,000-a-year management position in one of Donald Trump's companies. The show was hosted by the billionaire himself. Contestants took turns running various companies owned by the tycoon [*sic*; Trump would assign two teams various tasks each week—*Trans.*]. The [participant] who did the worst job would be eliminated from the game with Trump shouting: "You're fired!" ...

The future billionaire was born June 14, 1946, to Fred and Mary Trump. Donald's dad was remarkable. The son of poor Swedish [*sic*; German] immigrants who lost his alcoholic father at age 11, he managed to amass a $20 million fortune by constructing low-cost housing in New York.

Little Donald took after his father. When he was eight, he took a box of toy building blocks from his brother Robert and glued them into a "skyscraper" as tall as himself. The glue turned out to be so good that no one could dismantle the building....

Trump buildings.

In the early days after his university studies, Trump tried to get a position in an oil company, but the prospect of a long-term career did not inspire him. He decided to go back to his father and work on real estate development in New York. "There are many ways to make a career, but the surest one is to be born into the right family," Trump explained to his acquaintances....

In 1974, using seed capital from his father, Trump made his first independent deal. From the bankrupt Penny [sic; Penn] Central Railroad company, he bought the Commodore hotel, which had been built in the early 20th century and was by then quite dilapidated. Trump managed to persuade city officials to give him a 40-year property tax abatement, talked banks into lending him $70 million, and the Hyatt Corporation let him use its brand. And soon, on the site of the decrepit Commodore, the luxurious Grand Hyatt appeared.

Since the very beginning, Trump has been incredibly lucky. He began buying up land in Atlantic City, New Jersey in 1976, a few years before gambling was legalized there. By 1982, that land was worth more than $20 million.

But what really made him the biggest developer in New York was the construction of the Trump Tower....

Hypnotizing bankers.

...A lawyer who used to work with Trump once said: "Donald could walk into any bank and say: 'I need $25 million'—and no one would think of asking him for a financial report. They'd say: 'Donald Trump—$25 million. Here you go!' " But in the middle of 1990, everything collapsed. Donald Trump's company was unable to service its debts.... Bankers were horrified at the realization that their balance sheets were about to show a $9.8 billion loss. Trump tried to persuade them that everything would work out if they would just lend him a little more. And the banks relented. Trump's biggest creditors agreed not to take him to court and restructured his debts....

In November 2004, his casinos again went into bankruptcy proceedings. And this time, it looks like they will go up for auction. Nowadays, selling his name is becoming Trump's only truly big business. And most of his efforts are aimed at boosting his own recognition. For example, in 2000, he talked seriously about running for US president on the Reform Party ticket. In response, The New York Post published a cartoon in which a caricatured Donald Trump cheerfully says: "If I'm elected president, I promise the country that every year there will be a new first lady, and it will always be Miss USA!" Now he is producing his own Donald Trump cologne (with the "smell of luxury") and the Trump Signature menswear collection for aspiring businessmen. And last summer, he said he would fire US President George [W.] Bush for the war in Iraq....

Marketing Florida Condos to Moscow's Elite

By Anatoly Medetsky. *The Moscow Times*, April 22, 2008, p. 8, https://dlib.eastview.com/browse/doc/14209835.

At Bon, a hedonistic-themed Moscow restaurant created by legendary designer Phillipe Starck, an audience of well-heeled Russians dined in semidarkness amid fairy lights and ornamental hammer and sickles, crowns and hearts.

They were gathered to listen to a sales pitch for luxury condos in Miami, Florida, including three high-rise towers designed by Starck and a nearby beachfront tower called Trump Hollywood, named for billionaire coinvestor Donald Trump.

The most prominent of the prospective buyers, Federation Council Senator Valentin Zavadnikov, told fellow diners of his love for yachting off the Florida coast, where he skippers a Russian yacht in international races.

"I bought an apartment in Miami in 1992, but sold it in 1997," Zavadnikov said in a quick testimonial-style speech at the dinner last week. "I thought I would never go to America anymore. But now I go there every January, March and May."

Zavadnikov, a former Unified Energy System deputy chief executive who represents Saratov Province, is just one of the growing number of rich Russians spending time in Miami, now the most popular area in the US for Russian real estate investors, after New York.

The organizer of the dinner evening, US luxury construction firm The Related Group, brought together Zavadnikov, his well-heeled yachting team members, affluent golf players and international real estate brokers for a preview of properties in South Florida.

"People buy apartments there to send their families for the winter or to stay while they go yachting several times a year," Isabel Levin, an international sales broker for the company, said on the sidelines of the dinner. "A lot of them take out mortgages."

One of the projects touted by The Related Group is a downtown Miami compound of three 57-floor towers designed by Starck. Called IconBrickell, it will feature 90 replicas of Easter Island statues in the lobby and a 120-meter swimming pool once it is completed.

In the other—more expensive—project, the firm joined forces with Trump. Also under construction, the 42-story Trump Hollywood tower in the Hollywood Beach area of Miami enjoys a view of the Atlantic Ocean.

Prices range from $400,000 for an 80-square-meter studio at IconBrickell to $4 million for a 450-sq.m. three-bedroom apartment at Trump Hollywood.

Traditionally, South Florida attractions include beaches, casinos, golfing, posh shopping and dining, but the developers made sure they pointed out Trump Hollywood's proximity to an area of Miami known as "Little Russia."

A 2006 US census recorded 125,000 people with Russian ancestry living in three South Florida counties, a 19% jump since the previous survey in 2000....

Donald Trump to Sell His Name

By Khalil Aminov, Anna Ryabova, Olga Sichkar and Yevgeny Khvostik.
Kommersant, June 4, 2008, https://www.kommersant.ru/doc/899538.

The Trump Organization is considering the option of constructing luxury housing and hotels in Moscow, St. Petersburg and Sochi, reported the billionaire's son, Donald Trump Jr., yesterday at the "Real Estate in Russia" summit. In August 2007, with this aim in mind, the corporation registered the Trump trademark in Russia for services related to residential, commercial and hotel real estate.

Donald Trump, Jr., did not mention the amount of investment in the new market, but specified that before starting its own projects, the Trump Organization plans to sell the franchise to several Russian high-rise owner/developers, enabling them to build skyscrapers under the Trump Tower brand. While the US real estate market has been stagnant, the Russian market has seen a nearly 50% increase in the price per square meter, explained the billionaire's son, calling that discovery an eye-opener.

The Trump Corporation (TC) owns 1.6 million sq.m. of real estate in one of the most expensive areas of New York: Manhattan. They include the International Hotel & Tower, the Trump Tower, the Trump World Tower and 40 Wall Street. The primary owner is Donald Trump, whose worth is estimated by Forbes at $2.9 billion. TC [also] owns the Trump Taj Mahal casino, Trump Plaza, Trump Marina and 28% of Trump Entertainment Resorts. Trump co-owns (with the NBC corporation) the Miss USA, Miss Teen USA and Miss Universe beauty contests. Sales revenues [for TC] in 2007 totaled $10.7 billion.

Donald Trump made an attempt to access the Russian market four years ago. At that time, the billionaire's representatives negotiated with the Moscow authorities about the Trump Organization possibly taking part in the renovation of the Moskva and Rossia hotels. In May 2008, Lev Levayev, co-owner of AFI Development, paid the billionaire a visit. The meeting was of a private nature, AFI representative Natalya Ivanova told *Kommersant*: No agreements on joint projects in Russia have been reached yet.

Kommersant has so far managed to find one other developer who was interested in the Trump brand. In 2004, MosCityGroup co-owner Pavel Fuks wanted to acquire a Donald Trump franchise for one of his own projects. "I had the idea to use the name Trump Tower for one of the high-rises under construction for the Moscow City project (the Imperia Tower—*Ed.*), but we did not come to a mutually beneficial agreement," Mr. Fuks said, declining to name the franchise amount in question. According to another Moscow developer, the price for the Donald Trump brand varies from 20% to 25% of the project cost. The amount of investment in the Imperia Tower is estimated at $1.2 billion, so it seems Mr. Fuks would have had to pay Trump more than $200 million for the franchise.

In the US, projects under the Trump brand have a 20% to 30% markup.... "In Russia, this brand would not necessarily get the same response," comments Maksim Temnikov, a board member of the Mirax Group. Aleksei Belousov, commercial director of the Capital Group, agrees: "For Russian companies, the value of this name is not obvious: Even the quality standards developed by Donald Trump would have to be brought in line with Russian state construction standards."...

There is already one Trump brand product on the Russian consumer market: Since late 2007, the US [company] Drinks Americas Holdings has been selling Trump premium vodka in Russia for $40–$50. Granted, [local] market players say it has not had much success yet....

Georgia Getting Its Own Trump Tower

[No author indicated.] *The Moscow Times*, April 24, 2012, p. 7.

Tbilisi, Georgia—American property mogul Donald Trump flew into the former Soviet republic of Georgia on Saturday [April 21] to expand his global real estate empire, lending his name to a glitzy tower on the Black Sea coast there.

Unveiling a $250 million residential high-rise planned for the Georgian coastal resort town of Batumi, Trump said the Caucasus mountain nation had become a prime destination for foreign investment.

"I think you have a lot of investment opportunities in Georgia. It's amazing what's going on. It's one of the really amazing places in the world right now," Trump said. "You have a lot of opportunities beyond real estate in Georgia [too]," he added.

The five-star, 47-story residential building, called Trump Tower Batumi, is the first project to which the developer has lent his name in the former Soviet Union.

Often outspoken and always flamboyant, Trump, 65, has branched out from his core property developing business in recent years to become a celebrity in the US, in part thanks to his role in NBC's reality show "The Apprentice."

Georgia's economy was crippled by a five-day war with Russia in August 2008 and the global crisis that followed, which crimped foreign investment, forcing the former Soviet republic to rely on international aid.

Its recovery started in 2010, however, when foreign direct investment rose from $658.4 million in 2009 to $814.5 million. In 2011, FDI rose 20% year on year to $981 million.

"As Georgia becomes a player in the global economy, what's extremely important for Georgia is to have a brand like Trump coming to Georgia and showing the world that like Western development, Georgia is coming to the market as well," said Michael Cohen, the Trump Organization's executive vice-president.

Trump's partner and developer in the project, Georgia's Silk Road Group, one of the largest private investment companies in the South Caucasus, believes that it won't face problems in raising funds for the Trump Tower project.

"I know for sure that Trump's participation will be the key to the success of this project. It will cause interest among regional investors, as well as potential buyers of apartments in Trump Tower," said Georgy Ramishvili, chairman of the Silk Road Group.

"Trump is one of the most significant individuals in international business. Construction of the Trump Tower in Batumi will promote economic development not only in Adzharia, but in Georgia in general," Georgian Economy and Sustainable Development Minister Vera Kobalia said, Interfax reported. Trump Tower Batumi was designed by the New York firm John Fotiadis Architects.

Universe of Billionaires

By Aleksei Rozhkov. *Vedomosti*, June 18, 2013,
https://dlib.eastview.com/browse/doc/33923051.

Aras Agalarov will hold the Miss Universe contest in Russia— a show watched live by over 1 billion people. He will get some help from Miss Russia contest owner Rustam Tariko. The next Miss Universe pageant will be held in Moscow, announced its owner, American billionaire Donald Trump (whose fortune is estimated by Forbes at $3.2 billion).

During a live broadcast of the Miss USA contest, Trump invited Crocus Group founder and president Aras Agalarov onstage with his son Emin, and declared that Miss Universe will take place in Russia, according to a Crocus Group statement. The competition will take place in Crocus City Hall on Nov. 9.

An agreement to hold the show [in Russia] was signed by the Miss Universe Organization (co-owned by Trump and NBC Universal) and Agalarov's Crocus Group. Crocus Group holds all Russian broadcasting rights to the show and will be the competition's main investor, said Crocus representative Maria Zayats. She said the company plans to hold talks with leading Russian TV channels about broadcasting the event. The question of attracting coinvestors and other partners or sponsors is still open, says Zayats. Crocus is already discussing broadcasting issues with major Russian television channels, confirmed a source at one of the federal channels....

It was Agalarov's idea to bring the pageant to Russia, says his friend Tariko. Emin Agalarov, who is cultivating his own musical project, Emin, may perform his own songs at the pageant. One of his videos features current Miss Universe Olivia Culpo. Along with the winner's crown, she received a $45,000 grant to study at the New York Film Academy. A Russian has won the competition only once: In 2002, the title was awarded to Oksana Fyodorova, but she declined the crown.

An event of this caliber is an excellent opportunity to raise the Crocus venue to a new level, says Grigory Trusov, president of the Kontakt-Ekspert marketing agency. Although there won't be direct monetization, he compares it to the Olympics or the FIFA World Cup [if they were held] in a single stadium. Trusov estimates the expenses for holding the pageant—organizing, advertising, marketing, logistics, etc—at more than $10 million. Sponsorship packages for those wishing to associate their names with Miss Universe will cost hundreds of thousands of dollars, the expert estimates....

Crocus Group Owner Aras Agalarov: A Beauty Pageant Is More Profitable Than State Construction Projects

By Khalil Aminov. *Kommersant*, Oct. 24, 2013, p. 14.

Editors' Note—Miss Universe is starting in Moscow next week. This competition, held for the first time in Russia, is being financed by the Crocus Group. Crocus owner Aras Agalarov tells *Kommersant* why such events are useful for the country....

* * *

Question—How did the idea come up of holding Miss Universe in Moscow?

Answer—Well, you know, my son Emin is involved with music, as well as business. He decided to shoot a video with the winner of last year's Miss Universe pageant, Olivia Culpo, for his new single "Amor." To do that, he had to get permission from the organizers and the owner of the contest. (The company Miss Universe, Inc. belongs to the family of Donald Trump and the American TV channel NBC. —*Ed*.) While they were communicating, it came up that the pageant organizers had been thinking for a long time about holding the event in Russia; at that point, they had 17 applications from various countries under consideration. Miss Universe, Inc. told Emin that they had been to Russia and had not found a suitable venue, particularly in Moscow. Then Emin invited them [back to Russia], showed them Crocus City Hall, and they reported to Trump that it was the best venue in Moscow. My son negotiated with them, and the upshot was that he came back from the US with a proposal to hold a beauty pageant with nearly a hundred young women from around the world in our hall in Crocus City. I supported it. How could I say no to having Miss Universe at our venue in Moscow, with an audience of more than 1 billion viewers in 170 countries around the world? So that's how the Crocus Group got exclusive rights to hold this competition in Russia and [televise it in] the CIS countries....

Q—How much will it cost Crocus to put on the pageant? Why did you feel you needed to take part in this project at all?

A—The overall budget of the entire event is approximately $20 million....

Q—So, you are willing to spend $20 million to prove to the whole world that Russia is better than the foreign media make it out to be?

A—You have to understand, we can't spend $20 million just for that. In our case, several factors coincided. On the one hand, we do need to show the world that Russia is objectively different. On the other hand, after this transnational show, Crocus Group will gain international exposure.... From an organizational standpoint, Miss Universe is quite a complex event that requires a lot of preparation. Once it comes off, all the organizers will realize that Crocus

City Hall can accommodate an event of any status and with any number of participants. For example, the Grammys or the Oscars.

Q—Events of this status in our country can hardly be organized without approval from government officials. Did you get the go-ahead from upstairs?

A—I did have the opportunity to inform [some officials] about the upcoming event—particularly Vladimir Vladimirovich Putin and First Deputy Prime Minister Igor Shuvalov, during one of the last inspections at Far Eastern Federal University. That's a facility that Crocus built with [state] budget funds on Russky Island in Vladivostok for the 2012 Asia-Pacific Economic Cooperation summit. From that conversation, I understood that the authorities approved of holding Miss Universe in Moscow.

Donald Trump Plans to Build Office Center in Russia Similar to NY Trump Tower

[No author indicated.] *Itar-Tass Daily*, Nov. 9, 2013, https://sputniknews.com/voiceofrussia/news/2013_11_09/Donald-Trump-plans-to-build-office-centre-in-Russia-similar-to-NY-Trump-Tower-3765/.

MOSCOW—American billionaire and businessman Donald Trump plans to build an office center in Russia to be like New York's Trump Tower.

The businessman, who is in Moscow in connection with the Miss Universe 2013 beauty contest finals, told Itar-Tass that he planned to launch a business in Russia and was negotiating with Russian companies to build such a skyscraper.

Among the companies is Crocus Group of Russian billionaire Aras Agalarov. The company owner confirmed to Itar-Tass that there were plans for joint construction projects with Trump. "We began to discuss joint work in real estate a few days ago," Agalarov said. This year, Crocus participated in the organization of the Miss Universe show owned by Trump.

Russia's highest skyscrapers are located in the Moscow City international business center. The 339-meter-high Mercury City Tower, after the completion of the main construction work on Nov. 1, 2012, became Europe's highest. It is 33 m higher than London's Shard.

The Federation East Tower, which is under construction, may become the highest. The planned height of the 97-story tower is 385 m. The construction is expected to be finished in 2014.

The Russian developer company Crocus Group was founded in 1989.

Donald Trump in New Emin Video

By D. Garrison Golubock. *The Moscow Times,* Nov. 26, 2013, p. 16.

US billionaire real estate developer Donald Trump figures prominently in a new music video released by Emin Agalarov, an Azeri pop star and vice-president of Crocus Group.

Trump and Agalarov previously collaborated while organizing the Miss Universe 2013 contest, which took place in Moscow and was hosted by Crocus Group at Crocus City Hall, their sprawling expo and convention center on the outskirts of Moscow.

The Miss Universe contest features prominently in Emin's new clip: The video opens with Emin in a boardroom-like setting, sitting at a conference table with other suited businessmen looking at head shots of various Miss Universe candidates.

Emin then daydreams that he is back at his house, where he imagines himself to be surrounded by Miss Universe contestants, including Miss Russia, Miss USA, and Miss Ukraine, among a number of contestants featured. The contestants follow Emin around his mansion as he brushes his teeth, dances and plays the piano.

The mirage-like models frequently disappear and reappear, making Emin search for them. When Emin finally finds himself at a swimming pool surrounded by Miss Universe contestants in bikinis, he is suddenly jolted back to the boardroom, where his coworkers glare at him.

Trump, seated at the head of the table, calls Emin lazy and perennially late, eventually closing with his trademark phrase "You're fired!"

Crocus Group president Aras Agalarov recently announced that the company had started discussing joint projects with Donald Trump, who announced plans to construct a skyscraper in Moscow modeled after his Trump Towers in New York and Chicago, combining a hotel with office space and apartments.

If Emin's video is a premonition of what may come from his future collaborations with Trump, he will have to be careful not to snooze in the conference room.

PART ONE

The Trump Campaign (2015–2016)

Introduction

The events covered in this part begin just after Trump's announcement of his candidacy in June 2015, and end just before his presidential victory in November 2016.

The articles in Section 1.1 focus on the personalities of Trump and his various rivals (his fellow Republicans and his main adversary, Hillary Clinton), as well as how the various American personalities mesh with that of Russian leader Vladimir Putin. This section also includes some coverage about Trump's popularity in Russia, as well as commentary on the role of Russian and American media in the campaign.

Section 1.2 is more oriented to political analysis, leading off with an opinion piece by *International Affairs* editor Armen Oganesyan, who presciently suggests that Trump's pragmatism may win the majority of American voters. Other articles discuss the apparent foreign policies of Trump and his rivals (particularly regarding Russia), and identify trends in American and global politics. A particularly strong theme here is the tension between isolationism and internationalism. In the analysis that concludes this section, Dmitry Suslov discusses these two trends as a sort of dialectic in US political thought, identifying the latter as dominant since World War II and describing Trump as a potential game-changer.

1.1

Chemistry and Spin: Putin, Trump and Other US Candidates

Introduction

The articles in this section highlight the public personas of Trump and his presidential rivals, as well as the media's effect on public opinion in both America and Russia. Articles from late 2015 and early 2016 highlight Trump's attempts to portray himself as a "friend" of Putin, a PR move that Putin apparently reciprocated in December 2015 when he used the Russian adjective *yarky*: "He's a very *yarky* person, and he's talented—no question about that." Most US media outlets used the word "brilliant" as an English equivalent, and understandably so: The word in Russian is most often used for bright, vivid colors. However, unlike "brilliant," the word *yarky* carries no connotation of intelligence; a closer equivalent would be "striking" or "colorful." (Therefore, Trump himself strayed quite far by making the repeated claim, starting in April 2016, that Putin had called him a genius.)

This section also contains differing takes on the presidential primary race, featuring entertaining characterizations of the various candidates by Vladimir Frolov and Aleksei Baier. After Trump wins the Republican primary, coverage moves to his rivalry with Hillary Clinton. Commentators Aleksandr Vedrussov and Vasily Gatov intriguingly disagree on American media spin: Vedrussov sees a strong anti-Trump bias, whereas Gatov portrays Trump as a "Frankenstein's monster" created by conservative opinion-maker Fox News.

Also presented in this section are the results of Russian opinion polls on the Democratic and Republican rivals (a remarkable phenomenon in itself—how common is it for Americans to give their approval ratings of any candidates in a foreign election?). Aleksei Kovalyov argues that the Russian media are strongly biased in favor of Trump and against Clinton. As if to prove his point, Russian Federation Council representative Konstantin Kosachov blasts Clinton's "exceptionalism" in an October 2016 opinion piece. Meanwhile, Frolov cautions that given the mechanisms of American politics and trends in Russian-US relations, Russians should not expect Trump to be any more of a "friend" to Moscow than Clinton.

US Presidential Hopeful Trump Says He and Putin Would Be Pals

[No author indicated.] *The Moscow Times,* July 13, 2015, p. 2.

Donald Trump, a Republican business tycoon and television personality whose sights are set on the US presidency, said in a speech Saturday [July 11] that if he ascends to the White House in 2016, US-Russian relations will improve, as he and President Vladimir Putin would get along "very, very well."

In a speech that centered largely on the tough immigration rhetoric that has garnered him condemnation and praise, Trump asserted that he would have more positive results in dealing with China and Russia if he were president and said he could be pals with Putin.

Asked by an audience member in Las Vegas about US-Russia relations, Trump said the problem is that Putin doesn't respect current US President Barack Obama.

"I think we would get along very, very well," he said of Putin.

Trump's sentiments on Putin come in stark contrast to those expressed by Democratic presidential hopeful Hillary Clinton at a campaign event earlier this month.

"We have to be much smarter in how we deal with Putin and how we deal with his ambitions," Clinton said at an event in New

Hampshire. "He's not an easy man. * * * But I don't think there is any substitute other than constant engagement."

What President Trump Would Mean for Russia

By Ivan Nechepurenko. *The Moscow Times*, Sept. 3, 2015, p. 1.

Donald Trump might hope that he will have a great relationship with President Vladimir Putin if he gets elected to the White House, but the problem is that Russia's relationship with the US is driven by political elites in the two countries who have their own divergent interests, Russian America-watchers told *The Moscow Times* on Wednesday [Sept. 2].

Trump is the front-runner in US public opinion polls for the Republican Party nomination, but it is unlikely that he will win it and become president, experts agreed. Even if the Republican Party nominates him, he will be constrained by its long-term policies and the power of the US Congress, they said.

"He doesn't have a team, he is not connected with the establishment and he has already made many enemies," said Yury Rogulyov, director of the Franklin Roosevelt US Policy Studies Center at Moscow State University.

"He talks about finding common language, but this is not enough. Nobody will allow him to make a U-turn in US foreign policy. President Barack Obama said many things too [during his election campaign], but the political elite did not allow him to do much," he said in a phone interview.

Trump and Putin share many traits: They are direct, outspoken and like to make deals based on pragmatic interest. Putin is often credited with restoring a sense of pride in his country among Russians, while Trump's campaign slogan is "Make America Great Again!"

Both are antimainstream and self-confident people who don't feel constrained by political correctness. Both belong to closely knit systems: Putin is a graduate of the Soviet security apparatus; Trump belongs to the American corporate world. Both want to be portrayed as genuine men who are not part of the establishment.

Radiating confidence on every policy point he wants to pursue, Trump has already said multiple times that he will have a "great relationship" with Putin. It was the US that made Putin "the world leader," by not showing leadership itself, he claimed.

"I would be willing to bet I would have a great relationship with Putin," Trump told Fox News in June, shortly after announcing his campaign.

Trump didn't specify how he would build this relationship, saying that his confidence is based on a "feeling."

Moreover, the relationship would be so good that Putin would hand Edward Snowden over to the US, Trump told CNN in July.

"Look, if I'm president, Putin says [to Snowden] 'Hey, you're gone.' I guarantee you this," Trump said in a televised interview.

Snowden is a former US National Security Agency contractor who turned into a global surveillance whistle-blower and obtained temporary political asylum in Russia in 2013.

As an attempt to start building bridges, Trump has already offered Putin some praise.

"Putin has no respect for our president. He's got tremendous popularity in Russia; they love what he is doing, they love what he represents," he told Fox News.

According to Ivan Kurilla, a professor at the European University in St. Petersburg, the truth is that what Trump says about Putin is actually directed at Obama.

"While Russia has become an apparent failure for the Obama administration, Trump says that he can deal with Putin—just as during the last election, when Obama was proud of the 'reset' in the US-Russian relationship and Mitt Romney was calling Russia the main geopolitical foe. He was doing it in order to criticize the White House, not Russia," Kurilla said in written comments.

"The Kremlin is hoping that the future US president, whoever it will be, will change policy toward Russia, and I am confident that Moscow is ready to deal with him or her. But it remains a question whether the new American leader will be ready for such a turn. The election rhetoric will tell us nothing about that," he said.

Trump has promised to impose harder sanctions on Iran in order to make a deal "from strength," meaning that Iran's oil will not hit the market, increasing the chances that the price of oil—Russia's main export—will go up.

In addition, Trump said he would want to put more pressure on China, including an imposition of a tariff on its exports into the US. This could empower Russia in the eyes of the Chinese leadership and drive the two closer together.

Trump has also promised to crush militants of ISIS [Islamic State of Iraq and Sham] militarily. Given Russia's concern about the spread of terrorism south of its borders, this would be well received by Moscow.

Russian columnist for *Bloomberg View* Leonid Bershidsky has compared Trump with "brash, showy businessmen"—particularly Yevgeny Chichvarkin and Boris Berezovsky. The two fled Russia for London in order to avoid what they said was politically motivated criminal prosecution at home. Putin eats such people "for lunch," according to Bershidsky.

"Eventually, however, even Trump would come to understand that he was being mocked and manipulated, the Putin behavior that Obama can't stand. Trump's disappointment might produce an even more bitter confrontation than the one between Putin and Obama," Bershidsky wrote in a column published at the end of July.

Trump Slams Obama, Gives Putin an 'A' for Leadership

[No author indicated.] *The Moscow Times*, Oct. 1, 2015, p. 3.

Outspoken Republican presidential candidate Donald Trump on Tuesday [Sept. 29] called Russian President Vladimir Putin a better leader than US President Barack Obama.

"I will tell you that, in terms of leadership, [Putin]'s getting an 'A' and our president is not doing so well. They did not look good together," Trump said to conservative pundit Bill O'Reilly on Fox News' "The O'Reilly Factor" television show.

Putin and Obama met earlier this week on the sidelines of the UN General Assembly session in New York, where they discussed the conflict in Syria.

Trump also said in the interview he agreed with Putin's support for Syrian President Bashar Assad—a leader Obama has described as "a tyrant."

"Putin is now taking over what we started," Trump said. "I say there's very little downside with Putin fighting ISIS."

Odd Checks, Asymmetrical Balances

By Fyodor Lukyanov, research professor at the
Higher School of Economics. *Rossiiskaya gazeta*, Feb. 3, 2016, p. 8.

The [presidential] election campaign has officially started in the US. Iowa kicked off the series of primaries that will determine the candidates of the two main parties. Everything should clear up in the next couple of months, with a test of strength in the largest states.

How strong you are out of the gate is indicative here. [Republican] favorite Donald Trump has lost ground to Ted Cruz and almost fallen back to third place, barely managing to stay ahead of Marco Rubio. It's too early to draw any conclusions, but commentators do not rule out that the eccentric billionaire's lucky streak has run out. As a Republican Party candidate, that is. Nothing is preventing him from running as an independent candidate. Then he would really trip up his fellow Republicans.

The Iowa results confirm what has been said since the start of the campaign: Voters are fed up with a merry-go-round of essentially similar individuals, and are prepared to vote for politicians who position themselves as antiestablishment. Aside from Trump, Ted Cruz is perhaps the biggest challenge to the status quo. He does not have support from any of the [Republican] Party elite. He is extremely conservative but favors refreshing the Republicans' image, which is what won him the votes Trump was counting on. Interestingly, Rubio also had a strong showing. He is considered another alternative to the current political aristocracy, albeit a more moderate one. If the Iowa results are anything to go by, it can be assumed that Rubio could expect to win the support of [Republican] Party heavyweights: Compared to Trump and Cruz, he comes off as a safer bet and cuts a more respectable figure.

The Democratic Party results are no less interesting. Sen. Bernie Sanders, who is basically a communist by American standards, managed to achieve a draw with Hillary Clinton. No one took Sanders seriously, given Clinton's political weight and financial resources. However, she had to contend with American voters growing tired of the same old faces. It is unlikely that Sanders would be able to challenge Hillary in the long run: He does not have her administrative and financial resources. But a clear signal has been sent, and candidates will have to contend with the electorate's "rebellious" mood.

This is going to be an exciting campaign, especially given that just like Trump, Michael Bloomberg may also run as an independent. The billionaire and former Republican mayor of New York City apparently senses that the time is right for those who seek to distance themselves from traditional institutions, given the discord within traditional parties.

America stands at an important crossroads, and is experiencing the same processes manifesting themselves on a global scale. Traditional ruling political institutions are failing to address new challenges and circumstances. Of course, [this phenomenon] is easier to address within a single nation than in the global community as a whole: At least [a single nation] has a decision-making center. But even here, the centuries-old system of checks and balances (the American political system has always prided itself on being able to avoid extremes) is starting to fail. The system of checks (i.e., political forces and players) has changed, which requires a whole new set of balances. The system will probably find a new balance, but for now, we are seeing the old one crumble.

In a way, this is reflected in foreign policy. Assessments of Obama's presidency will vary widely: From an outside perspective, it is possible to assume that he understands very well (better that a lot of his colleagues and opponents in America) how the modern world works—and most importantly, how it doesn't. At the same time, he does not know what to do with this knowledge, and bases [his actions] on his own understanding of how to minimize risks.

That understanding is quite dubious. For instance, it seems that Obama strives to replace decisive and drastic actions (which he rightly believes would exacerbate existing problems) with decisive and drastic statements, and not-so-subtle hints. But this does not have the intended effect. You would think foreign policy players would appreciate prudence and caution, but instead they are jumping on this harsh rhetoric and taking response measures. Meanwhile, domestically, many [Americans] are upset by the disparity between words and actions, since it comes off as weakness and meaninglessness.

A striking example of this are the mutual recriminations following corruption accusations against the Russian president, which first came from a relatively low-level [US] official, but were then corroborated (albeit somewhat vaguely) by the White House.[2] I cannot speak for the American leadership's motives, but it is possible that the [US] administration actually sees this as "soft" and cautious pressure on Moscow to get it to change its policies—as if to say, "We are not rattling sabers here" (Obama does not like to do that). Meanwhile, this will probably create a far worse effect than any demonstrations of military force: After all, [the US] is essentially bringing criminal accusations against Russia's top official, which calls into question his political legitimacy. It is unclear how such steps can be combined with intensive negotiations on Syria and Ukraine, but one gets the sense that this is Washington's current notion of balanced politics. If that is indeed the case, then the American leadership should not be surprised that such an odd balance will be followed by a very unexpected asymmetrical response.

Losing the Trump Card

By Vladimir Frolov. *The Moscow Times,* Feb. 4, 2016, p. 5.

Donald Trump's campaign for the US presidency is losing momentum, and this is bad news for the Kremlin.

Republican voters in Iowa may have thwarted Russian President Vladimir Putin's wish to see the "doubtlessly talented" Donald Trump as the next US president. Trump, the "absolute leader of the presidential race" (as Putin described him back in December), came in second in Iowa with 24% of the vote, behind Sen. Ted Cruz at 28%. Trump failed to convert his handsome lead in the polls into actual votes, thanks to poor campaign management and an incoherent message.

Although Trump still enjoys a commanding lead in New Hampshire, which holds its primary on Feb. 9, and in South Carolina (Feb. 20), the loss in Iowa appears to have pierced a hole in The Donald's balloon of inevitability. His march to the Republican nomination may be about to crater, or at least prove more arduous and costly than it has thus far. Trump's train may have left the station, but it is not heading toward the White House.

Part of the reason for this is Sen. Marco Rubio, whose last-minute surge in Iowa to finish a close third (23%), has resuscitated the Republican establishment's hopes for a strong and unifying candidate who could actually govern the country. Rubio, not Cruz, is the real winner in Iowa, and his result changes the dynamic of the race as the Republican establishment and major donors begin coalescing around his candidacy.

Cruz, a conservative zealot hated within his own party, is likely to fade after New Hampshire if Rubio keeps gaining momentum. Jeb Bush will be pressured to withdraw from the race and should be lining up for a Cabinet position now.

It is not hard to see why Putin endorsed Trump before the voting started. Although Putin's sense of US politics is somewhat uninformed, this time around he knew exactly what he was doing: trolling the US political establishment. Trump's campaign message has been that American elites are morons and losers, and that a strong leader like him is needed to clinch advantageous deals for the US—particularly when negotiating with strong leaders like Vladimir Putin. A Trump presidency would shatter the US political system and leave the country distracted and weak—hence Trump's appeal to the Kremlin.

Trump's boast that he had met Putin once in New York and felt that he could build a strong and close relationship with Russia—cited by Putin as sufficient reason for endorsing him—was not based on anything in particular. Trump has neither a foreign policy platform nor foreign policy advisers, and his understanding of Russia is primitive. But his unmistakably Berlusconi style of leadership, his age and his aura of unrestrained masculinity is something that Putin finds appealing in other foreign leaders—George W. Bush, for example. Putin is known for his highly personalized foreign policy style, which sometimes hurts state relations, as US President Barack Obama and German Chancellor Angela Merkel have learned....

Rubio, a naturally gifted politician—often described as a Republican Obama—would be a tough challenger for [Hillary] Clinton, but the economy and demographics favor the Democrats and Obama's successful agenda. Barring an FBI indictment for mishandling classified information, Hillary Clinton could be the first female president of the US.

Clinton would reengage with Moscow and largely continue Obama's strategy, a combination of engagement and calibrated pressure. Yet, she has recently emerged as one of Putin's fiercest critics in the US....

A Clinton administration would likely be more interventionist and willing to use force than Obama's White House has been, which would not go down well in Moscow. Clinton was a leading advocate of using military force in Libya in 2011, and she recommended that Obama arm Syrian rebels in 2012. She supports establishing a no-fly zone and safe havens in Syria to protect civilians, which Putin rushed to preempt with a military intervention.

The Moscow-Washington relationship promises to remain a rocky one, and its management will require a steady hand, which a president Clinton is more likely to provide than a president Rubio, or, God forbid, a president Trump.

From Hillary to Trump: What the Kremlin Can Expect From the Candidates

By Aleksei Baier. *Slon.ru*, March 3, 2016, https://slon.ru/posts/64746.

While it may not have provided any definitive answers, Super Tuesday [March 1] in the US at least clarified a few things about the presidential race. Hillary Clinton emerged victorious for the Democrats, and Donald Trump is the Republican to beat. Both won seven states out of 11. For the Democrats, [Bernie] Sanders won four states, including his home state of Vermont. For the Republicans, Ted Cruz won his native Texas, as well as nearby Oklahoma and far-off Alaska. Meanwhile, Marco Rubio, the last hope of the Republican ruling establishment in its "stop Trump" project, finally won a state: Minnesota.

Now, it is possible to take a look at how the leading candidates plan to tackle US foreign policy—particularly, how they plan to build relations with Russia.

The USSR was naturally at the center of American foreign policy during the entire postwar period, and all problems that American presidents faced were in one way or another connected with Moscow: the loss of China, the Korean war, the [1956] events in Hungary, the Berlin Wall, the shock following the launch of the first Soviet satellite, Cuba, the Vietnam War and much more. Granted, starting in the mid-1990s, Russia exited the stage of US interests for about a decade. But it made a comeback by the 2008 presidential election, thanks largely to the efforts of cold war veteran John McCain, the Republican candidate in that election.

Since then, Russia has stepped up its activity in the global arena, and will most likely continue to play a central role in the current presidential race. Especially since by getting involved in the Syrian conflict, Moscow stumbled into an area of crucial importance for Americans—Islamist terrorism.

The Republicans are harshly criticizing Obama's foreign policy course, especially his weakness when it comes to Russia. This is exacerbated by the fact that both Cruz and Rubio are of Cuban descent. And for Cuban-Americans, hatred of Communism and Russia, which brought Communism to their island, is deeply ingrained....

But Clinton has a huge advantage in this regard. Without a doubt, she is the most experienced politician among the candidates, and knows firsthand how foreign policy works. As for her foreign policy course, that is no secret: This year, Hillary surrendered to the mercy of the winner. Eight years ago, her husband's faction, which controlled the Democratic Party at the time, failed to get her the presidential nomination. Instead, she was easily beaten by a young black senator, who has since formed his own coalition and built a party machine that got him reelected to a second term in 2012, despite predictions that he would lose. Now, Clinton is increasingly trying to play up her association with Obama—particularly because she essentially designed his foreign policy course.

So if she becomes president, [US] foreign policy may become much harsher than during the previous administration. Obama is extremely and almost pathologically patient, tolerant and cool-headed. He is more likely to wait things out than to act. Clinton is different—as her stint leading the US State Department has already demonstrated. She is a woman, and in American society, high-ranking women often have to prove that they are just as tough and decisive as men. When it comes to Russia, she has a small stumbling block—her failed "reset." She will have to prove that she has learned a bitter lesson. Here, she is a typical Democrat. Democrats have always started with a much more friendly approach regarding the Soviet Union, but often ended up with a quarrel and a confrontation....

Trump, on the other hand, responded in kind to Putin's praise (Trump loves being praised). He said that Putin was right in his [positive] assessment of [Trump's] character, and added that at least the Russian president is a leader, and not a weakling like Obama. Of course, it remains unclear why the weakling Obama is so disliked in Russia. And why America's staunchest foes in Russia, such as Aleksandr Dugin, support Trump of all people, whose campaign slogan is "Make America Great Again!"

Finally, after his Super Tuesday triumphs, Trump has basically cinched the nomination. Trump is the main reason why the nomination race among Republicans has turned into a farce and a freak show, where shameless lies and schoolyard name-calling have taken precedence over matters of ideology and policy. For [the Republicans], the democratic process has just regressed 150 years, back to a time when America was still young and uncouth.

What does Trump's victory mean for foreign policy, especially where Russia is concerned?

It must be said that Trump's platform is difficult to discuss. Western countries have not seen a politician like Trump at a national level since Italian partisans executed Benito Mussolini in the Alpine village of Giulino. He lacks a platform, has only a passing knowledge of the facts, but loves to gab and makes promises that are in direct violation of the US Constitution. When asked how he intends to fulfill those promises, he responds that everything will be just fine, since he has his eye on a few talented people who will take care of the details.

It is nevertheless necessary to think about how Trump would rule a superpower. He is the author of a literary gem titled "The Art of the Deal." Basically, that's his political credo. In his opinion, Washington is ruled by idiots who for several decades now have allowed "our partners" to take America for a ride. They simply don't have a clue how to negotiate.

Trump is an entrepreneur, but not all entrepreneurs are created equal. For example, Volkswagen, General Motors and even oil companies like BP are largely dependent on their corporate reputation, not to mention such "social network" companies like Apple, Google or Facebook. For them, pushing the little guys around is dangerous. However, Trump is in an entirely different line of business: He works in construction, building casinos, homes and golf clubs for the wealthy. You need connections in the local government for that, and nobody cares about the opinions of the average Joe. In this type of business, you negotiate with those who have clout. The rest can be ignored, bought off or sued. Judging by Trump's remarks, "the rest" includes Mexico, the European Union and China. Apparently, he doesn't know any other countries.

Russia is a whole other game for Trump: When he compliments Putin, Trump is showing respect for Russia. He understands that he will have to cut a deal with Russia. He will have to cut deals with other countries (and how!)—including with "rotten" Mexico—but he doesn't know it yet.

As for Putin, it seems he has been longing to sit down at the negotiating table with the American president and determine zones of influence (just as the European states once divided Africa). [Putin would say:] Here's your zone of influence, and here's mine—Central Asia, the Caucasus, Moldova, Ukraine and Belarus—and we'll stay out of each other's hair. We'll fight the Islamists together. And as for the Baltic states, Poland and Hungary—let's haggle. Trump has no ideology, so such a world order is all right for him. Thus, Trump's victory could signal a new dawn for Russian-American relations. Of course, there is one problem. While Trump's business has a mafia flavor, it is nevertheless above board as far as US legislation is concerned. It operates according to laws, court decisions and strict rules. Trump often successfully sues his business partners, clients and competitors. No one has thrown the chess board in his face yet. So it would be interesting to see what he would do and what court he would turn to when that happens.

Who's Afraid of Donald Trump?

By Aleksandr Vedrussov, director of the
Strateg-PRO analytical center. *Izvestia*, Sept. 1, 2016, p. 6.

Judging by the mudslinging campaign against Donald Trump in all mainstream American media, the mighty of this world are absolutely terrified that for the first time in decades, forces may come to power that would put the interests of the American middleclass above the profits of global megacorporations.

As paradoxical as it sounds, billionaire Donald Trump could turn out to be the politician that transforms America from a country serving the needs of the global capitalists to a sovereign state that defends its national (and not supranational) interests.

Speaking at the Republican National Convention in Cleveland, Trump made a proposal that is basically revolutionary for America: that it needs to move away from the policy of global domination at any cost and focus on solving domestic problems....

The fact that just about all of the party's major corporate sponsors—Coca-Cola, Microsoft, Hewlett-Packard, Apple, Motorola, JP Morgan Chase, Wells Fargo—have refused to support Trump speaks volumes....

We are seeing a very unique situation in American politics: A candidate for the highest post in the country from one of the two main parties is basically being turned into a pariah....

So why are such iconic representatives of the global corporatocracy, with their decades-long ties to the US government, so afraid of Trump coming to power?

First, this is due to the possible collapse of the painstakingly promoted Transatlantic and Trans-Pacific Partnerships that concern trade and investment between the US and the European Union and Asia (minus China). These aim to cement the leading role of megacorporations in determining the rules of the game on the global markets.

Trump has openly stated that he is categorically against handing over yet more of America's sovereignty to supranational agencies at the expense of the country's national interests. This position was overwhelmingly supported by the public, forcing Hillary Clinton (who is constantly trying to mimic being in tune with public sentiment) to make reserved statements opposing new integration projects for America.

Second, Trump's biggest and most unforgivable sin in the eyes of the global capitalists is his desire to establish not just constructive relations with Russia, but a partnership. A particular irritant was the American presidential candidate's willingness to "forgive" [Russia's annexation of] the Crimea and perhaps to even completely lift sanctions [against Russia] for the sake of a joint fight against global terrorism as embodied by ISIS (an organization banned in Russia).

The global corporatocracy went to a lot of trouble setting the Middle East ablaze, orchestrating a coup in Ukraine and driving a wedge between Russia and the EU. It is not about to allow Trump and Putin to establish order in Syria, Libya and Iraq; end the endless stream of refugees and terrorists into Europe; and make ensuring global peace and security a priority in international relations.

You can't cash in on peace and stability. But war—whether regional or global—is and always has been the best source of income for the global capitalists.

That is why the "hawks" representing corporate interests are betting on former US secretary of state Hillary Clinton, who won't hesitate to start a global conflict, as long as it makes her sponsors money.

That is why Trump, being a true American patriot and opponent of a global war, has come up against such fierce resistance from the American establishment. Let's hope that the American people have enough willpower and wisdom to make the right choice on Nov. 8.

In distant 1776, the Americans brazenly defied the British Empire and finally managed to gain independence (with Russia's help, incidentally). Perhaps now, 240 years later, it's time once again for the American people to fight for national liberation?

(Editorial)—Antidemocracy

By Maria Zheleznova. *Vedomosti*, Oct. 18, 2016, p. 6.

It turns out that an election on the other side of the world can be of interest to the average Russian, especially if it's an election with an unpredictable outcome. According to an October poll by the Public Opinion Foundation, more than half of all Russians (55%) know that Americans are going to elect a president in November. Moreover, Russians are fairly familiar with the election campaign (saying that it's an aggressive one): They know the names of the two main candidates, [those candidates'] respective positions on Russia, are aware that Hillary Clinton has some health problems, and have heard that the two candidates have debated.

Russians' sympathies lie with the Republican candidate. While in May, Donald Trump was viewed positively by 22% of the Public Opinion Foundation's respondents, in October that number stands at 38%. The share of Clinton supporters has not changed in that time—[it remains at] 8%. However, she is now viewed negatively by 61% [of respondents], compared to 45% [in May].

Such interest [in the US election] could be partly explained by the fact that half of the respondents believe it is important for Russia who will be the next US president. While 7% believe that a Democratic victory would be more in the interests of our country, 44% believe that about a Republican president. However, in both cases, the same percentage of responders (35%) believe that relations between the US and Russia will remain the same.

Nevertheless, it is unclear [to Russian respondents] who will win: About a third of respondents believe Clinton will win, with the same number betting on Trump. The rest are undecided. According to political analyst Yevgeny Minchenko, the fact that Russians see the end result as unpredictable is a sign that the Russian media are more or less objective in their campaign coverage, despite a slight bias for Trump. With the exception of the Ukrainian presidential elections of 2004 and 2010, which generated a lot of interest due to the two countries' closeness and the importance of Ukrainians' geopolitical choice, the 2016 US presidential election is perhaps the one in post-Soviet history that holds the most importance for Russians. This is due both to [the election campaign's] intensity and Russia's role in its agenda. In addition, both candidates embody stereotypes most Russians are well-familiar with: Trump is [seen] as an upstart businessman, while Clinton is a Soviet-style party apparatchik, Minchenko says. But the unpredictability of the final result in this particular campaign is more of a negative in the eyes of Russians: for the [Russian] audience, this is not the result of a struggle between a political David and Goliath, but instead an indication that both candidates are hugely unpopular. It's hard for those poor Americans to choose the lesser of two evils—we don't need a democracy like that over here.

White House and Television: Who Invented Donald Trump?

By Vasily Gatov. *Slon.ru*, Oct. 21, 2016, https://slon.ru/posts/75094.

The US presidential election is less than a month away. But the country's main television show has been running for almost two years now: Billionaire Donald Trump is running a campaign that will perhaps forever break the existing rules and boundaries of American politics. As a seasoned businessman, marketing expert and PR master, Trump has leveraged the power of the media, first and foremost the Fox News empire....

It's difficult to describe Donald Trump's views in the language of traditional political thought. In this sense, he is similar to [Liberal Democratic Party of Russia leader] Vladimir Zhirinovsky, a household name in Russia. But if we take a look at the programming Fox News has been airing for years, it is easy to see that the billionaire is simply taking advantage of the agenda that the television channel has been promoting among conservative Republicans for years.

If you look at Trump's economic platform, it more or less follows the tenets of the Republican Party—lowering taxes, reducing the government apparatus, and supporting business and investment with tax breaks for the wealthiest (so that they reinvest their capital in the economy). Fox News correspondents, commentators and news anchors have long toed that line—it's no coincidence that [the network's] owner and founder is Rupert Murdoch, a fan of Reaganomics and the policies of [former British prime minister] Margaret Thatcher, as well as an ardent opponent of anything that may seem "socialist." For years, hosts like Bill O'Reilly and Sean Hannity have waged a media war against any "Europeanization" of the American social and economic models (O'Reilly since the days of Nixon, and Hannity—since early Bill Clinton).

For them, as well as for Trump (who has "borrowed" their agenda), resisting such "socialist" projects as Obamacare is the continuation of the fight against communism at home. Communism is long gone, and Obama's and Clinton's "leftist leanings" on health care are highly dubious. Nevertheless, the ghost of communism continues to haunt Washington, as far as Fox News hosts are concerned.

Fox News has always taken an extremely conservative position on immigration, as well. Donald Trump was not the first to come up with the idea of building a wall stretching thousands of miles along the Mexican border—[the network's] conservative, anti-immigrant hosts have been talking about the need to punish [America's] southern neighbor pretty much since the days of Reagan. One popular myth among conservatives is the criminal and drug-running nature of Latin American immigrant groups. This is poorly disguised racism that has escaped the confines of political correctness.

A converted television viewer then rejects actual reality, choosing "faith in television."

The anti-immigrant agenda of Trump and Fox News is a classic example of all-encompassing media influence. Researchers beginning with George Gerbner, the founder of cultivation theory, have often noted that television audiences' views of the world around them "shift" away from objective reality. For example, ethnic crime has been the favorite subject of leading Fox News talk show hosts and correspondents for years. Their efforts have been bolstered by Fox's fictional dramas and sitcoms, which feature a disproportionately high percentage of Spanish-speaking criminals (and recently, Arab terrorists) relative to actual crime statistics, as well as in terms of the percentage of Hispanics (and Muslims) within the US population. Such media influence is called "cultivation." Over time, the viewer of various Fox shows stops acknowledging actual reality (especially when it comes to fears), choosing "faith in television."

For the vast majority of Trump supporters residing in the central and northwestern US, Hispanics are not even an issue—they are simply not a presence there, just as immigrants do not actually make up a significant proportion of criminals (or politicians, for that matter). However, Fox News tells us, "You just don't see it, but it's frightening," and the brainwashed TV viewer no longer accepts actual reality (where such a viewer may not even encounter Cuban, Mexican or Syrian immigrants, due to demographic or social factors). Instead, [such a viewer] accepts the following theory: I just don't see what my favorite TV show hosts see.

The second media effect that Donald Trump has successfully co-opted thanks to Fox News is the notion of a "corrupt Washington that must be destroyed." Recently, this theory has been supplemented with the idea of "rigged elections." Trump's falling ratings (as evidenced by opinion polls) are presented as a conspiracy of the political elite to keep him out of the White House. In communications and psychology, this is called the framing effect. Essentially, any of us who has raised children knows this logic trap. For example, in encouraging their child to adhere to certain behavioral norms, a parent might say: "See, adults don't act that way," using a behavioral frame that exists in their mind. In the case of a "corrupt Washington" and "stolen elections" that have yet to even take place, Fox News as well as Donald Trump are appealing to the existing frame of mind of the average American, who is tired of the monotony of American politics and politicians.

Indeed, Washington has many people who have held on to their seats in the Senate and the House for decades. Take, for instance, John Conyers, the doyen of the House of Representatives, who has been at his post for almost 52 years. Thad Cochran is the longest-serving Senator [currently in office], having been in his post for 43 consecutive years [*sic*; Patrick Leahy is the senior US senator; Cochran has been a senator since 1978—*Trans*.]. Representatives of the executive branch often return to their posts, and some have held them since the days of Reagan, Bush, Clinton and the other Bush.

The rhetoric and messages of traditional American politicians are also stale and woefully predictable, especially as far as their electorate is concerned. That is why Fox News is constantly hammering home the notion that "these Washington Big Kahunas aren't solving the problems of the average American" (which makes it strikingly similar to today's Russian television)....

Framing has always been the favorite weapon of demagogues and populists, and it is always firmly linked to the third whale on the Fox News/Donald Trump agenda—conspiracy theories. This is something that the Republican candidate has in common not only with [Fox News], but with Russian propaganda: The readiness to blame any problem on a conspiracy of external forces. When a "corrupt Washington" is not enough, other Illuminati are easily found—from the Freemasons to the "Chinese threat" (which has replaced the Russian one).

The only thing that Donald Trump and Fox News differ on is their take on Russia and its president. For businessman Trump, Russia "smells like money," and he has made several attempts to get on the Russian market (albeit unsuccessfully). As a corporate leader, [Trump] is attracted to Vladimir Putin's leadership style, which is much more similar to that of a CEO. Fox News, meanwhile, holds a fairly critical view of Russia and Putin—which is quite typical of US media outlets. Unlike Donald Trump, [Fox News] hosts are not comparing a "weak president Obama" to a "strong leader Putin."

With just a few weeks to go before the election, Fox News has assumed a much more tepid position on the Republican candidate; its hosts are even allowing themselves to criticize Trump and talk about his constant gaffes, factual errors and weak moral fiber. Of course, it's difficult to imagine Fox News endorsing Hillary Clinton, but Trump is nevertheless by no means a Fox News candidate. Murdoch & Co. would have preferred to see Texas Sen. Ted Cruz [as the Republican presidential nominee], since he has close and even friendly ties with the news channel.

The most interesting part is yet to come for the American viewer. But no matter who wins on Nov. 8, Donald Trump has already managed to greatly change America, which has gotten the idea that there is nothing in place to hold back populists and demagogues like him, who take the risk of going against the system and breaking the rules. Which means that Fox News reality has started to win out over actual reality.

Exceptional Case

By Konstantin Kosachov, chairman of the Federation Council's International Affairs Committee. *Izvestia*, Oct. 21, 2016, p. 6.

I believe that Hillary Clinton's policy article in *Time* magazine with the unequivocal title "Why America Is Exceptional" has given many people in the world something to think about. That's because this bombastic article, couched in the style of a high school essay, was published in the name of a former US secretary of state and now US presidential candidate from the Democratic Party.

Some passages written by the possible leader of the "free world" can only be quoted with great caution. After all, in a lot of countries, ideas of exceptionalism on any grounds are illegal. In particular, the Russian Constitution (Art. 29) forbids the propaganda of "social, racial, national, religious, or language superiority." Clinton's article is an almost quintessential example of such propaganda.

Of course, you could try to chalk this up to electoral "fever." That is, all of this is said and written purely for domestic consumption, where contentions of national exceptionalism and global superiority fall on the well-prepared soil of popular expectations and are generally par for the course in the US.

However, for the rest of the world, this is a culture shock, to put it mildly. After all, there have been no maxims of this kind and at this level probably since the 1930s and 1940s. We remember very well where talk about the "exceptionalism" of one particular nation led the world at the time and what price it had to pay. And today, this comes from the mouths of those who tomorrow may be at the helm of the biggest military arsenal in the history of humankind.

What is even more disturbing is that this is not being said by Donald Trump, the Republican candidate who is known for his eccentricity and political inexperience. On the contrary, the claims of America's exceptionalism and indispensability to the rest of the world are being uttered by one of the most high-profile female representatives of the US establishment in recent decades, who has been directly involved in a number of US foreign policy moves. And she admits quite openly and unpretentiously: If there is a fundamental idea that has guided and inspired her, it is that "the US is an exceptional nation."

At the same time, the author seriously asserts that America is indispensable and exceptional because of its values, and she even adds: "the values of freedom, equality and opportunity." Just how exceptionalism can go along with equality is a linguistic and logical puzzle—which, however, leaves the ideologues of American superiority completely unfazed for the simple reason that they draw a clear line between the domestic sphere and international relations.

What is a value within the state—respect for the rights of minorities and individuals, and the freedom to choose one's way of life—is completely rejected on a global scale: Here, everyone is supposed to march in one formation, while the right to dissent or follow an independent course is not allowed—and punished through outside intervention.

There is absolutely no doubt that the claim to national state exceptionalism—which may mean, for example, immunity from prosecution, among other things—is not a bid to make the world a better place but, above all, an open challenge to a multipolar, just, equal and democratic world based on the fundamental norms and principles of international law.

It was because of this logic of neoliberal messianism that the Middle East exploded, where far more people have been killed as a result of the bloody chaos created after "humanitarian interventions" than at the hands of the very same dictators against whom those interventions were made. The cure turned out to be far worse than the disease, but that absolutely does not keep Hillary Clinton from stating with confidence: "We need to continue leading the world. Because when America fails to lead, we leave a vacuum that lets extremism take root, emboldens our adversaries and discourages our friends."

The most amazing thing here is not hypocrisy: That would be understandable, considering the election context. However, a potential US president actually believes this. Even after Yugoslavia, Iraq, Libya, Syria and so on.

Although the subtitle of the article says that "America is indispensable—and exceptional—because of our values," [those values] are not immediately addressed. Previously, indeed, US ideologues and politicians prioritized "soft power"—the appeal of [the American] lifestyle, institutions and culture. Today, however, the former US secretary of state begins differently: "America is indispensable in part because we have the greatest military in history." And also "because of our network of alliances," which refers precisely to the military.

Therefore, the message to [US] allies and the rest of the world is absolutely unmistakable: We are the strongest ("Russia and China can't begin to compare"); we will continue the policy of aggressive leadership in the world; and all others had better be our allies, because "walking away from our alliances now would be a dangerous mistake"—in other words, you'll be sorry.

Against this backdrop, a quote in the article from Robert Kennedy, who called the US "a great, unselfish, compassionate country," as well as the author's own contention that "America has an unparalleled ability to be a force for peace, progress and prosperity around the world"—all of this looks starkly grotesque, and creates the impression that this is written for an audience with a secondary school education at best that takes little interest in the foreign policy of the past few years.

Although in his recent piece in *The New York Times*, well-known political commentator Ivan Krastev highlighted the fact that the global spread of English has become a problem for Americans themselves: "In our increasingly Anglophone world, Americans have become nakedly transparent to English speakers everywhere, yet the world remains bafflingly and often frighteningly opaque to monolingual Americans. While the world devours America's movies and follows its politics closely, Americans know precious little about how non-Americans think and live." Indeed, they often have no idea about how their words will echo outside [the US], which is why they are sometimes so frighteningly brazen.

The claims of Hillary Clinton and the US as a whole to national exceptionalism verge on real national chauvinism, which has always impeded normal communication. After all, full-fledged dialogue is only possible between equals. This makes the obsessive desire to portray oneself as a "force of good," which automatically designates all opponents as "forces of evil," look all the more dangerous....

Through the Looking Glass

By Aleksei Kovalyov. *The Moscow Times,* Nov. 3, 2016, p. 5.

From the word "go," Russian state media have been largely sympathetic toward Donald Trump. Even prior to the Republican primaries, they reported every minor bump and hiccup in his ratings. In September, Trump's against-the-odds campaign garnered more attention than Russia's own parliamentary elections. Most national outlets devoted extensive coverage to even the most minuscule revelations from the leaked Democratic National Committee and Clinton staff e-mails.

But it is an oversimplification to say state media went all out for Trump. They were less for Trump, more staunchly against Clinton. And here they followed President Vladimir Putin's own lead: In 2011, he accused the then-secretary of state [Clinton] of fomenting protests in Russia. Unsurprisingly, his media have not wasted an opportunity to portray Clinton as a Russophobic warmonger.

RIA Novosti, once Russia's largest and most respected news agency, has been in the vanguard of the agitprop efforts. To its credit, the agency's DC bureau has provided mostly objective and balanced coverage of the election. But the most popular of RIA's election dispatches, which garnered almost 200,000 page views, went so far as to claim "Clinton has problems with her head."

Few Russian media outlets endorsed Trump outright. Those that did are far from prominent. *Parlamentskaya gazeta*, a dull newspaper of record to the Russian parliament's upper chamber, was one such publication. In a September 2015 op-ed, it declared "Donald Trump a self-made man, a trait Americans love, as they love anyone who is the American Dream incarnate." It claimed Trump would be a better leader than Obama, who was a "single-issue president" (referring to Obamacare), or Clinton, who was "one of the worst secretaries of state in American history."

Open endorsements were largely absent from the more influential media. Indeed, RT, formerly Russia Today, was largely sympathetic to a Democratic contender, Bernie Sanders, and to third party candidates like Jill Stein. But when Sanders dropped out, RT threw its full weight behind discrediting Clinton.

As the election entered the final weeks, the Russian media focus switched to the supposed illegitimacy of the US election, implicitly backing Trump's claims about "large scale voter fraud."

On Oct. 23, Vesti nedeli [News of the Week], a weekly news summary show, did just that. In a long tirade, the program's host, Russian "chief propagandist" Dmitry Kiselyov, lamented "the downfall of the American media," criticizing outlets such as *Politico* for colluding with Clinton's campaign. Another news segment on Channel 1 called Donald Trump "just as evil" as Clinton, a "boorish adventurist" and a "swindler."

The most noticeable recent shift in the Russian state media coverage of the US election is the effort to frame its supposed illegitimacy in Russian terms. Fraud techniques at Russian elections are well-documented—from the so-called "carousels" (repeated voting with absentee ballots at multiple polling stations) to coercion and the use of "administrative resources" (support from the ruling party's political machine). Such fraud, witnessed in Russia's 2011 and 2012 elections, even led to large-scale protests.

Russian state media now have an easy message for their viewers: The same things will happen on Nov. 8. Voskresnoye vremya [The Times on Sunday], a weekly news summary show on Channel 1, even titled one of its segments "The Carousel Beckons," in reference to Russian-style electoral fraud.

Russia's propagandists are stopping short of saying that the US election will be just as fraudulent as the Russian elections have been. After all, that would require an admission of epic state wrongdoing. Rather, they seem more concerned with sowing seeds of doubt among their domestic audience.

Trump as a Mirror

By Aleksandr Frolov. *Sovetskaya Rossia*, Nov. 1, 2016, p. 3.

… The Gallup international polling agency recently asked people from 45 countries whom they would vote for if they could [vote in the US presidential election].

Russia was the only country whose inhabitants chose Trump. Trump got 33%, Hillary Clinton 10%, and 57% were undecided. Thus, the virtual "turnout" of 43% roughly corresponds to the actual turnout in the recent State Duma elections—making Trump's result [equivalent to] 77%. A very presidential rating. In short, we want [a US leader] like Putin!

Nevertheless, others confidently "voted for" Clinton.…

So all the assurances from Russian official propaganda that "all progressive mankind" [and] "all freedom-loving people" hate Obama and Hillary, and want Trump to win are, alas, not supported by facts. However, when the rest of the world "votes" for Clinton, that simply means that it sees Hillary as the lesser evil compared to Donald. The magnitude of these two evils can be measured mathematically. Journalists with the American weekly *Politico* tried to figure out how often both candidates gave listeners, to put it mildly, "inaccurate information," and fact-checked their speeches for one week in September. It turned out that Trump lied every 3 minutes 15 seconds, while Clinton lied every 12 minutes. Thus, we can say Hillary is four times more honest than Donald.

The comparison of Russia's [hypothetical voting] results with those of the rest of the world says something else, shedding light on the "special path" that Putin's Russia has chosen....

Trump's core electorate is concentrated in "the sticks"—in the most backward, depressed and reactionary states: the south and in the so-called Bible Belt; the former stronghold of slavery, decimated 150 years ago in the Civil War but not entirely bereft of nostalgia for those blessed days when blacks, women, Darwinians, atheists and other troublemakers knew their place. Now it is the bulwark of American "traditional values" and "spiritual bonds"; xenophobia in all its forms: racism, sexism, religious hypocrisy, hypersensitivity to the insulted feelings of "true white" Evangelical "Christians." All its hopes are currently riding on the badass macho billionaire who amassed his billions supposedly through honest labor. He'll whip things into shape!

Meanwhile, Trump's slogan of "Make America Great Again" is a mirror image of Putin's slogans. In Putin's view, Russia must get up off its knees before the West, while in Trump's view, America must get up off its knees before Moscow. It is sad, but the Gallup poll clearly shows that Trump and his American admirers have now become a mirror image of today's Russian mass consciousness. What is it about Trump that Russians find so beguiling? His toughness, his criticism of Obama, and most importantly, the fact that he supposedly deeply respects and highly values President Putin. Our TV propaganda is feeding viewers the line that the central issue of the Clinton and Trump debates was allegedly their attitudes toward Russia and Putin—and this, they say, is evidence of the giant strategic significance of Russia and its president in modern world affairs. Of course, it is tactically advantageous for the Democrats to portray Trump as a Putin toady and puppet. But what are the Republicans really saying, as opposed to how they are being portrayed on TV?

In reality, Republicans don't think much more of Putin than Democrats do. Suffice it to point out that Trump's running mate, vice-presidential candidate Michael Pence, called [Putin] a "small and bullying [leader]" who has proved stronger on the world stage than the Obama administration, and is now dictating his terms to the US in Syria and Ukraine. This is not an endorsement of Putin, Pence added, but an indictment of the weak and the feckless leadership of Clinton and Obama, [implying that] the Republicans are obliged to intervene in this situation as strong, decisive leaders. And that's what Donald Trump is going to do—"a man who is prepared to step onto the world stage as the leader of the free world." He will normalize relations with Russia.

However, we should clearly understand what "normal" is in the view of the US ruling class. It is the unconditional global hegemony of American capital in all spheres. And Obama, they say, frittered away this leadership, bringing America to a point where even Putin is walking all over it. Under Trump, this disgrace will end. So the promise to meet with Putin and normalize relations with him is nothing more than a promise to deal with the Russian president and put him in line. When Trump contends that Putin is greater than Obama, he means to say that Obama is smaller than Putin. He is by no means extolling Putin. He merely wishes to underscore Obama's fecklessness.

So before we get carried away with Trump, we need to understand what he has in mind. But right now, while zealously contrasting itself with the hated America, Russia is increasingly acting like the "Trump" half of America, mimicking its worst traits: parochial narrow-mindedness, and arrogance about its own spirituality, exceptionalism and specialness. Such is the irony of history.

This, however, does not mean that we should become like the "Clinton" half of America, which is what our liberals want; she is no better, as we have learned from our own experience. But is there really a different, "third way" for Russia? Yes, there is. But under capitalism, especially the kind that has formed in Russia under the rule of state-oligarchic capital, no third way is possible. Still in the thrall of capital, Russia is doomed to swing fruitlessly back and forth between Hillary and Donald.

Hillary or Donald, It's All Nuts

By Maria Lipman. *The Moscow Times*, Nov. 3, 2016, p. 4.

The reopened FBI probe into Hillary Clinton's emails has reversed the trend of previous weeks that had put her safely ahead of Donald Trump. One week before the presidential vote, the race is once again expected to be tight. The broad anti-Trump camp has returned to a state of being deeply worried, seeing his victory as a doomsday event. The truth is, Hillary Clinton is hardly a blessing either. Clinton, whose chances to win were estimated early this week at under 80% and falling, has been a long anticipated presidential contender. She formally announced her intention to run for president in 2007, but in fact her presidential ambition was a matter of course for much longer. Satirists even depicted her as a fetus clutching a "Hillary 2008" sign.

As she competed for the Democratic nomination in 2008, the expectation was that Clinton would become the first female president of the US. It was billed as a victory of social progress, the achievement of the dogged struggle for women's rights.

On the other hand, her anticipated rise to head of state, especially if she would have been chosen to run against Jeb Bush, gave reason for concern. The emergence of "presidential dynasties" did not look good in a nation that prides itself on its republican tradition.

In 2016, however, the shocking nomination of Donald Trump as Clinton's rival overshadowed both issues that made her unconventional—her gender and her "aristocratic" origin. Clinton is today reduced to a candidate of the establishment. By the same token, the race has been reduced to a confrontation between the establishment and its detractors, a conflict that is rapidly becoming a global trend.

If Clinton wins on Nov. 8, it will be a victory of conventional politics and political machines, over a preposterous challenger defying political and cultural conventions.

If Clinton succeeds in securing a victory, this would demonstrate the US's superiority over its former metropolis across the pond, which only a few months earlier failed to suppress its own antiestablishment revolt and voted for Brexit. It would also give an immense sense of relief to those in the US and around the world who abhor the prospect of Trump in the White House.

What a Clinton victory would not do, however, is quell an ongoing anti-elite revolt in American society. Trump supporters, embittered and angry as they are, will likely feel even more deeply infuriated seeing their candidate lose. Many have not forgotten the tricks that members of the establishment tried to play in order to prevent Trump's nomination as the Republican candidate. Trump's repeated statements about "rigged elections" fall on fertile ground. If their man does not win, his voters will have no doubt that the election has been stolen.

Trump artfully capitalized on the sentiments of the disenfranchised and alienated. Now that he has given them a voice, these Americans—at least 35% according to some estimates—will not give up. If Clinton is indeed elected on Nov. 8, the antiestablishment constituency will remain a huge challenge for her, even if they accept the result.

But the challenge is by no means limited to the domestic scene. Crisis is engulfing the European Union; a bloody war continues in Syria; the prospect of Russian-American confrontation is real; and the risks of terrorism are everywhere. The global order is rapidly crumbling, and it calls for a major revision or at least a fresh view of the foundations of international relations. As part and parcel of the American political establishment, Clinton is unlikely to rise to this task.

The tragedy of this campaign is not just that an infamous and insane candidate has a chance of winning, but that the victory of the seasoned and sane one is nothing for the world to look forward to.

As late as two months ago, Hillary Clinton unflinchingly praised America's "exceptionalism." "We are the indispensable nation and people all over the world look to * * * follow our lead," she said, seemingly oblivious to the spectacular failures caused by such morally righteous positioning. Interventionist policy guided by high principles—such as democratization or humanitarian concerns—has repeatedly led to disastrous consequences.

When it comes to Russian-American relations, the prospect of Hillary Clinton's presidency is also grim. Putin's Russia is an unpredictable and recalcitrant player. The president dismisses any criticism of his foreign policy and declares that if Russia's behavior is not to the West's liking, the West has nobody but itself to blame.

"We are provoked into protecting our interests, and then 'aggressive' Russia is accused of doing this or that," Putin said at last week's meeting of the Valdai international discussion club. "Why are you provoking us? Let us negotiate solutions instead."

Putin has made three things clear. One, nobody can force Russia to change its policy. Two, great power politics is back. And, three, the supposed right of smaller nations to act independently is meaningless unless protected by a stronger ally.

Ahead of a new administration being installed in the White House, Putin has increased the stakes and he looks unbending: It's the US that should change its course, not Russia.

Meanwhile the American establishment and its candidate are equally unwilling to contemplate compromise; they are exasperated and angry, anxious to punish Russia rather than negotiate solutions.

The heat of confrontation may subside a bit once the campaign is over, but it will not go away. Whatever discussions may be held they will hardly be constructive—at least for as long as both administrations, complete with their entrenched viewpoints, remain at either end of the negotiation table.

1.2

Forecasts and Analyses

Introduction

A major theme in this section is Trump's image as a "wild card" in American politics—a breaker of conventions. *International Affairs* editor Armen Oganesyan praises Trump for avoiding the clichés of both major parties' establishments, which the analyst lumps together as the "Bush-Clinton elite." Oganesyan even presciently suggests that Trump's new foreign policy of the "good deal" might just win over the American electorate.

Maria Lipman describes Trump as a breaker of taboos in American political discourse, comparing his firebrand quality to that of nationalist Vladimir Zhirinovsky in the 1990s. Although Lipman acknowledges that Trump has a shot at becoming president, she glibly says: "What does [a Trump victory] mean for Russia? Politically, not too much. US foreign policy has more constants than variables, and whoever wins the presidency will not have much freedom of maneuver: He or she will have to honor the existing alliances and obligations," thus maintaining America's self-image as a dominant power.

After the summer 2016 Republican National Convention, other Russian experts express the prevailing opinion that Clinton will win, although they disagree on whether she or Trump would be better for Russia. Mikhail Troitsky describes her as a "known evil" who would stabilize relations (as they can't get much worse), but Pavel Shankov comments that most progress in bilateral relations (e.g., arms treaties) has been achieved under Republican presidents. Besides, he says, "Russian politicians and pundits are gravitating toward" Trump.

Some analysts express a neutral view of who will win, but all of them overwhelmingly identify an internal crisis afoot in US politics. Diplomat Sergei Ryabkov says that the American public is fed up with the political establishment (more so than with Russia), and Dmitry Suslov argues that there is a deep divide between "isolationists" and "internationalists," as during the Wilson and FDR administrations. He predicts: "If Trump wins, the departure from the current consensus will begin in 2017. If Clinton wins, it will begin a little later. But it is inevitable."

Is Mr. Trump the Next US President?

By Armen Oganesyan, editor in chief.
International Affairs, No. 5, 2015, pp. 74–76.

"The American Dream is dead, but I will bring it back" is the slogan with which Donald Trump literally burst into the presidential election race. The billionaire who made his fortune through real estate development and sales has seriously scared both the Democratic camp and some of his fellow party members, the Republicans. Despite all the attempts to marginalize him, Trump is confidently winning support and building up an electorate for himself.

Donald Trump surely has his trump cards, and one of them is his financial independence, something he constantly stresses. The Bush-Clinton elite, encumbered with their clienteles, will never make America great—they have no chance of doing so, he tells his supporters. The Americans, who usually assume that all presidents have had lobbies behind them that financed their election campaigns and have largely controlled their policies, have been pleasantly surprised by Trump's uninhibited rhetoric, although he says he needs work more than rhetoric.

One distinctive feature of Trump's campaign is his assumption that one way to make America prosperous is to adopt a new foreign policy based on the notion of the "good deal." That is the positive aspect of his foreign policy doctrine. The negative side is his insistence that the US should be tough and resolute in negotiating such deals. In one of his campaign speeches, he lashed out against China for "destroying" the US economy by devaluing its currency and stealing jobs from ordinary Americans. Trump has mentioned China on several occasions, and despite his assurances that he is fond of the Chinese, the Celestial Kingdom is the number one enemy in his eyes. Unexpectedly, the number two enemy is Mexico, which, he claims, exports cheap labor and crime to America. "I would build a great, great wall * * * on our southern border and I will have Mexico pay for that wall," he said.

One more pet target of Trump's is big US corporations that locate their manufacturing facilities abroad to hire cheaper labor. He threatens to slap import duties of up to 30% on the goods they bring to the US.

The Republican candidate is convinced that unemployment in his country is at least twice as high as official statistics show. "I will be the greatest jobs president God ever created," he said. Much more than welfare allowances, Americans need confidence in the future and jobs that are secure and bring them what would be decent earnings by American standards. Hopping from subject to subject, Trump then goes back to the foreign policy theme and his ideology of making deals from a position of strength. Saudi Arabia, for example, must pay the US a fee for guaranteeing its security. That is a dubious thesis: Saudi Arabia is a regional power that itself has enough clout to make decisions on war and peace in the Middle East....

"One of the things that I heard for years and years: Never drive Russia and China together; and Obama has done that," Trump said. In talking about a visit to Russia two years ago, he said he would be able to "have a great relationship" with Putin and "get along" with the Russian people. Trump appears to be deliberately avoiding the Ukraine theme, and thereby obviously winning points from his fellow Americans, who are scared of anti-Russian rhetoric with increasingly frequent belligerent overtones.

Returning to his theme of fees that he wants foreign countries to pay the US, he insists that America impose dues for its global leadership on its potential adversaries and potential allies alike.

Trump was against the war in Iraq and deplored the US's human and financial losses in it. He doesn't believe that leadership necessarily means participation. He considers leadership a source of specific economic, mainly financial, benefits, among other things a skill to obtain lucrative deals through tough negotiations. He is convinced that there is no one in the current American political elite who is capable of bringing off such deals, that this elite is impotent, and that, as a result, America is a weakening superpower.

One naturally wonders what the odds are of Trump becoming president. In comparing him to political giants such as the Bush and Clinton family clans, many claim that his defeat is a foregone conclusion. On the other hand, the electorate is obviously tired of faces that are much too familiar, make déjà-vu speeches and use hackneyed clichés, and this may be to the advantage of the "loose cannon" Trump. His independent and obviously novel, if not indisputable, ideas have an appeal to them.

Critics claim that Trump's foreign policy views may scare voters instead of attracting them. "Maybe, but perhaps they don't understand the American people in the way that Mr. Trump does," says Jeremy Shapiro of the Brookings Institution. "He has tapped into a deep well of populist anger that runs through much of the Republican electorate. People are tired of the same old elites peddling the same old solutions, while the working class suffers through economic loss and cultural decline. They do not want any more efforts to explain away their anger in politically correct terms."

Nevertheless, Trump will have his work cut out for him trying to win ground from his eminent rivals, and the billions of dollars in his bank account can't do all the work. Both the Republican leadership and, naturally, the Democratic elite may close ranks against him. But both Bush and Clinton have rivals within their own parties, and at some point Trump may invoke his good deals theory and clinch a deal with some of them.

As for his foreign policy views, behind their questionable pragmatism and toughness is most likely a desire to seek agreement rather than try to force American attitudes and values on the rest of the world.

The latest ratings suggest that Trump is stably ahead of the other Republican candidates, including Jeb Bush.

Breaking Democracy's Morals: The Trump Phenomenon Makes US Politics Look More Like Those of Europe

By Maria Lipman. *The Moscow Times,* May 12, 2016, p. 5.

As Donald Trump has risen from a remote contender to the presumptive Republican presidential nominee, the US media commentary has been an unending flow of dismay, despair, anxiety and anger. Some commentators rather desperately discussed possible ways to prevent Trump from winning the nomination, but this proved meaningless when Trump won the Indiana primaries on May 3, and his remaining competitors withdrew from the race. Now the focus of the media analysis is shifting toward "Can he win?" the presidency.

While some of those who abhor a possible Trump victory try not to give in to fear, and claim that the Democratic party is built to defeat Trump or even forecast that 2016 will be a year of "Democratic routs," others find at least several reasons why November might bring on a "Trumpocalypse."

Since hardly anyone predicted Trump's current triumph, nobody can rule out another surprise—Trump becoming president of the US.

What does that mean for Russia? Politically, not too much. US foreign policy has more constants than variables, and whoever wins the presidency will not have much freedom of maneuver: He or she will have to honor the existing alliances and obligations, and will be unable to ignore powerful domestic interests or dominant ideas about US preeminence in the world.

As for Russia, US-Russian relations are defined, in the words of Andrej Krickovic and Yuval Weber, by a "fundamental disagreement about the genesis of the current world order." The US regards Russia as "a revisionist power bent on overturning the established order and challenging the US global leadership." In Russia, anything short of tough anti-Americanism is regarded as an unacceptable concession, while in the US, a softer Russia policy is seen as inadmissible appeasement. In Russia, the US of President Barack Obama is perceived as our main enemy, but at home, Obama is often criticized for being too soft on Russia. Any future administration, Krickovic and Weber write, will face strong pressure from both political parties to harden its Russia line.

Hillary Clinton will hardly resist this pressure. Although she served as secretary of state during the bygone era of the Obama "reset" of relations with Russia, she is anything but an appeaser. Rather, she is a hawk, not averse to using military interventions as a foreign policy means. It is true that Trump has made occasional overtures to President Vladimir Putin, and indeed mentioned that he would improve relations with Russia—"from a position of strength"—which can hardly be music to Putin's ears. But one should not take these statements any more seriously than Trump's declared intention to build a wall on the US-Mexican border or make US allies pay for the American military presence in their countries.

But even if this year's presidential race in the US does not matter too much for Russia in practical political terms, Trump's unexpected success is certainly important for us from a political-cultural standpoint.

Only eight years ago, the US was celebrating an amazing national accomplishment: The election of an African-American for president seemed to prove that the nation—if not fully, then at least in a very significant way—had overcome the legacy of slavery, followed by official and then unofficial racial discrimination.

Despite setbacks along the way, US history could be seen as a progressive advance from Abraham Lincoln's mid-19th-century line about a "government of the people, by the people, for the people" to the abolition of the poll tax about 100 years later, which finally granted voting rights to all adult citizens.

Theoretically speaking, in a universal democracy all the citizens are involved in making decisions about their country's affairs. In practice, however, decision-making is delegated to a small minority—the political elite that speaks and acts on people's behalf, but does not reflect the broad diversity of voters. Campaigning, the art of attracting and accommodating various constituencies, has evolved as a highly sophisticated, complex and costly industry. It helps promising political contenders reach out to their potential supporters and persuade them that [a given candidate] is the best person to serve the public, but also marginalizes unwanted influences and politically unwelcome views.

The competition between parties and candidates is fierce, and, especially in recent years, US society has grown more polarized. Still, this competition has remained within the established framework of moral propriety—so anybody appealing to ugly, xenophobic sentiments, whether racist, sexist, homophobic or otherwise, would be defeated in the early stages.

In retrospect, it seems almost inevitable that one day somebody would break the unspoken ban and reach out to those constituencies that had never subscribed to the language and values of the establishment, and had been skillfully marginalized by professional campaign specialists.

This year, it happened. Donald Trump tapped into the unappealing sentiments of those who felt excluded, disenfranchised and resentful. His success is due in large part to offensive language: opting for openly nativist rhetoric, aggressively attacking "non-Americans" ([including] Mexicans [and] Muslims), as well as women.

In the Russia of the 1990s, when we still had competitive politics, Vladimir Zhirinovsky played a similar trick. With his unabashedly nationalistic, aggressive language, he won the support of those who felt deeply disappointed and disenfranchised by the new, democratic government. On the televised election night, liberal intellectual Yury Karyakin exclaimed in shock: "Russia, come to your senses! You're out of your mind!"

Despite the long history of institutionalized democracy in the US, these days many progressive, liberal Americans seem to feel the same way as they realize that their democracy no longer has a bulwark against nativist, xenophobic politics. The Trump phenomenon makes US democracy look more like that of Europe, where nativist politicians have gained considerable success in recent years. It is also a disturbing realization to those Russian liberals who tend to blame ugly public sentiments and loathsome politics on state dominance and aggressive government propaganda.

The America Watchers

By Matthew Bodner. *The Moscow Times,* Aug. 4, 2016, p. 4.

Editors' Note—With the US presidential election entering its final stretch, observers in America and abroad are scrambling to forecast what a post-Obama US domestic and foreign policy would look like.

Russia appears to have a keen interest in the outcome of this election. Heading into November, the Kremlin is faced with two very different visions of America's future role in the world. On the one hand, there is Hillary Clinton's assumed doubling down on Obama's foreign policy platform. On the other is Donald Trump's blend of transactional neoisolationist populism, which would seem to fit better with Putin's desire for a reduced US presence on the international arena.

The Moscow Times polled several of Russia's leading experts on American politics to get the perspective from Moscow on what promises to be the most consequential presidential election in decades.

* * *

1. Who will win the election?

Dmitry Suslov, professor of American politics at Moscow's Higher School of Economics—Hillary Clinton will win, I predict. Election results in the US are usually determined by swing states, and independent voters who are more or less moderate and centrist. For these kinds of people, Donald Trump is just too radical. He succeeded in winning the Republican nomination because of his extreme and populist viewpoints. But, given the choice between him and Hillary Clinton, the conventional moderate American voter would vote for continuity and stability, rather than the kind of revolution that Trump brings with him.

Mikhail Troitsky, professor at the Moscow State Institute of International Relations; American foreign policy expert—I would certainly bet on Clinton's victory. But I wouldn't put all my money on Hillary becoming the next president. We will see what unfolds between now and November; [we will] see which issues pop up. For the moment, however, Clinton does have a better chance of winning than Trump.

Pavel Shankov, head of the Center for Applied Research at the Russian Academy of Sciences' US and Canada Institute (Russia's oldest US research outfit)—As has been the case since I started observing US elections in 2000, it's really hard to say anything before November. The victory of an experienced politician like Clinton still seems more probable, but Trump's campaign style is very aggressive. He might have a few aces up his sleeve. Already, Clinton almost lost several times to Bernie Sanders—a politician who is basically considered to be a communist by American standards—so her chances of winning are not entirely persuasive.

Andrei Sushentsov, program director at the Valdai Discussion Club and head of the Foreign Policy Analysis Group—I think Trump has a better sense of the zeitgeist in the American majority right now. That said, I think the Clinton campaign has better organization and greater capacity to get out the vote in decisive states. So, I think in the end Clinton will win.

2. This has been a very unorthodox election. How do you explain it to Russians?

D.S.—The American political system is in a process of unstoppable change, and both Donald Trump and Bernie Sanders are proof of this. Together, they showed that the American public is generally not okay with globalization. Today, people are basically saying, "We don't want that kind of tomorrow, so give us back our comfortable yesterday." Trump is exploiting those feelings.

The 2024 election will most likely be decisive in terms of American domestic politics. Clinton is the white knight of the Washington elite, and the Trump and Sanders phenomena show that the American people are becoming increasingly opposed to it. A Clinton victory would not stop the overall changes happening in the American electorate.

A.S.—The American elite has lost touch with the electorate. People have fewer economic opportunities, and this provokes all kind of conflicts in American society. Domestic and international security has once again become an important issue driving the election.

M.T.—The US is engaged in an overdue experiment in populist politics. What Trump is doing is a very shrewdly timed attempt to harness populism—in this case, anger at the impact of globalization on US society and economy—and to marry it to the democratic ideal of one person, one vote.

He has succeeded in doing this because he comes from outside the political class, and can therefore afford to shrug off political correctness. He can afford to appeal to racial divides, ethnic tensions and pent-up anger existing in American society.

Given the demographic changes taking place within the American electorate, this is probably the last time someone can play with such populist political tactics. Trump is betting on the white majority—of whom I guess less than 50% have college degrees—and it might be someone's last chance to run on a divisive, sexist, ethnocentric platform in America. The demographics are shifting away from the white majority.

P.S.—For many years, US politics was logical and explainable. Even with the really bad decisions, there was a certain logic at play. Trump, on the other hand, addresses those Americans who want to hear: "Make America Great Again."

That said, I still cannot understand Trump's own motivations. He's a businessman. Unlike in Russia, you don't go into politics to make money. In Russia, certain politicians manage to use their powers to benefit their business, and thus make big money. Maybe I'm an idealist, but it's a different system in America.

3. What would a Hillary Clinton victory mean for Russia?

D.S.—A Clinton victory would be very bad for US-Russia relations. Under her administration, American foreign policy would become even more ideological and even more anti-Russian. This would not be the end of the world, because this kind of foreign policy would become less and less supported by the American public. A fundamental change, a revolutionary change in American foreign policy is unavoidable. Either in 2020 or 2024, the US will put an end to the foreign policy consensus first established by Harry Truman in the 1940s [about the US maintaining an active leadership role in world affairs—*Ed.*]. This will be good for Russia.

M.T.—I think we have a better shot working with her. Trump is unpredictable, and it is better to stick with the "known evil," so to speak. Russia would have a chance of engaging in some substantive negotiations with a Clinton administration. Basically, with any new administration—or at least a predictable one—there is a chance to try some blank-slate negotiations.

P.S.—There's a weird relationship between Russian politicians and American parties. The general thinking is that Russian politicians work well with American Democrats. But if we look at the history of the cold war, it started under a Democratic president, Harry Truman. The first arms control treaty signed with a Democrat was in 2009, with Obama.

All previous arms control treaties were signed with Republican presidents. The Republican Party—I'm talking about the GOP of the 1970s, with Kissinger and "realpolitik"—was always very pragmatic. They had few ideological components.

Under a Hillary Clinton presidency, bilateral relations are not likely to improve. But there are very few opportunities for relations to get worse. There are rumors about potential cabinet and administration members that would be promising for Russia—names like Bill Burns, the head of the Carnegie Endowment and a former US ambassador to Russia. He's very smart, and well respected in Moscow. But then there are others, for example [Obama's former ambassador to Russia] Michael McFaul, who is still blamed in Russia for the general deterioration of bilateral relations.

And one thing is certain: Hillary Clinton and Putin would never understand each other.

4. What would a Trump presidency mean for Russia?

D.S.—The majority of problems in US-Russia relations are driven not by bilateral relations, but the fundamental difference in the way international order is understood.

If Trump prevails, the overwhelming majority of these problems would disappear by themselves. Trump would most likely be indifferent toward Russian policies in the neighborhood, and would likely not engage in democracy promotion and regime change.

On the other hand, Trump is the embodiment of unpredictability. George W. Bush also turned out to be completely different than we expected. For example, he campaigned against Clinton's liberal foreign policy, but after 9/11 he turned out to be much more ideological and interventionist than Clinton. A similar thing could happen with Trump.

M.T.—From what we are hearing, Trump is Russia's favored candidate. He talks about reneging on NATO commitments, recognizing the Crimea as part of Russia; he seems pro-Russia and wants to do business with Russia, and so on. But I would advise Putin to be cautious with Trump. He is extremely unpredictable, and we don't know who, for example, his national security adviser might be. What if he goes for someone really hawkish to prove to the bureaucracy he's a mainstream guy? In that case, we might get a policy even more adversarial toward Russia than Clinton's.

P.S.—Trump is controversial when it comes to Russia. Here he is perceived as a good dealer who would try to work with Putin, so this makes him a better option than anyone else. But he is hard to understand. The litmus test for Russian politicians is what each candidate says about Russia's actions in Ukraine—whether they were aggressive or defensive, basically.

Trump has said both things. But recently, he's been very positive about Russia and Putin. Naturally enough, Russian politicians and pundits are gravitating toward him.

Russia-US Relations After the Election: 'We Will Be Ready for a New Start'

By Russian Deputy Foreign Minister Sergei Ryabkov.
International Affairs, No. 5, 2016, pp. 26–39.

Editors' Note—This interview with Ryabkov was conducted in the summer of 2016 by Armen Oganesyan, editor in chief of *International Affairs*.

* * *

Question—Sergei Alekseyevich [Ryabkov], despite the hot summer months, there is no holiday season in international affairs. Even though some people still maintain that we are in isolation, Russia is present in virtually all main global political developments. This applies even to the US election campaign. I mean, of course, the recent statement by the US president that the hacking attack on the online resource of the Democratic Party may have been organized by Russian special services.[3]

Answer—The summer is indeed hot, both in the direct and figurative sense of the word. We are in the maelstrom of events and I believe that we are also generating certain waves.

As for the US, a bipartisan consensus based on an anti-Russian foundation has evolved there. We are faced with a situation where our country is being deliberately and consciously demonized and accused of almost every sin under the sun. The US ruling circles and all those they are dependent on have developed a certain complex with regard to Russia. They see us as an almost omnipotent evil, which points to some serious deviations in their perception of reality.

Now it has come to the point where we are accused of interfering in US internal affairs. We have repeatedly stated and reaffirmed that whoever becomes the next US president, we will respect the choice made by the American people. That Russia is trying to add electoral points to a particular candidate by hacking into some servers is a figment of the imagination of some spin doctors who are cashing in on all sorts of conspiracy theories, but in reality this is not possible.

I regret the fact that this story about hacking into the servers of the National Committee of the Democratic Party, which emerged in May but was not followed up at the time, came into focus at the height of a recent convention of the Democratic Party. Clearly, interparty conflicts have intensified in the US. We will probably see more black PR examples. This goes to show that there are not so many substantive arguments. Unfortunately, it has to be said that the present US administration has also been involved in some disgraceful machinations. This does not do it any credit.

Unfortunately, this is the kind of reality that one has to deal with. However, we take this in stride. All the assessments have already been made. The Russian presidential press secretary and the foreign minister have spoken up and I have simply nothing to add.

I do not trust words, especially the words of US politicians and US diplomats, regardless of their rank and standing.

Q—Sergei Alekseyevich, recently, the media have widely reported Donald Trump's remarks about the need to improve relations with Russia. How serious are these statements, in your opinion?

A—I do not trust words, especially the words of US politicians and US diplomats, regardless of their rank and standing. People should be judged by their deeds.

We have read the Republican Party program that was approved at the convention. We keep track of Donald Trump's remarks. We studied his speech at the convention. In the republican program on which he is running together with Mike Pence as his vice-presidential running mate, passages about Russia are written in the worst traditions of recent years. We stand accused of destabilizing the situation, being an aggressive power, posing a challenge to the US, and so on. I do not want to reproduce this phraseology. However, you know, this is what is stated in the program of the Republican Party, Mr. Trump being its candidate. So it is necessary to take a comprehensive view to see the whole picture.

Of course, he has sent signals that provide some grounds to expect changes. Whether these expectations will be fulfilled does not depend on us but only on the US side, on the choice that the voters make and on the policy that the next president will pursue. I will point out that recently Donald Trump's ratings have significantly declined.

Nevertheless, nothing prevents the future president of any party—be it Democratic or Republican—from reviewing Barack Obama's "legacy," which cannot be described as anything other than difficult, troublesome and problem-ridden. There is nothing to prevent a reappraisal of options and try to find a new point of departure, if not start from scratch (we also have no illusions in that regard). For our part, I can state with complete authority that we will be ready for a new start.

There is a phrase that has already become a cliché: "It takes two to tango." Now there is already one side ready to tango—ours—

but our American partners should make a choice for themselves whether they want to tango in the first place.

Q—How free will Donald Trump be in making the decision to review relations with Russia if he becomes president?

A—The election campaign in the US, as in any country, is developing according to its own laws. Less than three months remain before election day, but a great deal can change during this time. Election campaign canons probably also envision a certain adjustment of a candidate's image to improve his perception in the eyes of the public. So a candidate's traditional, established image as being "independent from the system" may be deliberately altered, for example, in order to add a "mainstream" touch. This is why no one in the US can seriously count on victory without taking into account the prevailing sentiments in influential social strata.

We are observing the same trends in Hillary Clinton's campaign. The Democratic Party program happens to contain ideas that were originally put forward by Bernie Sanders. [The Clinton platform] is absorbing everything expected to attract those who did not see it in the main candidate but preferred a rival with a "nonestablishment" image during the primaries.

Possibly, the candidate who wins this election will be able to overcome the inertia of the US apparatus. This has not infrequently been the case at different stages of US history. Will this happen in this particular case, especially in the sphere of Russian-US relations? Frankly, I would not give an affirmative answer because, first, Russian-US relations will probably not be a priority for the next US president and it will be some time before Washington starts seriously thinking about how to build a relationship with Russia. Second, regardless of political affiliation, the next US president will evidently confer on Russia with staff very often and thoroughly, while their behavior will be closely watched by the establishment, which believes that "no concessions must be made to the Russians" and that of late the Russians have done a great deal to undermine US interests. I have to say this again and again. We should not have any illusory expectations or empty hopes.

This reality cannot be reversed or altered. The inertia of US politics will remain a factor of impact, even though the US president has sufficient authority to overcome this inertia. History also shows that sooner or later the algorithm of our relations will change again, and they will be tuned in to a more positive wavelength. The barometer is sure to climb. As for when this happens, that depends entirely on the Americans.

Q—Sergei Alekseyevich, do Trump's well-known remarks mean that the American audience is tired of anti-Russian rhetoric and the tough anti-Russian course and that he is thus attracting an additional electorate?

A—I would not exaggerate the importance of statements that are made at various stages of the election campaign either by the candidates themselves or by representatives of their election campaign headquarters, not because they do not reflect particular sentiments. After all, US polling practices are well advanced, and public opinion evaluation procedures make it possible to identify the minutest "puffs of wind." However, I would not exaggerate the impact of statements that are made in the course of an election campaign, because there is a great distance between declarations and practical actions. Of course, it is a good thing that there are those in the US who are resurrecting the somewhat forgotten subject of establishing and developing constructive ties with Russia. By the way, we have not given up on this subject, and we keep saying that this is our objective. After all is said and done, it is up to our partners in Washington to make their choice. However, it is uncertain whether the slogan of "being friends with Russia" will play a positive role in the election.

How real is the US electorate's weariness of anti-Russian rhetoric? A certain segment of it probably feels the need for a positive alternative to the current anti-Russian free-for-all. However, the general fatigue of the American electorate is to a far greater extent related to problems that are growing in American society. Active politicians, the Washington establishment, senators and congressmen, and the big bosses on Capitol Hill lobbying for the interests of multinational corporations; their entourage, lunching at Washington's countless restaurants, sitting there over a glass of flat water and fixing their problems; all of these wheelers and dealers; all of these media hacks; this entire bunch, this superstructure that determines US domestic and foreign policy—unfortunately, none of them can respond to the growing scope of questions that are related primarily to the current difficult situation and prospects for the development of American society as such. This is the root cause of the protest sentiments within the US electorate. Here, Russia is actually "off the radar." However, we will see what all of this will look like in the future....

US Gives Another Reason to Believe Its Democracy Is Deeply Flawed

By Alex Gorka. *Strategic Culture Foundation Online Journal*, Oct. 23, 2016, http://www.strategic-culture.org/news/2016/10/23/us-gives-another-reason-believe-democracy-deeply-flawed.html.

The US has delivered another heavy blow against Russian-US relations.

Russian Deputy Foreign Minister Sergei Ryabkov said on Oct. 22 that Moscow finds it unacceptable that the US warned criminal charges will be brought against Russian diplomats if they appear at polling stations to observe the US election process on Nov. 8. Moscow chose to conduct the observations independently—not with the Office for Democratic Institutions and Human Rights (ODIHR) mission of the Organization for Security and Co-operation in Europe—because it does not fully accept the ODIHR methodology and criteria used for election assessment. Besides, that would involve additional restrictions on visiting polling stations in some states.

The idea to send a delegation of observers to the US has been rejected by the State Department.

According to State Department spokesman Mark Toner, the effort to send in diplomats was a "PR stunt."

Three states—Oklahoma, Louisiana and Texas—have even threatened to bring criminal charges against the diplomats if they appear at ballot stations.

By contrast, Russia sent personal invitations to US monitors asking them to observe the September parliamentary elections, and 63 accepted the offer. In total, 774 monitors from 63 nations received accreditation to observe Russia's parliamentary elections. In addition, US representatives visited Russia earlier as part of an OSCE/ODIHR monitoring mission.

Republican candidate Donald Trump has repeatedly claimed that the election is being "rigged," which Republican officials have disputed. "I'm telling you, Nov. 8, we'd better be careful, because that election is going to be rigged," he told Fox News.

According to Trump, his own primary election was "rigged" against him. Just think about it—the leader of a major political party believes that the US voting system is flawed! The candidate has said that some people voted despite being ineligible, some cast ballots many times and some impersonated dead voters. A poll conducted by *Politico* and [opinion research service] Morning Consult, released on Oct. 17 found that 48% of Trump supporters said they were "not too" or "not at all" confident that votes would be accurately counted on Election Day, and 81% of Trump supporters said they believe the election could be "stolen" from Trump as a result of voter fraud.

Around a quarter of Americans say they have "hardly any confidence" that their votes will be counted correctly, according to a recent AP/NORC survey.

According to Shyla Nelson, the cofounder of Election Justice USA (EJUSA), US elections are manipulated in many ways, including "voter suppression, unauthorized registration purges, district gerrymandering, gross exit poll variances, the privatization of voting machinery, and the lack of transparency in ballot processing—our elections will continue to rank among the lowest in the world in integrity."

Several key swing states use electronic voting systems with no backup paper trail. The system makes it virtually impossible for election officials to provide proof of how the election results were achieved. The reliance on electronic voting machines—often running on increasingly obsolete hardware and software—and online voting threatens public trust in US elections.

There are multiple examples of incidents that lead experts to question the security and reliability of voting systems across the country. A LawNewz report says cyberattacks and hacking into the voting system are a reality.

According to the OSCE/ODIHR Needs Assessment Mission (NAM) report, some 4.1 million citizens who are residents of US territories are not eligible, and some 600,000 citizens who are residents of the District of Columbia can vote in presidential elections but do not have full representation in Congress.

Around 5.8 million prisoners and ex-prisoners continue to be disenfranchised due to prohibitive and disproportionate legal regulations, or burdensome procedures for reinstating voting rights in a number of states. Women are generally underrepresented in public office, holding some 20% of seats in the outgoing Congress and some 25% of seats in the state legislatures. There are no limits on campaign spending. The paper concludes that there is a range of vulnerabilities in the conduct of American elections.

The 2016 Democratic Primary election was riddled with irregularities and fraud. In June, six Republican candidates from the June 2016 primary election filed Statements of Contest in Clark County District Court [in Nevada] based on NRS 293.410(f), which allows for an election to be contested on grounds that there was a possible malfunction in the voting or counting devices used to record and tabulate the votes.

A report by the nonprofit election integrity organization EJUSA is recommending that Democratic primary results in numerous states, including New York and California, be decertified, and that the paper ballots be recounted by hand in all states that show irregularities and where paper ballots are available. [It also recommends that ballots be] counted by hand in all future US elections.

With all the facts adduced above, it wouldn't be a big surprise if many Americans, as well as people in other countries who have been following events in the US, question the legitimacy of the election results. As one can see, there is every reason to express concern over the fairness of the Nov. 8 vote.

The US media have many times raised a ballyhoo over Russian elections being unfair.

Now they are doing their best to downplay the irregularities of the US voting system.

If the election system is fair, there is no need to prevent Russian diplomats from closely observing the procedures. After all,

Russia may be willing to take a page out of the US's book to perfect its own election system.

There is one more aspect worth mentioning here. By denying the diplomats their right to monitor the elections, the US is in violation of the 1961 Vienna Convention on diplomatic relations, which gives nations the right to monitor elections in other countries.

According to the document, the functions of a diplomatic mission consist in part "in ascertaining by all lawful means conditions and developments in the receiving state." Watching the vote is part of permitted diplomatic activities....

Good-Bye Familiar America? US Foreign Policy: A Forecast Until 2024

By Dmitry Suslov. *Russia in Global Affairs*, No. 4, 2016, pp. 83–91.

The presidential race in the US has entered its final stretch, meaning it is time to pause and take stock of events. Not surprisingly, the campaign has revealed profound fissures between Democrats and Republicans, which has been the case in all recent elections since 1996 (Bill Clinton and Bob Dole), but especially in 2000 (George W. Bush and Al Gore) and 2008 (Barack Obama and John McCain). No less important is the deep divide between the entire US foreign policy elite and society.

The nature and depth of the divide is reminiscent of the isolationists and internationalists during the administrations of Woodrow Wilson and Franklin D. Roosevelt. Indeed, it shows the limits of foreign policy consensus in the US, which first emerged in the 1940s when Harry Truman was president. The division grew larger after the US had declared victory in the cold war, then started actively working to shape the world to its ideas and values, which seemed universal at the time.

Consensus and challenges.

The foreign policy consensus shared by both Democratic liberal internationalists and Republican neoconservatives is based on four pillars:

1. Commitment to "global leadership";

2. Commitment to strengthening and broadening the "liberal international order";

3. Recognition of the inextricable link between the influence, safety, and prosperity of the US, on the one hand, and its leadership of the "liberal international order," on the other;

4. Commitment to spreading democracy. This implies the preservation and even expansion of the US global presence and greater intervention to resolve the most important international and even domestic issues and crises....

The current US foreign policy consensus received a huge infusion of legitimacy at the end of the cold war, which seemed at the time to confirm many of these assumptions. Today it is becoming increasingly clear that these axioms were illusory. Moreover, unlike the elite, which continue to believe in those principles and are desperately trying to prove their relevance, Americans are experiencing this the hard way.

A friendly world no more.

Twenty years after the greatest triumph of the West and the US, the world has ceased to move in a direction that is good for them. It turned out that globalization has a "dark side"—global financial and economic crises, overall vulnerability, and transnational security threats—and, in general, is working for non-Western countries much better than for the West. Against this backdrop, an unusually tough statement by President Barack Obama that the US, not China, will write the international trade rules in the 21st century, and Donald Trump's promises to bring industrial production back to the US are symptoms of the same disease. Globalization as it is no longer suits the US. It is decimating the middle class, reducing living standards, and fueling fears in American society that children today may be worse off than their parents.

The same applies to security. The end of the cold war failed to bring about Immanuel Kant's "perpetual peace." On the contrary, the world is becoming increasingly torn by conflicts, and is less governable and more hostile towards the US and the West in general. Transnational threats are growing in the wake of a renewed rivalry between great powers. The US, as the self-styled leader, is powerless to do anything about it. Washington's attempts to intervene and play the role of a "global policeman" have only made things worse (in Iraq, Afghanistan, Libya, the Greater Middle East and Ukraine).

The same goes for migration, which has become a major challenge to social development and identity, both in the US and Western Europe. American society was not prepared for the massive influx of Latin American immigrants. The melting pot, which worked so well for European Americans, did not simply falter, but collapsed. The white population, which will likely become a minority by mid-century, has found itself under siege. The growing terrorist threat from Islamic radicals has predictably prompted an even greater surge of intolerance.

Simply put, faced with the uncontrollable forces of globalization and a less hospitable world, American society—or at least a significant part of it—has started opposing the foreign policy consensus that the political elite has advanced for several decades. Society demands the familiar and friendly "yesterday" and instinctively seeks to fence itself off from an increasingly hostile world—whether nearby Mexico or overseas Europe, or the Middle East. Donald Trump is on the front lines of this protest. He is popular precisely because his populist statements resonate with public sentiment and the general rejection of the previous foreign policy consensus (and the elite behind it).

Importantly, all the Republican candidates and almost all Democratic ones (with one exception), who represented the traditional political elite and traditional foreign policy consensus during these elections, have failed miserably. On the contrary, the critics of the system, such as populist Donald Trump, socialist Bernie Sanders, and Tea Party leader Ted Cruz, have become the stars of the campaign. Against this backdrop, Hillary Clinton is the only representative of the Establishment and the champion of the status quo who has made it to the finals.

As a result of the chasm between the traditional elite and an angry electorate, for the first time since the first half of the 20th century presidential candidates are running campaigns based not merely on differences of opinion, but on fundamentally different foreign policy paradigms.

Returning leadership vs. returning greatness.

Shaped in the 1990s, Hillary Clinton's views of foreign policy represent a concentrated form of the traditional American foreign policy consensus. She is a proponent of US global leadership and the US-led "liberal international order." Moreover, Clinton is a true candidate of the American elite, who were disappointed in George W. Bush and Obama, considering the policy of the former excessively rigid and lopsided, and the policy of the latter too soft and accommodating. No wonder the majority of foreign policy elites began to coalesce around her during the initial stage of the election campaign. The Democrats were the first, as they believed that President Obama had not done enough to advance US global leadership, had done too little to promote American interests, and even less to promote American values. Later, when it became clear that the Republican candidate, Trump, was winning, neoconservatives scrambled to throw their support behind Clinton.

Even though Trump does not have a detailed foreign policy course and is guided mostly by his business instincts and pure pragmatism, he demonstrates a fundamental departure from the established US foreign policy paradigm. He understands the disaffected voters who, on the one hand, would like to fence themselves off from a hostile world and concentrate resources on domestic issues and, to be frank, put an end to globalization, but who, on the other hand, are not satisfied with the Obama administration's "weak" policies.

Judging by his remarks and the comments of his advisers, Trump intuitively leans toward classical political realism with a focus on national interests. He has little interest in values and the international order (as a set of rules and norms of behavior), and neo-realism, with its strict approach to global alignment of forces.

One of the key premises underlying Trump's foreign policy outlook is renouncing the link between the US's greatness, on the one hand, and its leading role in promoting the liberal international order in accordance with US interests and values (the American system of military, trade and economic alliances, international economic institutions, etc.), on the other. It is no coincidence that one of the most respected American diplomats, former ambassador to the UN, Iraq and Afghanistan, Zalmay Khalilzad, described Trump's foreign policy platform as a kind of throwback to the days of Franklin D. Roosevelt.

If the fluff of his outrageous and controversial remarks is removed from what he says, Trump's agenda is largely in line with the concept of offshore balancing, which has been promoted by leading American realists for several years. In accordance with this view, the US should reduce its direct presence in various regions of the world (except for where it is needed to protect US vital interests) and shift a greater burden of responsibility for security to its allies. It should take a very selective approach to direct involvement in crises, refrain from using military force as a primary foreign policy tool (specifically, give up occupation and nation-building missions), and reduce its democracy promotion activities. This concept (and the school of realism in general) also recommends that the US focus on relations with other great powers and develop policies towards them that will allow them to retain their superiority as long as possible.

Even with regard to specific foreign policy issues, Trump's controversial remarks, if, again, you separate them from the populist wrapper, are completely consistent with the leading American realists' recommendations. Thus, his statement that European countries should protect themselves and NATO should run its course is no different from calls by John Mearsheimer and Stephen Walt for a complete withdrawal of US troops from Europe (even now, despite the Ukraine crisis and the worsening standoff with Russia). It is especially resonant with what former US defense secretary Robert Gates said back in 2011: Washington might reconsider its approach to the alliance and its usefulness for America.

Trump's remarks about Russia and China and the role he assigns to relations with other great powers in his foreign policy agenda (if it can be referred to as such) are also broadly in line with the realistic paradigm. With regard to China as a major economic and political rival, the US has formulated a strict policy of containment. Trump has already made it clear that he will not try to build partnerships with Beijing, and not only because of the job drain to China.

A more constructive foreign policy has been proposed with regard to Russia, which is, of course, perceived as a great power, but not one that can pose a major challenge to the US or call into question its global superiority. Apparently, realist-minded advisers to the Republican nominee hope to use the proposed partnership with Russia to more effectively contain China. If this is the case, this factor may become one of the major irritants in relations between the two countries should Trump be elected president.

This does not mean, though, that if elected Trump will actually embark on a foreign policy course similar to that of Henry Kissinger or George H. W. Bush. Since the American elite, Congress, the government bureaucracy, and the media are against it, such a trajectory is simply impossible. For a larger number of employees in the State Department and the Pentagon, even the current US foreign policy is not tough enough and occasionally defeatist (remember the letter written by 50 employees of the State Department that called on Obama to start bombing Syria like the US did in Yugoslavia). With regard to Trump, there may be instances of sabotage or mass layoffs. Clearly, if he is elected president, his actual policies will be significantly different from his current statements. Already the choice of Mike Pence—a representative of the traditional Republican establishment with orthodox foreign policy views, including in relation to Russia—as a running mate demonstrates the inevitability of a major correction.

Departure is inevitable.

Major changes to US foreign policy will take place no matter what. It is hard to tell exactly how, but Trump, if elected, will make a major move away from the foreign policy paradigm that has been dominant in the US over the past 70 years. The US will be more hostile toward China, tougher and more pragmatic toward Europe, more pragmatic and neutral toward Russia, and more indifferent toward the Middle East. Most likely, there will be an attempt to once again reset US-Russia relations, this time on a new realistic basis of an informal "exchange of interests." US foreign policy will become even more one-sided, and the traditional bilateral

US-Russian nuclear arms control inherited from the cold war will eventually become a thing of the past. This is neither good nor bad. From the viewpoint of Russian interests, there are both positive and negative implications. In any case, it will not be the traditional policy of maintaining US "global leadership" or strengthening the US-led "liberal international order."

If Clinton wins, she will enjoy the support of the elite and the establishment of both parties on foreign policy issues for some time. The new administration will build on this to do what the Obama administration has not done or done poorly. However, the deep schism between the elites and society, and the rejection of the traditional foreign policy consensus by a large portion of the electorate will only grow deeper. Therefore, society will criticize Clinton's foreign policy through new populist leaders, and already in the 2020 elections she will be faced with new "Trumps." Popular protest against the status quo will erupt with a vengeance. In 2024, the candidate of the "anti-elite" may well win.

US foreign policy is entering an era of change—the most significant since the Truman administration. The cause of such changes lies in the discrepancy between the US foreign policy consensus reached at that time and forged in the 1990s, and the current (and, most likely, future) global trends. Maintaining "global leadership" in a multipolar world is impossible, and the "US-led liberal international order" in the traditional American understanding has not taken root. It is just a matter of time. If Trump wins, the departure from the current consensus will begin in 2017. If Clinton wins, it will begin a little later. But it is inevitable.

PART TWO

'Black Swan':
Responses to Trump's Victory

Introduction

On Nov. 5, 2016, Russian journalist Kirill Benediktov wrote his own blurb to a political biography of Donald Trump that he had just finished writing. The timing was vital: just days before the US presidential election. Benediktov titled the book *Chorny lebed* ("Black Swan"), based on a phrase popularized by American writer Nassim Taleb. Here is Benediktov's explanation of the title: "A year ago, no one took Donald Trump seriously. They called him a fool and a clown. Meanwhile, Donald Trump has turned out to be a classic 'black swan.' A 'black swan' is an event that comes as a surprise to the observer, has significant consequences, but can be easily explained—because it's baffling why no one actually managed to predict it."

Although Part One of this book showed that some Russian political analysts did take seriously the prospect of Trump becoming president, the Russian media as a whole erupted with astonishment once the election results were in. Part Two presents a range of reactions published in the days and weeks following Trump's victory, extending until his inauguration on Jan. 20, 2017.

These articles are divided into two sections. The first, loosely speaking, addresses the question: "How did this happen?" Commentary focuses on the political and ideological differences between Trump and Clinton, the makeup of the American electorate, the reasons that voters chose Trump—and, to a degree, even the implications for democracy writ large. The second section looks forward, considering the question: "What next?" Reporters and analysts make predictions about what Trump's foreign policy will look like in Europe, the Middle East, Asia and (of course) Russia. Some of these comments also range into the territory of international trends and the prospect of a new world order taking shape with the rise of this atypical, unpredictable American leader.

2.1

How Did This Happen?

Introduction

This section highlights immediate reactions to Trump's unexpected victory from several corners of the Russian media landscape—ranging from euphoria to cautious optimism to disgust, skepticism and even despair.

Coverage opens at an election-watching party in Moscow, where *Moscow Times* journalists interview several well-known Russian Trump supporters. The way they frame the Clinton-Trump opposition is emblematic: Journalist and political scientist Dmitry Drobnitsky speaks about the struggle between the "global elite" and "ordinary folks," calling Clinton a "soulless political machine." Kirill Benediktov describes Clinton as "100% ideologically motivated," and Trump as a "total political realist." Aleksei Zhuravlyov of the Rodina political party views Trump's "America first" policy as a boon to Russians: "If the US isn't the world's policeman, we can hope for cooperation."

The elation felt by this contingent of the Russian public at Trump's eventual victory bursts forth in Aleksandr Prokhanov's blog, published by right-wing newspaper *Zavtra* [Tomorrow]: "A giant explosion has shaken the world, setting all the continents atremble. The improbable has happened: Trump, the upstart, the maverick... has prevailed.... America rose up. It proved that our planet is not just the dried-out shell of the Earth's dead crust: It's also the deep magma, the chalice of fire, the womb that still has the energy to bear new civilizations and new values that today's world is longing for."

In the days following the election, Russian political analysts of all stripes struggle to make sense of what propelled Trump's win, and what implications it has for America and the world as a whole.

One observation shared by most of them is that the upset of Hillary Clinton, who represented a political dynasty, proves that democracy really does exist in America. For example, Andrei Movchan writes that the US middle class showed its rejection of socialist and bureaucratic trends. "Once again, the American people have shown that American democracy is not just a figure of speech covering up the subtle machinations of obscure elites."

Although Kirill Martynov also applauds the integrity of the US democratic system, he sees Trump's victory as a step backward toward old-style conservatism, rather than a step forward into a new era. "Trump has put the brakes on social progress, and you could say that the misogyny candidate won the 2016 election." Dmitry Oreshkin goes further, portraying Trump's win as part of a "global backlash" exemplified by Brexit, European nationalism and the continuing popularity of Putin in Russia. However, making an implicit contrast with the latter, he concludes: "America has one distinct advantage—it isn't afraid of making mistakes, since it always has a way of rectifying them through fair elections."

In contrast to the commentators above, Mikhail Fishman decries the presidential election as a defeat for democratic values: "The US political system has failed at its core. The bulwark of liberal democracy is sinking." Beyond American shores, he views Trump's triumph as validation for Putin's authoritarian leadership. Making a dig at the vagaries of the American Electoral College, he laments: "The hope for change in Russia has just been buried in the voting booths of Florida, Michigan and North Carolina." Oleg Kashin riffs sarcastically on much the same theme, pointing out similarities between the conservative heartlands of America and Russia—even using the Russian transliteration of "redneck" to describe both!

Trump Card:
A Donald Trump Fan Club Watched the Unthinkable Unfold in Moscow

By Ola Cichowlas and Matthew Kupfer.
The Moscow Times, Nov. 10, 2016, p. 2.

"Trump! Trump! Trump!" the crowd chanted, raising their whiskey-filled glasses. The group of men then turned back to watch the first exit polls from the US presidential election roll in on CNN.

It would have been an ordinary scene in Cleveland, Ohio or Jackson, Mississippi. But this venue was central Moscow, and the bar [was] filled with Russians, not Americans. Giant portraits of Vladimir Putin, Donald Trump and France's Marine Le Pen—the setting for many a selfie—hung in one corner, and several television screens broadcast American news.

The "Marathon for Trump" election-watching party brought together Russian fans of the Republican nominee. The event attracted an odd mix: pro-Kremlin political analysts, ultrapatriotic politicians, political strategists, and Russian Trump supporters dressed in campaign gear.

One of the men toasting Trump was Dmitry Drobnitsky, a Russian journalist and political analyst focused on the US. "Trump doesn't resemble the American leaders of the 2000s," Drobnitsky said. "We see that we're on the same side as him in the struggle between the global elite and ordinary folks fighting for their own interests."

He wasn't alone in those sentiments. Virtually all attendees believed that a Trump presidency would benefit their country and its relations with the US. At the start of the night, they seemed like an outlandish political fringe. Now, after Trump's historic and unexpected victory, they are decidedly mainstream.

Aleksei Zhuravlyov, chairman of the ultrapatriotic Rodina [Homeland] party in the State Duma and a man with connections to some of the organizers, hailed Trump's pro-Russian stance as he watched the early coverage. He expressed hope that Trump would join with Russia in waging war on terrorism, rebuilding something akin to the Soviet-American alliance in World War II. "We're under no illusions that this will be easy," he said. "But if the US isn't the world's policeman, we can hope for cooperation."

Kirill Benediktov, a political analyst and author of "Black Swan," a new political biography of Trump, praised the rise of pragmatism in American politics. "Clinton is 100% ideologically motivated, but Trump is a total political realist," he said.

The gathering wasn't all political science. Maksim Shevchenko, a prominent progovernment journalist who served as master of ceremonies, asked which of the women in the crowd would be willing to kiss Trump. (No one.) He requested that someone say something nice about Clinton. ("She taught us Russian women how to act when our husbands cheat on us!")

At one point, egged on by Shevchenko, guests even fantasized about civil unrest in the US. "I'd like to see the blacks come out * * * then the priests come out and say they're defending democracy," one intoxicated attendee slurred, before being ushered back to his table.

The drunk man's outburst may have been outlandish, but it was not fully out of line with the tone of the evening. Many of the attendees were members of extreme patriotic movements—people who say what the Kremlin cannot. For months, they have been gunning for a Trump presidency. One participant, Marina Kostycheva, a member of Rodina, admitted as much: "We act as the Kremlin's special ops and support Western parties loyal to Putin," she said.

As the evening began, the event seemed like the Russian Trump movement's swan song. Now, with Trump's victory, Russia's authorities may begin echoing the activists' rhetoric. When news broke on Nov. 9 that the Clinton campaign had admitted defeat, the State Duma burst into applause. Shortly thereafter, President Vladimir Putin sent Trump a telegram: In it, he expressed hope that they could help pull US-Russia relations out of their current crisis and build constructive bilateral dialogue.

"Trump represents the other face of the West," Drobnitsky said. Talking to Trump, he concedes, may be "more difficult" for Russia than Clinton. "But at least we won't be talking with a soulless political machine."

Hey Trump, Come on Over!

By Aleksandr Prokhanov. *Zavtra*, Nov. 16, 2016,
http://zavtra.ru/blogs/tramp_priezzhaj.

Donald Trump outplayed Hillary Clinton. Donald Trump is president of the United States of America. A giant explosion has shaken the world, setting all the continents atremble. The improbable has happened: Trump, the upstart, the maverick—with no highbrow advisers, no venomous political strategists, no wizards or sorcerers, no well-poisoners tormenting human souls—has prevailed. What sustained him wasn't the billions he amassed. It wasn't newspaper chains or financial moguls. What sustained him was the deep grassroots America that pulled itself up by its bootstraps on a fresh, rosy-cheeked continent. The America of settlers in cowboy hats, carrying the Bible in one hand and a Colt in the other. The people who docked on the Atlantic shores and dragged their bulky covered wagons into the West, built their bungalows and set up their own settlements among the herds of bison and the mustang-riding Indians.

This is the America of Jack London and [James] Fenimore Cooper, fearless sheriffs and pious pastors. This is the America of the great books of Hemingway, [F.] Scott Fitzgerald, Faulkner and Vonnegut. This is the America of those strong, simple-hearted lads with crew cuts who sat behind the wheels of Flying Fortresses and bombed Nazi breeding grounds in Europe to the tunes of Glenn Miller. This America of the Kennedys, the America of Neil Armstrong, looked like it was buried forever—lulled to sleep, intoxicated with folly, taken prisoner by bankers, nailed to the post of tolerance while being seduced by sweet-singing liberals and spooked by gay parades—but America rose up. It proved that our planet is not just the dried-out shell of the Earth's dead crust: It's also the deep magma, the chalice of fire, the womb that still has the energy to bear new civilizations and new values that today's world is longing for.

The old world is coming apart at the seams. It's unable to cope with the global uprising. It's still showing its teeth; it has trillions of dollars, mighty secret services [and] aircraft carriers with cruise missiles. But it has no more spirit. Spirit has abandoned the old world. Now its destiny is to curl up into a burnt scroll, whose ashes will be swept away by the hurricane of history.

Do you think Trump's victory is a miracle? No, it's history taking another deep breath. Do you think the revival of Russia after the collapse of [the Soviet Union in] 1991 was a miracle? No, it was the breath of history, which is stronger than any technology, any wizardry or magic spells. Mother History endures for a long time, dozing like a whale while people build flimsy houses and cute colored fences on its back. But the whale will wake up, flip its tail—and [there will be] no more houses of cards, no more monstrous liberal projects strapped onto Russia like a straitjacket.

Russia—through its suffering, its natural authenticity, its favor in the eyes of God—was the first on Earth to kick off the liberal boulder that had fallen on humanity. We have risen and we're on the move, like the spring: triumphantly and indomitably heralding the inevitable transformation of humanity.

The rumblings of Russian history have been heard on another continent. Skyscrapers have teetered. The ground has given way under Hillary Clinton's feet. Her husband's eyes are full of sorrowful tears.

President Obama—the peacemaker with cruise missiles in his fists, the Nobel laureate, the embodiment of lies and illusion—is now backing away from the White House as Trump sweeps in like a whirlwind. What will relations be like between America and Russia? How will Trump and Putin get along? . . .

The time has come to beat ISIS together. The time has come to fly to Mars together. The time has come to speak together—in English and in Russian—to utter the new word of life, to address humanity with the words of justice, universal love and truth. Let the two presidents, Putin and Trump, speak at the UN. And the [world's] peoples will hear the long-awaited words.

We are not idealists; [we are] not starry-eyed dreamers. We are covered in burns and raw wounds. We are grim doers and makers. But we believe that the world will be fair. [We believe] that the duplicitous liberals will not keep stinging people in the very heart, killing them with the poison of lies while singing sweet songs about freedom and human rights.

Europe has degenerated not because the music of Bach, Beethoven and Wagner no longer plays there. Not because the Cologne Cathedral and St. Peter's Cathedral have disappeared. Not because European thought no longer aims for the sky. It's because the peoples of Europe have fallen into the rapacious paws of petty schemers and cunning liars. Their time is over. Other Europeans will come—those who created Christian civilization, dreamed of immortality, uncovered bottomless truths in science and philosophy.

The Middle East—the mystical lands that gave birth to prophets, the lands from which the world's great religions arose—let these blood-covered and destitute lands no longer hear the whistle of cruise missiles and the explosions of multiple-launch rocket systems. Let the stained-glass windows of the mosques shine again. Let the noble pilgrims touch the sacred stone of the Kaaba in Mecca and pray to Allah not for revenge, not for wrathful punishment, but for grace and prosperity.

Donald Trump, put on a bullet-proof vest!

Donald Trump, don't trust the Wall Street bankers!

Donald Trump, come visit us in Russia! We have such snow, such evergreens, such great guys! We'll shoot our Colts at clay pigeons. We'll drink vodka. We'll go swimming in an ice-hole. You'll like it, Trump. Come on over!

Actor's Triumph: What to Expect From the US President-Elect

By Andrei Movchan, director of the Economic Policy Program at the Carnegie Moscow Center. *Republic.ru*, Nov. 9, 2016, https://republic.ru/posts/75969.

The morning after the US election, described by some as the second 9/11 (after all, it is the 9th of November [which is written "9/11" in Russian style—*Trans.*]), is an excellent illustration of the difference between the probable and the possible. An improbable event happened: The new president is a Presbyterian (of course, the great Ronald Reagan, Dwight Eisenhower and Theodore Roosevelt were Presbyterians too, but [Donald] Trump is the first Presbyterian president in 32 years); a businessman (Trump is the second businessman-turned-presidential candidate in US history, and the first businessman to be elected president) who specializes in gambling, beauty pageants, wrestling and real estate (all these industries have questionable reputations in the US); a man who has had serious problems with the IRS and gone bankrupt several times (as we know from "The Simpsons"); [a man] thrice married and twice nominated for an Emmy; a man who has repeatedly sold his name as a brand to various businesses; the author of what some would describe as a brilliant business plan of suing a bank because its demand to repay a loan hurts his business reputation; a TV host; a man whose jokes are often outright offensive; a man who openly disrespects American norms of behavior, tolerance and gender equality; and a harsh critic of NATO, free trade, confrontation with Russia and international efforts to combat climate change.

The people who voted for Trump were older and mostly male (53% of male voters voted for Trump and only 41% did for [Hillary] Clinton; among women, Clinton led with 54% while Trump was at 42%). Wealthier Americans preferred "The Donald" over his Democratic rival. Clinton had a big lead among voters under 44, among those whose income is under $50,000 a year, and especially among women. But still, 42% of women did vote for Trump, which means that we should question our views regarding American women and their mentality. Perhaps their feminist stance has been greatly exaggerated, and they secretly like the way the new president treats women.

Strange as it may seem, this election was decided neither by the rich (who supported Trump because he promised to reduce taxes) nor by the poor (who bought into his promises to "bring jobs back" from Mexico). It was decided by the middle class, which didn't get anything from Trump except ideas (the idea of fighting corruption, the idea of change, the idea of going back to traditional American values of freedom and enterprise, etc.). Trump's lead in the upper levels of the income pyramid is a mere 1% to 2%, but those who make $50,000 to $100,000 [a year] (31% of the US population) gave Trump a 4% lead over Clinton. Based on this, we can offer a speculative yet quite plausible theory: Trump was supported by US businesses (mainly small and medium-sized, which account for 51% of America's gross domestic product and provide jobs for 58% of America's labor force).

Markets responded to the surprising outcome of the election with increased volatility, but after a brief period of unrest, the situation quickly returned to normal. By the next morning (Washington time), international markets had recovered to their usual levels, except for the Mexican peso, which dropped by 10% and stayed there, horrified at the prospect of Trump building a wall at the border. (However, the peso was this low just recently, in mid-September, so you could say the Mexican market did not react to the news that much either.) Actually, there is nothing shocking about this second surprise of the day [i.e., the market rebound—*Trans.*]: Major investors are well aware that there is not much a US president can do, even if he dares to make a lot of promises. America has a strong foundation, and Trump will probably have to accept that during his time in the Oval Office, he won't be able to keep any of his controversial campaign promises except one: His friends the bankers and investors will still get those tax breaks after all. [As for the rest of the promises,] it's certainly hard to imagine the US leaving NATO (what would happen to defense contracts worth billions of dollars?), NAFTA (what about factories in Mexico manufacturing goods that US companies then export to other countries around the world?) or the World Trade Organization (how would US companies sell their products and services?). The same goes for imposing higher tariffs on Chinese goods (who else would the US borrow money from?). It's hard to imagine all these things, but it's possible, considering what happened with Brexit (some even call Trump's victory Brexit 2.0, and joke that the British and the Americans are basically still one nation). But even if anything like the above starts happening, it would have to go through the initial stages first: Bills would have to be drafted, discussed in committees, and approved by the Senate and the House. There are 191 Democrats in the new House. As long as they are able to get 27 Republicans to side with them, they can block any bill submitted by the president. The Republican majority in the Senate is even slimmer. Bills will be blocked, revised and sent back—which means that the markets will be aware of any coming changes long before they actually happen. So why worry about it today?

But while the new president isn't expected to surprise us economically, Trump's victory provides us with a lot of new (or long-forgotten) information about the social and political landscape in the US.

Once again, the American people have shown that American democracy is not just a figure of speech covering up the subtle machinations of obscure elites. Inept commentators accused American politics of being a family business (Bush-Clinton-Bush-Clinton), but now that myth has been busted. In fact, it is safe to say that it was fear of nepotism that turned many voters away from Clinton.

The Americans once again demonstrated that even if they fall for irresponsible rhetoric, at least it's always a different kind of irresponsible rhetoric. The idea of winning the middle class over with the vision of a welfare state works poorly in the US today. People prefer a state of opportunity and freedom (even if it's just another illusion). US voters are so tired of socialist rhetoric (which enjoys, at least so far, wholehearted support in Europe and is very popular in Russia) that they are willing to put up with the president's poor manners as long as he is not a populist (and Trump is a demagogue, not a populist). That's the thing about democracy: It's no more effective than dictatorship at bringing good leaders to power, but it's very good at getting rid of bad ones. So if Trump turns out to be as bad as many expect him to be (which may not happen, given that Trump is a brilliant businessman who always knows what to promise and how to succeed), in four years another president, probably a Democrat, will take his place (that is, as long as the Democrats learn their lesson and realize that they lost because of their dangerous penchant for socialism and bureaucratization).

It may seem to some that for Americans, the ideas of tolerance and feminism are more rhetorical in nature. Faced with a choice between a boorish male chauvinist on the one hand and a woman on the other, 42% of women chose the boorish chauvinist. A majority of voters chose a candidate notorious for his aggressive rhetoric against migrants over a candidate who was extremely tolerant. But we should remember that Trump is very inconsistent in his convictions. For example, he is a Presbyterian, and Presbyterians ordain women and allow same-sex marriage. Perhaps the American people can see through rhetoric; perhaps they know where Trump really stands and prefer real tolerance over hypocritical tolerance.

This goes to show that good old America, a land of equal opportunity (as in Samuel Colt's day), a land of freedom and conservatism, is very much alive and well. Yet Trump's victory in and of itself does not mean that public opinion in the US has been swayed by the Democrats' eight years in power. Trump won because of the way the US electoral system is set up. But his victory is nowhere near the landslide victories we often see in Russia (with the Kremlin candidate getting anywhere between 86% and 146% of the vote). As of 6 p.m. Moscow time on Nov. 9, Clinton was 150,000 votes ahead of Trump in the popular vote. If Trump had lost Florida and Pennsylvania (his lead in both states was a mere 1.5%), he would have lost the election fair and square.

Such a close win by Trump should make the Republican majority seriously consider their policies going forward. The wealthier voters supported Trump half-heartedly (his lead in this category is a mere 3%). Meanwhile, 51% of poorer people, who make up about 30% of the US population, voted for Clinton (compared to Trump's 42%). The Republicans now face an impossible mission: If they don't deliver on Trump's promises, in four years they will lose the support of radical isolationist voters who believe in an "America for white people," an "America that is self-sufficient" and an "America that doesn't care about the rest of the world." On the other hand, if they try to deliver on Trump's promises, the Republicans may get bogged down in things that would upset the markets, increase capital flight, increase the budget deficit and the sovereign debt, and perhaps even cause a new recession. As a result, the Republicans would lose the voters who thought Trump was an actor pretending to be an aggressive chauvinist but actually seeking to improve investment opportunities and the business climate in the US.

Furthermore, when Trump runs for reelection in four years, very young voters will have replaced 5% to 7% of his electorate, due to sad but natural reasons. Unless Trump manages to win over some new supporters, [shifting demographics] will greatly narrow his chances of reelection, as most young voters chose Democrats in this election.

It looks as if on Nov. 8, 2016, the US voted not to elect the 45th president, but to put an end to the long-standing policy of socializing the economy. Both the Republicans and the Democrats will have to accept the people's will. They have four years now to prepare their candidates (preferably new ones, not the same ones) for a new face-off, while a descendant of the McLeod clan, a military academy graduate, an actor, a businessman, a talk show host and an extremely rich individual serves as president.

As for us in Russia, we didn't win anything from Trump's victory (regardless of what the official [Russian] propaganda says, US leaders are always very pragmatic)—but we didn't lose anything, either. Still, we can learn an important lesson here. Since we like pointing at the US and saying it is no different from us, we have to come to grips with this new reality: The American people refused to support an elitist official who represented the interests of a small group of politicians and belonged to a "family" that had been in power for a long time, and voted instead for a tycoon with a questionable reputation (an "oligarch," to use a Russian term)—and America did not collapse. Even if just out of curiosity, I would like to live to see the day when the Russian people make the same kind of choice, especially since we have our own scandalous entrepreneurs who made their fortunes and created their businesses from scratch, who like risky statements, publicity stunts, sporting events and other things that the US president-elect does. And it doesn't really matter whether they prefer golf or cycling.

Four Years for White Men

By Kirill Martynov, politics desk editor. *Novaya gazeta*, Nov. 11, 2016, p. 5.

The US election result has its pros, and they are quite substantial.

First and foremost, the US election has shown that democracy works and must be respected. If the voters decided that they need a president like Donald Trump, then no one can alter that decision—

neither [US President Barack] Obama nor the infamous American establishment, which became the main target of Trump's election campaign. Modern political science defines democracy primarily as the fundamental ability to change a regime, and now that change has gone down in history, defying all odds. I don't like Trump, but I like democracy and I am prepared to accept its consequences—since as far as I know, there is no better political system.

In addition, Trump's victory has shown that the press is not an all-powerful propaganda tool after all. For a year, 90% of US media outlets claimed that Trump was the spawn of the devil, and that his election would be catastrophic for the country. However, voters decided otherwise. Therefore, this destroys the notion that democracy is a mere spectacle put on by the elite to serve their own interests—and that is also a good thing. For American media outlets, convinced of their own infallibility, this campaign should be a lesson: Running a propaganda campaign in the vein of the 1996 Russian [presidential] election under the slogan of "God forbid!" does not work in today's world. Thus, we can take a page from Trump's book and say that this election was society making a democratic choice against manipulators, which wouldn't be far from the truth.

Just before the US election, leftist philosopher Slavoj Zizek said that his vote would be for Trump, since the latter signifies the start of a mass crisis in the existing global order that would set off waves of change around the world. Such political reasoning based on the logic of "let's vote for the most odious candidate to spite the establishment" is hardly effective. In the end, Clinton's victory would also have brought about certain changes, maybe even more significant and positive ones—changes that took root over the past eight years under Obama (it seems that by 2016, everyone has forgotten that he was the first black US president).

This starts the list of cons associated with what happened in the US on Nov. 8—and I think they outnumber the pros. Trump was supported by rural America—the America that genuinely believes the country's greatest era was the 1950s to 1980s, when families were strong and social values were healthy. It could be that the changes in social consciousness over the past few years happened too quickly: People were expected to become more and more tolerant. So American society decided to take a pause. And even though a week before the election, Trump posed with the rainbow LGBT flag—the first Republican candidate to do so—he is nevertheless associated with a time when an American president could only be a white heterosexual man leading the appropriate lifestyle.

One issue that is getting fairly little attention here (out of political correctness, for one thing) is how this election was influenced by a latent distrust of women leaders. So what role did the Democratic contender's gender play on election day? It's one thing to publicly support gender equality, and quite another when you are given the choice to elect a woman as the national leader for the first time in history. Apparently, Americans turned out to be unprepared [for such a turn of events] and decided instead to vote for a man disliked by many. After all, the 19th Amendment, which gives women the right to vote, was adopted a mere 92 years ago, even though US democracy has been around since the late 18th century. The time for a "madam president" has not yet come. Trump has put the brakes on social progress, and you could say that the misogyny candidate won the 2016 election.

The economic and political risks associated with Trump's election are also being widely discussed around the world. America's [future] foreign policy strategy remains unclear, and the question of just how much the new US president really could be an isolationist remains open. This is the first time since the days of Roosevelt that the White House is insisting that America must concentrate its efforts on solving domestic problems. It makes no sense to say that Trump has brought down the system, or that he has once and for all put American liberals, university professors, feminists and East Coast journalists in their place. Right now, it looks as if Trump is a temporary anomaly, rather than the start of a new era in American politics. The new US president has been elected for four years, and it is already becoming apparent that he will be in store for a difficult reelection campaign amid a growing divide within the Republican Party, the deterioration of the two-party system and the consolidation of American society around a future opposition candidate—who will most likely be a man.

Transatlantic Backlash

By Dmitry Oreshkin. *Novaya gazeta*, Nov. 11, 2016, p. 6.

The night before the election, an absolute majority (if not all) of the polls and predictions except the *Los Angeles Times* handed Hillary the victory. On average, [her] chances were given as two to one or three to one. But in the end, Trump won, and his victory raised three big questions: What happened to the country and the voters? What happened to the forecasters? And what happened to the US electoral system?

Let's start with the latter: Absolutely nothing happened. It wasn't perfect, but voting was organized clearly and independently enough to bring about a result that was unexpected and that categorically does not suit the establishment. All sorts of nonsense tales from the Soviet crypt—falsified early voting ballots, electoral corruption, dead people on the voting registers, a coup in the event of a Trump win—went belly up. Voters voted, [electoral] commissions tallied up the ballots, and it turned out that the country wants changes. Whether that's for better or worse is another story. But as far as the election is concerned, it was open and honest. I had the opportunity to see that with my own eyes.

The Zhirinovsky effect.

The forecasters' error, in my opinion, can be explained by the "Zhirinovsky effect" that Russian polling experts discovered in the 1990s. All over the world, people tend to give pollsters socially acceptable answers. "Are you going to go vote?" "Yes, of course!" However, in reality, of all those who say that in Russia, no more than 60% will actually head to the polls. Perhaps that proportion is different in America. Polling experts have long realized this, so they adjust their predictions to compensate for [survey respondents'] desire to look good. In the '90s, the Russian media presented Zhirinovsky as a radical and a questionable character. But many people actually liked that about him. However, they preferred to avoid telling the truth when asked "Will you vote for Zhirinovsky?"

"No, probably not." So until polling experts learned to adjust for the "Zhirinovsky coefficient," his actual election results were always about 3% to 5% higher than predicted (and in 1993, during the "new political year," [they were off] by 12% to 15%!).

The US media also presented Trump as the bad boy your mother told you to stay away from. And it seems that not all of his sympathizers told pollsters the truth. When we are talking about a difference of two to three percentage points with a 3% margin of error, it's easy to make a mistake. Here's how it works: In the US electoral system, elections are determined by the states. In 48 out of 50 states, the winner [of the popular vote majority] gets all the electoral votes. The number of electoral votes each state gets is based on population: California has 55, Texas has 38 and Florida has 29. California consistently votes Democrat, and Texas [votes] Republican. It doesn't matter what the actual numbers are—we already knew that between those two states, Clinton would get 55 votes [and Trump would get] 38. However, Florida is a swing state. The gap between the winner and loser might be less than 1% (the exact number has not yet been established), but Trump definitely had the majority. So he got Florida's 29 electoral votes, putting him at 67 votes to Clinton's 55.

The same goes for other swing states: Trump won, but just barely. When it comes to predicting a result where the gap is about 1%, polling is powerless. Of course, [polling experts] should have picked up on a trend—after all, there is no way that over a dozen swing states all went a certain way at the last moment. But they didn't catch [the trend].

Unpopularity contest.

So now, what will happen to the US? On Monday, Nov. 7 [*sic*; Oct. 31—*Trans.*], *The Washington Post* wrote that the percentage of people who viewed Clinton negatively equaled the percentage of Trump detractors—both candidates had a [rating] of -22%. But their long-term trends were different. Hillary saw several peaks of popularity, the highest being in 2013, when she wrapped up her stint as secretary of state: [Her approval rating was at] 41%. Trump's popularity index has always been below zero. His lowest ratings (-52% and -51%) were in 1999 and 2015. Since then, you could say he has been gaining ground. Meanwhile, Clinton's ratings continued to fall. On the eve of the election, the two titans met at the -22% mark.

Trump knew what he was doing with his slogan "Make America Great Again!" Then there's [society's] fatigue from the corrupt fat-cat establishment, both red and blue. Trump's main assets were novelty, charisma, show business experience and the sympathy of the suddenly awakened American heartland—or, as geographers put it, the inner periphery. [This group] is stressed out and worried, feeling that its way of life is threatened in a social, economic and psychological sense (when it comes to traditional values). And rightly so! The eminent Pew Research Center predicts that by 2065, the proportion of whites in the US population will dip to 46% (it is now 62%), while Hispanics will make up 24% (today they are at 15% [sic; 18%—Trans.]), and blacks will make up 14% [sic; 13%—Trans.] (today they make up 12%). People think that by electing someone new, it is possible to reverse this global process and bring back the good old days. But that is delusional. At best, this process can be slowed down by a few decades—but at the price of significantly slowing the pace of development. However, it is just as impossible to convince voters of this as it is to stop migrants from moving to richer lands or to prove to a mad scientist that a perpetual motion machine is nonsense. You cannot resist a force of nature—all you can do is prepare the best you can.

Trump as a trend.

Here, America is hardly original: A conservative renaissance is sweeping the globe. We all have similar fears, whether we are French (Marine Le Pen), English (Brexit), German or Russian. In their own way, Putin and Trump are both riding the wave of a global backlash, even though they are going in different directions. Gratified to have gotten up off its knees, Russia is sinking into a very natural post-Soviet era of stagnation, doing its best to convince itself that this is just fine. After all, isn't that what the majority wanted? American conservatism is taking the opposite approach: Trump is planning to cut taxes, and to reduce bureaucracy and extreme liberalism following the Reaganomics model.

Is this bad or good? Time will tell. Trump's victory is shaky, the situation is complicated and [his] ratings are low. It will be hard for him to last in the White House for more than one term. America has one distinct advantage—it isn't afraid of making mistakes, since it always has a way of rectifying them through fair elections. And as the whole world just saw, that mechanism works perfectly.

The US Has Sneezed and Now Russia Will Catch a Cold

By Mikhail Fishman, editor in chief.
The Moscow Times, Nov. 10, 2016, p. 2.

The US, the most powerful nation on Earth, has just made its choice and voted for an unpredictable future. Never before in its 240-year history has America known so little about what will happen next.

What will Donald Trump's presidency look like? Will he repeal Obamacare? Will he try to put Hillary Clinton in jail? Will America deport tens of millions of undocumented immigrants or ban Muslims from entering the country? What will the US policy be in Syria? So far, these questions have no answers.

But the message that Donald Trump's sudden triumph sends is very clear: The US political system has failed at its core. The bulwark of liberal democracy is sinking. The West is divided, full of resentment and weak. The rules are changing. Like a shock wave, this simple message has blasted through national borders, encouraging autocracies across the world.

When Russian parliamentarians stood and applauded the news of Trump's victory, this was the exact sentiment they were cheering. They, along with President Vladimir Putin, didn't see it coming.

They viewed the US presidential election as a zero-sum game with the West that Russia has been playing during the last several years. Trump's unpredictability makes it difficult to predict how US-Russia relations will now evolve and how his administration will address the major issues that Moscow has put on the table—especially Ukraine and Syria.

But Trump's victory also delivers clarity to Russia's own political future. Putin is now heaving a sigh of relief; help came—a deus ex machina—at a vital moment.

These have been difficult times for Putin as a leader. Russians are finally beginning to feel the effects of their international isolation. And a fair degree of Western unity ensured that this status quo was unlikely to change. In 2003, during the Iraq war, Putin had been able to play upon differences and disagreements among Western powers. With the annexation of the Crimea, the war in Ukraine's Donetsk Basin region and now the Syrian conflict, Putin has lost his ability to maneuver....

Whatever plans Putin might have contemplated for his future, he has made some clear preparations for change at home. Sergei Kiriyenko, the newly appointed overseer of Russia's domestic politics, maintains a reputation as a reformer and a progressive. The Kremlin has also begun snubbing ultraconservative activists, and the reported torture of the jailed activist Ildar Dadin has become an issue at the highest levels of government.

In short, there was a fresh sense in the air that the regime might start loosening its grip. Political circles in Moscow had shyly begun anticipating a new "thaw."

Now, with Donald Trump as the new president of the US, this is no longer the case. This new "Trump world" is a global mess, and taking advantage of the disorder looks much more rational as a strategy. An outcast yesterday, Putin might even start seeing himself as the first among equals on the global scene. If he ever had doubts about running for another presidential term, now he will not hesitate.

The hope for change in Russia has just been buried in the voting booths of Florida, Michigan and North Carolina.

In Search of a Russian Trump

By Oleg Kashin. *Republic.ru*, Nov. 10, 2016, https://republic.ru/posts/75990.

A revolting rich guy with weird hair, bad taste, a thorny reputation, chronically spoiled relations with the press, and a young wife with fashion-model looks. Who might that be, do you think? [Rosneft CEO] Igor Sechin, of course, but if someone else came to mind—Donald Trump, for instance—that would hardly be surprising. There are not all that many truly unique types of people in the world. Some come into fashion and some go out of fashion: That's how it is in the film industry, show business and politics. Russia remembers how on the heels of iconic [former Moscow mayor Yury] Luzhkov, the authorities in the regions acquired a standard "experienced manager" look that quickly supplanted the heroes of the previous fashion—the first-wave democrats. But the "experienced managers" were in turn superseded by brusque law-enforcement and security officials or bureaucrats when Putin came on the scene. Even so, Moscow can only set the tone for its subordinates, the regions. No matter how special its path may be, Moscow itself is susceptible to global trends, and Trump is the new global trend. He's a challenge. How will he affect Russian political fashion?

It's not hard to find a Russian Trump. Igor Sechin is perhaps the most radical candidate, but it could be anyone: The people in and near power in Russia today look more or less alike. They are all rich; they are all generally rednecks; and they all would look more at home in the Trump Taj Mahal casino than in Silicon Valley coworking spaces. The ideal Russian Trump is, of course, Vladimir Putin. We don't need to go looking for him; he is constantly with us, and in another presidential election, he would once again promise to make Russia great again. That is obvious.

What's more interesting is society. The American campaign [for the 2016 presidential election], through its entire course, has repeatedly reflected our perennial public debate [in Russia]: Arguments about a general public that has suddenly become the chief conservative force; about a progressive minority doomed to be misunderstood by the vast majority; and about the limits of our authorities' populism and ideological flexibility have been raging here for a long time. And seeing that same debate suddenly played out in the American context serves as an excellent opportunity to take an outside look at ourselves....

We have the experience of confrontation between the prosperous, protest-minded Moscow intellectuals and the government, which subsequently went all out to draw the broad masses to its side (or pretend to). Now, America has offered the former Bolotnaya Square[4] a vivid model of the same confrontation, in which the minority can be dead right but doomed. Clearly, those seeking to aspire to something in Russia should study the American experience with a view to finding the magic word that would allow them to speak a common language with the majority. It is difficult to say what that word might be, but one thing is certain: It must be honest and not condescending. The classic postelection [cry of] "Russia, you've come off your rocker!"—think 1993, when the Liberal Democratic Party of Russia took first place in the State Duma elections—is paradoxically translatable into English right now, and carries the same meaning it's always had: "We thought we could ignore the opinion of those we consider rednecks." The time seems to be coming when such expressions ought to be recognized as indecent, and acceptable terms will need to be found to replace them.

And here is the main paradox. One way or another, the Americans are going to start looking to replace the existing relations between the "smart" minority and the "stupid" majority. Conclusions will certainly be drawn from Trump's defeat of the liberal left establishment; lessons will be learned and formulated in English on the pages of the same reputable media that all autumn were raising alarms over the advent of Trump. And then, perhaps, our "smart" Westernized minority—which is not always able to come up with something of its own, but is very sensitive to world intellectual fashion—will read the Americans' findings, accept them as a given and incorporate them. It's probably a naïve hope, but when some commentator from *The New Yorker* comes up with a way [for intellectuals] to behave so that some Joe from Oklahoma will choose them over Trump, perhaps it will also be possible for the Russian "creative class" to have such a conversation with Nizhny Tagil, so that it doesn't recoil in horror and think it would be better to have Putin than these [intellectuals] in charge. The American intelligentsia's failed campaign will teach the losers something (that thought had simply never crossed their minds before), and Russia's epigones of America's intelligentsia will also learn something. We have plenty of our own Trumps. And we have plenty of people who can explain convincingly and in great detail what a handful the Russian people are. What we don't have is people who know how to talk to the national majority on its level and in its language. The Americans, it turns out, have a similar problem. They will likely solve it, and we will look to them and solve it here, too.

Sergei Glazyev: 'Trump Needs Help!'

By Aleksandr Nagorny. *Zavtra*, Nov. 16, 2016, http://zavtra.ru/blogs/trampu_nado_pomoch_.

Editors' Note—[Sergei Glazyev], adviser to the Russian president and an academician of the Russian Academy of Sciences, answers questions from *Zavtra*.

* * *

Question—Sergei Yuryevich [Glazyev], how unexpected for you was Donald Trump's victory in the US presidential election?

Answer—It was quite predictable, and I had no doubt about it from the moment Trump took the lead in the Republican Party primaries. The fact of the matter is that any new political force spreads its influence like an epidemic, and these processes are described well by standard mathematical models in the form of an S-curve. Once a new idea takes hold in the minds of a critical mass of followers among the population, it begins to spread rapidly until it reaches a ceiling. The main question was the projected height of that ceiling: Would it cover half of the voters?

Unlike Hillary Clinton, Trump was a new politician whose ceiling of support was unknown, and that was the big mystery of his campaign. Hillary's ceiling was clear, since she was a well-known political leader of a well-known political force. From the beginning of the campaign, she was already at that level, and her objective was to drum up votes not "for Clinton," but "against Trump"—to wake up the masses of "sleeping" voters with the threat that the [country's] foundations would be shaken if the Republican candidate were elected. That was the target of her staff's most recent démarches: statements by well-known economists, politicians, show business celebrities and sports stars, [all] aimed at demonizing Trump. But it did not work, because for the target electorate, those defamations went in one ear and out the other. After Trump reached an exponential rise in supporters, the question was only whether he would be able to activate his entire potential electorate. As we can see, he did—maybe not completely, but enough to win.

Q—Why didn't you talk about your forecasts in public?

A—You have to agree that such forecasts would have played into the hands of Hillary Clinton, because they would have been proof of the myth that Putin supports Trump, and that the New York billionaire is practically his puppet.

Q—Maybe he is? But what do you think—how serious is Trump's intention to normalize relations with Russia and its president?

A—Very serious. Although we don't know either his true intentions or his obligations to the American establishment.

Q—But isn't Trump sort of "Mr. Antiestablishment"?

A—That's the heart of the matter—"sort of." American aggression—their hybrid war against the entire world, including our country—is caused not only by the paranoia of the neocons who set the tone in the Obama administration. The ruling elite in the US are ready to maintain their global dominance at any cost. Including world war....

Q—Let's get back to Trump. Will he lift the anti-Russian sanctions?

A—We shall see. If he lifts them, that will be an important preliminary signal of willingness to normalize relations between the US and Russia.

Q—You say "preliminary." But for you personally, such a decision would mean abolishing [your] persona non grata status in the US and other countries of the "collective West," right?

A—For me, these sanctions have no meaning. The US authorities have gone far beyond the bounds of international law by hounding undesirable Russian citizens all over the world. They have put me on sanctions lists twice, and no one knows how many such lists they have. They took on the role of global policeman long ago, and consider themselves entitled to arrest any citizens of other states who don't please them, anywhere on the planet. Trump says he believes this role is very burdensome for American taxpayers, and considers it necessary to concentrate on America's domestic problems.... The election of Donald Trump is a chance to avoid a world war, the embodiment of which was Hillary Clinton. But this is only a chance....

He needs help making strong, willful decisions that will undoubtedly be painful for the ruling elite, but a saving grace for the US as a whole.

Q—Something like Franklin Roosevelt's New Deal, which—like the legacy of Abraham Lincoln—the new 45th president of the US constantly refers to?

A—Yes, and here the American establishment must be shown that its aspirations for world domination not only run counter to the tide of history, but are also fraught with disastrous consequences for the US. Then it will be easier for Donald Trump to get rid of diehard paranoiacs like [Sen. John] McCain, who continue to fight the USSR and fan the flames of world war. To do this, we need to create a coalition of SCO and BRICS countries under a new global economic arrangement based on the principles of mutually beneficial voluntary cooperation, respect for national sovereignty, unconditional compliance with international law, and recognition of the diversity of economic cultures. [Such an arrangement] also precludes the forced imposition of liberal globalization, the use of force in world politics and interference in domestic affairs.

2.2

What Next?
Forecasts of a New World Order

Introduction

While some Russian analysts and commentators were grappling with how Trump's victory came about and what it meant for democracy, others were making predictions of what the world would look like with Trump leading America. Matthew Bodner of *The Moscow Times* summarized the views of leading experts in key areas of foreign policy. For example, Vladimir Frolov predicted that Trump would follow Putin's lead in Syria, but that Russia's alliance with Iran would thwart common efforts to fight ISIS. Bodner wrote that Trump seemed likely to back away from both Ukraine and NATO, based on his campaign promises. While these positions might be considered good news for Moscow, Trump's position on nuclear arms reduction boded otherwise: Given that his campaign speeches emphasized military development as a way of restoring American strength, Putin would probably find Trump difficult to work with on arms control.

In contrast to the emotional extremes—euphoria and despair—that dominated the postelection coverage in the previous section, notes of caution and skepticism prevail here. For example, Vladimir Mukhin gives evidence suggesting that even if Trump scales back support for NATO, Europe would marshal its own forces to pose an equally significant threat to Russia. Mikhail Troitsky argues that Moscow's whole Middle East strategy is in disarray: While Trump vowed to make fighting terrorism his top priority, he also promised to take a tougher line with Iran—Moscow's ally in Syria. And one condition for normalizing relations with Russia could require Moscow to jump on the bandwagon and get tough with Tehran. Vladimir Frolov writes that Trump's views on Israel could also place Putin in an uncomfortable position: The US president-elect vocally supports Israeli settlements on the West Bank (and implicitly opposes a Palestinian state), but Putin would be hard put to agree with him, since that would alienate other Middle East nations with which he has been trying to forge alliances in his Syria campaign.

On the subject of European politics in general (aside from military strategy), Russian commentators were more optimistic. Their prevailing opinion is that the new generation of Western leaders are friendly to Putin. They cite the French presidential primary victory of François Fillon, who wanted to end anti-Russian sanctions; the rise of Austrian right-wing politician Norbert Hofer, who also decried the sanctions; not to mention the recent victories of pro-Russian presidents in Bulgaria and Moldova. What's more, European Commission head Jean-Claude Juncker said (as quoted by SCF journalist Peter Korzun) that he "would like to have discussions on a level footing with Russia." Even award-winning journalist Andrei Kolesnikov, who can generally be depended upon to cut his president down to size, acknowledges: "Now, [Putin] is a global leader in his own right. And this image has been bought by the West: Putin is successfully peddling fear in the West and threats domestically. And now he is king of the hill." Of course, Kolesnikov adds with a dash of sarcasm, if Western countries (including the US, under the presidency of Donald Trump) become Russia's friends, how will Putin keep up the "besieged fortress" mentality that has so effectively mobilized domestic support?

On the eve of Trump's inauguration, as American media coverage grew harsher, a new theme emerged in Russian news coverage: sympathy. For example, Fyodor Lukyanov begins his analysis of Trump vs. Wilsonian democracy with the bold statement: "By all indications, opposition to the new occupant of the White House is going to be fierce from day one." In the same vein, after Trump's comments on Russian hacking allegations at a January press conference, Russian commentators portray him as caught in the machinations of Washington. Konstantin Kosachov is quoted in *Izvestia* as saying: "Judging from his statements today, both Donald Trump and his team are under horrendous pressure from those who oppose improving relations with Russia." Aleksei Pushkov praises him for resisting anti-Russian trends in America: "Essentially, he is being forced to continue the policies of Barack Obama regarding Russia. [Trump] made it clear that he will not do that."

Even when Trump spoke against Russia—for instance, its role in the hacking scandal—*Izvestia* reporters Tatyana Baikova and Aleksei Zabrodin toned down his response a bit: "[T]he president-elect said that Russia could have been behind the attacks on Democratic Party servers." (According to a transcript of the conference published in *The New York Times,* Trump's response was more assured: "I think it was Russia.") Nikolai Zlobin acknowledged the toughness of Trump's remarks, but explained it away as follows: "Trump spoke harshly about Russia in order to prove that he has no ties with it."

The theme of Trump's "Russia ties" become more prominent in the global media throughout 2017—and that is the subject of Part Three of this book.

The Shape of Things to Come

By Matthew Bodner. *The Moscow Times,* Nov. 10, 2016, p. 6.

What to expect in US-Russian relations during the Trump presidency.

Donald Trump will be the next president of the United States. A Trump presidency is perhaps the least predictable in American history, but one thing seems certain: A sea-change in US-Russian relations is on its way.

Relations between the two historical superpowers are the worst they have been at any point since the end of the cold war. Successive crises in Georgia, Syria and Ukraine have put the two on a collision course.

Hillary Clinton's widely anticipated victory was expected to double down on an adversarial policy. An experienced hand on Russia, Clinton did not approach Moscow with any sense of optimism or naïveté. She was expected to revisit the issue of arming Ukraine, and play hardball with the Kremlin across Europe and the Middle East.

Trump was less specific about his policy in these regions, but he regularly praised President Vladimir Putin and talked of the need to work together with Russia. In a way, Trump is likely to attempt his own version of Barack Obama's failed 2009 "reset" in relations with Russia. While Trump and Putin may see eye to eye on a lot, there are areas where they might butt heads.

The Moscow Times looked at several areas that will define US-Russian relations under President Trump.

Syria and the Middle East.

The most dramatic change under President Trump may come in the Middle East. Russia's military operations there severely limited President Barack Obama's options. Moscow has staked significant domestic and international reputation on its support for Syrian President Bashar Assad. Trump, like Obama, won't change that. But, unlike Obama, he is likely to embrace it.

Efforts to work with Russia in Syria over the past year were highly personalized. Any chemistry between Secretary of State John Kerry and Russian Foreign Minister Sergei Lavrov failed to bring results. Dialogue is virtually nonexistent. Trump, however, has different priorities and is a very different beast from the Obama administration.

"You're not fighting Syria any more, you're fighting Syria, Russia and Iran, all right? Russia is a nuclear country," Trump told Reuters two weeks ago, warning US intervention would spark World War III.

The president-elect is likely to accept whatever fait accompli Russia presents him with as he enters office in January. This, more than likely, will be a military victory for Assad over the opposition, says Russian foreign affairs expert Vladimir Frolov.

Trump's own vision on how to combat ISIS remains unclear, and he declined to elaborate on it during the campaign. That said, at a rally in early September, Trump pledged to "convene [his] top generals and give them a simple instruction: They will have 30 days to submit to the Oval Office a plan for * * * defeating ISIS."

"Any nation who shares in this goal will be our friend in this mission," he said.

Trump will have to reconcile obvious contradictions in his approach to the Middle East. He has slammed détente with Iran, and specifically said the Iran nuclear agreement was a bad deal. But he will need to work with Russia and Iran in Syria. Meanwhile, his Islamophobic rhetoric on the campaign trail, if turned into policy, may undermine relationships with Arab allies in the fight against ISIS.

Ukraine and sanctions.

When Russia shocked the world by starting military operations in Syria in September 2015, it did so with an eye on Ukraine. By leveraging influence over Assad, the Kremlin thought it might be able to persuade Washington to make concessions over Ukraine and sanctions.

That turned out to be a miscalculation. Obama stressed Ukraine would be treated as a separate issue; and in diplomatic circles, "compartmentalization" became the new buzzword. Russia was told in no uncertain terms that sanctions would only be dropped if the February 2015 Minsk agreement was implemented in full.

So far, this line has held in both Washington and in Europe. But much of the West's commitment to the policy has hinged on the dual leadership of the American president and German Chancellor Angela Merkel, who may herself be on her way out. Across Europe, commitment to the policy of sanctions against Russia is faltering.

Trump is certain to reassess America's commitment to Ukraine. In July, [he] was asked if he would recognize the Crimea as Russian territory. Yes, he replied. He "would be looking (*sic*) into that."

If campaign positions are any indication, Trump is also likely to ask European leaders to assume most of the burden in Kiev. "Where's Germany?" He asked in an August 2015 interview. "I mean, we're like the policemen of the world."

Trump is opposed to arming Ukraine with lethal military equipment.

NATO.

Trump's Ukrainian policy is tied in with his opinion of the 28-member NATO military alliance. The president-elect has openly criticized the alliance as an outdated structure too focused on Russia, and ill-suited for combating the challenges of international terrorism.

In a July interview with *The New York Times*, Trump suggested he would not honor Washington's defense commitments to NATO members in eastern Europe. While Obama underwrote moderate deployment costs, Trump wants members to pay up for American defense in full.

"If we cannot be properly reimbursed for the tremendous cost of our military protecting other countries," Trump said, "then yes, I would be absolutely prepared to tell those countries: Congratulations, you will be defending yourself."

Such words are music to the ears of the Kremlin, which has protested against increased NATO presence near its borders. They are also likely to make nations like Poland and the Baltics more jittery. Life under the Soviet yoke remains a real and significant national memory for these nations.

At a rally in April, Trump hinted that the US might even withdraw from NATO if other members do not increase contributions. "Maybe NATO will dissolve," he said. "That is OK, [it's] not the worst thing in the world."

Counterterrorism.

If Trump abandons Ukraine and forges a relationship with Russia in Syria, it could open the door for a potentially fruitful area of cooperation: international counterterrorism and intelligence sharing. The US and Russia have tried to work together in this area before, but the Ukraine crisis put a stop to it. Disagreements over Syria have only deepened the rift, despite the common threat of Islamic terrorism.

Trump owes much of his victory to promoting a hard-line, offensive war against terrorism. In many ways, he probably looks to Putin on this issue. The Russian president has pursued ruthless counterterrorism strategies in Russia's southern Caucasus region. Trump has said Russia would be a key partner in the war against ISIS.

But Trump might find himself frustrated in attempts to make a good counterterror deal with Russia. Even before the breakdown in relations, cooperation has not been without problems, and Russia reportedly only ever shared partial information on threats. After the Boston [Marathon] bombing, US officials alleged Moscow could have helped prevent the attack if more information had been shared.

Moscow has also on occasion tried to use the counterterrorism banner to further its own aims—for example, to legitimize its tough actions in Chechnya, says Mark Galeotti, an expert in Russian security affairs.

Arms control.

A cornerstone of US-Russian relations has always been arms control treaties. Every US president has tried to negotiate cuts to nuclear arsenals; not all of them have succeeded.

Beyond criticizing the New START treaty signed early in Obama's presidency, Trump does not seem to have touched on nuclear reductions while campaigning. But it is an issue his administration will have to address.

New START was the high-water mark of Obama's attempted reset in relations with Russia. Both sides continue to work toward reducing arsenals to the agreed 700 missiles and bombers, and 1,550 warheads by 2018. But the treaty expires in 2021. Trump must, therefore, begin negotiations on the future of US-Russian arms control by the end of his first term.

Trump is faced with two options: New START has a provision for extension to 2026. The alternative is harder: start from scratch to negotiate a new treaty.

To secure a new treaty, Trump will have to resolve ongoing disputes with Russia over adherence to the landmark 1987 Intermediate Nuclear Forces (INF) Treaty. Both sides have accused the other of violating INF in recent years. The Kremlin will also likely want to see US concessions on things like missile defense and hypersonic weapons.

Trump considers himself a deal maker. In the 1980s, he reportedly even offered himself up as a one-man arms control negotiator with the Soviets. Considering that his stated platform devotes significant attention to military armaments and restoring a perceived loss of American strength, Putin will find Trump difficult to work with on arms control.

Trump well might prove a difficult challenge for Putin. While he adopted populist positions during the campaign, his next two months will be focused—perhaps for the first time—on forming serious policy positions. What emerges from this process depends heavily on who Trump surrounds himself with.

In many ways, the only certainty is that we are entering uncharted territory in US-Russian relations. Predictable enmity is now out the window.

Will Donald Trump Abolish NATO?

By Vladimir Mukhin. *Nezavisimaya gazeta*, Nov. 11, 2016, p. 2.

Donald Trump's unexpected victory in the US presidential election seems to be prodding the leadership of the European Union to finally make the decision to establish its own army on the continent. European Commission President Jean-Claude Juncker regards this as an "inevitable process" because, in his opinion, the US will eventually stop ensuring Europe's security. As is known, in the course of his election campaign, Trump has repeatedly stated that America should stop being "the world's policeman" and focus on dealing with its domestic problems.

However, according to the EU leadership, there are additional reasons for establishing an independent army. These include Great Britain's decision to exit the EU, the escalating migration crisis, the threat of the proliferation of terrorism in Europe, and finally, the so-called threat allegedly coming from Russia. Even before the US election results were announced, EU foreign policy chief Federica Mogherini promised to draft proposals on strengthening the military component of European security and defense policy by the end of November. In September 2016, France and Germany put forward a plan to create a joint military force that would match NATO's military capability. The plan is due to be finalized next month.

So far, Mogherini has not officially supported Juncker's idea of establishing a European army. Nevertheless, on Nov. 7, addressing the chiefs of the general staffs of EU member countries in Brussels, she said that on Nov. 14, she intended to discuss with the foreign and defense ministers of EU member countries an Implementation Plan on Security and Defense. According to her, it contains three priorities: enabling the EU to respond to conflicts and crises; further enhancing security and defense capacities of EU partners; and strengthening the EU's capabilities to protect European citizens. The first steps along this path will apparently be related to Juncker's proposals to deploy EU civil and military operation command headquarters in Brussels. It is also planned to conduct these operations outside the EU.

The main lobbyists for the establishment of Europe's own army are Germany, France and the Czech Republic—the latter, as is known, proposed addressing this issue at an EU summit back in August 2016. Some countries (Latvia and the UK) did not support the idea, while many took a neutral stance, counting instead on the US's announcement to boost NATO's capabilities in Eastern Europe. However, after Trump's victory, the situation is apparently changing. And the EU is now counting on its own forces, which was precisely what Juncker said. "[Europe] owes a great debt of thanks to America, but they will not ensure our security in the long term. We have to do that for ourselves, and that is why we need to take a new approach to the European Defense Union, including [the long-term goal of] establishing a European army. That is the direction in which we are already heading, even if many Europeans are not yet aware of that fact," Juncker said.

Understandably, the EU leadership wants to create a collective security system with a joint military command, similar to that of NATO. It is no accident that Juncker proposes deploying EU military headquarters in Brussels, where the North Atlantic alliance is headquartered, and which has a NATO force command and control system already in place....

"I do not see it as a big military problem if the Pentagon's soldiers leave Europe or reduce their presence there," commented military expert Lt. Gen. Yury Netkachev. "The core of European large combined units and military units deployed near our borders will not change." The general is convinced that "the combat command and control system that existed in NATO can be easily integrated into purely European structures if the alliance is reformed. Say, if a European army is established, the four new battalions that are being formed in the Baltic region, which are under the command of the 16th Polish Division, will only slightly change their composition, while their command and control system will remain the same." However, the expert stressed that if there is no US military assistance, the EU army will have to find funding at the expense of European states' resources. "This problem could be somewhat offset if somewhat neutral states, such as Sweden and Finland, join the European army. However, this scenario is not beneficial for Russia. The possible dissolution of NATO, unfortunately, will not reduce military threats for our country," Netkachov says with certainty.

"After Trump's victory, US military policy in Europe won't make an immediate U-turn," Aleksandr Kanshin, deputy chairman of the Russian Defense Ministry's public council, told NG. "The US has its own interests here. And as US president, Trump will have to defend them." In his view, right now it is very difficult to say exactly how the role of NATO or Washington in it will change. But it will change, the expert believes. "One can only hope that Russian-US relations would finally improve, including when it comes to global security issues. Meanwhile, real military threats coming from NATO countries are unlikely to diminish in the foreseeable future. And the EU's attempt to establish its own army is further evidence of that. Although I do not think that it will be so easy to establish independent military structures in EU countries. This would take time and resources, including an increase in military budgets. Would European society accept that? I believe that this is unlikely. At present, Europe has many other problems to deal with: an unstable economy, terrorism and illegal migration. An army would not solve these problems."

Two Faces of American Capitalism

By Dmitry Yevstafyev. *Ekspert*, Nov. 14, 2016, p. 23.

The outcome of the US election probably doesn't mean that the US has finally split into small-town America and postmodern America—a division that emerged in the 1990s and has been becoming increasingly pronounced. Hillary Clinton and Donald Trump showed Americans—but most important, the whole world—two faces, two models of American capitalism. The first is American globalist capitalism, which the world has by now grown accustomed to and is based on American military and political hegemony, both of which depend on the nature of allied relations. The second is Trump capitalism—at least the way [capitalism] was formulated by the businessman-showman, demonstrating the priority of internal, not external sources of US might—which means redirecting resources to restructuring domestic obligations and alleviating the most painful symptoms of modern America's ill health.

Trump's slogan, "Make America Great Again," meant essentially one thing: Right now, as of 2016, America is not great in the sense and to the extent that a sole superpower should be great. And some time is needed so that, after putting its house in order, it can once again demonstrate its greatness to the whole world. Attempts to read any signs of isolationism in Trump are naïve. Basically, the difference between Clinton's and Trump's positions was simple: global leadership today or the day after tomorrow. However, both have something in common: the great-power present. If you have any doubt, just read the US president-elect's Gettysburg speech, which will probably soon be considered historic.

However, the problem is not that Americans showed and were shown two capitalisms: white-collar capitalism and blue-collar capitalism. Only a very naïve person would see Donald Trump as a mouthpiece for the interests of the American middle class. The two faces of capitalism have always existed in the US. What's more, foreign capitalism has always been a source of resources to compensate for the social vulnerabilities and ineffectiveness of domestic capitalism, as symbolized by cities such as Buffalo, Detroit and Pittsburgh, which have turned into relics of America's former industrial might, as Trump has repeatedly said.

The relatively prosperous eight years of Obama, after the not-quite-successful reindustrialization under [George W.] Bush, were ensured exclusively through the massive and continuous inflow of funds into the American economy from abroad, which are in effect being eaten up by the American public.

Global American capitalism is a combination of a technological rent collection system and an even more important system of stimulating capital inflow to the US. The first system is based on the unmatched potential of global communication and marketing, while the second is based on the equally global potential of projecting military power and political influence (including far beyond fabled "soft power").

These days, America's domestic problems are almost inseparable from its foreign policy problems. Over the past 30 years, the American economy has become too globalized to even consider restructuring the domestic economy without affecting [US] foreign economic—and therefore foreign political—obligations and circumstances. It would be wrong to think that the elite groups behind Hillary Clinton did not see the problems of small-town America, ignored them, or believed that everything would fix itself. They just had no idea that the situation was so acute, and bet too heavily on the progressive part of American society, thus depriving themselves of support from "real Americans." However, there is no doubt that the American elite were earnestly preparing to create opportunities to at least simulate an American revival.

Of course, no American president or American political elite as a whole can afford to change the traditional development model unless the situation becomes truly critical. And for all the complexity of the challenges facing America today, the situation is not critical, even though the first alarm bells are ringing: for example, the failure to implement local renewal programs (in places like Detroit and New Orleans—a significant part of [the latter] remains devastated after Hurricane Katrina, which happened over a decade ago) or to ensure social stabilization (stabilization through inaction, if you will) in hopelessly depressed suburbs, where fighters for a bright African-American future are now beginning to take up arms—for the first time since the 1970s.

The problem is that in the new era of slowing globalization, the two capitalisms cannot coexist: The US's ability to ensure their coexistence on credit is nearly exhausted. Therefore, the US's ability to be a global stabilizer at its existing level of military might has been exhausted. In order to play its global role, the US will need far more resources. If America's domestic problems become a factor in global politics, catastrophic consequences will ensue for the global balance of forces that has evolved over the past 30 years—a balance that suits the majority of players.

No matter what the advocates of a multipolar world might say, the US still has tremendous say over the set of models that may guide the future of the world, even if it cannot dictate that future as such. Let's face it: In the era of slowing globalization, a world with the US's active participation would be very different from a world without it, even if none of the aspiring countries manages to achieve the status of a full-fledged center of power.

Let's look at the breakdown of the media-assigned roles in the US election campaign before it finally spun out of control and lost a sense of proportion. Clinton focused mainly on foreign policy but underscored the social problems of today's America, disingenuously asserting that nothing should be changed right now, or else it will get worse, and that it is better to deal with the symptoms than try to change the world. On foreign policy, Trump pushed the notion of revamping the system of America's foreign ties, and on domestic policy he in fact raised the possibility of fundamental changes and the need to forcefully address key issues, primarily social ones.

Hillary Clinton had practically no domestic agenda. She said that relations with [US] allies should remain a priority. However, on the whole, the election campaign impressed a simple idea on the minds of globalists and Atlanticists throughout the world: In a world of slowing globalization, everyone but Americans should tighten their belts. And if [other countries] suddenly begin to focus on their own domestic problems, [a stance] that Donald Trump waxed eloquent about, everyone will suffer, including countries that allow themselves to criticize the sole superpower.

To a very large extent, jack-in-the-box Donald Trump's transformation from a fringe outsider into a real contender for the presidency (including from the US media's standpoint) suspiciously coincided with a clear slowdown, if not the actual collapse, of the much-touted geopolitical projects of the Barack Obama period.

As for the Trans-Pacific and Transatlantic [Trade and Investment] Partnerships, the US's partners/satellites, even super-loyal ones like Germany and France, sensed the US's need for these projects and began to squeeze concessions out of Washington. That was probably when the idea emerged to show the world an alternative to the familiar American liberal globalism that the [US's] allies find humiliating every once in a while.

"There will be no more concessions: We've got enough troubles of our own." This is essentially what the American elite wanted to tell the whole world. They managed to do just that.

Granted, the civilized world was spooked by the prospect of America's problems growing into global problems. That is because the so-called Western world is in principle unable to stand up to increasingly acute global challenges. The most that Europe, Japan and US satellites from other regions can do is tactically play for time as they wait for the Americans to come and start saving everyone, even at the cost of the total destruction of everything. That is what Saudi Arabia is doing, for example. Despite its colossal military budget, it has proved unable to cope with half-naked Houthis.

A perfect example is a hysterical article by former NATO secretary-general Andreas [*sic*; Anders] Fogh Rasmussen to the effect that the US should retain and even strengthen its status as the world's police officer, expanding the policy of interventionism as advocated by Hillary Clinton. Naturally, when he talked about the US as the world's police officer with a monopoly on interventionism, Rasmussen was bound to understand that this would mean subjugating the geoeconomic capabilities of American allies to the interests of American global leadership. And most important, if small-town America suddenly won, then the civilized world would have to loosen the purse strings on a far greater scale.

The globalized world felt very uncomfortable when shown the prospect of ending up out in the geopolitical cold if the US, figuratively speaking, deemed it more appropriate to deal with domestic issues—above all, straightening out [America's] system of excessive social obligations. This despite the fact that many realized that in practice, everything would be far more low-key and calm under Donald Trump, and existing obligations in Europe, let alone in East Asia, wouldn't be axed (although the conversation with [US] partners would be much tougher).

It is also significant that now the "inconceivable" scenario has begun to play out, the new American administration has completely free rein in making certain demands on its allies.

The American elite were unprepared for Trump's election as the US president. The elite who have reigned in the US over the past 30 years—and who have long come to regard the division into Democrats and Republicans as just a manner of speaking—were unprepared for the need to change tomorrow, as it were. The formula of one Soviet leader [i.e., Yury Andropov—*Trans.*] can probably be applied to the American ruling class and "service" strata: They did not know the country they live in.

The problem is not that the US lacks sufficient resources to implement Trump's mandate even partially, or that there's no way to get hold of those resources without a major shakeup of the American economic system. (Granted, it's by no means certain that the Bolivar[5] of the American economy, who could not carry the two American capitalisms, would be able to withstand a major shakeup, even a temporary one.) The problem is that the US's allies are neither politically nor economically ready to substantially change the system of distributing obligations and to finance the new US president's efforts to resolve long-standing economic problems that were previously regarded as unimportant in comparison to building a global postmodern society.

And not because they don't want to, but because there are almost no resources left to do so: The world economy may have an even smaller safety net than American white-collar capitalism does. I believe that neither Donald Trump, nor the garrulous European leaders, nor their reticent Asian colleagues nor experts have realized yet just how close the world has come to the collapse of the fundamental principles that in fact constituted globalization.

After all, small-town America in reality voted neither for Trump nor for Clinton: It voted against the society that was brought about by globalization, which the US has been promoting with misguided enthusiasm over the past 30 years.

Will Trump Tear Up the Nuclear Deal With Iran?

By Nikolai Bobkin. *Strategic Culture Foundation Online Journal*, Nov. 20, 2016, http://www.strategic-culture.org/news/2016/11/20/will-trump-tear-up-nuclear-deal-with-iran.html.

Donald Trump's victory in the US election and the coming changes in the country's foreign policy are still a headline story for the global media. Although there have been only cautious hints about the possibility of normalizing US-Russian relations, opponents of such a policy are already speaking up. One scenario being mentioned predicts a new conflict between the US and Russia after Trump moves to pull the US out of the agreement over Iran's nuclear program that was negotiated by the P5+1 [i.e., the five permanent members of the UN Security Council, plus Germany—*Trans.*]. Attempts are being made to portray any review by Washington of the terms of the Joint Comprehensive Plan of Action (JCPOA) as a disaster for Tehran and an obstacle to Moscow in the normalization of relations with the next US administration. But is this really a problem?

In Tehran, they are calmly waiting to see how the American president-elect's foreign policy unfolds. In the end, snippets from Trump's campaign speeches are more useful for showing how he thinks than for predicting his future political decisions. In any event, from Iran's perspective, Donald Trump is a more promising figure than Hillary Clinton. His refusal to focus on deposing Assad at the expense of fighting ISIS, his promise to destroy ISIS, his call for Saudi Arabia to provide ground forces in the battle against terrorism, his acknowledgment of US responsibility for the lack of stability in Iraq, his desire to normalize relations with Russia—all this is significantly different from what Clinton had promised.

Tehran has taken note of the fact that in a Nov. 11 interview with *The Wall Street Journal*, Trump praised Iran and Russia's role in the war on terror. Under certain circumstances, such an approach could pave the way for Iran and the US to cooperate in the battle against ISIS, alongside Russia. That possibility was never entertained under Obama.

Iranians have also pointed out one more detail: Trump has never stated that US policy toward Israel is unalterable, and has even hinted at a willingness to review previous US commitments to that country. In a *New York Times* interview, he questioned whether it made sense to provide Tel Aviv with billions of dollars in military aid every year. He also affirmed his support for a two-state solution in Palestine and has refused to recognize Jerusalem as Israel's capital.

But perhaps this is just wishful thinking on Tehran's part. While addressing the American Israel Public Affairs Committee, Trump chided Clinton and Obama for having "treated Israel very, very badly," and offered assurances of his own love for Israel.

Regardless, Iran does not yet see the election of US President Trump as a direct threat to its nuclear agreement with the P5+1. Iranian Foreign Minister Javad Zarif has noted that Tehran is determined to stay faithful to the JCPOA, but that "this doesn't mean we do not have other options."

What options would those be?

It is logical to assume that this means that Iran is allowed to review the terms of the nuclear deal without detriment to itself. After all, many in the Islamic Republic [of Iran] believe that from the standpoint of Iran's interests, the current nuclear deal is not the best option. Ayatollah Ali Khamenei has repeatedly charged that the agreement is filled with ambiguities. The Iranian leader has warned that the JCPOA could cause great damage to Iran, both now as well as in the future. Iran's Supreme National Security Council and the Islamic Consultative Assembly (Majlis) also approved the agreement, but included caveats that the government must take into account.

It is possible that Trump might give Iran the chance to withdraw some of those caveats. He did not express concerns about the nuclear deal from the standpoint of the nuclear nonproliferation treaty. Trump pointed to something else in his criticism of the agreement, namely the fact that lifting the sanctions and unfreezing Iran's assets ($150 billion by his estimate) has opened up Iran's markets for many countries, but not the US. "Did you notice they're buying from everybody but the United States?" he exclaimed.

This new US president, who aims to use trade as a foreign policy tool, naturally yearns to correct this situation. And a change in the US position—especially the restoration of trade and economic relations with private US companies—is also an intriguing prospect for the Iranians, who are having serious difficulties establishing trade and financial ties with the West. One example might be the currently stalled deal to buy over 100 Boeing airplanes from the US. Incidentally, Trump also expressed his ire on this topic: Why is the Obama administration preventing the Iranians from buying from Boeing, which only encourages Tehran to purchase Airbus [planes] from Europe? Because, as Trump said when the nuclear deal with Iran was finalized, the US is "led by very, very stupid people."

But it's quite unlikely that Trump intends to go back to square one in the nuclear negotiations with the Islamic Republic of Iran. As Walid Phares, one of Trump's foreign policy advisers, said after the election: "Ripping up is maybe a too strong of word. * * * He will take the agreement, review it, send it to Congress, demand from the Iranians to restore few issues or change few issues, and there will be a discussion." Iran got the message.

Nor does the outgoing Obama administration believe that Trump will rip up the nuclear deal. State Department spokesman Mark Toner, noting that the agreement with Iran is not a legally binding treaty, emphasized that it is in America's best interests for it to remain in effect. If Trump decides to withdraw from the deal, Iran will begin to revive its nuclear weapons program.

How Will Russia Respond to Trump?

By Mikhail Troitsky, political analyst and international relations specialist. *RBC Daily,* Nov. 23, 2016, p. 5.

Barring clear progress in relations with the US before the summer/fall of 2017, Moscow will again have to acknowledge irreconcilable rivalry with Washington.

Many in the Russian expert community currently expect relations with the US to improve under the new administration. However, the pessimists disagree with the optimists, pointing to the seriousness of US-Russian differences, and the conviction held among [US] administration officials and members of Congress that Russia is one of the US's most dangerous adversaries in the modern world. In addition, according to the pessimists, the president-elect and his future national security adviser, Gen. Michael Flynn, are the only ones [in the new administration] to have publicly expressed a position on Russia. And even Flynn seemingly changed his opinion [on Russia] in the final weeks before the election.

Of course, if a US president shows a strong will and gets personally involved in forming a policy on relations with Russia, the resistance of the administration and, in part, Congress, can be neutralized. For example, in 2009, despite being surrounded by skeptics, Obama initiated a "reset" [in US-Russian relations] immediately after an acute conflict over Georgia. As it later turned out, even [then] secretary of state Hillary Clinton, who pressed a symbolic "reset" button together with Russian Foreign Minister Sergei Lavrov, was a skeptic.

How might relations develop between the two countries in the first months of the new administration? Moscow risks disappointment if it attempts to immediately achieve ambitious goals like getting NATO not to extend membership to post-Soviet states or the US not to deploy missile defense systems in Europe.

During the election campaign, Donald Trump promised to modernize and build up weapons, including nuclear ones, and developing missile defense is a sacred cow for the Republicans. So the Trump administration is unlikely to be interested in Moscow's willingness (if any) to resume arms reduction negotiations on, say, strategic nuclear weapons.

It cannot be ruled out that Trump's promise to pressure [the US's] European allies to increase their defense spending would only strengthen NATO as a whole and may jump-start efforts to enhance security coordination within the European Union. In any case, it is hard to imagine that Mr. Trump could manage to get NATO to publicly abandon its "open door" policy, even if he really wanted to.

Trump's consideration of prominent Republican politicians committed to the ideas of Atlanticism (Mitt Romney, for example) to fill the post of secretary of state may indicate that he has no plans to seriously revise relations with NATO.

This means that if in the first few months of his presidency Trump is seriously interested in changing relations with Moscow, the most likely fields for interaction would be Syria and the sanctions imposed by the US and its allies against Russia in 2014. The president's future national security adviser, Michael Flynn, believes that the main threat to US security is "radical Islam," not just "violent extremism"—the terminology used by the Obama administration. So the Trump administration could drop support for the "moderate opposition" [in Syria] and agree to join Moscow in using massive force against radical groups that are banned in Russia, including ISIS, without regard for collateral damage.

If this cooperation between Moscow and Washington in Syria in the spring of 2017 proves effective, it could provide additional impetus to the idea of lifting sanctions against Russia and ending the US's policy of isolating Moscow. Nevertheless, coordinating the fight against Islamic radicals would likely be hampered by a number of difficulties in addition to the notorious mutual mistrust that exists between Russian and US law-enforcement, security and military agencies.

First, there is the matter of which side would determine the priorities of a joint operation. Second, it would be extremely difficult to overcome disagreements about the contours of a final settlement of the conflict in Syria, including the fate of [Syrian President] Bashar Assad, without which it would be hard to set common objectives for the operation. Finally, if the US really does wage an intensive military campaign in the Middle East under the banner of fighting "radical Islam," would Moscow benefit from sharing political responsibility with Washington for such an approach, bearing in mind the position of Russia's Muslim population and Russia's relations with, for example, the Persian Gulf monarchies?

But the biggest dilemma for Russia could come when the Trump administration says what it would like to get from Moscow in exchange for agreeing to relax the sanctions and abandon, for example, unconditional support of Ukraine in the conflict with Russia. One US condition would likely be for Russia to join [the

US] in pressuring Iran to get Trump's promised tougher terms on the Iranian nuclear deal (Iran would be required, for example, to refuse to support Hezbollah in Lebanon).

A key condition of the Trump administration for normalizing relations with Moscow would most likely be Russia's suspension of activities that Washington perceives as attempts to weaken the US and change the rules of the game in world politics. Russia might have to meet several criteria to comply with the relevant conditions: from halting hostile cyber operations that Washington blames on Moscow, to refraining from increased Russian military activity along the borders with NATO countries or support for radical nationalist parties in EU countries.

Ultimately, Russia will have to reexamine its views of the US: from viewing the strategic rivalry between Moscow and Washington as virtually insurmountable, to accepting the US as a positive force in international relations. Is such a shift in official assessments possible? It cannot be ruled out a priori. The first indicator will be the conditions and format for the parties' interaction in Middle Eastern hot spots. However, domestic considerations could intervene.

Whether a conservative reset takes place between Moscow and Washington will most likely depend on the agenda for the [2018] Russian presidential election. In recent years, the Russian media have portrayed the US as an important determinant of many processes in Russia: from the "externally funded" protest movement to food countersanctions in response to the sanctions imposed through US pressure.

Under such conditions, not using US-Russian relations as part of the election campaign would mean abandoning an important lever of influence on voters. Therefore, only one of two flashy messages would be effective: "The US is continuing its course to subdue and possibly destroy Russia" or "through tough and skillful maneuvering, we managed to persuade the US to take our core interests into consideration." No middle-ground arguments—for example, about the new [US] administration continuing an uncertain position toward Russia—would be effective.

The message about reaching a compromise with the US without incurring losses for Russia would allow the authorities to end discussions about the feasibility of Russia enduring economic deprivations [due to international sanctions]. However, barring clear progress in relations with the US before the summer/fall of 2017, Moscow will again have to acknowledge irreconcilable rivalry with Washington.

It is therefore possible that Moscow's attitude toward the US will again drift, as it has since the presidency of George W. Bush and then under Barack Obama—going from high expectations, to the belief that "administration officials are not allowing the [US] president to carry out his intentions," and then ultimately ending in the final verdict: "The new president was unwilling to cooperate on an equal footing."

What Will the Middle East Look Like Under Putin and Trump?

By political analyst Maksim Suchkov, expert on the US. *Republic.ru*, Nov. 23, 2016, https://republic.ru/posts/76411.

The first telephone conversation between Russian President Vladimir Putin and US president-elect Donald Trump took place a mere six days after the election. According to an official press release, the conversation was friendly and focused on the need to "normalize" relations between the two countries. Predictably, the first contact between Putin and Trump made Russian commentators cautiously optimistic about the possibility of a major improvement in relations between Moscow and Washington, and at the same time showed the West that its worst fears of having Putin and Trump team up in a formidable tandem were materializing.

Throughout the campaign, US commentators kept saying that Trump had no experience in international affairs and Putin would definitely outsmart him. This was based on the "praises" the Republican candidate had been singing about the Russian president, but in reality Trump's fondness for Putin has been greatly exaggerated. The true purpose of Trump's remarks was to expose Barack Obama to further criticism for being "weak and passive."

So, there is no reason to believe that Trump will be Putin's "puppet." On the contrary, Trump's respect for Putin merely indicates that the flamboyant billionaire, too, is eager to assert himself as a rough and tough leader.

As a businessman, Trump has had the reputation of a tough negotiator, so it is unlikely that cooperation between the US and Russia on Syria or any other issue will be as smooth as many are thinking in Russia. And it's not just because Trump is unpredictable. As much as Trump may be interested in working with Putin, it will be hard for him to maintain this commitment throughout his term, because that would mean having to overcome numerous bureaucratic and political obstacles on a daily basis—including the bipartisan consensus on Russia that has emerged in Washington in recent years.

Syria is, of course, the biggest challenge for the US and Russia in the Middle East. So far, Moscow and Washington have been backing opposing sides in the conflict and pushing two incongruous narratives about the situation in Syria. But now there is a lot of potential for cooperation between Russia and the US on postwar settlement issues: working on a new Syrian Constitution, forming a provisional government and rebuilding the country. In both Moscow and Washington, policymakers realize now that it is necessary to put an end to the military conflict and let diplomacy do its work. But there is no clear understanding as to how this can be done specifically. The official Russian synopsis of the first telephone conversation—which said that Putin and Trump "agreed that it was necessary to join efforts in fighting our common biggest enemy, namely, international terrorism and extremism" and discussed "ways to resolve the Syrian crisis along these lines"—may indicate that the Russian leadership is in fact trying to identify some of the first steps along this path.

If Trump really manages to focus on fighting ISIS and Islamic extremism, that may open the door to working with Moscow on this issue further down the road. So far, his administration appointments corroborate this theory. Incoming CIA director Mike Pompeo and national security adviser Michael Flynn have consistently advocated prioritizing this threat. Regular intelligence sharing and joint combat missions against extremists would be a perfect option for Moscow. As a climax, the Russian and US Air

Forces might launch a joint offensive against the ISIS capital of Raqqa—probably before 2017 is over. In reality, though, many other factors may come into play. There are too many unknowns about Trump's future policies, especially considering that the Pentagon and Congress are going to oppose this cooperation. The latter is already working on a new round of sanctions against Russia due to its actions in Syria and Ukraine. The goal is, first, to put in place legislative restrictions to limit Trump's future foreign policy experiments; and, second, to show the president-elect from the very start where the red lines are.

Before Trump takes office on Jan. 20, 2017, Moscow will probably do its best to promote his ideas internationally and to create the most favorable conditions for their implementation. In recent months, Moscow has been bracing itself for the possibility of Hillary Clinton winning the election and implementing her policies in Syria: imposing a no-fly zone and ramping up financial, military and political support for the Syrian opposition. As a result, Moscow has created infrastructure in and around Syria to contain Hillary Clinton's plans. Those containment capabilities can now be used as bargaining chips in dealing with the new administration, and their removal could be presented as some of the concessions Moscow is willing to make. The most likely approach for Russia looks like this: On the one hand, the Kremlin will try to send the US president-elect as many "positive messages" as it possibly can, while on the other hand it will seek to strengthen its positions on the ground in Syria before inauguration day, so it has enough bargaining chips for the future deal. The Aleppo offensive by the Syrian Army, and Russian air strikes against Idlib and Homs Provinces are all part of this plan.

The situation on other fronts in the Middle East may be a bit trickier. The most overlooked aspect is the potential fight over Iran. Moscow's tactical alliance with Tehran and some semblance of consensus on a broad range of regional issues are not a given; they require constant efforts on Moscow's part. Perhaps Trump will be able to mend fences with the Sunni Gulf monarchies (even though local elites are currently skeptical about such a prospect). At the same time, the Trump administration will almost certainly try to revise the Iranian [nuclear] deal, in which the Obama administration invested so much political capital, to bring it more in line with US (and Israel's) national interests. If Trump chooses the more confrontational scenario with Tehran, as recommended by some of the people already appointed to key positions in his administration, it will be harder for Russia and the US to bring their positions closer.

Regional powerhouses will play an increasingly prominent role in the Middle East, and both the US and Russia should learn to work with them. There are just a few such powers left: Egypt, Iran, Israel and Turkey. In recent years, Moscow was able to establish working relationships with them (with varying degrees of success). Now it has to prepare for a new reality: Regardless of what regional rulers think about Trump's victory, absolutely all of these countries are objectively interested in starting a new chapter in their relationships with the US. No wonder Egypt's President Abdel Fattah el-Sisi was first to congratulate Trump after his victory. If Trump decides to seize this opportunity to win back the trust of America's long-term allies and manages to do so, Moscow will have to look for a new modus operandi in dealing with these states.

Finally, another important factor is whether the Trump team will promote some kind of "strategic vision" with respect to the Middle East like that of the neocons on George W. Bush's team. In addition, Trump will have to address the dilemma that Barack Obama has been struggling with for eight years: Does America need a bigger presence in the region, or would it be wiser to minimize its involvement here and focus on the Asia-Pacific region instead? Or perhaps even focus just on its own domestic issues? Based on the strategic choice Washington makes on this issue, the US and Russia may engage in cooperation or, on the contrary, end up with even fiercer confrontation.

Time is also of the essence. The four years Trump will have in the Oval Office may not be enough to fundamentally fix US-Russia relations. But it is more than enough time to make things even worse. Therefore, Moscow and Washington should, first, have a clear and, more importantly, realistic understanding of what specifically they would like to achieve, at least within the next two years. Second, they should remain open to all opportunities to improve relations, like the ones they have today. If they have this bare minimum, they could then attempt to normalize relations. But that's all they can expect at this point. In recent history, efforts to improve relations between Russia and the US have often failed because the Kremlin and the White House expected too much.

Europe Turns Toward Russia in Major Foreign Policy Change

By Peter Korzun. *Strategic Culture Foundation Online Journal*, Dec. 1, 2016, http://www. strategic-culture.org/news/2016/12/01/europe-turns-towards-russia -major-foreign-policy-change.html.

Jean-Claude Juncker, the president of the European Commission, believes that Europe does not need to depend on US foreign policy regarding its relationship with Russia.

In his interview with Euronews, the European Commission president said that he "would like to have an agreement with Russia that goes beyond the ordinary framework, bearing in mind that without Russia, there is no security architecture in Europe." Mr. Juncker noted that "Russia must be treated as one big entity, as a proud nation." The president emphasized that he "would like to have discussions on a level footing with Russia." He thinks that President Obama was wrong to say that Russia was only a "regional power."

There are reasons for Mr. Juncker to make such a statement at this particular moment.

With Donald Trump in office, the US's European policy is expected to go through drastic changes, and a period of uncertainty will last in Washington at least until Jan. 20 [when Trump takes office].

This is also a time when so-called "pro-Russian" politicians will be gaining more clout in the Old World. Actually, they are not exactly pro-Moscow but rather pro-national, putting national interests at the top of their priority lists. For them, the interests of their countries are more important than the priorities of the US or the EU. They believe that normalizing relations with Moscow is in their national interests, [so they want] to make that part of their foreign policy plans.

Two weeks ago, such leaders came to power in Bulgaria and Moldova. The EU's image has been damaged in both countries, where the public believes that economic progress is too slow and nominally pro-EU leaders are failing to tackle corruption.

François Fillon—a politician advocating rapprochement between Russia and the EU—won the center-right nomination for the French presidency on Nov. 27. His victory means that two "pro-Russia" candidates—François Fillon and Marine Le Pen—will probably face off in the April 2017 presidential election.

A presidential election will take place in Austria on Dec. 4. Norbert Hofer of the Freedom Party has a good chance of winning. Judging from what he has said during the election campaign, Mr. Hofer will consider pulling out of the EU and visit Moscow if elected president. He promised "to show my strong commitment to the withdrawal of sanctions against Russia because I am firmly convinced that sanctions hinder communication."

If the Italian referendum on Dec. 4 says "no" to major government overhaul plans, then a snap election will become a possibility to benefit Italy's Northern League party, which advocates the improvement of relations with Russia. Its leader, Matteo Salvini, has visited Moscow and the Crimea a number of times, and called for lifting the EU-imposed sanctions.

Some signs confirming a change in the EU's policy on Russia are largely gleaned from the headlines. In late October, the EU lifted a cap on Gazprom's use of the OPAL pipeline in Germany, paving the way for Russia to expand Nord Stream's capacity and bypass Ukraine as a gas transit route. Nord Stream 2 has recently been supported by London. German Vice-Chancellor Sigmar Gabriel is an outspoken advocate of the project....

Meanwhile, the idea to recognize Russia as a global power and make it part of the global US-Russia-China equation is being floated among US foreign policy pundits. In his recent comments on MSNBC's "Morning Joe," Zbigniew Brzezinski, a well-known foreign policy guru, said, "America is needed to pull together some larger coalition that can deal with global problems. And in that larger coalition * * * America, China and a changing Russia could be preeminent." Actually, what Mr. Brzezinski is suggesting resembles the Yalta Conference held in February 1945.

Indeed, a "big three" format talk is the right place to address global issues: trade, finances and a global security architecture. Will Mr. Trump listen to what foreign policy pundits say? In any case, the pivot to Russia is becoming a global trend.

What Are the Implications of Israeli-US Conflict Over UN Resolution?

By international relations expert Vladimir Frolov. *Republic.ru*, Dec. 27, 2016, https://republic.ru/posts/77973.

The Barack Obama administration has for the first time declined to block an anti-Israel resolution at the UN Security Council (in February 2011, the US vetoed more or less the same draft), provoking an acute crisis in US-Israeli relations. The attempt by US president-elect Donald Trump, in response to Israel's request, to pressure the Obama administration and force it to impose a veto was unprecedented in US foreign policy. It is not part of American tradition for presidents-elect to interfere in current foreign policy issues before their inauguration. President Trump will most likely disavow the American position with regard to this resolution and side with [Israeli Prime Minister] Benjamin Netanyahu (he has already written on his Twitter page that "things will be different" at the UN after Jan. 20), but the Middle East policy agenda he has outlined threatens to cause an even bigger political and military crisis in the region, burying—for a long time, if not forever—the prospects for an Arab-Israeli peace settlement....

In recent years, Netanyahu has striven to ensure that the Palestinian problem stops being perceived by Israel's international partners as a central issue—as the determining factor in their relations with the Jewish state. Netanyahu has positioned Israel as an effective fighter of international terrorism and a source of advanced technology....

So Netanyahu is pinning all his hopes on Trump's future administration, with which he is building relations through the president's son-in-law, Jared Kushner (Trump is considering appointing him as a special envoy to broker a Palestinian-Israeli settlement); through Trump's chief political adviser Steve Bannon; and through billionaire Sheldon Anderson [sic; Adelson—*Trans.*], a sponsor of rightist Republicans who owns media assets in Israel. Israel's attempt to stop the UN Security Council's resolution with Trump's help is unprecedented, as are the direct accusations against Obama and Secretary of State Kerry of being in cahoots with the Palestinians and promoting the anti-Israel resolution (Israel's ambassador to the US even promised to give the Trump administration Israeli intelligence data purportedly confirming that conclusion, which in and of itself is an amazing move in relations between allies). Netanyahu's problem is that Trump's declared stance on the Palestinian-Israeli peace process and his initial cabinet appointments may actually complicate Israel's position and destabilize the situation in the Middle East.

Without going into detail, in the course of his election campaign and after his victory, Trump indicated that he would support Israel on the settlements and on maintaining control over the West Bank, and would even recognize Jerusalem as Israel's capital, relocating the US Embassy there from Tel Aviv. Trump's and Netanyahu's positions against the nuclear deal with Iran and the need to counter Iranian expansion in the region are equally close. Trump has effectively proclaimed the return to the "no gap between the US and Israel" policy that was pursued by George W. Bush without particular success for the peace process.

To implement those plans, Trump has appointed a rather controversial figure as the new US ambassador to Israel: David Friedman, a New York-based bankruptcy lawyer known for his extremist views on the Palestinian-Israeli peace process that are totally at odds with official US policy. For example, Friedman actively supports building more settlements and even having Israel annex the occupied territories in the West Bank; rejects a two-state solution to the Palestinian-Israeli conflict; and opposes talks with the Palestinian National Authority. Needless to say, he also supports relocating the US Embassy to Jerusalem (which, incidentally, is required under a law passed by Congress in 1995 that all previous presidents have suspended via executive order, due to national security considerations).

Trump's attempts to implement these ambitious plans will lead to a new Arab-Israeli conflict. Moving the US Embassy to Jerusalem would risk a third intifada and the PNA's annulment of its decision to recognize the state of Israel in keeping with the 1993 Oslo agreements. A new surge in violence in Palestinian territories would nullify positive breakthroughs in Israel's relations with Arab states. Netanyahu and even his ultraright Defense Minister Avigdor Lieberman oppose annexing the entire West Bank. Neither is particularly enthusiastic about assuming responsibility for governing 2.5 million Palestinians (Lieberman, for example, has stated that there are more important problems for Israel than the US Embassy). Both understand that an alternative to the two-state solution is Israel's transformation into an apartheid state with isolated self-governing Palestinian "Bantustans." The position of Trump and his ambassador strengthens the position of the Israeli ultraright, making Netanyahu redundant.

The big question is whether Trump, faced with Middle East realities, will be able to change his position quickly or substantially adjust it (for example, making the embassy relocation purely symbolic, "laying the cornerstone" and authorizing new building projects only in settlements that have been agreed upon with the Palestinians, [and/or] halting the seizure of new lands).

An escalation of the Palestinian-Israeli situation with this US position would be an unpleasant surprise to Moscow, which would probably be unable to abandon its support for the Palestinians so as not to further complicate its relations with the Islamic world. The problem is also that Trump's team seems to be intent on a "holy war with radical Islam," interpreting this concept in the spirit of George W. Bush's "axis of evil," with Iran as the main target. It is hard to imagine Moscow supporting such a reckless misadventure, let alone participating in it in any way. Granted, the example of the Syria campaign shows that the bounds of the possible are now quite wide.

Battle of Ideas in Washington

By Fyodor Lukyanov, research professor at the Higher School of Economics. *Rossiiskaya gazeta*, Jan. 11, 2017, p. 6.

American political battles are taking on whimsical forms. A significant part of the political establishment (both Democratic and Republican) has officially recognized but not reconciled itself with the president-elect. By all indications, opposition to the new occupant of the White House is going to be fierce from day one.

It just so happened that the subject of Russia became the weapon of choice for Trump's opponents. This means that Russia will be at the center of discussion. [It may also come under] pressure in order to tie the hands of the new administration. This is not about Russia, which is an important factor in American politics, but far from the only one. American society and its political class are currently battling over their country's role in the coming years and maybe even decades.

In January 1992, US president George H. W. Bush said in his annual State of the Union address that America had won the cold war. "There are those who say that now we can turn away from the world, that we have no special role, no special place. But we are the United States of America, the leader of the West that has become the leader of the world. And as long as I am president I will continue to lead in support of freedom everywhere, not out of arrogance and not out of altruism, but for the safety and security of our children. Strength in the pursuit of peace is no vice; isolationism in the pursuit of security is no virtue."

A quarter of a century later, Donald Trump, the man who is going to be sworn in as president, said during his campaign that when it comes to foreign policy, his motto is "America first." "No country has ever prospered that failed to put its own interests first. * * * We will no longer surrender this country, or its people, to the false song of globalism. The nation-state remains the true foundation for happiness and harmony."

The remarks [of the two presidents] are divided by the era of a unipolar world that has been the subject of contentious debate. What does this mean in terms of American policies? After Bush (who lost his reelection bid in 1992 and did not get the chance to fully enjoy American dominance), all US presidents (Clinton, [George W.] Bush and to a lesser extent, Obama) acted on the assumption that America's goal is to change the world and, if necessary, countries that get in the way of global changes or do not fit into the picture. This notion has been a part of American culture since the country's inception, but until the late 20th century, it was not possible to put it into practice, especially on a global scale.

Donald Trump has announced that he will abandon this goal, which is seen not just as a sudden change of course, but basically as a betrayal of national ideals. Meanwhile, the newly elected president's flamboyant style aside, his views are nothing new for the American political tradition. Appealing to nationalism ("America first"), prioritizing domestic affairs and consolidating the masses against the aristocracy—such a toolkit is usually associated with the seventh US president, Andrew Jackson (1829-1837). The Jacksonian worldview contrasts with the Wilsonian one: The 28th US president, Woodrow Wilson (1913-1921), was the founder of the liberal world order. And while he never personally succeeded in bringing his ideas to life since he was unable to overcome the opposition of the isolationist establishment at the time, his ideas in many ways shaped the course of policy after World War II, and especially after the cold war.

The struggle between the two legacies—Jackson's and Wilson's—has always been a part of the US's foreign policy debates. Such was the case during George W. Bush's first term, for instance. However, overall, Washington is used to the liberal, interventionist Wilsonian paradigm dominating [politics]—it has become almost an axiom. Trump's turn to a different approach that is just as deeply rooted in American politics signals the end of the liberal model and serves as a reminder that political development is cyclical. And most likely, this trend is here to stay for the foreseeable future (then a new cycle will begin again). But understanding this inevitability will take time and will apparently be quite painful....

'There's No Reset Button. We're Either Going to Get Along or We're Not'

By Tatyana Baikova and Aleksei Zabrodin. *Izvestia*, Jan. 12, 2017, p. 1.

US president-elect Donald Trump gave his first press conference nine days before his inauguration. During the press conference, which lasted about an hour, he responded to the leading media outlets' questions, including on key domestic and foreign policy matters.

As some in Russia have pointed out, the remarks by the next occupant of the White House indicate that he is coming under serious pressure from anti-Russian forces. Despite that, Donald Trump made it clear that he may adjust his policy in favor of a pragmatic improvement in relations with Russia. "There's no reset button. We're either going to get along or we're not. I hope we get along, but if we don't, that's possible too." That was the American leader's response to a question on Russian-American dialogue.

"Judging from his statements today, both Donald Trump and his team are under horrendous pressure from those who oppose improving relations with Russia. Right now, the president-elect does not have any counterarguments to defend his position in favor of cooperating with our country. So he is maneuvering, stalling for time and trying not to make any sudden moves. Right now, I suspect that even Trump himself does not know whether or when there will be progress [on this issue] after the inauguration. Relations with the US are not going to get easier under Trump in any case, but they could become more pragmatic. All in good time," Konstantin Kosachov, head of the Federation Council's international affairs committee, told *Izvestia*.

The press conference began with a brief speech by US vice-president-elect Mike Pence, who said that the American people are tired of "fake news." Donald Trump also demonstrated he has no patience for intentionally distorted information when he interrupted a CNN journalist asking a question by saying he does not intend to speak to representatives of media outlets that publish fake news.

[The press conference] devoted particular attention to the hacker attacks that were allegedly orchestrated by Russia. In responding to that question, the president-elect said that Russia could have been behind the attacks on Democratic Party servers [*sic*; Trump actually said: "I think it was Russia"—*Trans.*], but added that other countries also launch hacker attacks against the US. He also stated that Washington is developing a defense system against such attacks.

Aleksei Pushkov, member of the Federation Council's defense and security committee, explained in a conversation with *Izvestia* that Donald Trump is in a situation where he is forced to reckon with the mood of the American political elite.

"Right now, the mood is one of hysteria about Russia and its so-called interference in the US election. This situation has been created artificially, but has a direct impact on the tone set in the media and in Congress, where a new bill on proposed sanctions against Russia has just been submitted. As president-elect, Trump cannot completely ignore the extremely tense atmosphere with regard to Russia. At the same time, he has confirmed willingness to cooperate with Moscow in the fight against terrorism. During the election campaign, he identified this as the main area of cooperation. As for the degree of cooperation with Russia in other areas, he will determine that later on as president. I think that given the current touchy atmosphere, we can hardly expect more clarity from Trump," the politician said.

In Aleksei Pushkov's opinion, Trump is acting within the framework of the existing system, which is in many ways monopolized not only by Russia's enemies, but also by Trump's enemies, who are trying to impose their position on him.

"Essentially, he is being forced to continue the policies of Barack Obama regarding Russia. [Trump] made it clear that he will not do that. Under Obama, there was no cooperation between the US and Russia on terrorism, only talk. However, there will be progress in that direction under the new head of the White House," the senator said in conclusion.

According to Nikolai Zlobin, head of the Center for Global Interests research center, the main purpose of Trump's press conference was to tell the American voters how he plans to separate his job as president from that of head of a multibillion-dollar corporation. In addition, journalists had amassed a lot of questions for Donald Trump that he tried to answer.

"Trump has been silent for a long time about Russia and the hackers. He needs to dispel suspicions and accusations against him as much as possible. Admitting that Russia was behind the hacking of several US political organizations is very important for him in terms of getting Congress to approve his candidates to cabinet posts. His remarks are driven by domestic trends in the American political process. But I think that the subject of Russian hackers is becoming a thing of the past. In addition, being the owner of a large corporation implies that he may come under pressure where his property and investments are concerned. This is a new matter for America. So it is important for Trump to explain how he will resist such pressure from other countries. Trump spoke harshly about Russia in order to prove that he has no ties with it," Zlobin believes.

According to the expert, Trump is going to start actively building a new system of computer security and start working on relations with Moscow.

"I think that by summer, we are going to see some serious changes in American politics. Overall, I don't see any reason for him not to have good relations with Russia. Vladimir Putin is known as a pragmatic politician in the US. And today, Donald Trump has also shown himself to be a pragmatic politician who is not prone to all sorts of ideological theories. In this sense, it will be easier for Putin and Trump to find common ground," Nikolai Zlobin said in conclusion.

PART THREE

The Story of Trump's 'Russia Ties'

Introduction

This part focuses on the controversy around Trump's alleged collusion with Russia before he was elected—a theme that was touched on marginally before the 2016 election, but assumed much greater importance in the media (both Western and Russian) throughout 2017. Two key events on the American side that sparked reactions in Russia were the January 2017 release of the Department of National Intelligence Report, which concluded that the Russian government had used cyber espionage and media influence to interfere in the US election; and special counsel Robert Mueller's investigation into contacts that took place between Trump campaign personnel and Russia.

Because the Trump team's personal contacts with political, diplomatic and other figures in Russia and Eastern Europe go back further in time, they are the subject of the first section (3.1). Events discussed here include professional interactions, specific conversations and meetings that took place well before Trump was elected; however, some articles included in this section were published a year or more after the fact, because the Russian authors were responding to subsequent research by US investigators.

American intelligence findings are the focus of Section 3.2, which presents Russian responses to allegations and evidence of Moscow-sponsored hacking of American computer servers during the presidential campaign. Like the articles in Section 3.1, much of this material was published after the US election—some of it quite shortly before this book went to press.

3.1

Contacts With Russia and Ukraine

Introduction

As Trump's campaign heated up through the first nine months of 2016, news reports started to emerge about members of his team having contact (current or past) with key figures in Russia and the former Soviet Union. The Western media in particular made inferences between these ties and Trump's enthusiastically pro-Russian campaign platform, even hinting that Trump was Putin's "puppet."

The articles in this section start with Paul Manafort's appointment as Trump's campaign manager, delving into prior details of his work with former Ukrainian president Viktor Yanukovich, as well as Ukrainian and Russian business magnates. Although Manafort's activities in Ukraine date back to 2006 or earlier, they took on added significance after Trump was elected president—particularly in late October 2017, when Manafort turned himself in to the FBI following an indictment by Mueller.

A second group of articles centers on a meeting between Donald Trump Jr., Trump's son-in-law Jared Kushner and Russian attorney Natalya Veselnitskaya. This meeting, arranged by Trump's old acquaintances Aras and Emin Agalarov, took place at Trump Tower in June 2016, but the American press did not pick up the story until the summer of 2017, in connection with an ongoing investigation of Trump's ties to Russia. The coverage here includes Veselnitskaya's own rebuttals against allegations that she had promised the Trump team compromising material on Hillary Clinton.

Next comes a Russian perspective on contacts that key members of the Trump team (including Kushner and foreign policy adviser Michael Flynn) made with then-Russian ambassador Sergei Kislyak during the presidential transition period. For the sake of context, we will note that Kushner and Flynn tried to establish a "back channel" of communication through Kislyak after the election—by which time Trump had appointed Flynn as US national security adviser. Then, in late December, after Obama decided to expel 35 Russian diplomats as a punitive move for Moscow's alleged interference in the US election, Flynn told Kislyak (in a phone conversation monitored by the FBI) that the Trump administration would review Obama's decision, and asked Moscow to refrain from retaliating. Putin agreed and Trump expressed gladness at that decision.

On the Russian side, press secretary Dmitry Peskov denied there was anything inappropriate in Kislyak's conduct: "This is his job. He was talking about bilateral relations." However, Flynn got into trouble at home—because he technically had no right to conduct such negotiations, and because he later concealed his contacts with Kislyak—and resigned his position in the Trump administration in February 2017.

While all of the evidence of ties between the Trump team and various figures in Ukraine and Russia made a great splash in the US media, Russian sources downplayed the significance of these interactions, much of which they knew about during the heat of the campaign. For example, political analyst Vladimir Frolov writes in July 2016 that "it's unlikely that Manafort is being influenced by Moscow these days"; asserts that a 2015 speaking engagement by Flynn in Russia "doesn't make him an agent of Russian influence"; and dismisses allegations of Trump's collusion with Russian intelligence as "pure conspiracy theory." After the election, however, in a February 2017 analysis, Frolov does cite evidence of a "Russian trail" in behind-the-scenes plans to settle the Ukraine conflict. In an Aug. 1 article (included in Section 4.4, below), Frolov explicitly accepts the evidence of Flynn's contact with Kislyak, citing it as a key event in the diplomatic war that escalated in the first months of the Trump administration.

Trump Changes Horses

By Igor Dunayevsky and Aleksandr Samozhnev.
Rossiiskaya gazeta, June 22, 2016, p. 8.

US Republican presidential candidate Donald Trump has fired his campaign manager, Corey Lewandowski. Most local commentators say that such a significant shake-up should be interpreted as Trump's transition from his triumphant primary bid to the electoral race culminating in November 2016, where he is likely to face a pitched battle with ex-secretary of state Hillary Clinton for the post of 45th president of the US.

Trump has appointed as his right-hand man Paul Manafort, a conservative and fairly well-regarded political consultant, albeit with a somewhat controversial reputation in local circles (for instance, he was once an adviser to ex-president of Ukraine Viktor Yanukovich—*Ed.*). [In March 2016,] the post of "convention manager" had been created for Manafort. This job was given key importance, so the new appointee brought in his own team to help him consolidate power on the campaign trail.

According to *The New York Times*, Trump decided to change horses in midstream on the advice of political allies, sponsors and his own children who work for his business empire. [All of these people] pointed out Lewandowski's lack of experience managing a national campaign. Trump campaign headquarters announced the dismissal in a laconic press release that thanked the now-former manager for his work.

Lewandowski had headed the Trump team from the outset of the election campaign in the summer of 2015. At that point, the campaign resembled a ragtag gang with a colorful ringleader and an entourage of henchmen that disregarded all the usual rules and regulations, flouting their opponents' unbending, ironclad political techniques by attacking them from one side after another. In taking this approach, Lewandowski interpreted his role of chief strategist in a rather unconventional way: He distinguished himself by showing unconditional personal loyalty to the candidate, rather than trying to give him advice on campaign tactics. Lewandowski's mantra could be summed up in four words: "Let Trump be Trump." He described Trump as working on a grand scale, interfacing with voters at mass "show rallies" that drew thousands of people, sometimes even tens of thousands—especially in the languishing American hinterland.

And it worked. The Lewandowski mantra held true. So it continued until roughly the end of March, when it became clear that the billionaire was in first place in the primaries. But at the same time, it was growing more likely that he would not garner the 50% of delegates' votes required for automatic victory. In that case, the winner would be determined on the spot at the Republican National Convention in Cleveland, Ohio, in July. This would render the outcome of the primaries almost meaningless: The deciding role would be played by the convention attendees. And the businessman's advisers could do nothing about it. Trump was losing steam, and Lewandowski had no other strategy.

As a result, Trump has put his money on Paul Manafort, hoping that [the latter] can help him consolidate Republican voters (many of whom regard the billionaire with unconcealed hostility, due to his explosive rhetoric) and find common ground with the party elite. After all, an unprecedented number of prominent Republican politicians still adamantly refuse to support Trump. At one point, his ratings did go high enough to bring him neck and neck with Clinton. But then, in a routine interview [with *The Wall Street Journal* on June 2—*Trans.*], he suddenly accused a federal judge of bias in a litigation case against him. Trump said the bias was due to the judge's Mexican origin and the fact that Trump himself had previously called illegal immigrants from Latin America "rapists." The businessman caught a barrage of accusations of racism.

Meanwhile, as Trump was calling on his party to rally around him, there was a tooth-and-nail battle going on covertly within his own staff, between Manafort and Lewandowski. The "old guard" took Lewandowski's side, believing that their approach of "letting Trump be Trump" had brought him victory, and that attempts to change the billionaire's image would only turn off his voters. Lewandowski himself had strained relations with the conservative elite who were trying to get Trump to change his behavior;

[Lewandowski also] clashed regularly with the press. Manafort, by contrast, took on the role of Trump's ambassador to Washington, trying to patch up dialogue with the party leadership and with Republicans in Congress.

In this context, saying goodbye to Lewandowski seems logical. Trump is aiming to win at any cost, and his campaign manager was running more risks than solving problems. Lewandowski's dismissal and Manafort's approval lead commentators to conclude unequivocally that Trump is trying to convince Republican doubters that he is willing to listen to their advice and build bridges for a common purpose, which the Republican National Committee frames as follows: Don't let Hillary Clinton win a third term for Barack Obama. As for Lewandowski, despite the dismissal, he still seems to expect that Trump (if he wins) will reward him with a position in the administration or some other bonus....

Republican Party of Regions

By Aleksandr Panov. *Novaya gazeta*, Aug. 24, 2016. p. 10.

Going out with a bang.

Hillary Clinton's campaign staff and US media outlets broke a story about now-former Republican campaign manager Paul Manafort's activities as adviser to former Ukrainian president Viktor Yanukovich. Meanwhile, the Ukrainian Anticorruption Committee has discovered an unreported "secret ledger" and records showing $12.7 million paid to Manafort. *The New York Times*, CNN, NBC, the Associated Press (AP) and *Politico* have each conducted their own investigation. What interests the American media the most is compliance with the law: Did Manafort declare his income, and did the lobbying firms he employed to promote Yanukovich's interests in the US obey the [American] law on foreign agents [i.e., the Foreign Agents Registration Act, or FARA—*Trans.*]? Violation of this law could mean up to five years in jail and a $250,000 fine.

They are also looking into a possible link between Manafort's money and a change in the Republican Party platform at the recent national convention in Cleveland, where a point about providing the Ukrainian authorities with "lethal defensive weapons" was removed.[6] More broadly, [the media are studying links between Manafort and] the views of Donald Trump, who is willing to rethink the status of the Crimea, does not intend to rush to the aid of East European NATO allies at the drop of a hat, and calls the Russian president a brilliant and talented politician.

Unlike Obama.

Manafort denies receiving $12.7 million from the Party of Regions' secret ledger (in addition to his official salary as a PR man and lobbyist). The Ukrainian Anticorruption Committee is calling on the FBI to investigate, but there are some indications that it is already doing so.

After Donald Trump read an AP article about the secret payments his adviser had received from Yanukovich's people, he decided that Manafort could not keep his job as campaign manager any longer. Donald doesn't like it when someone other than himself is the center of attention, his detractors say sarcastically. Trump's inner circle—his son Eric and son-in-law Jared Kushner—also called for Manafort's resignation.

According to the official version, Manafort tendered the resignation himself, and Trump thanked him for his work. A seasoned lobbyist, Manafort really did help his candidate—especially during the Republican National Convention in Cleveland. During behind-the-scenes negotiations in the best traditions of "shuttle diplomacy," he helped enlist the support of a significant segment of the Republican establishment. More importantly, he thwarted a planned mutiny of delegates who were planning to hold a fresh vote of the primary results and block Trump's nomination as the [party's] official presidential candidate.

In this sense, Manafort did his job and can walk away. But the influential lobbyist is not walking away inconspicuously, as members of his profession tend to do.

"Paul Manafort's resignation is a clear admission that the disturbing connections between Donald Trump's team and pro-Kremlin elements in Russia and Ukraine are untenable," said

Hillary Clinton's campaign manager Robby Mook. And he added: "You can get rid of Manafort, but that doesn't end the odious [sic; odd] bromance Trump has with Putin."...

From Savimbi to Yanukovich.

Republican political consultant and lobbyist Paul Manafort, 67, has worked for the Ford, Reagan and [George H. W.] Bush administrations, as well as for international clients as infamous as guerrilla leader [Jonas] Savimbi of Angola, president Mobutu Sese Seko of Zaire and president Ferdinand Marcos of the Philippines. In 2005, Ukrainian oligarch Rinat Akhmetov, who was Manafort's client [at the time], brought him onto the Viktor Yanukovich team, where he became [Yanukovich's] political strategist—or "spin doctor," as they say here [in the US].

The practice of hiring Western consultants was widespread in the post-Soviet space. An American team of spin doctors had worked for Boris Yeltsin in 1996. That subject even inspired a Hollywood film: "Spinning Boris" [2004]. It's a comedy.

According to the American media, Manafort took the lead on Yanukovich's team, which was disappointed with the job done by Russian PR specialists during the Ukrainian presidential race in 2004. Officially, the American was on the Party of Regions payroll as a political consultant for six years, from 2006 to 2012 (although [fact-checking Web site] PolitiFact reports that Manafort had unofficially advised Yanukovich as far back as the 2004 election). Manafort tried to control everything from [Yanukovich's] hairstyle and suits to his manners. He convinced Yanukovich to learn English, to make speeches in Ukrainian when visiting the country's western regions, and to speak Russian in the east. Some say he even got Yanukovich into the habit of blow-drying his hair....

The duties of Manafort's team also included working with the American press to promote a positive image of Yanukovich and simultaneously to criticize his opponents—such as former prime minister Yulia Timoshenko, whose release from prison was being demanded by all Western leaders.[7]

Today, Manafort says that Yanukovich was a pro-Western president, not pro-Kremlin, and that thanks to [Manafort's] PR efforts, American companies—[in sectors ranging] from energy to farming—secured lucrative contracts in Ukraine. However,

The Times of London cited "a senior Ukrainian prosecutor" who reported that in 2006, Paul Manafort had organized a series of protests in the Crimea against Kiev and [the prospect of] Ukraine joining NATO; [these protests were] led by Yanukovich's Party of Regions. The protests forced NATO to cancel a planned international military exercise. Thus, under Manafort's leadership, Yanukovich "laid the groundwork for Russia's annexation of the peninsula, which Donald Trump has now suggested he would recognize," *The Times* writes.

Rick Gates, a Manafort aide in the Trump campaign, [previously] worked with two well-known Washington lobbying firms, Mercury LLC and Podesta Group Inc., which set up meetings for the Ukrainian leadership with influential Senate and House representatives. AP reported that these firms were paid $2.2 million. Curiously, Mercury founder Vin Weber was a senior adviser to Republican presidential candidate Mitt Romney in his past [2008] campaign bid, and John Podesta—a cofounder of the other lobbying firm that worked for Manafort and Yanukovich—is now leading the campaign of Trump's rival, Democratic candidate Hillary Clinton....

Manafort denies his participation in financial transactions involving the two Washington firms. However, their staff members told AP on condition of anonymity that Trump's former campaign manager had called their offices to personally check on the lobbyists' work.

Secret books and a GRU interpreter.

... Even after Viktor Yanukovich fled to Russia, Manafort's involvement in Ukrainian political campaigns did not end. The most recent one he served on, in October 2014, was for the Party of Regions' successor, the Opposition Bloc. Several members of the [bloc's] parliamentary faction told *Politico* on condition of anonymity that Manafort had advised their project in 2015 as well. That year, he flew to Ukraine six times to meet with the leaders of the bloc, although they had stopped paying money to his firm....

In response to the *Politico* investigation, Manafort sent a brief Twitter message to the editorial office that he has had no contract and done no business with Ukraine since 2014. As for *The New York Times's* assumption that he had received payments from the

Party of Regions through a "secret ledger," he described it as unfounded, stupid and senseless. At the same time, he did admit that such payments were made, but not to him personally....

The American media have been paying particular attention to Konstantin Kilimnik, a former military translator who journalists claim used to work for GRU [Russia's Chief Intelligence Administration]. Before he met Manafort, Kilimnik worked at the Moscow office of the International Republican Institute (IRI). In 2006, Kilimnik started working as Manafort's interpreter, and then became his right hand in Ukraine, heading up his Ukrainian office. Detractors see evidence here of the Trump adviser's "ties to Russian intelligence."

In addition to "spinning Yanukovich," Manafort's team of American advisers, assisted by the [alleged] former GRU operative as their interpreter, tried to forge business ties with Russian partners. In late 2006, Manafort helped set up a direct investment fund in the Cayman Islands. Under the name Pericles, the fund used millions of dollars provided by Russian oligarch Oleg Deripaska to buy a Ukrainian cable TV company. However, the company soon closed. A Cayman Islands court is processing a legal filing to recover Deripaska's money, *Politico* writes. Court documents filed in the case show that Manafort and his partners received $7.35 million from Deripaska in investment fund management fees.

Trump headquarters does not want Manafort's dismissal associated with Ukraine or Russia. Last week, according to people close to Trump, new high-profile American media figures joined the Trump team to "shake up" the campaign [because] Manafort was not up to the task. However, [sources] in the US and the rest of the world tie the dismissal primarily to the former campaign manager's "Ukrainian skeletons in the closet." There is no doubt that the topics of Russia, [Trump's] bromance with Putin and the millions that "went missing" during Manafort's time as Yanukovich's adviser will come up during televised debates with Clinton next month. And the American press is not going to leave the Manafort firing alone.

Why Donald Trump Is Not a Putin Agent

By Vladimir Frolov. *Slon.ru*, July 25, 2016, https://slon.ru/posts/71242.

Republican presidential candidate Donald Trump's controversial interview with *The New York Times*,[8] in which he expressed opinions that resonate strongly with Russian foreign policy interests, hit the American public like a bombshell. The transcript has sparked a wave of articles in leading American publications, including pieces by Anne Appelbaum and Nobel laureate Paul Krugman. Most of these experts draw the discomfiting conclusion that wittingly or unwittingly, Trump is acting in Russia's interests....

More impressionable observers have begun to talk openly about Trump being "Putin's puppet," and alleging that his businesses and election campaign (which he initially financed independently) depend strongly on money from Russian oligarchs close to the Kremlin (those mentioned most often are father and son [Aras and Emin] Agalarov). Entire investigative journalism reports have been written about Trump campaign manager Paul Manafort's ties to former Ukrainian president Viktor Yanukovich and Russian businessman Oleg Deripaska.

American [*sic*; British] political analyst Sam Greene says that the theme of Trump as a Putin agent has become a media trend. But this, of course, is nonsense.

How can we not welcome this?

Moscow probably does like a lot of what Trump says. His foreign policy initiatives could seriously weaken the US's position in the world and destroy relations with key American allies in Europe and Asia, which would inevitably ease American pressure on Russia. We know that Trump and his team intend to substantially restrict the US's security commitments, including American nuclear guarantees to NATO, Japan and South Korea; to abandon the promotion of democracy abroad and [efforts to] overthrow authoritarian regimes; to cooperate with Syrian President Assad and Russia in fighting ISIS (an organization banned in Russia); to withhold supplies of lethal American weapons to Ukraine; and to establish constructive relations with the Russian leadership.

The Kremlin probably also likes Trump's intentions to ditch the Transpacific Partnership (TPP) and halt talks on the Transatlantic Trade and Investment Partnership (TTIP), [both of] which Moscow views as threats that would consolidate American dominance in the world.

Trump's vows to restore relations with "superpower" Russia are seen by Moscow as his willingness to recognize Russia's right to its own sphere of interests in the post-Soviet space. When the possible future president of the US says (and his political advisers confirm) that NATO security guarantees should take effect only after an audit, that means the end of the NATO-centric system of security in Europe, which Moscow can only dream of. When US House of Representatives ex-speaker Newt Gingrich, who is now on the Trump team (and used to be an active supporter of NATO expansion), says that the US would not start a nuclear war over Estonia—which is "in the suburbs of St. Petersburg"—what could that be but a ringing acknowledgment of Russia's zone of influence?

In the words of Vladimir Putin (who has twice in the past year called Trump a "striking" and "talented" politician): "How can [Russia] not welcome that?"

Dubious helpers.

It's much less obvious whether Moscow is doing anything to promote Trump's candidacy and whether it's helping his election campaign, which would be a violation of US laws. Of course, if it had the ability to do so, the Kremlin would gladly use it. After all, [the leaders] there believe the US and the European Union are doing exactly the same thing by replacing pro-Russian leaders in the post-Soviet space and the Middle East. But in reality, Moscow has no such ability.

The US is not France, where opposition parties like Marine Le Pen's National Front can borrow millions of dollars from foreign banks. In America, foreign funding for electoral campaigns is strictly prohibited. Hints that Trump's business empire, and consequently his campaign, are in some way dependent on Russian money look inconclusive; no real evidence has been found that Trump has any business projects in Russia or with Russian partners. Yes, he wanted to build a Trump Tower in Moscow, but that didn't work out.

Much has been said about Moscow's influence on Trump's campaign manager, Paul Manafort. The basis for this conclusion is that Manafort worked for years as a media adviser to Viktor Yanukovich, when the latter was prime minister and president of Ukraine. But those who jump to such conclusions are not aware that all the time Manafort was an adviser to Yanukovich, the Kremlin was trying to get him fired, as it considered him a channel of American influence (this was one of the reasons Moscow distrusted Yanukovich, too). Apparently, Viktor Fyodorovich [Yanukovich] realized that the Kremlin was trying to strengthen its control over him, and for that reason he did not fire Manafort. But the American adviser played no political role. Instead, he used his access to Yanukovich's officials to promote his own business projects in Ukraine. One of these was the failed project with Oleg Deripaska to acquire some media assets in Odessa. In other words, it's unlikely that Manafort is being influenced by Moscow these days.

Another supposed channel of Russian influence on Trump is his foreign policy adviser Carter Page, who worked in the early 2000s at Merrill Lynch's Moscow office, and had some business projects with Gazprom and its top managers. Page actually does parrot Russian news propaganda on Ukraine, even the allegations that Washington was trying to annex Ukraine and that the acquisition of the Crimea was Russia's legitimate response to American aggression. But it would be hasty to infer from this that Page is carrying out a Russian intelligence mission and whispering Russia's opinions in Trump's ear. Page looks more like a typical Moscow expat from the Vladimir Putin fan club. In July, Page came to Moscow to speak at the New Economic School, and he also gave a lecture to [political scientist] Aleksandr Dugin's students, criticizing US policy for its "hypocritical focus on democratization, inequality, corruption and regime change." There is no evidence of contact between him and Russian officials. His ties to Trump are superficial, and he plays no public role in his campaign. It's unlikely that this person would occupy any foreign policy post in a new US administration.

Another figure from Trump's foreign policy team is Gen. Michael Flynn, former director of the Defense Intelligence Agency, who was spotted next to Vladimir Putin at a gala for Russian TV channel RT in Moscow in late 2015. Flynn, who had been fired by [US President Barack] Obama for maltreatment of subordinates and conflict with other members of the presidential team, came to Moscow as a paid speaker. But to view him as a conduit for Kremlin policies is simply ridiculous. His views are similar to Russia's when it comes to combating terrorists in Syria, and he was willing to speak at RT for money, but that doesn't make him an agent of Russian influence; he's more like a "fellow traveler."

What merits closer scrutiny is the mysterious episode that occurred at [sic; prior to] the Republican [National] Convention, when the party's foreign policy platform was being drafted. As a result of direct intervention by unnamed Trump advisers, a call for America to supply lethal [defensive] weapons to Ukraine was struck from the text. And yet Trump's campaign staff showed no interest in any other part of the platform; they left the content up to right-wing conservatives. What and who dictated the wording on Ukraine? This is an interesting question, and it does give cause for suspicion. But it was most likely not a direct order from Moscow. Were there any informal consultations with [the Russian] Embassy in Washington via third parties? That will probably be the subject of an FBI investigation.

Russia's hand in America's election.

The controversial publication of electronic correspondence from the Democratic National Committee on WikiLeaks [in July 2016] may actually show some real signs of Russia's attempted influence on the US presidential election. [These e-mails] were leaked by two groups of hackers that American cybersecurity professionals believe have ties to Russian intelligence services. The timing of the publication (right after the Republican convention and right before the Democratic one) and its contents (which show that the DNC supported Clinton in the [primary] race against Bernie Sanders, using methods that were less than above-board) attest to the initiators' intent to inflict some reputational damage on Clinton.

And also to convince Sanders supporters to (at the very least) not go to the polls. Perhaps hoping to neutralize the media effect of these publications, Clinton's campaign staff launched a counterattack: Democratic campaign manager Robby Mook appeared live [on CNN] and accused Russia of meddling in the US campaign on the side of Donald Trump.

The Obama administration took this situation very seriously. It was the topic of several intelligence meetings in Washington last week. There is apparently some basis for the allegations that Russian intelligence interfered in the US election campaign—although the Kremlin, as usual in such cases, denies everything.

Indeed, the hacking and leaking of DNC correspondence looks like a classic "offensive tactic": releasing damaging information about the target, demoralizing her supporters and indirectly promoting [one's own] ally. But nobody can claim that this [leak] would have any electoral effect. This operation—even if we imagined it was cooked up in Russia—shows a total lack of understanding of the mechanisms that drive American politics, as well as an overblown perception of one's own ability to influence them. Such actions are unlikely to change anything in a country with a population of 300 million, independent media and billions of campaign dollars in play.

On the other hand, if the goal was more modest—e.g., a tit-for-tat against Clinton for trying to discredit Russian leaders via the Panama [Papers] (which Moscow believes were leaked by American intelligence services)—then this "offensive tactic" can be considered a success: [It made] plenty of noise, pleased the [Russian] leadership and had no practical effect. No one could have counted on the latter, anyway. Anyone who ties this [operation] to Trump assumes he was in the know about a top-secret Russian intelligence mission—which is pure conspiracy theory.

Wearing us out with an arms race.

Official Russian media make no secret of their affinity for Trump and their negative attitude toward his rival, Hillary Clinton. But is that proof of Russian [government] support for Trump? No. Who in the US watches Russian TV channels [that broadcast] in Russian? Even English-language RT—which is "pumped for Trump," as they say—has such a small audience in the US that it's ridiculous to speak of any electoral impact. The reason why Russian TV likes Trump lies in Russian domestic politics. It's just one more way of legitimizing the Russian authorities when even a US presidential candidate says that Vladimir Putin is a strong leader who's doing everything right. [This is] a very compelling argument for the average Russian.

A much more important issue is how Trump would put his foreign policy agenda into practice if he gets elected. The problem remains that the leaders of the Republican Party don't want to be associated with his platform. Some of them are even planning to vote for Clinton; they consider Trump a threat to American democracy.

The implementation of Trump's foreign policy plans would only exacerbate global turbulence, leading to acute regional crises and proliferation of nuclear weapons. No matter how attractive the prospect of a globally weaker America may be, it's not good for Russia. On the other hand, certain aspects of Trump's proposed solutions are already being implemented by the Obama staff: For example, they are refusing to supply lethal weapons to Ukraine; and they are cooperating with Moscow to resolve the Syrian crisis, rather than forcibly overthrowing the Assad regime. Moreover, demands to increase US allies' [financial] contributions toward joint defense are customary for American foreign policy, although Trump has expressed them in tougher language than before.

So far, Moscow sees a Trump presidency as a "window of opportunity" to maneuver, assuming that it should expect nothing from a Clinton presidency but an even fiercer confrontation. Moscow does understand the problem of Trump's lack of [political] experience. And there are concerns that his populist calls to "Make America Great Again" may result in an attempt to restore the US's leadership role the way Reagan did during his first term: by wearing Russia out with an arms race.

The Crimea for Lease: A Russian Trail in Settlement Plans for Ukraine

By Vladimir Frolov, expert on international relations. *Republic.ru*, Feb. 27, 2017, https://republic.ru/posts/80078.

Over the past few weeks, plans for a peaceful settlement in Ukraine have been popping up in the media like mushrooms after a rain. They are addressed primarily to the Donald Trump administration, and the incumbent and future leaders of France and Germany.

All of the initiatives have three things in common: (1) They reflect a desire to go beyond the unviable format of the Minsk agreements of September 2015 and February 2015 [for a settlement of the Donetsk Basin conflict]; (2) the initiators are Ukrainian politicians and experts who are in one way or another oriented toward Ukraine's old political elites from the days of [former Ukrainian presidents] Leonid Kuchma and Viktor Yanukovich (the latter himself came up with a "peace plan" in a letter to Trump and in an interview with Western media on Feb. 21); and (3) the "initiatives" essentially—albeit not completely—serve the interests of those among the Russian political elite who favor ending the fruitless geopolitical confrontation with the West....

The biggest splash came from a story in *The New York Times* on Feb. 19, alleging that Trump's personal lawyer Mike Cohen (who is mentioned in the well-known "intelligence dossier on Trump" as a key contact with Russian representatives) delivered a Ukrainian peace plan to former national security adviser Michael Flynn.[9] The plan was drafted by a group of Ukrainian politicians led by Andrei Artemenko, until now a little-known Supreme Rada deputy from the Radical Party, with mediation from Felix Sater, a Russian-born New York businessman with a rather unsavory reputation, and hand-delivered to Flynn days before he resigned over "unauthorized" talks with the Russian ambassador.

This alone has the makings of a spy thriller: Cohen had no authority to promote such initiatives at the National Security Council. Artemenko's confusing statements that his plan was approved by Vladimir Putin's key advisers (immediately denied by the Kremlin), as well as his well-known links to pro-Russian politicians in Ukraine and some Ukrainian "political émigrés" in Moscow, only thicken the plot. Meanwhile, the plan is quite realistic and, according to a *New York Times* editorial, deserves attention as a basis for a solution to the "Ukraine stalemate."

The Artemenko plan basically offers a comprehensive solution to the Crimea and Donetsk Basin issues. First, Ukrainian voters would decide in a referendum whether the Crimea would be leased to Russia for a term of 50 or 100 years (in an interview with the Ukrainian Web site strata.ua, Artemenko reduced the term to 30 to 50 years) with a subsequent referendum on the final status of the Crimea. Then the border and the separatist regions of Donetsk and Lugansk Provinces would be placed under Ukraine's control (with amnesty for most participants in combat operations) and a 72-hour safe corridor would be provided for all those who choose to leave for Russia, which would mean the dismantling of the [self-proclaimed] Donetsk and Lugansk people's republics. Then a nationwide referendum would be held on whether to grant the Donetsk Basin special [autonomous] status, followed by local elections. The reconstruction of the Donetsk Basin's ruined infrastructure would be financed by Russian lease payments for the Crimea. All Western sanctions against Russia—both the Crimean and Donetsk Basin sanctions—would be lifted.

Even though the Artemenko plan met with a hostile reaction from Ukrainian politicians, and the [Ukrainian] Prosecutor General's Office initiated a criminal case against the lawmaker on charges of high treason, it would actually be a better deal for Ukraine than the Minsk agreements. The latter benefit primarily Russia, giving it an opportunity to drastically change Ukraine's state system and policy without resorting to military methods of influence.

The purpose of the Artemenko plan is to restore Ukraine's sovereignty over the Donetsk Basin and to abolish the DPR/LPR as tools for maintaining Russia's political control over Ukraine. The "long-term lease" of the Crimea is a more acceptable formula for Ukraine than simply an agreement to transfer it to Russia. The Minsk agreements turn Ukraine into a Bosnia, while the Artemenko plan allows it to remain a single country....

Other settlement plans—one by Sergei Taruta, another billionaire, former governor of Donetsk Province and Supreme Rada deputy, and [the other] by Konstantin Kilimnik, a former aide to US political adviser Paul Manafort, who worked for Yanukovich and then for Trump—aim to solve the problem of the legitimate political representation of the Donetsk Basin's separatist territories. Kilimnik's plan proposes bringing back Yanukovich and his old team, while Taruta's plan calls for reinstating the powers of the local and regional council deputies who were elected in 2010 under a special Ukrainian law. The idea is clear: The incumbent DPR/LPR leaders will never be legitimate, and although the Minsk agreements do stipulate holding free and fair elections in these territories under the auspices of the OSCE, few believe in their feasibility. So the Taruta plan is quite workable (nobody has any illusions about a Yanukovich comeback)....

Finally, Yanukovich's plan—presented in the form of a letter to the US, German and French leaders and rather resembling testimony in support of his own alibi—also promotes the idea of reconfiguring the Donetsk Basin's elite through a referendum on the status of the Donetsk Basin, and Kiev's subsequent direct talks with Donetsk and Lugansk. It would be naïve to think that Viktor Yanukovich has matured enough to come up with a plan like that on his own in Rostov on Don. Unlike the Artemenko plan or the Taruta plan, a Moscow trail is quite obvious here....

Of course, Moscow would like to resolve the Ukraine issue as part of the European security issue, packaging the Donetsk Basin situation into new agreements with the West on recognizing the entire post-Soviet space as Russia's sphere of influence, where Russia would have the same rights to intervene as the USSR had in Warsaw Pact member countries. Moscow is irritated by signals that under Trump, Washington does not plan to include Ukraine in a vaunted "big deal" [with Russia], while the resolution of the conflict in eastern Ukraine is being put forward as a precondition for further bargaining." The new "selective reset," where Washington cooperates with Russia only on issues that are beneficial to the US (for example, nuclear disarmament) but refuses to address issues that are of principal importance to Moscow as part of a package approach (the precedence of Russia's interests in the post-Soviet space) is of little interest to the Russian leadership. But it would be difficult to get written guarantees from Trump recognizing Russia's sphere of influence in the CIS. Hence there are two possible scenarios: Change nothing and continue to dream about a post-Western world where Ukraine is given to Russia (Russia could wait forever), or deal with the concrete problem of withdrawing from the Donetsk Basin saga and finally closing the subject of the Crimea, proposing solutions and making reasonable compromises in a direct dialogue with Kiev without Trump....

Russian Lawyer Tells State TV She Met Trump Jr. to Ask for 'Help'

[No author indicated.] *The Moscow Times*, Aug. 5, 2017, https://themoscowtimes.com/articles/russian-lawyer-tells-state-tv-she-met-with-donald-trump-jr-to-ask-for-help-58581.

The Russian lawyer who reportedly met with Donald Trump Jr. to offer him compromising material on Hillary Clinton told state television she wanted to "ask him for help."

"It was a private meeting," Natalya Veselnitskaya told the Rossia 24 channel's Vesti news program. "I asked for help. Help to spread a story that I had come across in my professional capacity."

Veselnitskaya said she met with Trump Jr. in June 2016 on behalf of her client Russian businessman Denis Katsyv, who was accused of money laundering in the US in connection with the Magnitsky Act. The law was signed by President Obama in late 2012, and introduced the first post-Soviet sanctions against Russia, punishing individuals who were allegedly involved in the death of lawyer Sergei Magnitsky, and targeting officials involved in corruption.

Veselnitskaya told the interviewer she had wanted to speak to Trump Jr. to tell him about William Browder, Magnitsky's employer. Browder was the cofounder and head of Hermitage Capital, which was a leading foreign investor in Russia until 2006, when it was targeted by corporate raiders with government ties. After Magnitsky died under suspicious circumstances in a Moscow prison, Browder successfully lobbied for Washington to pass the Magnitsky Act.

Veselnitskaya accused Browder of a "financial scam" and [described] her meeting with Trump Jr. as "innocent."

"[The request to Trump Jr.] was a completely normal request to everyone who could provide any kind of support in US Congress, so that the Congress [legislators] would know what really happened in our country with Browder."

"As I've said before,[10] [the meeting] had nothing to do with [Trump's] rivals or the presidential election," Veselnitskaya told the program. "That never happened; that's not true."

Her story contradicts reports by *The New York Times* that Trump Jr. had agreed to meet with Veselnitskaya after she offered him compromising material on his political rival Hillary Clinton ahead of the US election.

Trump initially denied the account, saying he had met Veselnitskaya to talk about a Russian ban on adoptions by American families. When probed, he admitted that such an offer had been made but dismissed Veselnitskaya's information as not "meaningful," saying it "made no sense."

Veselnitskaya's comments to Russian TV came the same day that *The Wall Street Journal* reported that special counsel Robert Mueller had called for a grand jury to look into allegations of possible Russian interference in the US presidential elections. Veselnitskaya's meeting with Trump Jr. will be a major focus, the newspaper reported.[11]

In the interview, Veselnitskaya said she had not once been invited to US Congressional hearings to tell her story, calling the investigations politically motivated. "They don't want the truth there at the moment; they need an enemy," she said. "Some because they are looking to undermine Trump, some because they want to fuel the conflict with Russia."

Kremlin Not Surprised by Media Reports on Eavesdropping on Russian Ambassador to US

[No author indicated.] *Itar-Tass Daily*, Jan. 25, 2017, http://tass.com/politics/927204.

The Kremlin is not surprised by media reports about eavesdropping on telephone conversations of Russian Ambassador in Washington Sergei Kislyak by the FBI; this situation is a source of dissatisfaction, Russian presidential spokesman Dmitry Peskov said on Wednesday [Jan. 25].

He noted that the issue at hand is media reports, not some official information. "However, we are aware of US media reports that found confirmation that not only the ambassador but also some heads of state—of Germany, France and other European countries—were eavesdropped on actively. I do not know how things stand now," the Kremlin spokesman stressed. "Therefore, this can hardly be considered a piece of news, and this is hardly a piece of news that gives rise to satisfaction on our part."

The NBC TV network reported on Tuesday that the FBI eavesdropped on telephone calls between President Donald Trump's national security adviser, Michael Flynn, and Russian Ambassador in Washington Sergei Kislyak in December 2016, but "found nothing improper."[12] According to a source interviewed by the TV channel, US intelligence agencies "merely listened in as part of routine eavesdropping on Kislyak."

Senator Blasts Resignation of Trump's National Security Adviser Over Russia Contacts

[No author indicated.] *Itar-Tass Daily*, Feb. 14, 2017, http://tass.com/politics/930717.

US National Security Adviser Michael Flynn's resignation over contacts with Russia's ambassador may signal that President Donald Trump has not yet attained sufficient independence at his post, senior Russian Sen. Konstantin Kosachov wrote on his Facebook page on Tuesday [Feb. 14].

Kosachov, who chairs Russia's Federation Council (upper house of parliament) committee for international affairs, said Flynn can hardly be considered a pro-Russian politician. However, compared with many other high-ranking US officials, he was "open for dialogue and was in Moscow," and had contacts with the Russian ambassador.

"Given the current deadlocked bilateral ties and the lack of cooperation on key global issues, this is certainly better than nothing," Kosachov noted. "Dismissing the national security adviser for contacts with Russia's ambassador (ordinary diplomatic practice) is not just paranoia, but something much worse," he stressed.

"Either Trump has not gained the desired independence and he is being consistently (and not unsuccessfully) pushed into a corner, or Russophobia has already engulfed the new administration from top to bottom," he added. Earlier reports said US President Donald Trump had accepted the resignation of his national security adviser Michael Flynn, who acknowledged that he had inadvertently provided US Vice-President Mike Pence and others with "incomplete information" on his contacts with Russian Ambassador to the US Sergei Kislyak.

Claims published by *The Washington Post* earlier suggested Flynn had discussed the US anti-Russian sanctions with Kislyak.[13]

The telephone consultations presumably took place a month prior to Trump's inauguration.

The paper said some officials in the administration thought the talks between the would-be national security adviser and the Russian ambassador might have sent an irrational and theoretically incorrect signal to Moscow that the sanctions, which the Obama administration had introduced in the wake of the 2014 reunification of the Crimea and Sevastopol with Russia, could be eased.

Rendezvous Without Hope for a Reset

By Igor Subbotin. *Nezavisimaya gazeta*, March 13, 2017, p. 9.

The new American administration's Russia policy is still hazy, even though the US leadership has made several public statements about the Kremlin's course on the international arena....

The likelihood that Trump will offer Putin to push the reset button now is very small when you consider the number of recent scandals that have broken out around Trump and his associates.

Trump's conciliatory tone toward Moscow waned considerably after his former national security adviser Michael Flynn was forced to resign due to charges of [unauthorized] contact with the Kremlin: fateful telephone conversations with Russian Ambassador to the US Sergei Kislyak. After this scandal, the White House released a series of statements on Ukraine reminiscent of the Obama administration's rhetoric. Later on, Attorney General Jeff Sessions became another target of the "Russian agent hunters." He, too, had talked with Kislyak but did not tell the Senate [about those conversations during his confirmation hearing—*Trans.*]. The *Wall Street Journal* recently reported that the US president already intends to review his policy toward Russia.

Commenting on CNN about Kislyak's meeting with Trump representatives, [Putin's spokesman Dmitry] Peskov explained: "This is his job. He was talking about bilateral relations. He was talking about what is going on in the United States so we have a better understanding in Moscow. This is what is being performed by every ambassador of Russia abroad, every ambassador of the United States abroad, including in Moscow, because the more [an] ambassador talks to people in his country of residence, the better job he does."[14] The spokesman added that Russian diplomats had such contacts with the Hillary Clinton team, too....

Dancing With Washington

By political analyst Vladimir Frolov. *The Moscow Times*, June 8, 2017, p. 4.

Russian President Vladimir Putin danced circles around US television host Megyn Kelly on June 5, deflecting her questions on Russia's meddling in the US presidential election.[15] But he stopped short of denying it....

Putin redirected media attention to cyber hacking and the media frenzy over Russia's ambassador to Washington, Sergei Kislyak. But this deflection masks the real issue: Russian attempts to discredit one US presidential candidate, and bolster the one Moscow fancied.

It sidesteps the issue that has potential legal consequences for Trump's presidency—the possibility of collusion between the Trump campaign and Russia's operation to meddle [in the election]....

Former CIA director John Brennan told the House Intelligence Committee in May that US intelligence agencies detected a series of suspicious contacts between Russian government officials and Mr. Trump's associates. But he acknowledged that the contacts might have been benign.

It is also unclear which Russian officials were in contact with the Trump campaign. Ambassador Kislyak does not count, unless he actually requested US policy changes in exchange for Russian illicit services before the election. His meetings with Gen. Flynn and Jared Kushner during the transition are a different story, unrelated to the campaign. Those contacts might have been improper for US officials, but not for the ambassador.

Kushner's request for a secret channel with the Kremlin is bizarre, but not unprecedented in the history of presidential transitions.

Kushner's meetings with Russian banker Sergei Gorkov of the state-owned VEB [Vnesheconombank: Russia's Bank for Development and Foreign Economic Affairs—*Trans.*], which is subject to US sanctions, may raise more red flags. But those meetings are only significant if lifting sanctions was discussed in exchange for Russian loans to bail out Kushner's real estate projects.

The Trump administration's rush to lift sanctions on Russia right after the inauguration looks suspicious in this context. But it could also reflect genuine policy preferences made public during [Trump's] campaign. The FBI's interest in Kushner's role in running the campaign's digital operation may be of more significance here.

The fact that US intelligence may have intercepted some conversations between Russian officials discussing ways to influence the future Trump administration and then, after the election, effusively congratulating themselves on Trump's victory is so far merely an interesting anecdote that does not reveal exactly which Russian officials the US [government] had tapes of (members of the Russian parliament do not count).

This remains a murky story, and it might be wise not to over-connect the dots. But it is now consuming more and more of the US political space and has created tight constraints on Trump's Russia policy, denying Moscow hopes for a quick change in tone with the US.

On the other hand, with the disruption and distraction this is causing in Washington, it is still a net gain for Russia geopolitically. Anti-Russian hysteria in the American media is good for Putin's reelection campaign in 2018.

Russian Ambassador Kislyak on Meeting With Trump Adviser Flynn: 'There Were No Secrets'

[No author indicated.] *The Moscow Times,* Aug. 7, 2017, https://themoscowtimes.com/news/kislyak-says-there-were-no-secrets-discussed-during-flynn-meeting-58591.

In his first public appearance since his return from Washington, Sergei Kislyak said his meeting with Donald Trump's former national security adviser Michael Flynn was part of his job description.

"Any diplomat, Russian or not, works to better understand the political situation of the place where he is stationed," Kislyak said during the "Press Conference" program on Rossia 24 state television on Saturday [Aug. 5].

Kislyak's name has been at the center of spiraling allegations of collusion with the Russian authorities by people close to Trump. Flynn was forced to resign just one month after taking up his position as Trump's first national security adviser on allegations that he had had been in contact with Kislyak around the US election campaign to discuss the lifting of US sanctions. Kislyak's name has also been connected to Attorney General Jeff Sessions and Trump's son-in-law Jared Kushner.

In the broadcast, Kislyak denied all claims of inappropriate dealings. "It was completely correct, and calm, absolutely transparent," he said of his meeting with Flynn. "There were no secrets—not from our side, in any case." He said the two men had discussed issues of mutual interest between the US and Russia, including terrorism.

But the lifting of US sanctions imposed on Russia over its role in the Ukraine conflict and the annexation of Crimea had not been on the agenda, he said. "I was instructed [by Moscow] not to discuss the issue of sanctions." Kislyak insisted. "We don't discuss sanctions with anyone. And be certain that I fulfilled my instructions faithfully."

Kislyak, who was Russian ambassador to Washington from 2008 until July 2017, also denied Russian involvement in last year's presidential elections, and said his country had been "fully prepared for either one [candidate] or the other."

The Russian ambassador told Russian TV that he believes American antagonism towards Russia is a manifestation of the country losing its superpower status. "I was amazed to hear CNN commentators talk about ethnic Russians in the US as a category to be investigated," he said. "When people go to those lengths, it means the country is psychologically ill."

3.2

Spying on the Competition: The Hacking Scandal

Introduction

This section focuses on the technical side of the "Russian trail," starting with covert activity in 2015 and early 2016 by Russian hackers, who accessed some correspondence of American military and political leaders. The fact that some of the material included confidential e-mails from DNC officials, which were then leaked to the press and used by the Trump campaign to discredit rival Hillary Clinton, sparked heated debate in the American media about Russian "meddling" in the presidential election.

As with the stories of personal contacts (see Section 2.3, above), Russian media coverage of the hacking incidents is rather matter-of-fact. Although the Kremlin denied any connection with the hacked e-mails when they were leaked on July 22 (just before the Democratic Convention), most political commentators in Russia acknowledge that their government's involvement was at least plausible. For example, expert Dmitry Oreshkin tells *The Moscow Times* in July 2016 that the Kremlin was using an old Soviet tactic of information warfare; however, the goal was not to sway the election results, but to "conjure up feelings of chaos" in the US.

In the wake of Trump's presidential victory, Maksim Suchkov dismisses the hacking accusations as "a deliberately constructed narrative" by American media or intelligence agencies. He gives two possible theories behind the story: (1) members of the Democratic Party leaked the e-mails themselves, then Democratic leaders tried to hide the dissent within their own ranks; and (2) the Democrats' attempts to shift focus onto Russian hackers in the run-up to the election were intended to discredit Trump as a candidate (and now as president).

Once the accusations flying around the American media became codified in the Department of National Intelligence Report in January 2017—which expressed a high degree of confidence that the Russian government had interfered in the US election not only through cyber espionage, but through Russia-sponsored media—the tone of commentary from Russia heats up markedly.

The brunt of this criticism is directed not against alleged Kremlin spies or pro-Trump colluders, but against the paranoid Washington establishment. Vladimir Bruter writes in *Izvestia* that the intelligence report's conclusions are based on invalid assumptions that overestimate Russia's impact on American media and society in general. Yulia Latynina, while expressing absolute certainty that "the Kremlin really did try to interfere in the US election," also turns the cold war-style accusation back on the US. She writes that the Democrats are using the interference allegations in a "brilliant disinformation campaign" that traps president-elect Trump in a double bind: "If he doesn't acknowledge the Kremlin's interference, he's denying the obvious. If he does, then he's also acknowledging that he became president as a result of that interference by a foreign power."

This view does not differ markedly from remarks by Russian Security Council chief Nikolai Patrushev in a *Rossiiskaya gazeta* interview: "The impression is that the US Democratic Party is trying to get back at Russia for its own failures and miscalculations." Patrushev maintains that it was not Russia's influence, but "failures in US domestic policy that led to such election results."

In the more liberal *Republic.ru*, analyst Tatyana Stanovaya also finds fault with the Obama administration, claiming that it created a political vacuum in which Russia has felt increasingly free to expand beyond its traditional borders of influence: "If there is an opportunity to promote an alternative agenda in the media, Moscow is going to do so within the framework of general informational competition. And if suddenly there is a chance to hack the Democratic Party's servers, why pass that up?"

Spying on Uncle Sam

By Hannah Berkman. *The Moscow Times,* July 28, 2016, p. 5.

Computer hacking, international espionage and damaging leaks—what sounds like a Soviet-era fable might, in fact, have some truth to it.

On July 22, on the eve of the US Democratic Party Convention, WikiLeaks released some 20,000 internal party e-mails from the DNC. The most damaging ones revealed the committee had championed a rear-guard action against the challenger candidate Bernie Sanders in favor of eventual nominee Hillary Clinton.

Fallout was swift. DNC chairwoman Debbie Wasserman Schultz resigned. The Clinton campaign then accused the Kremlin of being behind the leaks, echoing cybersecurity experts' claims that Russian hackers breached the DNC and Clinton Foundation systems in June. Her campaign manager said the leak was meant to play into her Republican opponent Donald Trump's hands.

The US media have long connected Trump's campaign to the Kremlin, pointing to his pro-Putin advisers and Russian business ties. Could it be that Russia has decided to actively meddle in the US presidential election?

The evidence mounts. US intelligence agencies told the White House that they have "high confidence" that the Russian government was involved in the hack, *The New York Times* reported July 26.[16] President Barack Obama called it "possible," citing experts, but stopped short of a full-blown accusation.

As a country that has been suspected of similar behavior in the past, Russia's involvement is possible and even plausible, international affairs analyst Vladimir Frolov told *The Moscow Times*. After the initial hack was reported in June, three cybersecurity firms have concluded that a Russian trail is present in the leaked files.

The firm handling the DNC's breach, CrowdStrike, reportedly has experience with the "Russian espionage groups" in question. The groups had "advanced methods consistent with nation-state level capabilities," and one of the two groups responsible had access to DNC servers for a year.

After Schultz's resignation, Julian Assange, the WikiLeaks founder and vocal critic of Clinton, told reporters that he had timed the leak to coincide with the convention. Assange, who has been living in self-imposed exile in the Ecuadorian Embassy in London for four years, has well-reported links to Russia—even hosting an interview show in 2012 for Russia Today, a Kremlin-sponsored propaganda outlet.

The DNC wasn't the only organization targeted. Around the same time, Russia was accused of hacking into the Clinton Foundation, the Clinton campaign and e-mail accounts of US lobbyists, policy groups, law firms and consultants.

The Kremlin has denied the accusations, calling them "absurd." When initial reports came out, Putin's recently appointed Internet adviser, German Klimenko, suggested that someone "simply forgot the password."

Intelligence officials from various countries have previously accused Russia of breaching their systems, including a three-week string of cyber attacks in Estonia in 2007 and a 2015 hack into Germany's parliament. Both attacks disabled the countries' government Web sites and systems for days.

If Russia is indeed behind the leaks, it might be following one of several possible objectives. One prominent explanation is an attempt to discredit Clinton for what is seen as a smear campaign against Putin. The Kremlin does not actually believe it can influence the US election, analysts say, but it does see an opportunity for retaliation.

"The DNC is a secondary target," Frolov says. "Even if Russia didn't find anything to directly harm Clinton's chances, they found a good information war weapon, and they released it at the opportune moment."

A scandal is exactly what the Kremlin wants, says Dmitry Oreshkin. The political analyst sees Soviet logic at play, describing a zero-sum game "where a point lost for the West is a point gained for Russia." Rather than calculatedly aiming at a particular election result, the leaks were meant to "conjure up feelings of chaos" in the US, Oreshkin argued.

The Kremlin favors Trump over the more Russia-skeptic Clinton. A Trump presidency is seen as a "window of opportunity," because [the Republican candidate] has already spoken of restoring relations, Frolov said. The Russian media have painted him as a nonestablishment candidate who will keep the US out of others' affairs and pull back from NATO.

However, experts disagree on Russia's feelings toward Trump's erratic behavior. According to Frolov, Russian officials harbor feelings of apprehension about his inexperience and volatility. Oreshkin, meanwhile, sees Trump's unpredictability as a plus for Russia, a chance to increase feelings of chaos.

One of Trump's advisers told Bloomberg that he "wouldn't be surprised" if the Russians were behind the WikiLeaks scandal, but his campaign chairman [Paul Manafort] described the claims as "pure obfuscation."...

The US media are easily manipulated, says Vasily Gatov, a media analyst and senior fellow at the University of Southern California's Annenberg Center [on Communication Leadership and Policy]. "Since Russians blame Obama for everything, the American media decided they should blame Putin for all sins, including the rise of Trump," he said. "Putin may want to screw Hillary, but he's certainly not betting on Trump."

A more pertinent threat to US interests comes from Trump's isolationist foreign policy. His populist voter base is pushing for a noninterventionist US, which could undo alliances cultivated over decades.

Then it would be Trump who's playing into the hands of Russia, and not the other way around.

One Hack Too Far

By Vladimir Frolov, international affairs analyst.
The Moscow Times, Oct. 13, 2016, p. 5.

Last Friday [Oct. 7], the US Intelligence Community (USIC) publicly blamed the Russian government for directing "compromises of e-mails from US persons and institutions, including from US political organizations."[17] It claimed that the disclosures of hacked e-mails on [Web] sites like DCLeaks.com and WikiLeaks "are intended to interfere with the US election process," while "only Russia's senior-most officials could have authorized these activities."

The hacking of the DNC computer networks was first disclosed in mid-July. CrowdStrike, a private cyber intelligence firm brought in by the DNC to investigate the hacks, identified with a "high degree of confidence" two groups of hackers with links to Russia's intelligence services.

Cozy Bear (CozyDuke or APT 29), ostensibly working for the FSB, Russia's domestic intelligence service, breached the networks in mid-2015. It collected intelligence and personal data undetected until April 2016, when another group of hackers, Fancy Bear (Sofacy or APT 29), purportedly working for GRU, Russia's military intelligence service, broke into the same network, unbeknownst to the first group. This second hack raised some flags for the system's security....

In a recent Bloomberg interview, President Vladimir Putin denied that Russia "on a state level" had anything to do with the e-mail hacks. At the same time, his claim that "the important thing is the content that was given to the public, not the search for who did it" suggested more than a cursory knowledge of the matter.[18] His further claim that the Russian government did not possess the kind of sophisticated sense of US domestic politics necessary to pull off such a tricky game sounded lame. The Russian Foreign Ministry maintains a granular understanding of the intricate details of US presidential and party politics. The Russian

Embassy in Washington keeps about a dozen diplomats on the beat. It is not, as some claim, that the Russians suddenly discovered the DNC last year.

While the publicly available evidence linking Russian intelligence to the hacks is inconclusive, and may even suggest a false flag operation to entangle Moscow in a brawl with Washington, the USIC had a high degree of confidence in Russian involvement, even in July. The fact that they publicly named Russian intelligence as perpetrators suggests that they have definitive proof.

The question is: What was Moscow really trying to accomplish? Cyber operations to collect intelligence are normal spycraft. The DNC and RNC are legitimate targets for Russian HUMINT and SIGINT [human intelligence and signals intelligence] operations, as are private e-mail accounts and cell phones of key US policymakers. You get intelligence by eavesdropping on people with access to real secrets.

Initially, it appeared the Russian hacking was just about that—at least the Cozy Bear part of it in 2015. There were two notable scoops. First, the hacking of a private e-mail from former NATO Supreme Commander Gen. [Philip] Breedlove in early 2015 in which he unsuccessfully lobbied the Obama administration to send advanced antitank weapons to Ukraine (it was reassuring to know the White House was not serious about stopping Russian armor in eastern Ukraine). Second, a private audio recording by Hillary Clinton in which she opposed plans to develop a new nuclear cruise missile for US strategic bombers. Otherwise, the intelligence value of the trawl was small.

When the Russian hacking was discovered (due to the destructive rivalry between Russian intelligence services, who failed to deconflict on the target), Moscow found itself sitting on a pile of Beltway gossip of limited intelligence value, but with some potential for influence operations. Perhaps some "genius" suggested it should be made public to trash Hillary Clinton, intensely disliked for her public role in supporting the mass protests in Moscow in 2011. No thought was apparently given to the likely impact on future US-Russia relations, particularly if Clinton got elected, and what the US response might be. As is customary with intelligence operations, the Foreign Ministry was not briefed on the plan.

It is unlikely that the Kremlin really hoped to influence the results of the US presidential election or viewed Trump's victory as likely. That would have signaled a degree of incompetence that Moscow is still incapable of. Rather, the point of the exercise was to send a message that Russia mattered and could do bad things that the US, in Moscow's view, has been doing to Russia. It worked, but not exactly how Russia had hoped. It made Russia a negative issue in the campaign.

Subsequent releases of hacked Clinton campaign e-mails, including personal e-mails from her campaign chief, John Podesta, reveal signs of a classic "active measures" campaign to smear Clinton and provide ammunition for Donald Trump's attacks on his opponent in the race. They contained signs of falsification and doctoring typical of such campaigns, while the timing of the release—the night *The Washington Post* published a damaging audio recording of Trump discussing sexually assaulting women[19]—suggests a tightly coordinated effort, with WikiLeaks playing an unsavory role.

It did not help Trump, but has hurt Russia's relations both with the US and the likely future American president, Hillary Clinton. This may no longer be the work of Russian intelligence services, as the Russian state media have mastered the art of active measures on a scale unimaginable by the KGB. For months, Russian state media have been running a character assassination campaign against Clinton, highlighting every loony right-wing conspiracy on the market, including spurious assertions of Clinton's complicity in founding ISIS (a terrorist organization banned in Russia—*Ed.*). This shows a glaring disconnect between Russia's foreign policy interests, which require a workable and civil relationship with US leaders, and the interests of propaganda driven by personal ambition to the detriment of the nation's greater good. There is little that Russia has gained from this effort other than bad press.

The operation destroyed what little trust remained between the two countries, and at the sensitive moment of negotiations between [John] Kerry and [Russian Foreign Minister Sergei] Lavrov on Syria. It also put US President Barack Obama in an awkward position: Not retaliating is politically unfeasible. Publicly naming Russia is just the first step. Economic and technology sanctions appear to be the most likely next step. At the same time, Washington wants to maintain the option of reengaging Russia on Syria and is wary of escalation by cyberattacks.

Moscow needs to find a way to defuse the crisis. Offering secret talks on permissible rules of cyber warfare and cyber intelligence collection might be one way to do it. Better managing its intelligence services would be another.

Attacks From Moscow: Did the US Believe in Russian Hackers?

By American studies expert Maksim Suchkov.
Republic.ru, Dec. 20, 2016, https://republic.ru/posts/77631.

For more than two weeks, the topic of hacker attacks supposedly initiated by Russia remains the top news story in leading American newspapers and TV channels. The theory that [Russia] was behind the hacking attacks is generally accepted by the American establishment—unless you count Trump and his supporters, who have reacted sarcastically to the idea of foreign interference in US policy. The subject is getting a lot less attention in Russia. Our experts are either keeping mum or are skeptical (especially in off-the-record conversations) about the Americans' line of thinking. As for politicians, it makes no sense to start forcing the issue at this point: [Relations] with the outgoing administration are already a done deal, and certain hopes are being pinned on cooperation with the coming one.

It is noteworthy that during the first wave of discussions about the hacker attacks in the US, immediately after materials from the Democratic National Committee and e-mails of Clinton's closest allies were leaked to the press, the main motive for "Moscow's interference" was presented as the desire to discredit the US electoral and political systems. Now, a different reason is given: to directly help Donald Trump win the election.

Regardless of whether [such allegations] are true, Russia's involvement in the cyber attacks has become the main factor in relations between the two countries. What will the consequences be?

If we assume that the idea of Russia's influence is a deliberately constructed narrative (by the US media or special services), as Russia claims, then there are at least two theories as to which groups in the US stand to gain.

The first theory was voiced by Craig Murray, a supporter of Julian Assange and former British ambassador to Uzbekistan: According to him, the leaked materials were given to WikiLeaks by members of the Democratic Party leadership who were sick of the "corrupt dealings of the Clinton Foundation" and the unfair way the DNC was treating Clinton's rival Bernie Sanders during the primaries. In other words, even if Russians hackers were involved, as far as Murray is concerned, WikiLeaks got the materials from disillusioned Democratic Party supporters, not from [Russian hackers]. If we assume that is indeed so, then the idea that the Kremlin interfered [in the election] was invented to hide dissent and betrayal within the ranks of the Democratic Party from the American public.

A second theory is that the Democrats' attempts to shift focus onto Russian hackers in the run-up to the election were intended to lower Trump's ratings. Now that Trump is president-elect, they are instead aimed at proving to the average American that Trump is not only unqualified to serve as US president, but is actually a threat to American interests, since he is prepared to sell them out to Putin: Yesterday's prize was victory over Clinton; tomorrow's might be an agreement on Syria, or (even worse) a lucrative oil deal. This theory pairs nicely with criticism over ExxonMobil CEO Rex Tillerson's nomination for secretary of state.

There are indeed plenty of reasons to be skeptical. For a long time and at various levels, there has been talk in the US of "specific examples of Moscow's involvement," but no concrete evidence has ever been provided. Moreover, when members of relevant Congressional committees requested the proof that the CIA supposedly had, the agency refused to release it, claiming its sources were confidential. That caused a sensation, since such a thing is unheard of in America with its system of checks and balances, where the legislative branch has the right to oversee the work of the government, including intelligence services.

This also raises a lot of questions for the intelligence community about interagency cooperation: Why did the CIA act as Russia's chief accuser, rather than the NSA with its legendary omnipotence, the scope of which was exposed by Edward Snowden? After all, electronic espionage and hacker attacks fall specifically within the NSA's jurisdiction....

It should be mentioned that at the moment, Moscow is not able (and not exactly in a rush) to prove it did not hack the Democrats' servers. The situation is complicated by the fact that hypothetically speaking, our country does have a motive: Russian-American relations are in dire straits. A controversial and dirty election campaign for [Russia's] geopolitical foe, a lackadaisical approach to handling secret information involving the ruling party's main protagonists, and a slew of materials compromising its top representative—all of this created a convenient opportunity to once again knock the "rotting American system," as well as to complicate the election for the front-runner, who also threatened to continue a policy of confrontation with Moscow. The suspect also has the means to commit such a crime—intellectually and technically, Russia is one of the few countries that could have carried out such cyber interference. Of course, entities that are not affiliated with any government and also happened to gain from the whole affair should not be ruled out.

There is another theory that complements Moscow's aggressive behavior toward Washington: The only area where Russia has parity with the US is nuclear weapons. If the cyber attacks were initiated by Russia, the intention was to show its capabilities in this area and prove to the Americans that now there is another field where Russia can do just about anything the US can. On the other hand, [the hacking] can be seen as an attempt to prevent the US government and the agencies affiliated with it from interfering in Russia's domestic affairs, including the 2018 presidential election. In other words, it's an attempt to create a kind of deterrence mechanism. Unlike a harsh method such as nuclear deterrence, this is a softer approach that works at the propaganda level. If that is the case, then from now on the two countries have their work cut out for them in building relations in this area, and creating a system of mutual checks and balances like the one that existed during the cold war.

Of course, all of this conceals a circumstance that Moscow (if it really were behind such actions) must have taken into account. If a candidate that [Russia] tried to "sink" using such methods ended up winning after all, it's very likely that in response, he or she would unleash the entire might of the US's electronic intelligence against Russia (or any other party that carried out the cyber attacks), as well as use political and economic leverage against it. Given Clinton's personality, there's no doubt that this is exactly what she would have done. The fact that Russia decided to take such a risk is not exactly surprising—lately, our politicians have gotten used to putting it all on the line. Whether such a move is rational is another question. After all, in the end, the hacker attacks were not the reason Clinton lost. In this sense, the Democrats' reaction is understandable." In order to clear its good name, [the Democratic Party] must shift focus from the contents of the [leaked] information to the method through which it was obtained. For the average Trump voter, a "Russian trail" in the US election sounds just as implausible today as it did during the campaign. A popular argument for that part of the electorate is that those who are talking about Russian hackers today are the same people who on the eve of the Iraq invasion were convinced that Saddam Hussein had weapons of mass destruction.

The problem is that even if it turns out tomorrow that the hacker attack was carried out not by Russia, but by "somebody sitting on their bed that weighs 400 pounds," as Trump had quipped earlier, it still wouldn't alter the already negative view of Russia among the American establishment. Regardless of whether it is socially or politically valid, the theory of "Russian interference" plays an important role: A maverick like Trump, who does not play by the rules of American politics, needs to set certain limits on the course he charts so as not to impinge on US interests—and [his] declared "friendship with Russia" just so happens to be a major red line. Congress is going to draw red lines via legislative acts, while the media will do so via propaganda pressure. In this sense, it no longer matters who is really behind the illegal leak.

The fact that Russia ended up as the scapegoat is an accurate reflection of our country's place in US politics, [which is that of] a marginal topic replete with the usual set of negative stereotypes. For all those interested in establishing a positive agenda between the two countries, it will take a long time and a lot of work to change this paradigm. For example, Henry Kissinger, the patriarch of American diplomacy, confirmed this when he said that what happened is nothing out of the ordinary for US-Russian relations: "I don't doubt that the Russians are hacking us and I hope we're doing some hacking there." The position of the US administration that will take over on Jan. 20, 2017, will be of utmost importance. If it chooses to put the brakes on the matter and focus instead on building cooperation with Moscow as promised, then perhaps this crisis could be overcome with minimal damage to bilateral relations.

America Comes Out on Different Sides of Russia

By Sergei Strokan. *Kommersant*, Jan. 9, 2017, p. 1.

Preparations for the changing of the guard in the White House, which will take place Jan. 20, when president-elect Donald Trump is inaugurated, have drawn definitive battle lines regarding relations with Russia. One camp, which agrees with the outgoing Barack Obama administration's accusation that Moscow interfered in US domestic politics, wants to take a harder line [against Russia]; these include a significant number of Congress members—both Democrats and Republicans—as well as leaders of intelligence services. The other camp, which seems determined to normalize relations with Russia, includes Donald Trump himself, his team and a group of Congressional Republicans who have refrained from criticizing the Kremlin. For the first time in US history, the "Russian question" is becoming a litmus test of American patriotism.

It has effectively disrupted the Democratic-to-Republican transition in the White House. The reason for this unprecedented split that has divided the American elite into "us" and "them" is the issue of relations with Russia, which is becoming more hotly contested as the inauguration of the 45th president of the US draws nearer. In an ABC TV interview, outgoing President Barack Obama called on Republicans and Democrats to put aside their differences to confront the external threat to America that he believes Moscow poses. "We have to remind ourselves that we're on the same team," warned Mr. Obama. "Vladimir Putin is not on our team." In his opinion, a situation where some Republicans trust the president of Russia more than [they trust] their Democratic compatriots is unacceptable.

And now, the main political event of early January—the unveiling of a joint report by three intelligence agencies (the National Security Agency, the Federal Bureau of Investigation and the Central Intelligence Agency) about the Russian leadership's alleged interference in the US presidential election—has further deepened the rift between the two camps in Washington.

Since the 25-page public version of the document and its classified version (double the size) were presented to Barack Obama and Donald Trump,[20] the sides have not changed their positions on the Russian question.

Mr. Trump's reaction to the classified portion of the NSA-FBI-CIA report was clearly not what its authors expected, having put their professional reputations—and perhaps their careers—on the line. Trump said [afterward] that he'd had a "constructive meeting and conversation with the leaders of the intelligence community," and that he had learned a lot. He even permitted himself the following pleasantry: "I have tremendous respect for the work and service done by the men and women of this community to our great nation." However, the president-elect remained adamant in his overall opinion. He once again cast aside the theory that Russia could have affected the election results through hacker attacks, including by tampering with voting machines.

After the meeting with the intelligence services, Mr. Trump posted new comments on Twitter, further riling up those who oppose his idea of normalizing relations with Moscow. "Having a good relationship with Russia is a good thing, not a bad thing," he wrote in one tweet. "Only 'stupid' people, or fools, would think that it is bad." [In another tweet,] Donald Trump responded to critics: "Both countries will, perhaps, work together to solve some of the many great and pressing problems and issues of the WORLD!" He added that both sides, America and Russia, "have enough problems without yet another one."

The unwillingness that Donald Trump is showing on the eve of his inauguration to go along with the opinion of the intelligence community about alleged Russian interference in the presidential election, as well as his promises to prioritize relations with Moscow, threaten a prolonged confrontation within the American political elite.

Under these circumstances, the publication of the intelligence report certainly does not settle the question of alleged cyber attacks by Russia and other foreign states: In fact, it moves the debate to the floor of Congress, where it will very likely drag out for many weeks and months.

This possibility was confirmed by the hearings that began last week in the Senate Armed Services Committee, chaired by John McCain.

"There is no national security interest more vital to the United States of America than the ability to hold free and fair elections. * * * That's why Congress must set partisanship aside and work together to respond to cyber attacks," said Republican Sen. McCain, thereby echoing Democratic President Obama's key point: Interparty consensus is necessary to counter the "Russian threat."

It was announced that the Senate Armed Services Committee will form a new subcommittee on computer security and cyber weapons, to be headed by well-known Kremlin critic Sen. Lindsey Graham. Sens. Graham and McCain stated that Congress is drafting a new bill to tighten sanctions against Russia, and urged president-elect Trump to stay the course set by the Obama administration in relation to Moscow.

A joint interview with Lindsey Graham and John McCain, aired yesterday on NBC's "Meet the Press," reveals a notable change of tone being taken by Trump's irreconcilable critics toward the new White House administration during the run-up to his inauguration.

In response to questions from NBC, the senators essentially disavowed their previous theory that Donald Trump's victory in the election had come about through Moscow's interference. Instead, they tried to persuade the president-elect that their actions were not directed personally against him, but against external forces that threaten America: [namely] Russia, which they must join forces to fight.

"I think he's worried that inquiring into what Russia did in the election is going to undermine his credibility and his legitimacy," Lindsey Graham said. "[But] quite frankly, I haven't heard any Democrat at all of prominence say that we doubt that Donald Trump won." Then he addressed the incoming head of the White House: "Putin's not the reason that Clinton lost and Trump won. I don't think anybody's saying that. So Mr. President-elect, that's not what we're trying to do. What we're trying to do is find out what the Russians did in our elections and make sure that other people including the Russians won't do it next time."

Putting aside the question of the legitimacy of Donald Trump's presidential victory and instead focusing on the ongoing debate about Russia is a new move by the anti-Moscow hard-liners, who are [now] making persistent efforts to negotiate with the new administration on joint actions. Such a move could lead to a certain convergence between the new administration and Congress, most of whose members have a much more critical attitude [toward Russia] than Donald Trump. When he commented on his meeting with the leaders of the NSA, FBI and CIA, Mr. Trump strongly disagreed with only one of their contentions: that Moscow had impacted the outcome of the vote. However, he made one other notable acknowledgment in those post-meeting remarks that could be interpreted as accepting the theory of Russian influence on American politics.

To wit, the US president-elect said: "Russia, China, other countries, outside groups and people are consistently trying to break through the cyber infrastructure of our governmental institutions, businesses and organizations including the Democrat [sic] National Committee." In this regard, Donald Trump has already announced his intention to develop a plan within his first 90 days of office to "aggressively combat and stop cyber attacks." In turn, former Republican Sen. Daniel Coats, [Trump's likely] candidate for national intelligence director, has already said that for him, "the top priority will be to ensure the safety of America, and [we] will use all possible ways to do so." It is noteworthy that Mr. Coats would never be taken for a Moscow sympathizer: He is on the sanctions list of [Westerners banned from travel to] the Russian Federation.

Thus, the pitched battle for a new Russian agenda in the White House—[a debate] that in recent weeks has effectively made the Moscow issue a criterion of American patriotism—might prompt Donald Trump to at least dial back his current promises to normalize relations with Russia. Outgoing Vice-President Joseph Biden voiced the opinion of hard-liners in a PBS News Hour interview, where he made it clear that Moscow was not the only one counting on Mr. Trump. "Grow up, Donald. Grow up. Time to be an adult. * * * Show us what you have," American political veteran Biden, 74, instructed the 70-year-old American leader.

His voice just might be heard, judging from a statement made yesterday by the new White House chief of staff, Reince Priebus, in an interview with Fox News Sunday: [Priebus] confirmed that Donald Trump does not deny the intelligence services' findings that Russia tried to influence the US election. This was the first official indication that the future administration is willing to compromise with its critics in the intelligence community and Congress; moreover, it's an acknowledgment of a "Russian trail" in the American election campaign.

Five-Fake Report

By political analyst Vladimir Bruter, expert at the International Institute for Humanities and Political Studies. *Izvestia*, Jan. 11, 2017, p. 6.

The US intelligence report about alleged hacker attacks by Russia against political institutions in Washington is based on five fake premises.

They are all well known, both within the American intelligence community, and among American political analysts and experts.

This fact in itself essentially negates the informative value of the report, turning it into just another propaganda piece. And it's for very good reason that the NSA, the largest US intelligence service, essentially disagreed with the report's contention that "Putin and the Russian government aspired to help president-elect Trump's election chances when possible by discrediting [former] secretary [of state] Clinton and publicly contrasting her unfavorably to him." Whereas the "CIA and FBI have high confidence in this judgment," the report says that the "NSA has moderate confidence."[21]

So, what are the fake premises on which this "analytical" document is based?

Fake Premise No. 1: Russia is actively interfering in the American media space.

In point of fact, Russia is simply not present in the US media space. You can't be misled by the figures cited in the report that show an increase in the Russia Today television channel's audience, because no matter how much RT's ratings may be growing, they are minuscule compared to [those of] American channels. RT's influence on the American electorate is inconsequential: The way things stand, it's simply impossible that it could have had any impact on the process and outcome of the election—and the authors of the report are well aware of that.

Fake Premise No. 2: Russia's interference had an impact on the election outcome.

In point of fact, the whole electoral campaign had minimal impact on the election outcome. Both principal candidates garnered approximately the number of votes they were expected to. Therefore, external forces made no special impact, nor could they have. Clinton lost not because of some external enemy's machinations, but because of her resounding defeats in a number of key states that Democrats hadn't lost in more than 20 years: Michigan, Ohio, Pennsylvania and Wisconsin. The cause of Clinton's defeats in the Midwest—the so-called "Steel Belt"—is not some plot hatched in the Kremlin, but the difficult economic situation in this industrial region of the US. This is the home of the people who are most disgruntled with the dominance of globalization and the virtual economy. They don't watch RT, they don't read Russian newspapers over breakfast, and they don't even have much idea who Putin is.

Fake Premise No. 3: There is a pro-Russian lobby in the US that influenced the outcome of the election.

This is not true. Russia has no forces that could affect elections in the US. We have no lobbyists in the US, no pro-Russian nonprofits, and no agents of influence in the American political elite or even the expert elite. There is no member of Congress who would consistently and vehemently advocate changing the nature of US-Russian relations. A reasonable question arises: "How is Russia influencing [the US], and through whom?" Theories about online communities can only make us smile.

Fake Premise No. 4: There is a link between the Russian information campaign and the number of votes cast for Trump.

There is no proven link between voting for Trump and [having] pro-Russian sympathies. In general, Democrats are even fonder of Russia than Republicans. Moreover, according to polling data, relations with Russia have never been a priority for the voters who swung the election. They are basically uninterested in foreign policy; the most important things to them are jobs and stability. Russia cannot influence these people in any way.

Fake Premise No. 5: The authors of the report deliberately conflate Russia's intentions to sway the Western community with some [alleged] results of Russian propaganda.

This is roughly the same as claiming that [radio station] Voice of America destroyed the USSR. Such statements are humiliating—most of all for those who make them.

Russian TV and hackers actually defeated Clinton? Neither the CIA nor the FBI believes that. So, why keep talking about it with a stubborn sense of purpose that should be put to better use?

There are three main reasons.

First, the outgoing administration would like to leave a legacy of relations with Russia that are so badly spoiled that Trump (and Tillerson, Kissinger, etc.) would be hard put to repair them any time soon.

Second, members of the establishment want to restrict Trump's freedom of action as much as they can. In effect, they have been trying constantly to make him admit that his victory was the handiwork of the quasi-mythical yet all-powerful KGB, [an admission] that would delegitimize him even before he officially takes office.

And finally, third: This [report] was a peculiar kind of "20:20 hindsight" on the part of the CIA and FBI: a petty and belated comeback bid after the big game was already lost—partly through the fault of the intelligence services [themselves]. They were quite aware of the fact that Clinton's previous "mistakes" would actually have made her ineligible to run in the election. Suffice it to mention the passages about [Russia] using hackers to publicize information about Clinton that the intelligence services were trying to hide. One can only ask: "Why were they trying to hide it, and how is that compatible with democratic elections in a democratic country?"

How should Russia respond? The answer is very simple: We shouldn't. The Democrats' reign is over. It ended ingloriously, and it makes no sense to look back on it.

This is the difference between politics and history.

The main thing now is the future—and let's hope that the new American administration will find the strength to stamp out the ridiculous and senseless mistakes of the outgoing administration. Russia is ready to help [them] do that, but will always keep its own interests in mind and protect them.

Carefully, consistently and scrupulously.

Watergate for Trump

By staff commentator Yulia Latynina. *Novaya gazeta*, Jan. 11, 2017, p. 5.

In 1972, President Nixon's administration authorized the wiretapping of Democratic Party headquarters for electoral purposes. Two years later, that wiretapping triggered an impeachment [process] for President Nixon.

In 2015, Kremlin hackers broke into Democratic Party servers during the US presidential campaign. And now the US ruling elite is doing everything it can to make that hacking [episode] trigger president-elect Trump's impeachment.

They want to trump up a new Watergate for Trump.

The difference between this situation and Watergate was that Nixon actually authorized the wiretapping himself. But in this case, you can find neither hide nor hair of Trump.

What's happening with president-elect Trump and the Democratic Party hacking story is a brilliant disinformation campaign.

Let's go through the key moments of this campaign in order.

On Jan. 6, the office of the DNI (US Director of National Intelligence) submitted a partially declassified report based on data from the FBI, CIA and NSA. According to the report, the president of Russia is personally responsible for the hacking of servers at Hillary Clinton's campaign headquarters, in an attempt to get Trump into the White House.

I have no doubt that the Kremlin is behind the hackers. The hacker groups Cozy Bear and Fancy Bear used Russian-language versions of software; worked from 9 a.m. to 5 p.m. Moscow time with breaks on Russian holidays, including those celebrated only at the Lubyanka [headquarters of the Russian Federal Security Service—*Trans.*]; and, unlike other hackers, were never in dire financial straits or hungry for monetary gain. These hackers showed a rare degree of altruism, targeting only those who incurred the Kremlin's wrath—from WADA [World Anti-Doping Agency] to Angela Merkel's party servers.

But I do have other questions. First: How did the Democratic Party itself—as well as the FBI, CIA and NSA—respond to this hacking? Answer: They didn't.

The Democrats first got wind that their servers were being hacked back in September 2015. That was when FBI agent Adrian Hawkins called the Democratic [National Committee] office to warn about a likely breach. The call was fielded by technical support associate Yared Tamene. Tamene was not authorized [to handle the call] and, as he later explained to *The New York Times*, could not even verify whether the caller was really an FBI agent. Hawkins called again a month later (!)—and again Tamene [fielded the message]. Then another month later.

For seven months (!), no one in the FBI made any attempt to talk to the Democratic leadership. It wasn't until seven months after Hawkins's [initial] call that the Democrats contacted computer security specialists from CrowdStrike.

Those servers got hacked not because of the amazing abilities of Fancy Bear, but because of the outrageous negligence of DNC associates. In March 2016 (i.e., six months after Hawkins [first] called), Clinton campaign worker Billy Rinehart got hooked by a run-of-the-mill phishing lure: He received an e-mail from Google asking him to go to their Web site and enter a new password, and he followed the instructions. Believe it or not, the same hook also caught campaign chairman John Podesta.

How can we explain such carelessness?

Very simple. Since Watergate, every American politician takes it as gospel that when someone hacks or taps a political opponent, the one who wins out is the one who got hacked. Besides, the campaign documents didn't contain anything incriminating for Clinton.

The only one to benefit from the e-mail scandal was Clinton herself. CNN and MSNBC repeatedly explained to their audiences that if the Kremlin was working for Trump, then they should vote for Clinton.

But immediately after the election, President Obama saw the light. He said that he'd underestimated the degree of interference, and that the hackers' activity had influenced the outcome of the election.

The question arises: If these terrible Russian hackers had so much influence over the election, why did no one start fighting them in September 2015?

Only now that Trump has already won the election have the Democrats come up with this ingenious explanation: It wasn't the American people who carried Trump to victory—it was the Kremlin. It's all because of those enemies of the nation!

You may ask: If there was no point in hacking those servers, why did the Kremlin do it? I'll answer with another question: Why [did the Kremlin get involved in the conflict in] the Donetsk Basin? And why [did it] make a porno film [in 2005] about [then-Georgian president Mikhail] Saakashvili and [then-Ukrainian prime minister Yulia] Timoshenko? Most of our geopolitical operations achieve their goal only in the sense that their real goal is money laundering.

When the American DNI tells me that the Kremlin wanted to influence the election and that it celebrated Trump's victory, I completely agree. But when the DNI tells me that the Kremlin influenced the election, then you know what? There's a big difference between wanting and doing.

To prove the unprovable, the DNI report stoops to the level of devoting an enormous amount of space to Russian television. It contains adorable graphs and even cartoons, one of which shows a giant [RT editor in chief] Margarita Simonyan stepping over the White House. That image is from the intro to her RT show [*sic*; her former show on Russian REN TV—*Trans*.]. But what does it have to do with the American election? Are we supposed to believe that RT has grown more influential than *The Washington Post*, *The New York Times*, MSNBC and CNN combined?

This opening move in the chess game to get Trump impeached is simple and ingenious. It's based on a Big Lie—and, like every good Big Lie, it contains a grain of truth. The Kremlin really did try to interfere in the US election. It's now up to Trump to respond. If he doesn't acknowledge the Kremlin's interference, he's denying the obvious. If he does, then he's also acknowledging that he became president as a result of that interference by a foreign power.

A World Without Illusions, Myths

By Ivan Yegorov. *Rossiiskaya gazeta*, Jan. 16, 2017, p. 1.

Editors' Note—In an interview with *Rossiiskaya gazeta*, Russian Security Council Secretary Nikolai Patrushev tells who is behind hacking attacks on the Internet and why Obama has spoiled relations with Russia, as well as what threatens our country's security the most.

* * *

Question—Nikolai Platonovich [Patrushev], the past year was notable for the constant accusations against Russia on the part of our Western partners, particularly the outgoing US administration. Understandably, all those words could have been ignored if they were not backed up by tangible and clearly hostile actions.

Answer—The policy of the outgoing Barack Obama administration, aimed at discrediting our country, was not accidental. The point is that Washington is not ready to accept the fact that the US's global leadership strategy is increasingly giving way to processes such as the formation of a multipolar world order and the building of an equitable international security architecture. The Obama administration strove to preserve its dominating role in the international arena, actively involving acquiescent Western countries in its reckless misadventures.

While making groundless accusations against Russia, the US was silent about the fact that its policy has often involved gross violations of international treaties and obligations, fomenting territorial disputes and creating new dividing lines—be it in Europe, the Middle East or the Asia-Pacific region.

Unfriendly actions at odds with international law have effectively led to an unbridled surge in terrorism, a deepening of the Sunni-Shiite divide and the civilizational divide more generally, as well as humanitarian disasters in certain countries and regions.

The danger of these resultant challenges and threats spreading elsewhere, including to Russia, has forced us to take measures to strengthen our security and required us to adjust [our] foreign policy....

Q—The new US president will be inaugurated in a few days. Will strategic interaction between Moscow and Washington change once Donald Trump is in office?

A—At least the US president-elect is not making remarks about Russia being a threat or evil. Barack Obama's policy not only pushed Russian-US relations far back, but also largely predetermined the vector of Russia's interaction with NATO and the European Union over the past several years. Unfortunately, this was not confined to anti-Russia rhetoric alone. Here are just a few examples.

The number of calls by NATO ships from non-Black Sea member states into the Black Sea has tripled. The number of flights by tactical and reconnaissance aviation along Russian borders has almost doubled, and that of airborne early warning aircraft has increased by a factor of nine.

A firm course has been set to further expand the alliance, with Montenegro, Macedonia, Bosnia and Herzegovina being drawn in at an accelerated pace. The deployment of elements of a US global missile defense system continues in Europe. In addition to putting the Aegis Ashore complex on combat alert in Romania, there are plans to go ahead with establishing a missile defense site in Poland. A decision was made to deploy US missile defense systems in the Republic of Korea. Under the pretext of a so-called forced response to Russia's heightened activity in the Arctic region, NATO leadership is taking measures to reinforce the bloc's northern flank.

The West's consolidated efforts are aimed, among other things, at undermining integration processes that involve our country [and at] devaluing the idea of the "Russian world" as a whole, which jeopardizes the security of not only Russia, but a large number of [other] countries.

As for the White House's decision to declare 35 Russian diplomats personae non gratae, it was the largest one-time expulsion of diplomatic mission personnel since the cold war.

The impression is that the US Democratic Party is trying to get back at Russia for its own failures and miscalculations. Generally, American citizens are not particularly interested in the situation in the international arena. They are concerned by the situation at home. And it is precisely failures in US domestic policy that led to such election results.

Of course, in light of these factors we cannot talk about fundamental changes in Russia-US relations with the election of Donald Trump as the US president. We have no illusions about strategic restrictive measures being rolled back any time soon.

Consistent and painstaking work will be required in all areas, including those where it was terminated or scaled back. We are ready for such work—naturally, on the basis of equality and mutual respect. After all, it will be crucial for stability in international relations as a whole—which, I am convinced, is also in keeping with the fundamental interests of the American people.

I believe that certain opportunities for constructive engagement with the US will open with regard to antiterrorism efforts, information security and some other areas. If the Donald Trump administration is interested, we will be ready to resume full-scale consultations with our American partners via the Russian Security Council.

'Dangerous but Predictable': How Russia Spooked the World With Hackers and Prostitutes

By Tatyana Stanovaya, director of the analysis department at the Center for Political Technologies. *Republic.ru*, Jan. 12, 2017, https://republic.ru/posts/78445.

At a confirmation hearing in the Senate Committee on Foreign Relations, candidate for US secretary of state Rex Tillerson said he believes Russia poses a danger, but it is not unpredictable in advancing its own interests. [This] compromise formula, designed to find common ground between the advocates of dialogue with Russia and those who support sanctions, actually makes no sense: Predictability as a characteristic is a priori at odds with one of the most pronounced qualities of Putin's regime: the opportunistic nature of its interests and excessive dependence on external factors. Predictability is only possible when a state has a strategic foreign and domestic policy. To Moscow, this remains an unaffordable luxury.

The perception of Russia as a dangerous state began to evolve after the annexation of the Crimea, but in practice appeared only in 2016. "Now they will have to take us seriously," those in the Kremlin rejoiced, clearly underestimating a new problem: Regardless of the position that various forces in the West take in terms of tactics for building relations with Russia, as far as the global community goes, Vladimir Putin is becoming a figure who needs to be brought to heel. The difference here is only in approaches: Whereas Obama says Moscow should be dealt with harshly, Trump proposes trying to put Russia in its place "nicely."

After [the annexation of] the Crimea, the mastermind of the anti-Russia line has been German Chancellor Angela Merkel, who accused Russia of redefining the world security architecture established after World War II. [She alleged that] Russia had violated all international norms, which became a starting point for a global discussion: What could generally be expected from it now? Before long, the camp of those who thought Russia was too weak to bother with switched to the camp of alarmists (which was originally very small) who see Russia as a threat to the civilized world. That transition was due not only to the fact that Moscow had indeed spooked the world with its special operation in the Crimea; the problem was that the policy of containment as a form of exerting pressure on Russia had shown its limitations.

The lack of consensus on sanctions, the pragmatism of big business looking for any ways of circumventing them, the general chaos of global politics, and the weakening of the US's role, as evidenced by the Syria conflict, led to a situation where the critics of Moscow needed new convincing arguments to vindicate their alarmism and their position on Moscow's actions. That was how the demonization of Russia began. It resulted from the West's limited opportunities to influence Putin's policy. Meanwhile, he had given ample cause to fear him before. Gas wars with [Ukraine] that interrupted supplies to Europe; trade wars with Moldova, Georgia and Belarus; the influx of Russian spies; saber-rattling (including nuclear saber-rattling)—all of that existed even before the Crimea. After the onset of the geopolitical crisis, there was more reason to fear Moscow, but the country's policies remained the same.

The current list of gripes against Russia is rather meager: [It is accused of] planting fabricated news stories, blogger activity, cyber attacks, and promoting Russia's position via pro-Russian media outlets that are not exactly popular, to put it mildly. That said, can Russia's aspiration to establish contact with Western politicians be called a threat? Some are bought off, others are lured, while still others are blackmailed using their own weaknesses—be it women, drugs, or God knows what else. However, can strategic alliances [and] strong institutionalized political relations be built on the fear of exposure? Moscow's actual influence on American domestic political processes remains so weak that it makes you wonder about the psychology behind the changing perception of Russia.

A country defeated in the cold war and pushed to the periphery of world politics, Russia, with its small economy but enormous ambitions since the Crimea, has moved beyond the bounds of its "traditional zone of influence" and started playing its own game. The very fact that Moscow has an interest in elections in the US, Germany, France and East European countries; in the Brexit vote or the referendum in Italy; the fact that it actively defends these interests by all available methods—[all of this] is perceived as disproportionate given Russia's weight, like a river swelling and breaching its banks when everyone thought it had dried up. And this is definitely not about Russia throwing its weight around, but rather about it losing its neutrality during the past two years when it comes to the domestic affairs of other states. When it comes to the domestic affairs of its "partners," the Kremlin has acquired the status of an active player who is no longer satisfied with merely rooting from the sidelines. And the West is probably spooked not so much by the danger posed by that influence as by the sheer fact that the stage was taken by a player who has over the past 25 years been considered a geopolitical castrate, disgruntled but impotent.

The vulnerability of the West itself, which assumed the role of world conflict manager and then clearly failed when faced with one of the most formidable challenges of the century—international terrorism—has played into Russia's hands. Barack Obama recognized the US's former policy in the Middle East as ineffectual, but did not come up with a new one. The Syria crisis is the West's failed litmus test on managing global threats. Against this backdrop, Russia chose the simple but effective tactic of taking advantage of the opportunities it was given. The Kremlin occupies vacant niches, and chaos is replaced by the kind of order that Moscow is able to establish. It is difficult to imagine a Russian military operation in Syria amid a ground operation by international coalition forces. Moscow's attempts to "influence" the US election should be viewed from the same angle: If there is an opportunity to promote an alternative agenda in the media, Moscow is going to do so within the framework of general informational competition. And if suddenly there is a chance to hack the Democratic Party's servers, why pass that up?

Politics is not only the art of the possible. In terms of how the situation in the US could be influenced, Russia had the same means as any other relatively well-off country. Politics is also the art of the desirable: The readiness and motivation to go from an observer to an actor. And it is precisely in this respect that Russia has changed, making its post-Crimea foreign policy extraterritorial—that is, going outside its traditional zone of influence. Add here another new principle: the readiness to act first and hammer out the details later, but under new, changing conditions, as was the case in Syria. Russia has demonstrated its geopolitical capabilities outside its traditional zone of influence—but, going back to Tillerson's remarks, does this make it dangerous?

The danger of Russia is certainly not in cyber attacks or video footage of Western politicians allegedly partying with prostitutes. The danger of Russia directly depends on only two factors. The first is having strategic long-term interests that define the vector of its foreign policy in relation to territories and partners. Does Russia have such interests in practice and not just in theory—for instance, the well-known "projects" to create a common security zone from Lisbon to Vladivostok, a single missile defense system, and Russian-European energy interdependence, which have remained the dreams of the Kremlin romantics? In reality, Russia's interests and its steps based on these interests are reactive, tactical, recklessly adventuristic, short-term, and often simply desperate. Had there been no revolution in Ukraine, there would have been no annexation of the Crimea; and, consequently, there most likely would have been no Syria campaign. The problem with Tillerson's position is precisely that Russia's strategic interests are unrelated to its tactics. The second factor is the number of vacant niches on global issues, since chaos in the international arena is only going to grow, given the US's new policy of noninterference. Russia is seeing a lot of windows of opportunity, due in part to Trump coming to the White House. As its strategic planning crisis continues, Moscow is going to approach those opportunities relying on the same situational factors and often short-term goals. The deflation and fragmentation of the West is going to expand the bounds of the possible for Russia, giving it more room to maneuver. As its horizons and choices expand, it will become increasingly unpredictable amid the absence of a long-term strategy and the erosion of the legal framework in international affairs. All of this sets the stage for greater unpredictability, making Russia more dangerous, at least for the part of the world that perceives Putin's ideology and values as alien.

PART FOUR

President Trump: The First 200 Days of Foreign Policy

Introduction

The final part of this book begins with Donald Trump's inauguration and covers highlights of roughly his first 200 days in office, up to his signing of the Countering America's Adversaries Through Sanctions Act on Aug. 2 (Day 194). The passage of the sanctions act was a landmark event, because Trump in effect joined with Congress to declare who the US considers adversaries and allies—the latter being Europe and NATO, and the former being Iran, North Korea and (to the surprise of many) Russia.

Tracing the main lines drawn in this legislation, Part Four contains four sections devoted to distinct areas of the Trump administration's foreign policy: Europe, the Middle East (including Iran), nuclear policy (with North Korea figuring prominently) and Russia (understandably, the topic that inspired the most contentious commentary in the press).

With regard to all these areas, journalists and political analysts find the maverick American president inconsistent and unpredictable. One example is his apparent reversal of opinion on NATO: "I said it was obsolete. It's no longer obsolete." Another is the fact that his first foreign visit was not to Russia or Western Europe, but to a Muslim country—Saudi Arabia. In the area of nuclear policy, Trump is viewed as sending mixed messages: gearing up for an "arms race" and yet also claiming to be open to negotiation with Russia. The theme of Trump's inconsistency comes out most strongly, of course, when both houses of Congress overwhelmingly pass the sanctions act and Trump does not veto the legislation. Perhaps the most interesting factor here is that even when Russian commentators are most confused, disappointed and even outraged by Trump's decisions, they do not impugn his character, honesty or intelligence—unlike their counterparts in the West, particularly in the US. Instead, they (generally) portray him as a sympathetic "everyman" trapped in the machine of the American political establishment. At the very worst, they call him weak, unable to quell the internal turmoil within Washington. Perhaps, in a curious way, the Trump presidency has inspired a more nuanced picture of the US political system in the Russian press.

4.1

'Paying Their Fair Share': Europe and NATO

Introduction

Coverage of Trump's policies on Europe and interaction with EU leaders was marked by several key events: the Munich Security Conference in late February 2017, the NATO summit in Brussels and Group of Seven meeting in Sicily (both held in May); and the G-20 summit in Hamburg in July.

Reports from Munich highlight a potential rift in relations between the US and its European allies. Leonid Shestakov comments that speeches by Trump's delegates (Vice-President Michael Pence and Secretary of Defense James Mattis) about every NATO country needing to pay its fair share for security guarantees came as a "cold shower." On the other hand, Aleksandr Mineyev writes that Pence's remarks in Brussels were more reassuring to European leaders. In a more detailed article in *International Affairs*, Dmitry Danilov goes as far as saying that Trump has reversed his policy: Comparing Trump's public statements in January (when he called NATO "obsolete") and his delegates' remarks in February, he concludes: "Trump had been forced to backpedal: He tried to blackmail Europe and failed." Indeed, Trump's remarks at an April 12 meeting with NATO Secretary General Jens Stoltenberg seem to support Danilov's contention; CNN reported the president as saying: "I said it was obsolete. It's no longer obsolete."

Be that as it may, the Russian press continues to cite tensions between Trump and the West: for example, his threats to pull out of the Transatlantic Trade and Investment Partnership (TTIP) and his June 1 announcement that the US would quit the Paris Climate Agreement. Stanislav Kuvaldin describes the latter decision as "perhaps the most fundamental shift in the US's new global standing."

Russian commentators also make much of Trump's visit to Poland in early July, one purpose of which was to make an agreement for the US to sell its liquefied natural gas to Poland. This deal, they say, was an attempt to foil Germany's ambitions to be Europe's gas hub, as well as an irritant to the EU's most influential leader, German Chancellor Angela Merkel. However, there is an interesting counterpoint in Russian journalists' interpretations of how Trump's gambit would affect Russia. Andrei Kolesnikov writes that Trump is resisting the trend of solidarity with Western Europe to court Poland independently, thus "stealing" it from Russia's zone of influence. On the other hand, a commentary in *Ekspert* sees a silver lining for Russia: Putin could leverage more advantages from a divided West.

Munich: Cold Talk

By Yevgeny Shestakov. *Rossiiskaya gazeta*, Feb. 20, 2017, p. 1.

The Munich [Security] Conference is a place where you are likely to come across quite a few familiar faces from the world of big politics, including both current and former officials, those in retirement and in reserve....

Russian Foreign Minister Sergei Lavrov says he had about 25 bilateral meetings in Munich, as well as a meeting on Ukraine among the foreign ministers of the Normandy Four [France, Germany, Ukraine and Russia]. According to Russia's top diplomat, he did not meet with anybody from the US: He did say hello to [US] Vice-President Mike Pence, but they did not talk. "Politicians will now be studying the signals sent by the US in Munich. What I heard is that the US wants to work together with its European partners to address the international issues that concern Washington today," Lavrov said after the conference. Russia is waiting for Washington to finalize its foreign policy team, the minister explained, so "we can get a clearer picture, once we engage in professional-level dialogue, of how the general ideas being expressed by President Trump and his vice-president are going to take shape as specific policies."

Moscow prefers not to draw hasty conclusions regarding the future of Russia-US relations based purely on Mike Pence's remarks in Munich, especially since a large part of his speech was devoted to future dealings between the new US administration and Old World political elites.

What is the European Union worried about?

It would be wrong to think that the EU is worried about Ukraine or, say, about the current status of its dialogue with Moscow. [This year's] Munich conference has shown that Old World political elites are preoccupied about their own future—about how they will survive under the Trump administration. They are especially bothered by the question of what price Europe will have to pay for the security guarantees provided by the White House—and whether there is a way to avoid paying the bill.

US Vice-President Mike Pence and Defense Secretary James Mattis made it abundantly clear that the haggling match with Brussels is on and that all Europeans who reject the deal as offered by Washington will be left to deal with their problems on their own. A certain participant even described the speech given by the US vice-president as an ultimatum to Europe. The White House is trying to get its partners to cough up additional funding for NATO upkeep. Just listening to Pence was enough to convince anybody that it would make no sense for the Europeans to argue with the new US administration—if anything, it would only cost them more. "If you keep faith with us, we will keep faith with you" was the central idea the US vice-president sought to impress on the Europeans. Pence said that Europe and the US "must be strong in our military might" in order to protect their way of life. "We will strengthen our military, restore the arsenal of democracy," Pence said. After presenting Washington's extensive plans to build up its military, Pence explained that the White House expects its European partners to take similar steps: Plans call for "renewed resources to defend [ourselves] from the known threats of today and the unknown threats of tomorrow." Pence's speech shows that the Trump administration is determined to mobilize Europe to confront new challenges. But what are those challenges? Apart from international terrorism, the threats most frequently mentioned by the American representatives were North Korea and Iran. We [Russians] did not make the official "enemies of America" list; Pence mentioned Russia only in the context of the Ukraine conflict. Yet to Europe, his speech was a cold shower—not unexpected, but cold nonetheless. As German Foreign Minister Sigmar Gabriel pointed out, if it were to increase defense spending to 2% of its gross domestic product [a NATO-wide benchmark set in 2014, and reaffirmed by Pence in Munich—*Trans.*], Berlin would have to raise an additional 25 billion euros. But Gabriel was the only high-ranking European official who ventured to publicly question whether such defense spending was feasible—and, more importantly, cost-effective.

Europe at a crossroads.

Speaking at the Munich conference, German Defense Minister Ursula von der Leyen made a rather unorthodox statement given the context of the forum: "NATO is not self-evident, not for America and not for us Europeans," she said, as quoted by *Deutsche Welle*. [She also explained:] "The crises and conflicts have opened our eyes: Whoever wants security needs their own powers and capabilities." Yet her NATO colleagues opposed the idea of Europe developing its own defense strategy and, on the contrary, advocated the need to strengthen the NATO umbrella. [German] Chancellor Angela Merkel connected the European dots for her listeners: "We need the military power of the United States to protect Europe's borders," Merkel said, presenting her vision of the security situation. According to her, NATO serves Europe's interests, but it equally serves the interests of the US. Yet Merkel chose not to argue with the Trump administration about defense spending, confirming that Germany is ready to boost its military budget. Speaking on one of the Munich conference's key panels devoted to the future of the West, British Foreign Secretary Boris Johnson asked, "Who needs the EU [to protect free trade] when you've got NATO?" It seems like this idea does not look too outrageous and is winning supporters. [However,] EU top diplomat Federica Mogherini strongly criticized the idea of increasing Europe's contribution to NATO's projects. Security, she said, is not just about spending more on defense; you also have to spend more on humanitarian issues and development. German Foreign Minister Sigmar Gabriel, too, advocated caution when ramping up defense spending, arguing that military measures do not always increase security. But there were not many critical remarks of this kind expressed about the US president's plans. The prevalent mood was to go along with the US, as exemplified by Poland. Polish President Andrzej Duda called transatlantic ties a source of power for the Western world, which it should not shy away from using to push back enemies. Lithuanian President Dalia Grybauskaite agreed, saying that EU security cannot be ensured without the US....

Seducing Europe

By staff correspondent Aleksandr Mineyev, Brussels.
Novaya gazeta, Feb. 22, 2017, p. 5.

The Donald Trump administration conducted a week-long special operation to soothe the Europeans, who were starting to consider the White House one of today's "challenges"—almost on a par with international terrorism and Russia. "No!" assured Washington's messengers in unison.

From Thursday to Monday [Feb. 16–20]—beginning with the G-20 foreign ministers' meeting in Bonn and the NATO defense ministers' meeting in Brussels, continuing with the Munich Security Conference and ending with the US vice-president's visit to Brussels—Secretary of State Rex Tillerson, Pentagon chief James Mattis and Vice-President Michael Pence tried to persuade their interlocutors that they had misunderstood the American president.

At a press conference in the glassed-in lobby of NATO headquarters, a BBC journalist asked Pence whom [European leaders] should listen to: Pence, who professed his unwavering support for Europe; or Trump, who praised Britain for its "smart" decision to exit the EU? Was there any guarantee that the tall American guest would repeat today's assurances at a press conference tomorrow?

Pence repeated the prepared response he had given already in Munich: that he had not come to play the "good cop" and was not taking it upon himself to smooth out his boss's rough edges. Instead, he said, he was following [Trump's] direct instructions: "[T]he President directed me to go to Munich and come here to Brussels with a very specific message."

In that message, Trump seeks to alleviate concerns about substantive issues that alarmed European leaders during his election campaign. These include the US's attitude toward NATO, the EU and European integration, as well as the Russian-Ukrainian knot. Readers are reminded that in electoral debates and interviews, Trump called NATO an obsolete organization and the EU "a vehicle for Germany"; he also said he would consider recognizing the Crimea as Russian and making friends with Putin.

Indeed, NATO is now 70% funded by the US, which supports its operations with intelligence, military transport aviation, precision-guided weapons and other expensive, state-of-the-art resources.

Since the cold war ended, European members of the alliance have consistently reduced their military spending; only in recent years, since [Russia's annexation of] the Crimea, did they start reversing that trend. According to Secretary General Jens Stoltenberg, [European allies and Canada] increased [defense spending in 2016] by 3.8% ($10 billion). NATO has set a goal for all its members to raise their military budgets to at least 2% of their gross domestic product. So far, only five of the 28 member countries have reached that benchmark. And they are not the richest ones.

Pence raised this issue in a conversation with Angela Merkel. [He said] America is unhappy with the Europeans' defense dependency ("the patience of the American people will not endure forever"). Germany's military budget is currently 1.3% of its GDP. The chancellor promised to raise it to 2%, acknowledging that Europe cannot fight the threat of jihadism (and other threats) alone, without America.

Differences of opinion on NATO concern only funding and cost-sharing mechanisms, not the role and purpose of the alliance.

NATO Secretary General Jens Stoltenberg expressed appreciation for the US's contributions: creating a line of deterrence along the alliance's eastern ("post-Crimean") borders; increasing the number of US troops in Europe; and deploying American subunits in NATO's East European member states. He promised to do everything possible not only to increase NATO's military spending, but to work with the EU to make [that spending] more efficient.

America and Europe feel that they are on the same page with respect to Russia. Containing Russia is one of NATO's goals—despite all Trump's appearances of appeasing the Kremlin and befriending Putin.

"In the wake of Russian efforts to redraw international borders by force, we [the US] will continue to support efforts in Poland and the Baltic States through NATO's Enhanced Forward Presence Initiative," Pence said.

The US will continue to hold Russia accountable for implementing the Minsk agreements. In [Washington's] opinion, Moscow must start by deescalating the violence in eastern Ukraine in order to move on to the political points of the accords. The political process is effective only when the guns are silent.

"We urge both sides to abide by the ceasefire that was scheduled to begin today," Pence stated at the NATO press conference. "While the United States will continue to hold Russia accountable * * * we will also search in new ways for new common ground with Russia, which President Trump believes can be found."

Judging by the Munich Conference attendees' tepid reaction to his words about finding "common ground" with Moscow, this idea does not inspire any enthusiasm on the continent right now.

As for European Council President Donald Tusk, Pence brought him Trump's assurances that the US wishes to further its collaboration with the EU.

"Whatever our differences, our two continents share the same heritage, the same values, and above all, the same purpose: to promote peace and prosperity through freedom, democracy, and the rule of law. And to those objectives we will remain committed," the US vice-president told journalists after his conversation with Tusk. Tusk himself described [that conversation] as "open and frank." In diplomatic language, that means contentious.

But Pence praised the EU for its achievements in developing a common market, and marveled at the freedom with which goods, capital, services and people move within the EU. He noted the historic significance of EU enlargement, the introduction of a single currency, and the development of common approaches to security policy. The EU has brought the peoples of Europe peace and prosperity, and the US is going to join efforts with it to achieve the same throughout the world.

Europeans are also disturbed that Trump is against multilateral free trade agreements. [For example,] he pulled the US out of the Trans-Pacific Partnership agreement. [Also] in jeopardy is the "deal of the century"—the Transatlantic [Trade and Investment] Partnership (TTIP), which has been in the works for several years and is officially still being negotiated. It probably has somewhat more hopeful prospects [than the TPP].

For the US, economic isolationism with respect to, say, Southeast Asia is not quite the same thing as isolation from the ideologically and economically kindred EU.

Last week, the EU demonstrated its desire to stick to the course of free trade: The European Parliament ratified the [Comprehensive Economic and Trade] Agreement with Canada. This agreement is far ahead of its time. Many experts and politicians see managed globalization, not protectionism, as paving the way and setting the standard for future trade agreements.

No matter how cynically our propagandists may use the word "values," they probably make a more durable bonding cement than interests. They moderate one's reliance on [others'] "common sense." [Values create] a feeling of commonality from the inside out.

Granted, in the case of the EU and the US, there are also many shared interests. These are the two largest economies on the planet. [They make up] almost half of the global economy. No one else has any basis to call itself a great power (in any case, definitely not Great Britain, since its exit from the EU).

US-EU trade has created 14 million jobs on both sides of the ocean. US trade with Russia is insignificant by comparison. For the EU, Russia is a substantial trade partner, but not compared to America.

Contradicting the "early" Trump, his vice-president swore allegiance in Brussels to the principles of a free economy that would ensure global economic growth while fostering peace and prosperity in the world.

Pence's visit gave European leaders a chance to ease the tension and establish contact with the new people in Washington on a personal level. After his talk [with Pence], Tusk said that a "post-Western age" (a phrase used by the organizers of the Munich Conference [in a preconference report]) has not arrived, and that the united West, bound together by shared values, is alive and well. Jean-Claude Juncker, patting Pence's shoulder during their official handshake, said in his typical tongue-in-cheek manner: "I do not think that the moment has come to divide the US and the EU."

Judging from the general tenor of talks at the Munich conference, as well as conversations on the sidelines of the EU and NATO [meetings], Europeans' suspicions about the new White House boss have not yet been allayed. But both sides are trying.

The American vanguard's deployment to Europe has laid the groundwork for Donald Trump's visit to Brussels. The new NATO headquarters complex, which is across the street from the current one (and was [initially] supposed to hold its grand opening in March, in the presence of Hillary Clinton as the [US] president), will host Donald Trump in May for its first NATO summit.

Munich Shows Western Elite's Total Discombobulation

By Igor Subbotin. *Nezavisimaya gazeta*, Feb. 20, 2017, p. 1.

At the Munich Security Conference—whose announced theme was "Post-Truth, Post-West, Post-Order"—US Vice-President Michael Pence made several statements whose content was reminiscent of the previous American administration. The politician promised Europe not only to preserve the former [US-EU] partnership, but to hold Russia accountable for its policy in eastern Ukraine. The vice-president's remarks, which conflicted with what President Donald Trump had said earlier, added to the confusion among European politicians and experts.

"The United States has been faithful to Europe for generations, and we will keep [that] faith," Pence announced in Munich. "We share a past, and * * * we share a future. * * * The United States is now and will always be your greatest ally." Pence assured European leaders on Trump's behalf: "The United States of America strongly supports NATO." The vice-president pointed out common values upheld by America and Europe: freedom, democracy, justice and the rule of law.

Vowing to maintain military cooperation, Pence made sure to remind [America's] European partners about the need to fulfill their financial duty to NATO....

NG editor in chief Konstantin Remchukov, who attended the Munich conference, assessed the US vice-president's remarks as follows: "One gets the impression that Pence was building on the groundwork laid by the previous administration months ago. He used terms like 'deescalating the conflict' in Ukraine. Conceptually, that demand originated with Obama a year ago. And yet Trump said at a [July 2016] rally in Florida that even though he thinks NATO is great, not all countries are paying their fair share."

According to Remchukov, Pence's speech was not intended to reassure the Europeans. "The split goes deeper," Remchukov said. "He's really indicating how uncertain things are in all respects. The liberal order that was established on the basis of an entire regulatory framework and has been the dominant practice since 1945 is now in substantial jeopardy. Trump is saying no to the TPP and notifying NAFTA (North American Free Trade Agreement) partners that they will have to renegotiate if they want NAFTA to function in an amended form. He's definitely sending signals that there will be no more business as usual in the global economy."

As an illustration, Remchukov cited the shock expressed by Munich conference chairman Wolfgang Ischinger at the fact that Trump claims to have equal respect for Vladimir Putin and Angela Merkel. "[Leaders] in Europe find that unbelievable," Remchukov said. "Another factor is that they all recognize that without the US, security in Europe cannot be achieved. Anyone who's in the know considers it an illusion that Europe is capable of ensuring its own security without America. Of course, Pence's goal is not to reassure Europe—and he can't do that anyway. Recently, basic perceptions of predictability in relations between Europe, America and the rest of the world have been undermined." They cannot be restored with just one or two visits, he says.

"In Munich, I remembered a few interviews Obama gave during the TPP talks, when he stated the following in no uncertain terms: This agreement is a way to establish trade rules for the 21st century that will include everyone, even those countries that are not part of the TPP—namely China," Remchukov continues. "That was an explicit challenge to set new rules for trade. Now that Trump is withdrawing from the TPP, it's clear that the Americans won't be able to impose new rules for the 21st century. But does this mean that Russia, China and other developing economies should be brought on board to work out those rules? There's been no answer to that question."

Remchukov reports that with Trump now in office, confusion reigns in the Western expert community. "From my numerous contacts, I have the impression that all the minds of Western analysts and experts are in great disarray," he says. "I've been meeting with them for 30 years, and I've never seen them so discombobulated. These former prophets have nothing left of their old self-confidence. None of the analysts I spoke with—European or American—know what to say; they can't predict anything. There's a feeling that the cold war has reached an unexpected juncture: The traditional cold war between us [Russia] and the West, including information warfare, has acquired a new layer—a cold war within America, between pro-Trump and anti-Trump forces."

NATO: Trump's Burden

By Dmitry Danilov, professor at the Moscow State Institute of International Relations and head of the department of European security at the Russian Academy of Sciences' Institute of Europe.
International Affairs, No. 3, 2017, pp. 29–47.

US President Donald Trump called NATO an obsolete organization and demanded that the European allies should contribute bigger "fair shares" to European security. This includes, among other things, total fulfillment of their obligation to steadily raise their share of military expenditures up to 2% of their GDPs. This caused consternation among the European leaders and the fears that America's role and guarantees would be eroded, transatlantic unity weakened and the role of NATO undermined. Trump's unconditional acceptance of Brexit as the Brits' wise move fanned doubts in the new American administration's wholehearted devotion to the strategic alliance with Europe/EC and its ability to remain NATO's responsible leader.

On the other hand, Brexit deprived the EU and Europe of the leader that ensured European interests in the relations with the US, in the transatlantic alliance and within NATO-EU cooperation. Trump's declared readiness to revive cooperation with Russia despite the Ukrainian crisis questioned the earlier agreements and decisions to contain Russia.

Led by the Obama administration, Europe toughly responded to [the annexation of the] Crimea; today, in the light of the Trump administration's renovated Russian strategy, Europe is no longer sure that the US will remain the political linchpin of transatlantic policies. Although the new administration has already confirmed its political assessment of the Ukrainian crisis and Russia's "destabilizing" role, it also hinted at its readiness to move closer to Russia (and to lighten the sanction pressure) if there is bilateral progress on the issues of arms control and counterterrorist struggle.

The Europeans have to take into account that Trump has identified the "2% problem" as the key one on his transatlantic agenda and the main point in his diplomatic contacts with the European allies. The burden-sharing issue figures prominently in the media coverage of contacts between the allies and at the press conferences that sum up such contacts. It remains to be seen whether the 2% benchmark on which the Europeans and Washington had agreed long before Trump became president can be achieved at all and whether it will become the transatlantic landmark, let alone a priority of the European NATO members.

'Burden-sharing': history of the issue.

… The sharing of burdens and responsibility within the North Atlantic alliance has been on the agenda from the very beginning: It determined [NATO's] existential parameters, the constantly changing transatlantic balances and policy. In fact, the alliance was set up because Europe could not ensure its own security and adequately pay for it. Having assumed the responsibility for Euro-Atlantic security, America became its leader. At all times, the political role and independence of Western Europe were limited by the fact that it was not part of North American defenses: It "protected" the US and Canada at home, while America remained its main defender. After the 9/11 terrorist attacks against the US, its European allies went out of their way to confirm their solvency and pay the Atlantic bills by contributing to America's defenses: for the first time in its history, NATO invoked Article 5 on collective defense of the Washington Treaty.

This contribution and Europe's widescale involvement in the NATO counterterrorist operation in Afghanistan was the weightiest argument in favor of the continued transatlantic balance. On the other hand, NATO's withdrawal from Afghanistan inevitably exacerbated the dilemma of burden-sharing/re-sharing included in the post-Afghan agenda and the Alliance's Wales Summit of September 2014. Washington deliberately avoided direct pressure and relied on the Alliance's political and diplomatic channels to give its European allies a chance to independently arrive at "the right decision."

The summit approved the common budget benchmarks: the 2% level of their annual defense expenditures as a share of GDP during the next decade, the fifth part of which (20%) should be spent "on major new equipment, including related research and development." Everybody knew, however, that this political commitment that presupposed regular reassessment of progress was not a program obligation of the Alliance's heads of state and government. A new agenda in the context of the Ukrainian crisis demanded that the allies should play by the rules yet it cannot be regarded as a starting point of a new transatlantic balance.

Transatlantic relations: from chemistry to math.

After he won the presidential election late in 2016, Donald Trump formulated a foreign policy platform of his own, adjusted relations with [America's] European allies accordingly and, as might have been expected, changed radically the rules established by the previous administration. For the first time in NATO history, "responsibility distribution" was directly tied to the sums this or that country paid for solidarity, which is in fact for European defense. The newly elected president used this to consolidate the positions of his administration within the renovated partnership with the Europeans. This exacerbated the entire set of problems related to the nature of US-European relations, the role of NATO, the US's "responsible leadership," and the readiness and ability of European allies to support America. This is not about the sums Europe should pour into common Euro-Atlantic security: This is about its debt to the US. Today, Washington looks at Europe's "fair share" as a "debt of honor" and a criterion of future transatlantic relations....

Trump has trapped Europe in an extremely tough and deliberately politically incorrect manner. Today, it must persuade the American president, its key ally, whom many find unpalatable, that it is as loyal as ever, that it is willing and, most important, able to follow the leader. Trump will have to loosen his grip to be able to rely on the European allies; their abilities are limited, yet the US global agenda and its leadership are impossible without them. This means that the transatlantic balance will be determined not so much by the correlation between America's toughness and Europe's flexibility, but by their ability to arrive at a common platform for their future solidarity.

For a new American card game with Europe, the American president selected a hand of three trump cards: burden-sharing, American guarantees and the Russian joker. The stakes were clear from the very beginning: Europe "owes vast sums of money" to the US (to "the American people," not to President Trump); the debt should be paid and Washington will insist on it; and the US will find common points with Russia if this suits American interests. His "fair claim" has provoked political fragmentation, which has made it much harder for Europe to arrive at a concerted "European answer": Today, it is not quite clear which Europe the American president has in mind and with which he intends to reach the "2% agreement."

The UK is leaving the EU. Does that mean that the place of the European leader and the US special partner will be vacant? Will Berlin fill the void? Will Germany, with its defense expenditures of 1.2% of GDP versus Britain's 2.2%, move to the forefront as the leader? Washington has broadly hinted: If Germany wants America on its side in its race for leadership, it will have to pay. During US Secretary for Defense James Mattis's first meeting with German Defense Minister Ursula von der Leyen, he thanked her for Germany's leadership in NATO and invited both countries to start a strategic dialogue. Berlin, however, deemed it necessary to point out: "There is no debt account in NATO. To relate the 2% defense spending that we want to reach in the next decade solely to NATO is wrong. The defense spending also goes to UN-peace missions, into European missions and towards our contributions to the fight against ISIS terrorism."

It seems that the European NATO allies of Germany will follow suit, which means that Trump will have to revise his set of European political instruments. On the other hand, not all European allies are on Germany's side: As distinct from Old Europe, some of its opponents have already responded to the American support of their request to contain Russia by increasing their contributions to defenses. This new split inside the "European pillar of NATO" provoked by Washington is fraught with strong negative effects: an escalated crisis of European integration, lost reference points needed to tune up the transatlantic balance, mounting anti-American sentiments in Europe, and the crumbling foundation of American leadership and its global role in Europe.

This transatlantic rearrangement leaves no space for Europe as an equal partner and no space for an independent game with Moscow. Russia is in a better position: no rules of the game either with the Americans or Europeans should be changed to respond to "Trump's challenge": The "sanctions" imposed due to the Crimea cannot change Russia's position. Its interest is clear. Russia will be ready to support Washington's program of international and European security: (1) if the Trump administration declines to pour money into an absolutely unjustified "Baltic project" of stronger European defenses against Russia; (2) if confrontation with Russia makes it harder for the US to achieve its priority (global) aims; (3) if Moscow proclaims deescalation and rapprochement for pragmatic reasons; (4) if the EU agrees, in the final count, to drop the Clinton/Obama sanctions.

The sides have clarified two issues: struggle against international terrorism and ISIS and revival of arms control talks. Today,

Moscow still looks at Donald Trump's election slogans of "obsolete" NATO not as a chance to weaken the transatlantic alliance (or the US or the European Union) but as a "window of opportunity," a chance of a U-turn leading to Russia/the US/Europe/NATO cooperation in response to the very real and mounting challenges to international security. To achieve this, is it necessary to block the "Ukrainian" push to contain Russia as being very dangerous for Europe, decrease the mutually unjustified risks and start moving toward normalized Russia-the West relations up to and including the settling of the Ukrainian crisis in full conformity with the Minsk agreements.

So far, political dynamics prevail over political analysis and planning yet Trump has become more emancipated and his ability to change and flexibly respond to changes while sticking to his guns looks more pronounced. While preparing for the NATO summit in Brussels scheduled to the end of May his administration considers the "2% issue" as its central topic. To answer the questions of whether the Europeans are ready to respond to Trump's call to pay the debts and to what extent their problems and deficits may affect the transatlantic balances, we need to scrutinize the European obligations to increase their defense expenditures within NATO.

Trump's 2%: what's at stake.

President Trump and the key members of his administration reconfirmed the US's dedication to the transatlantic alliance and NATO. This means that the potential of American revisionism is somehow limited. In fact, Trump cannot move aside from NATO: This would do no good either to his position or that of the US, whose "might" he promised to strengthen. As the leader of NATO, he tried to blackmail his European allies and failed.

First, he had to beat a hasty retreat. Washington used the Munich Conference of Feb. 17–20, 2017, and the visits of US Defense Secretary James Mattis on Feb. 15 and Vice-President Mike Pence on Feb. 20 to Brussels/EU/NATO to clearly confirm its loyalty to common values and NATO.

Second, the current political context and the unfolding electoral cycle in Europe do not allow Germany and France and their Old European partners to retreat under Trump's unjustified pressure. In fact, the American president who challenged Europe with an "uncompromising choice" could have hardly expected Europe to accept it. On the whole, Europe is growing more and more independent partly thanks to the Trump factor and the response of the European political class. The strengthening populist and nationalist forces in Europe cannot be regarded as the resource of the American president. In fact, a vector of opposition to American diktat is growing stronger....

After the February "explanations" of American policies, Europe should merely use political and diplomatic wording to accept greater responsibility and increase its financial contribution to the NATO budget. In fact, this was registered as a common European position (including obligations to increase defense spending) adopted by the Wales Summit of 2014. The Europeans should consolidate their positions on this comfortable platform; they should not respond to Trump's attempts to raise the stakes so as not to bind themselves with additional and burdensome obligations. On the eve of the meeting between Merkel and Trump of March 17, 2017, NATO Secretary General Jens Stoltenberg gave a politically correct answer to a politically incorrect question about Germany's inability to reach the 2% level: the subject would be discussed "yet I expect the President will talk with her about it as well; this is simply about all of us doing what we all said that we would do." He pointed to the demands of the time and agreed with Washington: "To provide for our common defense and in the ever-changing threat environment in which we live, that's [the increase in spending] more important now than ever."...

This means that Washington and the Europeans have no reasons to quarrel at the May summit in Brussels; in fact, they have already approved a draft of an agreement: The US and the Trump administration will receive "guarantees" and reassurances that the Europeans will increase their share of the burden in exchange for reaffirmed American leadership and guarantees....

If Europe fails to fulfill its obligations outlined within NATO, Trump might use that as an instrument of pressure to increase his influence on the allies and consolidate US leadership in NATO when establishing new US-Europe balances. On Feb. 20, 2017, Mike Pence said: "We have a president who is stepping forward, he is expressing American leadership not just on the issue of funding but also on his call last year that NATO should evolve to * * * widen its tactics to include counterterrorism as a major focus and NATO has begun to do that. We must be as I said before, we must be as dominant in the digital world as we are in the physical world. And the United States is committed to continuing to work with our NATO allies to achieve that objective for the security of all the nations in our alliance."

This means that the American NATO agenda consists of counterterrorist struggle and cyber security, rather than containment of Russia, as one of the priorities. The US will insist on its idea about the future of NATO in full conformity with its leadership in the sphere of finances. This means that the new US Administration will assess NATO's efficiency by its ability to work under American leadership to overcome the terrorist threat and address other strategic tasks formulated by Washington. Trump's financial formula addressed to Europe—you should pay more—means in fact "if you disagree with the American agenda in the joint transatlantic enterprise, you will pay for your projects yourselves."

Translated into contemporary American, this means: we have already done everything we needed to do in our relations with Russia; the time has come to get down to real business (probably together with Moscow). On the whole, this position perfectly fits the NATO "Warsaw" approach to Russia: containment + dialogue. (Mike Pence: "Be assured, the United States, as well, will continue to hold Russia accountable, even as we search for new common ground, which President Trump firmly believes can be found.")

The European card might prove useful in domestic political struggle in the US, both to President Trump and his enemies and opponents. Facing the worst type of confrontation with the American political establishment and Congress, as well as exacerbated confrontation between political elites, forces and groups of interests in the US, Trump will be probably able to demonstrate to Europe that America can be tough. Depending on specific circumstances that might take the form of rotation of American contingents at the Eastern flank; of using trade and economic pressure instruments up to and including talks on the Transatlantic Trade and Investment Partnership (TTIP), etc., or of harsher American anti-Russian sanctions and supplies of lethal armaments to Ukraine. Strange as it may seem, the same instruments might be used by Trump's opponents in the US Congress.

If these instruments are used either by Trump or his opponents, Europe will be the loser. This, however, gives Europe a chance to become an external stabilizer. Indeed, to preserve stability, the American political class and the elites should reach a consensus on Europe and European security, since US priorities are concentrated elsewhere—in China, Syria/ISIS/the Middle East, where Europe has no strategic role to play. On the other hand, no complications or even worse European positions in the American strategic arrangement will force Europe to considerably increase its contribution to NATO, at least amid the current economic and political limitations and tension.

Strange as it may seem, today more money poured into the common European defense industry increases the risks of Europe's even greater dependence on the US. Those countries that have no military-economic potential to speak of (the Baltic countries, Romania and Poland) will probably discover new horizons opened by closer ties with the US and multidimensional spin-off, including in their economies. The European leaders (France and Germany) and the EU as a whole will gain nothing from Washington's firmer position in Europe; it will increase the risks and cause potential losses in the form of a weakening European defense autonomy, [as well as] the common European and export markets of arms and defense technologies.

This means that the opportunity to enjoy short-term political and, in some cases, economic dividends produced by bigger defense budgets will enfeeble Europe and its leaders in the long-term perspective outside the "Trump period." Different political and economic expectations of European countries from their defense investments, in the context of their relations with the US among other factors, objectively provoke an even more obvious split within the frames of the common European Security and Defense Policy and lower the common European political denominator in NATO.

This means that the "Trump effect" will probably not significantly affect the burden-sharing situation in the mid-term perspective. The economic situation; Brexit; competing social, economic and political tasks; factors of domestic politics, including the change of the elites in Europe; and the desire to strengthen Europe's competitive positions in its relations with the US and other external players should be considered weighty factors that will continue to interfere with the growth of defense spending in European countries. At the same time, however, there will be an obvious movement toward the specified and confirmed benchmarks. Some countries will be ready to demonstrate that they correspond to the new transatlantic accents of the new administration, which will exacerbate the dilemma of "fairer" burden-sharing, both transatlantic and European.

The Foundation of the West Is Shaken, Its Future Uncertain

By Andrei Akulov. *Strategic Culture Foundation Online Journal*, June 2, 2017, https://www.strategic-culture.org/news/2017/06/02/foundation-west-shaken-its-future-unsertain.html.

There are signs that the very foundation of what is known as the West appears to be shaken with something new coming to take its place. Some experts said that Trump's election in the US signaled the end of the liberal order. Some saw his victory as "the night the West died." Now the prediction appears to be confirmed.

Europe "must take its fate into its own hands," remarked German Chancellor Angela Merkel, reflecting a new transatlantic rift that has emerged after the recent NATO and Group of Seven summits. According to her, while Germany and Europe would strive to remain on good terms with America and Britain, "we have to fight for our own destiny." "The West has become smaller, at least it has become weaker," Sigmar Gabriel, Germany's Foreign Minister, chimed in. Martin Schulz, the German chancellor's center-left rival in the upcoming September election, joined in, calling Trump "the destroyer of all Western values." According to him, the US president is undermining the peaceful cooperation of nations based on mutual respect and tolerance.

So there is consensus within the ranks of the German political elite regarding the role of the US. German politicians say it openly in the name of a United Europe led by Berlin.

Germany, the European No. 1, does not consider America as the West's leader anymore—a role it has indisputably held since the end of World War II. The US does not like this, but there is nothing to be done about it.

According to [a tweet by] Richard Haass, president of the US Council on Foreign Relations, "Merkel saying Europe cannot rely on others & needs to take matters into its own hands is a watershed-& what US has sought to avoid since WW2." *The Financial Times* believes the chancellor has committed a blunder. Right or wrong, she has done it, and it changes a lot.

The idea of Europe taking its destiny into its own hands, at least in terms of ensuring its own security, is not new. The US and the UK going separate ways from the rest of Europe is not a new trend, either. It had come into focus before, but it was unthinkable for a German leader to openly say such a thing. Just as it was unthinkable for NATO to be left out in the cold.

According to *Die Welt*, Germany, France, the Netherlands and Denmark have led a drive to prevent next year's summit of NATO heads of state from taking place in Turkey. Eighteen European Union nations and Canada agreed with the decision to prevent the meeting from taking place in Istanbul. NATO defense ministers are expected to make a final decision when they meet in June. According to the report, the favored proposal envisions the meeting at NATO's new headquarters in Brussels.

The conflict had been smoldering for some time before threatening to go public. Germany even considered withdrawing its military from Turkish soil. An ally with the second largest standing force is on the brink of leaving the alliance or, at least, just keeping up appearances as a member without actually being one. As Montenegro joins the bloc, a trend in the opposite direction is also becoming visible. It's not in the headlines, but Slovakia may soon leave NATO.

The EU is in deep trouble and on the verge of being torn apart. Internal divisions are a well-known trend. Germany and the northern European states are calling for austerity policies, which is prompting resistance from weaker eurozone economies. The EU leader has become extremely unpopular among large countries like Italy, Spain and Greece. The members of the "Visegrad group"—

Poland, Hungary, the Czech Republic and Slovakia—appear to be a bloc within a bloc.

The divisions are deepening. Poland and the Baltic states are more pro-US than pro-German. Europe could become divided while implementing the "multispeed" concept [the idea that different parts of Europe need to integrate at different rates—*Trans.*].

With all the discussions under way, ensuring security without the US and the UK seems to be a tall order. The European deterrent is to be based on and closely connected with the US-led NATO. The much-vaunted concept of a European rapid reaction force looks more like a pipedream.

No matter who wins the September election in Germany, the stance on the US role will not change, as the view is shared by all major candidates. It's hardly possible to say exactly what is in store, but changes will come. Evidently, from now on, it's hard to talk about such thing as Western unity. It is vanishing right in front of our eyes.

NATO and the EU are going through changes that are shaking the foundation the West was built upon. There will be no such thing as the West-Russia pattern. Rather, Moscow will have to deal with the separate groups of states that will emerge once the West's unity bursts at the seams. Sanctions and other things will simply die away. The groups may differ in their views on the issues the West has been unanimous on until now, and the very term "the West" may lose its relevance. The things that had seemed to be unimaginable before have happened, with new poles of power emerging to change the political landscape of the Euro-Atlantic region and the contemporary world.

The Whole Earth Minus the US: The Consequences of America Exiting the Climate Agreement

By Stanislav Kuvaldin. *Republic.ru*, June 2, 2017, https://republic.ru/posts/83602.

Donald Trump's official statement that [the US] is exiting the Paris Climate Agreement, which he made in the White House Rose Garden at 11 p.m. Moscow time on June 1, marks perhaps the most fundamental shift in the US's new global standing. This is not even so much about what obligations the US is shirking but how other countries reacted to the news. By all indications, national and business leaders are determined to continue striving to meet the goals [set in the Paris Agreement] despite the American authorities' U-turn on the matter.

In order to understand the significance of Trump's step, it makes sense to examine the 2015 Paris Agreement and why it became an international reality.

First, prior to the US's exit, the agreement united a record number of countries—practically all recognized states. Now, by exiting the agreement, Trump is proposing that the US join the ranks of such nations as Syria and Nicaragua, which did not sign the Paris Agreement.

Moreover, the reason Syria is not on the list is not of its own doing—that is only because a civil war is raging in the country and many did not consider the Bashar Assad government, which represents the country at the UN, as representative of all Syrian people. That is why it was not invited to join the agreement. For its part, Nicaragua, led by former Sandinista leader Daniel Ortega, decided against signing because it believes the agreement is too mild and does not oblige wealthy nations to make the necessary [emissions] cuts.

So it looks ridiculous for the US to suddenly find itself in the company of two outsiders that for one reason or another ended up not being party to the agreement.

The Paris Agreement is a set of voluntary obligations taken on by states in order to prevent the earth's temperature from rising more than two degrees Celsius compared to preindustrial levels. The aim is to reduce climate impact by cutting human greenhouse gas emissions—primarily carbon dioxide and methane, as well as other gases created by human agricultural and industrial activity.

Each country is going to determine the best approach for it to tackle this issue. The agreement does not require all nations to immediately start reducing greenhouse gases. For certain developing nations, it is assumed that it is impossible to fight poverty and ensure economic development without temporarily increasing emissions. In that case, it is proposed that [those nations] set a time frame for when they will reach their peak and start reducing emissions. However, developed states must start reducing emissions [right away]. This brings us to the question of why nations around the world decided to make these commitments.

This can hardly be explained merely by scientific data on climate change and humans' impact on it. Although the practically complete consensus [on global warming] in the scientific community is a significant factor, it is hardly the only one forcing politicians, economists and entrepreneurs to come together to solve this problem. After all, states don't always rush to restrict economic activity—even if all scientists in the world advise it.

Clearly, social pressure also played a role in the political decision-making. Unlike in Russia, climate change and the need to adopt urgent measures to reverse it are part of the "progressive" agenda for many social forces. This has become a focus of public opinion and cannot simply be ignored. However, that is hardly enough to bring about a global agreement.

Such all-encompassing agreements are always based on material factors, and in this case, it would help to recall the lessons of Marxism and say that this agreement became possible due to the development of productive forces....

Thus, the Paris Agreement became possible largely because alternative energy sources stopped being the stuff of science fiction: Over the past 40 years, prices per kilowatt of energy produced by solar power have become 100 times more affordable and continue to fall....

This resulted in oil companies (such as Shell and Total, for instance) making significant investments in renewable energy sources simply because this energy market trend can no longer be ignored. It was this shift—which is driving new technologies, creating new jobs, reducing dependence on oil exporters, and changing the energy market and the economy in general—that laid the groundwork for the Paris Agreement.

All nations recognized that they stand to gain by taking part in this process. Take China, for instance, which used to be wary of any attempts to limit the use of certain types of energy (namely coal). Today, it is a world leader in manufacturing turbines and solar panels, which speaks to serious shifts in the global economy.

Trump decided to ignore all these considerations by withdrawing the US from the Paris Agreement after taking a few months to think it over. In fairness, it should be added that Trump decided to leave the door open a crack, stating that he is prepared to renegotiate the terms on which the US would participate in the agreement. However, even Trump's rhetoric here speaks volumes: He called the agreement reached by countries around the world "unfair" for America. Thus, he has demonstrated that he believes the US to be just a passive party to a process it has no influence over.

Such a situation seemed impossible a few years ago. [Today,] America does not see itself as a world leader, and assumes that the world is ready to take advantage of it. At the same time, it is now possible for a major agreement that concerns global economic policy to remain intact even after the US exits it. Moreover, the rest of the world is starting to get increasingly tough with America and its inadmissible actions.

Prior to Trump's announcement, the leaders of Germany, France and Italy published a joint statement to the effect that the Paris Agreement is not subject to renegotiation. For his part, [French President] Emmanuel Macron also issued a virtually unprecedented appeal to the American people, where he said the decision [to exit the agreement] was a mistake and called on everyone to unite in tackling common challenges....

Perhaps such a strong reaction to Trump's move is explained by the fact that under the terms of the agreement, countries may only exit it four years after its entry into force (in November 2016). More specifically, the matter is not up for discussion for the next three years; there is also a year-long waiting period. So basically, the US would only be able to exit the agreement after Trump's term expires. This means that perhaps the US won't leave it after all.

Nevertheless, everything that is happening today is very telling. Leading world countries now see America as a strong power that is impeding progress on a major breakthrough, and doubt the decision-making abilities of its leader. They are even prepared to engage directly with the American public, bypassing the US leadership. Meanwhile, the US president is convinced that America is being slighted by the rest of the world, which it must protect and isolate itself from. Clearly, Russian citizens know what that feels like. As for the Americans, they are about to find out.

How Trump Is Stealing Eastern Europe Right From Under Russia's Nose

By Andrei Kolesnikov, program director at the Carnegie Moscow Center. *RBC Daily*, July 5, 2017, p. 5.

Self-isolation has many advantages, especially when it comes to the domestic audience—for instance, you constantly feel strong and independent, as someone who does not "bargain with sovereignty." At the same time, you risk being sidelined in international politics. Russia's current leadership was hoping to gain from a European schism, with the continent veering increasingly to the right. But for the time being, it's Donald Trump who is busily splitting up the European Union as a passive Russia looks on.

In advance of what promises to be a historic but probably meaningless handshake at the G-20 summit in Hamburg between the two enfants terribles of international affairs, the American president is going to visit Warsaw on July 6 in what promises to be a triumph. He will be greeted there by throngs of sincere, hand-picked flag-waving fans—for it is in the interests of Poland's current right-wing populist leadership to establish good relations with the US in light of its former leadership's terrible relations with the EU. Then there's the possible gas deal (the first American tanker carrying liquefied natural gas is already dropping anchor at Poland's shores).

The US administration is looking not only for an ally in Poland, but also a Poland in the broadest sense of the word—one that translates to almost all of Eastern Europe. Theoretically, this would mean the Visegrad Four (besides Poland, it includes Hungary, the Czech Republic and Slovakia) as well as the nations that joined an alliance based primarily on energy interests called the Three Seas Initiative (12 nations of Central Asia and Eastern Europe, so basically almost the entire post-Soviet bloc, plus Austria). That summit also took place in Warsaw, and Trump was also there.

He is interested in building "his own" Europe as a counter to "Old Europe," which doesn't understand him. Russia is not even considered a player in this scenario—it remains on the sidelines, ready for a historic handshake. [For their part,] East European countries are trying to get the EU into a tug-of-war with Trump.

I would agree with Bulgarian political analyst Ivan Krastev that European rivalry is playing out along the lines of Macron vs. [Hungarian Prime Minister Viktor] Orban. Now, Trump is jumping into the fray. "Old Europe" is going to pay close attention to his maneuvering in "new Europe." Emmanuel Macron made a preventive friendly gesture by inviting Trump to Paris to celebrate Bastille Day on July 14. Whose handshake will be firmer, Macron's or [Law and Justice Party leader Jaroslaw] Kaczynski's? And how does Putin's hand that he is extending to Trump play into this?

The expression "firm handshake," made famous in the Yeltsin era, is most likely all that can be expected from the two leaders' meeting on the sidelines of the G-20 summit. So as to avoid disappointment, officials on both sides worked to lower expectations for the meeting, which does not resemble negotiations in any way. What will they actually talk about? [Anti-Russian] sanctions? But who would lift them? Trump has his hands tied by the American system of checks and balances that the founding fathers set up.

Syria? That's a subject getting more controversial by the minute. North Korea? China, not Russia, has leverage [over Pyongyang]. All that's left is returning embassy "dachas" in Maryland and New York, but that's a bit trite for a "historic" meeting.

The problem is that tackling small items does not work without a big goal that can unite both sides. Any actual cooperation is thwarted by a lack of ideas or even a vague outline of a "big deal"—something that neither the Russian nor the American leadership is able or willing to come up with. When Richard Nixon, another US president who was not the most conventional, and Leonid Brezhnev, who wasn't deemed particularly smart (even though he had keen political intuition until he got sick in late 1974) got down to serious negotiations—during the Vietnam War, no less—they had a goal. It was simple—to establish normal, pragmatic relations. As Brezhnev's speechwriter Aleksandr Bovin wrote in his memoirs, the general secretary had gone through a war and genuinely wanted to establish peace, including through compromise. In his memoirs, Henry Kissinger (who made a symbolic, rather than meaningful, appearance at the Primakov Readings forum in Moscow) wrote about how the unofficial communications channel between Moscow and Washington (aka the back channel) functioned—the real one, not the one Jared Kushner set up, which has already been discredited. In a word, if you want to accomplish anything, you need to understand your objective and then throw at it all the resources at your disposal. Currently, we have neither a goal nor political will.

What will Trump talk about in Warsaw, where he is expected to give his big speech? Packaging Putin together with the Ukrainian issue, a touchy subject for both Poland and the West, will not be easy. The same goes for a relationship formula for the US and Europe, which is still a single political unit that Trump decided to break up. But saying that out loud would be going too far. Poland is turning into a right-wing populist hybrid authoritarian state modeled on Russia but without becoming Russia's ally—on the contrary, it continues to distance itself [from Moscow]. The EU's East European members will find it difficult to maneuver between the institutions of America and Europe, the latter being led by a strong Franco-German alliance.

Does Trump have any idea of how many disagreements he could rekindle and how dangerous it is for the West to toy with the Poles' emotions? Probably not. And yet someone managed to explain to him that in Poland, he would be greeted like a hero—like Batman—and be a most welcome guest. [He knows] that [Poland] is where he could theoretically win over half the EU—the countries that believe they are second-rate EU members wronged by EU bureaucracy and international corporations that sell Eastern Europe second-rate goods (at least that's what officials in the Czech Republic, Hungary and Slovakia think). "With some products, we are in fact Europe's garbage can," Czech Minister of Agriculture Marian Jurecka said recently.

Like his predecessors, Trump is building a Washington-Warsaw axis, not so much knowing but rather sensing its strategic importance. However, this [US] president is of a completely different political leaning than his predecessors, while Warsaw is not what it used to be (the same could be said of all members of the Visegrad Four, whose founders included such greats as Lech Walesa and Vaclav Havel, who sought to join Europe, not separate from it). However, that axis remains important. On July 6 in Warsaw, Trump will devalue his handshake with Putin on July 7 in Hamburg without even realizing it. An ecstatic Twitter barrage is all that will remain of it.

The World Comes to Those Who Wait

[No author indicated.] *Ekspert*, July 10, 2017, p. 7.

The G-20 meeting in Hamburg was perhaps the most eagerly awaited summit of 2017. And not so much because of its agenda, but because of the first personal meeting between Vladimir Putin and Donald Trump—between the old Russia, which has been protecting its interests for many years, and the new America, which for the first time in decades is being forced to at least acknowledge those interests exist....

It is already possible to say that the talks were a big success for Russia. For one thing, they were very timely for Putin (and the Russian president is known for being a brilliant tactician who knows how to leverage such moments)....

Were Washington and Brussels (or rather, Berlin) in agreement, it would be easier for them to oppose Putin—which they actually tried to do within the framework of the Obama-Merkel duumvirate supported by François Hollande. Now, however, there is no such agreement, largely because Berlin is unwilling to accept Trump's views. "In recent days, Angela Merkel has sharply criticized America's isolationist policy, as well as the US's planned exit from the Paris Climate Agreement. She wants to work together with other European leaders to confront Mr. Trump, and that is exactly what her German voters want from her," the German weekly *Der Spiegel* wrote.

This particular opposition is spilling over into the symbolic realm, too. For example, during the G-20 leaders' photo shoot, Trump was put at the far right [of the group]—on the fringe, as far as possible from the center, where Merkel stood. And then something interesting happened: French President Emmanuel Macron came down from his spot in the second row and stood to Trump's right, thus closing out the first row. It was unclear whether he was asked to do so because America's protocol people were incensed, or whether it dawned on him that this would be a way to suck up to the American leader. If the second theory is correct, it seems that dissension in the West is deeper than it appears.

Yes, of course Trump would like to find common ground with Merkel—and Europe would like him to. "The trip [to Hamburg] offers [Trump] the chance for redemption after a catastrophic visit to Brussels in May," writes *Politico*. But this is hardly possible; the disagreements are simply too strong.

Very interesting prospects are opening up for Moscow in this respect. Both Trump and Merkel would like to achieve real agreements with Putin, but with minimal consultation with each other. (On some issues, they even hold opposite positions.) Germany, the self-declared paragon of European values, finds itself fighting an isolated battle to give Putin's rogue state its political objectives for the benefit of Germany, Inc., writes *Forbes*. Berlin wants to become Europe's gas hub, so of course Trump's longing to supply liquefied natural gas to Poland is absolutely out of the picture [for Merkel]. As is his desire to pit Eastern Europe against Western Europe ([former US defense secretary Donald] Rumsfeld's famous "old Europe vs. new Europe" principle), which Trump unveiled during [his] visit to Poland.

The incident again proves that the world comes to those who wait....

Macron Displaces Merkel

By Maksim Makarychev. *Rossiiskaya gazeta*, July 17, 2017, p. 6.

France has held its traditional Bastille Day celebrations, Emmanuel Macron's first as head of the Fifth Republic.

The limelight during the festivities was on US President Donald Trump, who visited France along with his wife Melania.... Afterward, the US president said with obvious pleasure that France has a great president, a great leader; Paris is beautiful; and that he'd be coming back.

It should be recalled that the first communication between the "isolationist Trump" and the "globalist Macron"—who in the French election was supported by American Democrats—did not hold out promising prospects. In addition, the French president reacted very sharply to the US president's statement about withdrawing from the Paris Climate Agreement. However, in a matter of weeks the situation changed to such an extent that Trump has started to trust Macron, speaking with him as an equal and gradually making him his preferred European partner. For his part, the young French leader who does not conceal his ambitions is cleverly taking advantage of the obvious differences between the US and Germany, and Trump's noticeable irritation with German Chancellor Merkel. Macron is gradually building a new transatlantic Paris-Washington axis in the teeth of the traditional Anglo-Saxon model, particularly as there are still a lot of questions in US-British relations. Suffice it to recall the American leader's constantly postponed—under various pretexts—visit to London. After the weak Hollande, whom Trump pointedly ignored, Macron is getting France back in the great geopolitical game, forcing both sides of the Atlantic to reckon with it.

Moreover, in the face of the shaky political future of Merkel, who, other than chairing the Franco-German Ministerial Council, was virtually invisible in Paris, Macron is becoming more than just Washington's main European partner. He really could lay claim to the role of Europe's new leader. In these circumstances, the rivalry between the German chancellor and the French president on the issue of European leadership is becoming more and more apparent. And Macron is outshining Merkel, who for many years was the "European leader by default," concludes Agence France-Presse. Moreover, the agency adds, Macron is showing flexibility in dealing with Trump, while Merkel is maintaining a firm relationship with the American leader, continuing to criticize him for protectionism and withdrawing from the climate agreement, which he announced six weeks ago.

In Paris, the dynamic and energetic Macron scored more points. First, he persuaded Merkel that it was necessary to establish a euro zone budget and develop a Franco-German fighter jet. On the other hand, he showed that he is capable of persuading even his tough American counterpart. At least, in an interview with *Le Journal du Dimanche*, Emmanuel Macron reported sensational news. According to him, Donald Trump said he "would try to find a solution [for the US to return to the Paris Climate Agreement] in the coming months. We spoke in detail about what could allow him to return to the Paris deal." "Donald Trump listened to me. He understood the reason for my position, notably the link between climate change and terrorism," Macron said. However, so far it is not clear whether Trump's promise was merely a response to getting the royal treatment or whether he really can abandon his grandstanding.

4.2

Let's Crush ISIS Together: Terrorism and the Middle East

Introduction

Key occasions for the Russian press to comment on the Trump administration's Middle East policy were the Munich Security Conference; President Trump's speech before Congress on Feb. 28; the chemical attack in Syria on April 4, along with the US air strikes launched in response; Trump's visit to the Middle East in late May; and the first face-to-face meeting between Trump and Putin in early July, at the G-20 summit in Hamburg.

Trump did not attend the Munich conference, but Fyodor Lukyanov writes that Washington's views were coherently represented by Sen. Lindsey Graham, who condemned the Obama administration for lifting the sanctions against Iran in 2015. From the more heated remarks against Tehran that representatives of Israel and Saudi Arabia delivered in Munich, Lukyanov concludes that the Middle East is a unique microcosm of today's world: "This is where everything is happening at once, and where all major interests represented in the international arena at large are colliding."

Counterterrorism efforts are a case in point. When Trump spoke to Congress, he reiterated his campaign pledge to fight ISIS; but Peter Korzun in a March 7 article expresses disappointment that the president did not mention Russia as a partner in that fight—only America's "friends and allies in the Muslim world." The journalist drew a connection between this omission and Trump's efforts to distance himself from Russia after dismissing Michael Flynn as national security adviser in mid-February.

The following month, Korzun also criticizes Trump's decision to launch air strikes against Syria in response to the deadly sarin attack, arguing that Trump had previously espoused a noninterventionist policy. The tone here is representative of other commentary in the Russian press at the time in that it simultaneously faults Trump for weakness and Washington as a whole for sowing global discord: "The US president was not able to stand tall and not bow under pressure.... Overnight, it became clear that Donald Trump is no longer the one calling the shots in Washington. The 45th president has lost. The Washington establishment has won." On the other hand, Gevorg Mirzayan praises the White House for treading carefully between military toughness and diplomatic finesse: Trump opted for "a beautiful, courageous but limited strike ... without strengthening the enemy and without causing particular damage to those who are fighting that enemy." Mirzayan intimates that Trump might even have coordinated the response with Putin.

One point of Middle East policy area that Trump surely did not coordinate with Moscow was his four-day visit to the region, in his first trip abroad as president. The trip starts with Saudi Arabia, where Trump and King Salman sign an arms deal worth hundreds of billions of dollars. Sergei Strokan comments that in light of Trump's highly publicized travel ban against citizens of several Muslim countries, the choice of the Arab flagship of Saudi Arabia "confirmed his reputation as the most unpredictable US president, capable of drastically changing his position depending on the circumstances."

The main goal of the visit to Riyadh was to forge a military and political alliance in the Middle East that Washington itself dubbed an "Arab NATO." Some Russian experts doubt that such an alliance is feasible. Andrei Akulov comments that attempts to create such alliances in the Middle East date back to World War II, but that all have failed because the key actors—which include Saudi Arabia, the UAE, Jordan and Egypt—have different strategies and goals. In addition, the alliance is explicitly pitched as a Sunni partnership against Iran. Akulov concludes that Trump's bias against Iran makes the US unfit to mediate in the Middle East—"hardly anybody but Moscow is fit for the role." Leonid Isayev adds that the American president does not have a clear understanding of the situation in the region, largely due to a shortage of experts at the State Department; Trump is only doing what America's traditional allies in the Arab world expect, and indicating which parties he is prepared to negotiate with in the future.

Aleksei Khlebnikov also comments on Trump's lack of a clear strategy in the Middle East, but the outcomes of the Putin-Trump meeting at the G-20 summit gave him cause for optimism about cooperation between Russia and the US, particularly with regard to Syria and counterterrorisam. Trump's motivations, according to Khlebnikov, are that he wants to avoid getting embroiled in another Middle East war; he is not looking for direct confrontation with Russia; and that he wants to score more political points in America by demonstrating "an approach to Syria that is different from Obama's soft and indecisive policies."

Moscow Proposes Trump Take a Different View of Iran

By Andrei Ontikov. *Izvestia*, Feb. 1, 2017, p. 3.

Moscow is keen to seek a compromise on the Iranian nuclear program with the administration of US President Donald Trump, who has repeatedly criticized the international agreements already reached on the issue. Politicians and experts believe that Russia will be able to persuade the new head of the White House to keep Washington's signature on the document, because that would allow the US to improve cooperation with Tehran on resolving other important issues for the Middle East region. And Moscow and Washington will get the first opportunity to harmonize positions on this issue in mid-February, when the foreign ministers of the G-20 meet in Bonn. Granted, it is still not clear who will represent the US, because Donald Trump's nominee for secretary of state, Rex Tillerson, has still not been approved by the Senate.

During the election campaign, President Donald Trump repeatedly criticized the agreement that six mediators (Russia, the US, China, Germany, France and Great Britain) made with Tehran regarding Iran's nuclear program. And he has continued to criticize it after taking office, even promising to unilaterally remove Washington's signature from the document. Later, his foreign policy adviser during the election campaign, Walid Phares, explained that this might not mean a total renouncement of the deal but its revision.

"Iran is located next to Russia, and the prospect of the resumption of the military part of its nuclear program concerns us. Therefore, we do not wish to abandon the deal that was brokered with great difficulty by the US, the European Union, us and Iran itself," Andrei Klimov, deputy chairman of the Federation Council's international affairs committee, told *Izvestia*.

The senator recalled that Iran is also an important player in Syria and the fight against terrorism in the Middle East. And if Donald Trump wants to make progress on Syria, he needs to compromise with Iran. According to Andrei Klimov, the Iranian nuclear issue is sure to be raised in one form or another at the upcoming G-20 summit, which will take place at the level of foreign ministers in Bonn, Germany, in the latter half of February.

"Donald Trump is a new partner for us, and we need to understand what he is planning to do and how. But there are some logical axioms that allow for a solution," Andrei Klimov commented.

Tehran has made it clear that Iran intends to resume the nuclear program if the US pulls out of the deal. [If it does,] according to Ali Akbar Salehi, head of the country's Atomic Energy Organization, work [on the program] would get up and running quickly, not only at previous parameters, "but also at a much higher level from a technological standpoint."

The Islamic Republic was quick to keep its promises: Already on Jan. 30, media outlets reported that Iran had test-fired a medium-range ballistic missile. This is a clear violation by Tehran of UN Security Council Resolution No. 2231.

It is not yet known whether Washington will withdraw its signature from the agreement that took more than 10 years of painstaking negotiation by all interested parties. However, in the opinion of Dmitry Zhuravlyov, general director of the Institute of Regional Studies, this danger really does exist.

"Donald Trump is very reminiscent of 1970s-era conservatives. Their logic was simple: Anything that could pose a danger to the US must be destroyed. If the consequences of pulling out of the deal are explained to him, he will surely take heed. He is a sane person. Moreover, judging from a recent telephone conversation between the Russian and American leaders, he is ready to listen to us. But there is also a danger that fundamental decisions will be made before we have time to communicate our position," Dmitry Zhuravlyov said....

Will Tomorrow Come?

By Fyodor Lukyanov, research director of the Valdai International Discussion Club. *Rossiiskaya gazeta*, Feb. 22, 2017, p. 6.

The Munich Security Conference wound up Sunday [Feb. 19] on a frightening note. A key area of discussion had been the Middle East. Remarks about Syria were relatively calm....

However, the main focus was not Syria but Iran, and on this topic the participants laid it on thick. First came Iranian Foreign Minister [Mohammad Javad] Zarif, who spoke, as always, vividly and in brilliant English, emphasizing common concerns. Then the fireworks went off—[in speeches by] American legislators, Israeli Defense Minister [Avigdor] Liberman and Saudi Foreign Minister [Adel] al-Jubeir. The speakers seemed to be competing to see who could most masterfully lambaste Tehran as the main problem in the Middle East, and in fact the whole world.

The most coherent remarks came from US Sen. Lindsey Graham, who outlined the approach that apparently prevails in Washington. Graham condemned the agreement on Iranian nuclear weapons that had been brokered by the previous administration; however, he did not talk about denouncing that deal and restoring the sanctions. He simply promised that Iran would be held accountable for everything else [besides the nuclear program—*Trans.*]: supporting terrorism, destabilizing the Middle East, [pursuing a ballistic] missile program, suppressing rights and freedoms, etc. In other words, without canceling the accords already reached, Congress intends to simply impose sanctions against Iran for other reasons. That would render the nuclear deal meaningless, since punitive measures would be applied all over again. In this sense, members of Congress—who by and large are not fond of the current White House—do see eye to eye with the administration: Trump's stance is aggressively anti-Iranian.

It is not clear how fast or how far the US is willing to go, [even] with the explicit endorsement of Israel and Saudi Arabia. Tehran seems to consider these threats a bluff for now, but is not about to underestimate them either. This shift in international mood is also important because Iran has a presidential election coming up in May....

One more reason why the latest anti-Iranian wave is vitally relevant: Iran is a key country, both on the battlefields of Syria and at the negotiating table in Astana. The Astana talks are bringing results not only because Russia and Turkey managed to cooperate, but because they also brought Iran on board. Of course, there is a risk posed by the fact that the drivers of this process, which is so critical to the entire Arab world, are three non-Arab countries. It cannot progress further without the involvement of key powers in the Arab community, especially the Gulf countries, just as final decisions can be made only in Geneva, under the authority of the UN. However, an attempt to exert pressure on Iran could make Tehran part of the problem, rather than part of the solution. And Iran certainly wields a lot of leverage, as one of the most influential countries in the region....

All discussions of regional policy—whether they happen in Munich, Moscow, Astana or Geneva—make one thing clear: The Middle East continues to be not only a center of crucial events, but a unique microcosm of the world. This is where everything is happening at once, and where all major interests represented in the international arena at large are colliding.

Trump to Halt Plan to Fight Islamic State With Russia

By Peter Korzun. *Strategic Culture Foundation Online Journal*, March 7, 2017, http://www.strategic-culture.org/news/2017/03/07/trump-halt-joint-plan-fight-islamic-state-with-russia.html.

Normally, a new US president is treated benevolently by Congress, with lawmakers giving wide leeway for initiatives coming from an administration. It's different in the case of Donald Trump. He enjoys no honeymoon period, with all his activities obstructed in each and every way.

Under the circumstances, the president may have to shelve a joint plan to combat [ISIS] with Russia amid the scandals related to the ties of the president and administration officials with Moscow. "I don't know Putin, but if we can get along with Russia that's a great thing. It's good for Russia; it's good for us; we go out together and knock the hell out of ISIS, because that's the real sickness," the president told Fox News in late January.

Today, the administration says it is scaling back, at least for the time being. That's what President Trump stated at a Feb. 16 news conference held right after the firing of his national security adviser Michael Flynn. "It would be unpopular for a politician to make a deal." "It would be much easier for me to be so tough—the tougher I am on Russia, the better."...

On March 4, Dmitry Peskov, Russia's presidential spokesman, stated that Moscow was ready to continue the fight against ISIS without the help of the US. The statement was made in the wake of Palmyra's liberation from ISIS.

Opposed by Democrats and Republican orthodoxy, Trump has had to backtrack, losing initiative. The fight is not over. The president speaks directly to those who support him. A wave of pro-Trump rallies have hit America. Rallies are scheduled in some 50 cities.

The president's first "big" speech in Congress greatly strengthened his position, increasing his number of supporters and sympathizers. It really gave him a bump. The plans to increase military expenditures have also helped strengthen his support base among the military brass and circles close to the US defense industry.

The success of the ongoing fight against ISIS and subsequent contribution to the peaceful settlement of the Syria crisis is extremely important for US international standing. Russia has greatly increased its clout in the Middle East and plays a key role in the fight against terror. It is the only actor who can effectively mediate between the parties pursuing different aims in Syria. It has just prevented a clash between Turkey and Syria in Manbij.

The problem of ISIS is not limited to Iraq and Syria. There is a great probability that Russia and the US will have to cooperate on Libya and Afghanistan....

Russia has more leverage than the US with key actors involved in the conflict, including Turkey, a NATO member, the Syrian government and Iran—a country that cannot be ignored. Russia is on speaking terms with Saudi Arabia, Jordan and the Kurds. It has a leading role in the Astana process. Its Aerospace Forces and experts greatly influence the situation creep.

Moscow has been playing the role of mediator to prevent clashes between Syrian and US forces on the ground. The refusal to coordinate efforts with Russia will reduce US influence on events in Syria and thus diminish its clout in the Middle East.

Acting on its own, the US will willy-nilly have to significantly increase its forces in Syria and the region in general. There are signs the process has already started. It has been reported recently that the Pentagon's plans envisage a major US Army deployment in Syria before an assault on the ISIS capital of Raqqa. Even so, it has no resources to go it alone. A major military operation in Syria is doomed to be unpopular in the US after the bitter experience in Afghanistan and Iraq.

It means America needs allies, partners and comrades in arms. "We will work with our allies, including our friends and allies in the Muslim world, to extinguish this vile enemy from our planet," President Trump told Congress on Feb. 28. A success will enormously boost his position and weaken the position of critics. He definitely needs Russia to achieve this success.

The two nations would benefit if they use the experience of the past (the [1975] Helsinki Act) and divide the pertinent issues into baskets. One basket should include controversial matters to be addressed at a round table. The issues that unite the two nations should be put into another basket. The fight against terror is one such matter.

If success is achieved on this issue, the process would encompass other areas of the relationship. Refusing to coordinate activities with Russia on Syria is tantamount to shooting oneself in the foot. No one wins, everyone loses. Donald Trump would lose more than anyone else at a time when he badly needs breakthroughs and achievements.

US Strikes Syria: Trump Is a President Who No Longer Calls the Shots

By Peter Korzun. *Strategic Culture Foundation Online Journal*, April 8, 2017, http://www.strategic-culture.org/news/2017/04/08/us-strikes-syria-trump-vpresident-who-no-longer-calls-shots.html.

The US delivered a strike against Syria, firing 59 cruise missiles overnight on April 7 in a major foreign policy reversal. The Tomahawk cruise missiles were launched from US ships in the Mediterranean Sea toward Shayrat air base in the western Syrian province of Homs. The act of war was committed upon the order of the president, who once warned against US involvement in foreign conflicts. Just a few days ago, Donald Trump said he was no longer focused on making Assad leave power....

The attack ordered by President Trump indicates a drastic policy change. Before the strike, influential American media outlets had called for making Russia's position a decisive factor for defining further US policy.

As Dennis Ross, a counselor at The Washington Institute for Near East Policy and a US News contributor, put it, "If Russia chooses to deny that the Assad regime—the only Syrian party in the war that has an air force—was responsible for this attack, the message will be loud and clear: No cooperation with the Russians in Syria is possible." There is more to it. "If the Russians join us in condemning the action, imposing sanctions on the regime and insisting that Assad now permit complete access to ensure the destruction of the remaining chemical weapons on hand, we will at least have something to discuss," he said.

[It is] the very same thing all over again—outright pressure and the language of ultimatums are offered as tools to pressure Moscow into complying with US demands....

Now, what do we have? Donald Trump has reneged on his campaign promises, deliberately creating a crisis in the Russia-US relationship. Russian President Vladimir Putin regards the US air strikes on Syria as an act of aggression against a sovereign state delivered in violation of international law under a far-fetched pretext.

Now the US president is trapped. The attack against Syria took place a few days before Secretary Tillerson was to meet Russian President Putin on April 12. An improvement in the relationship would have been possible if President Trump were adamant in his desire to do what he said during the election campaign. But he wasn't. He wanted to make deals, and that's what Moscow was ready for. Now the prospects for progress are dim.

The US president was not able to stand tall and not bow under pressure. He failed to stick to his guns. April 7 is a special date. Overnight, it became clear that Donald Trump is no longer the one calling the shots in Washington. The 45th president has lost. The Washington establishment has won.

By taking a shot at Syria's government, President Trump undercuts the main goal of doing away with ISIS, thus making it a winner. No wonder the group lost no time intensifying its combat activities in Syria right after the American strike. Israel supported the US action, and it is very likely that it will see ISIS militants at its border soon.

Attacked by the Americans, Damascus could respond in kind. That creates added danger for US forces on the ground. There'll be other implications of this military action, which was committed under a false pretext. And there is no light at the end of the tunnel, since no conflict settlement is possible without Russia and Iran—the influential actors opposing the use of force by the US.

Obviously, America is sliding into another Middle East war with no definite goals defined, falling into the same trap over and over again.

Uncle Donald's Show

By Gevorg Mirzayan. *Ekspert*, April 17, 2017, p. 13.

... Over the past two weeks, any Russians who for whatever reason did not unplug from the media might have gotten the impression that Russian-US relations have sunk to a new low. US President Donald Trump carried out a missile strike on a Syrian air base, thereby betraying his own values, his voters' trust and the affection of Russian citizens who sincerely regarded him as a decent guy. Experts disagreed over the causes of Trump's move (his enemies won out, he can't stay on track, he channeled his inner cowboy), but they said in unison that Russian-US relations were seriously affected; that the thaw [in US-Russian relations] was over before it even began; and that Trump refused to cooperate with Moscow, deciding instead to stick with tradition and contain [Russia].

However, there was also another viewpoint. Its proponents believe that the whole affair with the US response to the chemical weapons provocation is nothing but Trump's tactical move to deal with domestic political issues: At this point, he did not choose to sacrifice his foreign policy concept, and the bombing does not conflict with it in any way. Most important, [this theory goes,] Trump's decision to bomb the Syrian air base will not exacerbate relations with Russia. Our country allowed the Americans to carry out a limited strike that was mainly for show, because it wanted to avoid scenarios that would have been more unfavorable—for both Trump and (above all) Russia itself. So, everything that has happened since the attack bears out the "optimistic" theory—because it was based on rationalism, not emotions, and it posited Trump as an intelligent and sensible person, not the madman that some activists on both sides of the Atlantic make him out to be.

Fairy tale for Trump.

The Khan Sheikhoun case—which was in fact what started this crisis—was a provocation, pure and simple. What's more, as often happens in the Middle East these days, the story is poorly cobbled together and easily seen through....

The West and [other] enemies of the Syrian president immediately named the toxic agent as sarin, and said it was dropped by Bashar Assad's aircraft on defenseless citizens. Experts, as well as simply sensible people, immediately dismissed that theory on both counts. First, the horrifying video footage of the clean-up after the tragedy refutes the sarin theory. People were running around without hazmat suits; the victims' breathing was labored, but not painful; and [there were other] symptoms of injury [inconsistent with toxicity]—all of this shows there was not a trace of sarin anywhere nearby. According to some reports, opiates could have been used.

Second, even if this action was deliberate, the perpetrators should be sought according to the principle of "who stands to gain." Topping the list of potential organizers is the Syrian opposition itself, whose fate before the attack was sadly obvious. Assad's forces were advancing, forcing [the oppositionists] to choose between death and political compromise with Damascus—and the West ditched them. Literally a few days before the incident, Donald Trump confirmed that he was not going to overthrow Assad, closing the book on the opposition's verdict. Its defeat was just a matter of time, and the only chance for survival was the kind of action that could sweep all the pieces off the chessboard.

Some external forces were also interested in provoking the situation. Saudi Arabia needed the civil war in Syria to continue as long as possible, and thus needed to prolong the life of the Frankenstein known as the Syrian opposition. The Turks were unhappy with their place in the Middle East triumvirate, and could have used the provocation to raise the stakes to blackmail Russia and Iran. Part of the US establishment wants war with Iran on the Syrian periphery and is nostalgic about the US military presence in the Middle East under [George W.] Bush. And finally, certain circles in Iran also need a war with America—to strengthen their positions within the Islamic Republic itself and prevent the victory of the current head of state, Hassan Rouhani, in the [May 19] presidential election....

Giving a jab.

Of course, Donald Trump understood the alignment of forces very well and clearly saw the "Assad-sarin" theory coming apart at the seams. Nevertheless, he had to stick to it and even act according to its logic.

The problem was that the US media began to position this story as a test of America's leadership—Trump's leadership. TV screens and newspaper pages featured gruesome pictures and horrifying stories of children who had lost all their relatives and [now] hoped only for the beacon of freedom and democracy to shine its righteous light. If Trump had not lit it, he would have been accused of weakness (which was at odds with his image as a strong leader who would not coddle America's enemies—an image that he peddled throughout his election campaign and has generally used as the basis of his foreign policy strategy) or premeditated betrayal of American interests to serve Russian interests. After all, Assad's guilt was already compounded by Russia's guilt: According to a number of Western media outlets, the Kremlin either played a role in organizing the chemical attack or intentionally covered up Assad's mistakes. If Trump had not reacted, it would have looked like he was shielding his "bosses at the Lubyanka [Federal Security Service headquarters—*Trans.*]." And such a show of weakness or protecting the Kremlin (much less a combination of the two) would pave the way to impeachment. "We weighed * * * the risk associated with any military action * * * against the risk of inaction," said Trump's national security adviser, Herbert McMaster. And the risk of inaction weighed more.

On the other hand, the action toward which Trump was being prodded (a full-scale military response, with further military-political support for the Syrian opposition) came with its own risks, which were just as great as the risk of inaction. First, Trump would be handed his own proxy war—not even an Afghanistan or an Iraq, but a Vietnam (since he'd be fighting in Syria indirectly against Iran and Russia). It's one thing to be in conflict with Iran, much to Israel's pleasure; but it's quite another to end up with hundreds of coffins with American soldiers in them, much to the [US] electorate's displeasure. Second, by supporting anti-Assad action without a ground operation, Trump would be strengthening Assad's enemies, who are also America's and Israel's enemies—for example, Saudi Arabia and those much-talked-about terrorists from ISIS (who are banned in Russia). Third, and most important, a US invasion of Syria would call into question the entire modernization of US foreign policy, based on pragmatic spending cuts and higher efficiency. In his foreign policy doctrine and his inauguration speech, the president stated that he no longer wanted to change unsuitable regimes with bombs; he wanted to do so through seduction, by strengthening America's image as a real "city upon a hill"—an idol of modern-day nationalism. An invasion of Syria, however, would bring back [George W.] Bush's foreign policy, which essentially overstrained the US and impaired its global influence.

This is precisely why the White House opted for an intermediate strike—a beautiful, courageous but limited strike without [assuming] any obligation to continue [the offensive], without strengthening the enemy and without causing particular damage to those who are fighting that enemy. In the wee hours of April 7, two US Navy destroyers launched nearly 60 cruise missiles—each worth almost $1.5 million—against the Shayrat air base. According to Donald Trump, the Syrian warplane with chemical weapons on board had taken off from that base. As it turned out, this beautiful and very costly strike caused minimal damage (only a few facilities, as well as old aircraft, were destroyed, while the runway remained intact)—but after that, the Pentagon announced that the issue was basically closed. "The strike was intended to deter the regime from using chemical weapons again," said Pentagon spokesman Jeff Davis. According to Trump, this (not the overthrow of Bashar Assad) is "the vital interest of the United States." Even though the US president stated that he had "changed" his attitude toward his Syrian counterpart, he did not put Obama's idea about regime change back on the agenda, adding that he is not going to send troops back to Syria.

Putin to the rescue.

Right after the strike, Moscow publicly expressed outrage, of course. According to press secretary Dmitry Peskov, the Russian president stated: "This strike does not bring us closer to the end goal in fighting international terrorism. On the contrary, it creates a serious obstacle to building an international coalition to fight [terrorism] and effectively resisting this universal evil." Russian experts also talked about [the US] violating international law (which has already been violated many times before), about the Americans setting a precedent by carrying out a strike against a sovereign country (which was not unprecedented, because before Syria, the US also bombed Yemen and Pakistan), and about [the US leadership's] desire to overthrow Assad after all.

However, the hard facts tell a different story. For example, damage [from the US strike] was minimized because Moscow, warned [by American military officials] in advance, removed its aircraft and most personnel from the air base. Yes, Russian missile interceptor systems were silent. However, 36 Tomahawks failed to reach their targets, which was not just happenstance: From all indications, they were shot down by Russian electronic warfare systems. [This interception was] not a public act, but a real test of these systems and a way to save face (along with the public outrage [expressed by Russian officials]). Moscow had promised to defend Syrian airspace, and it did defend it partially—but did not enter into open confrontation with the US by making visible use of its antimissile systems. Everyone understands very well why the missiles fell, but nobody will officially blame that on the Kremlin; thus, there will be no public challenge to the US, either.

Yes, some people claim that the warning to the Kremlin was worded like an ultimatum, and that [the Russian military] was not given much time to clear the base. But it's important to understand that Trump is no fool: He realized that Vladimir Putin might have responded by flatly refusing and activating all the missile-defense assets in Syria, not to mention delivering a retaliatory strike on the warships from which the missiles were launched. He did not respond [that way], possibly because there was no ultimatum in the first place: Trump asked, and Putin agreed. After all, out of the three possible responses Trump could have made to the chemical weapons incident (keeping silent, landing a knockout punch, or giving a jab), the third was the most beneficial for Putin, too. It's no good for Russia if Trump is ousted, let alone if the US invades Syria and Trump renounces his neo-isolationist foreign policy.

In the end, Trump's plan worked—somehow or other. First of all, [his own] country eased up pressure on him: US media outlets were compelled to write glowing articles about the new president....

What's more, Trump proved that he is not Putin's agent. *The Washington Post* wrote: "Just two weeks ago, Russia was in the driver's seat in Syria, as the lead military and diplomatic player in a peace process involving Turkey, Iran, the Kurds and rebel groups, all orchestrated by Putin. The most important part of this was that the United States was not getting in the way. In an instant * * * when * * * Tomahawk missiles came crashing down around a Syrian air base, that all changed, and since then, the Kremlin has been fighting a rearguard action aimed at dulling the Trump administration's ultimatum."

Hand over Assad, please.

Those fairy tales about the ultimatum freed Trump's hands to start a proper dialogue with Russia. Without that [idea] in the background, Secretary of State Rex Tillerson could hardly have flown to Moscow as planned.

As a matter of fact, the majority of US media outlets did not criticize that visit largely because they thought the secretary of state was going to present Moscow with an ultimatum. Far from dispelling that rumor, the US administration encouraged it in every possible way....

Contrary to expectations, however, there was no ultimatum at the talks: Experience must have told Western politicians that little could be obtained from Putin with threats. Moreover, upon arriving in Moscow, Tillerson abruptly softened his rhetoric and even tried to avoid actions that could be perceived as provocations. In particular, he chose not to meet with selected representatives of the Russian nonestablishment opposition or to jump on the bandwagon of rabid accusations against the Kremlin of complicity in the Syrian chemical attack....

The reason for such circumspect behavior was that Tillerson had come to Moscow to make a deal. America, which cannot overthrow Assad by force, needs Russia's consent and assistance to remove him by proxy. This has nothing to do with personal dislike for the Syrian leader: Assad's departure would be portrayed as a crowning victory for Trump and seriously strengthen his position in the US....

Let's start talking.

The Kremlin takes a skeptical view of that proposal. After all, Assad's departure would have very negative consequences for Moscow. First, it would seriously complicate the tactical situation in Syria: At this point, Assad binds together all progovernment forces [and] symbolizes resistance and the war on terror. Second, if the president is ousted (rather than departing voluntarily upon the completion of peace talks and the end of the civil war), that would be a serious blow to Russia's authority, not to mention the consequences for Iranian-Russian relations. Moscow has spent too much effort to prove to everyone that, unlike the US, it does not betray its allies. So if Assad really is up for sale, it would only be in exchange for very serious compensation.

What might Trump have offered in exchange? A showcase return to the "Western family" (from which Russia could be expelled at the drop of a hat for new transgressions, since it has never been considered a full-fledged member of that family)? No thanks, we've been through that....

However, the inability to seal a big deal doesn't mean that Tillerson's visit was unproductive. It was essentially the first meeting between the Kremlin and such a high-ranking official from the new administration and the Kremlin, during which the parties set in motion the process of normalizing Russian-American relations....

Moscow is willing to wait, and even willing to put up with elements of anti-Russian rhetoric from the Trump administration (realizing that these remarks are made for domestic political consumption). Until that time comes, the most important thing is for the White House not to take any real action to deepen unnecessary confrontation. Here, however, not everything depends on the US: The chemical weapons incident has shown that Trump will have to respond to possible new provocations, which are probably just around the corner (after all, the Syrian opposition has also discovered Trump's Achilles' heel). And then, if Trump can't pull off a repeat of the current show, that's when the real test of Russian-US relations will begin.

We Have Contact

By Yevgeny Shestakov. *Rossiiskaya gazeta*, May 11, 2017, p. 8.

Negotiations between Foreign Minister Sergei Lavrov and US Secretary of State Rex Tillerson, which took place Wednesday [May 10] in Washington, will likely determine the future dynamics of Russian-American relations.

[The diplomatic leaders] talked about restoring real interaction between the countries on the Syrian track, which could eventually build a much-needed atmosphere of trust for discussions at other international venues. Lavrov came ready to answer questions of interest to the White House concerning key aspects of intra-Syrian [conflict] resolution. Readers are reminded that a memorandum on the formation of four "deescalation areas" in Syria was signed in the capital of Kazakhstan [on May 4]; the guarantors are Russia, Turkey and Iran.[22] [Ahead of the signing,] *The New York Times* described [the proposed agreement] as "one of the most detailed suggestions to emerge in recent months in the rocky negotiations to halt the war." Washington generally endorses the idea of "zones," but with an important caveat: The White House considers Tehran's participation in the project a risky step. Experts from the guarantor states have until June 4 to prepare a detailed map of the deescalation areas and to agree on a mechanism to halt hostilities there.

However, US President Donald Trump may have gotten the impression that [the guarantors] want to leave his country and the US-led international coalition out of the game: The deescalation plan was one of the main topics covered in the most recent telephone conversation between the presidents of Russia and the US [on May 2]. The White House and the Kremlin reported that the leaders' conversation was constructive. But the American side still had questions. Some of them were voiced by US Secretary of Defense James Mattis. "Who is going to be ensuring [that the zones] are safe? Who is signing up for it? Who is specifically to be kept out of them?" Mattis rattled off the US military's concerns about details of the Syria memorandum. Mattis added that the Defense Department is interested in clarifying these matters because it is involved [in the conflict].

The chief of the Russian General Staff had talked with his American counterpart, the chairman of the Joint Chiefs of Staff, about how the deescalation zones would be set up. Judging from Mattis's reaction, despite previous positive assessments, the White House was not sure about the feasibility of the Astana plan and wanted to understand what role its guarantor countries would assign to the US-led coalition. According to a source in Lavrov's delegation, what made Washington most doubtful was Iran's participation in the peace plan. The White House had hoped to receive confirmation from the Russian foreign minister that the Iranian Armed Forces, as well as groups associated with Tehran that are fighting on the side of Damascus, would not be deployed in the deescalation zones or recruited as monitors of the peace plan. According to RG sources, Lavrov offered Tillerson explanations about provisions that are not spelled out in the Astana memorandum, but were negotiated by the guarantors of the deescalation zone agreement.

Ahead of the meeting between Lavrov and Tillerson, their diplomatic corps had convened experts from the two countries for behind-the-scenes meetings in Vienna in a "2+2" format. There, too, [participants] discussed the points of the Syria agreement that raised questions at the White House. These included a possible ban on flights by US-led coalition aircraft over the deescalation zones. According to [Russian] Deputy Foreign Minister Vladimir [sic; Mikhail] Bogdanov, the possible "involvement of Americans in the role of monitors in those areas must be discussed by military officials and experts, taking into account the views of the guarantor states." However, the mere fact that such an idea has been proposed indicates Washington's potential wish to participate in an arrangement that would allow the US to seize the initiative in the intra-Syrian settlement process.

The change of venue of the Lavrov-Tillerson talks—which took place at the American capital, rather than the Arctic Council [ministerial meeting] slated for the end of the week in Fairbanks, Alaska—was another indication of how important the Astana initiatives are to Washington. [It also showed] sincere motivation on the White House's part to have the Russian foreign minister meet with the US secretary of state. The Astana memorandum was supported by representatives of more than 25 armed opposition groups operating in Syria.

According to a source in the Russian delegation, a pilot deescalation zone will be set up in southern Syria, in areas along the Israeli border; this idea, too, was discussed at the Lavrov-Tillerson talks. The Russian president's press secretary, Dmitry Peskov, commented: "These zones will make it possible to preserve the territorial integrity of Syria, [and] avoid a situation where the country is divided into some ephemeral zones of influence."

Russian and American military officials had already renewed their agreement on aviation cooperation in Syria. But Wednesday's negotiations between Lavrov and Tillerson marked a substantial step forward in bolstering geopolitical interaction between Moscow and Washington in Syria....

President Trump Pushes for 'Arab NATO' in the Middle East

By Andrei Akulov. *Strategic Culture Foundation Online Journal,* May 23, 2017, https://www.strategic-culture.org/news/2017/05/23/president-trump-pushes-for-arab-nato-middle-east.html.

President Donald Trump's visit to Saudi Arabia on May 21 signals a lot of things. The religious center of the Muslim world was the first stop on the president's first trip abroad. The largest arms deal in US history was signed, and a renewal of the American-Sunni Muslim alliance was announced after a period of relative "nothingness" or stagnation during president Obama's tenure. Donald Trump addressed more than 40 Muslim leaders at the Arab Islamic American Summit in Riyadh.

The president called on the leaders to unite to "drive out the terrorists," adding that Muslim countries had to "fulfill their part of the burden"—not just wait for American intervention. Sounds very much like the calls for the US's NATO partners to increase their share of the burden. The eradication of [ISIS] is presented as the main objective, but the containment of Iranian influence in the region topped the agenda.

The Saudi capital was decorated with images of the US president and the Saudi king side by side. The slogan said that together the two will prevail, indicating the renewed bond between the economic partners and military allies opposing the common enemy—Iran—together with the Arab Gulf States and Israel, which was the next stop on the president's trip. Jordan and Egypt have a history of constructive relations with the Jewish state, while Saudi Arabia and the United Arab Emirates (UAE) formally view it as an enemy, despite reports of clandestine contacts.

In the headline address, Trump signaled his intention to end engagement with Iran and declared his commitment to Sunni Arab nations, signaling a return to the policy of building alliances, regardless of differences in approaches concerning certain issues or human rights records. The US administration has made a choice, picking a side in the geopolitical struggle. "From Lebanon to Iraq to Yemen, Iran funds arms and trains terrorists, militias and other extremist groups that spread destruction and chaos across the region," Trump told dozens of Muslim heads of state attending the summit.

The idea of an "Arab NATO" is not new. The Arab (Sunni) military alliance has until now been seen as part of a continuing trend in the Middle East. Since 2013, Saudi Arabia has been actively pushing for increased regional military coordination. An attempt to create a response force of 40,000 was made in 2015 to bring together troops from Egypt, Jordan, Morocco, Saudi Arabia, Sudan, and a few other Gulf nations. The concept never came to fruition because of internal disputes.

Some attempts have been made, such as the February 2016 Saudi Arabia-led massive military exercise, called Northern Thunder, which included military assets and troops from around 20 different countries. The only functional participation has come from the GCC states—Egypt, Jordan and Pakistan—but it was a step on the way to integrating Sunni Muslim states' forces.

Meanwhile, Saudi Arabia and the UAE have either established or are preparing three military bases strategically located around the western shore of the Red Sea and on the Gulf of Aden to counter Iran. In January 2017, the Egyptian Navy established a naval force in the Red Sea. The Red Sea force will utilize naval equipment and helicopters to be acquired from Russia.

This year, the idea to revive the project was discussed during the visit by Crown Prince and Defense Minister of Saudi Arabia Mohammed bin Salman (March 13–17) and by Egyptian President [Abdel Fattah] el-Sisi (April 3) to Washington. In both cases, the sides agreed upon the need to establish an Arab analogue of NATO to deter the growing influence of Iran in the region.

Initial participants in the coalition would include Saudi Arabia, the UAE, Bahrain, Qatar, Kuwait, Egypt and Jordan, with the US playing an organizing and supporting role while formally staying outside the alliance it would lead in practice. For the Arab countries involved, the alliance would have a NATO-style mutual-defense component under which an attack on one member would be treated as an attack on all, though details are still being worked out.

The idea of forming a military alliance is bolstered by the defense cooperation deal the US president signed with Saudi King Salman, pledging $110 billion effective immediately and up to $350 billion over 10 years. The largest military package includes littoral combat ships, THAAD missile defense systems, tanks, armored personnel carriers, missiles, bombs and munitions, communications, and cybersecurity technology.

The concept is seen as a way to strengthen US standing in the region and make the allied states increase their financial contribution to regional security. The deal will create tens of thousands of new jobs in the US defense industry and make the future bloc dependent on American arms, while keeping other arms exporters away.

The US plans are extremely hard to implement. Arab countries have always been riddled with disagreements. The key actors—Saudi Arabia, the UAE, Jordan and Egypt—have different strategies and goals. The Middle East has seen a number of attempts at joining military forces since World War II: the Arab League's Joint Defense Pact, the Middle East Command, the Middle East Defense Organization, the Baghdad Pact (officially known as the Middle East Treaty Organization), or indeed the Gulf Cooperation

Council (GCC). None of them succeeded, due to internal and external strife.

Arab leaders again failed to reach a consensus on Iran at the Arab League Summit in Jordan on March 29, 2017. The divisions prevented them from including any direct condemnation of Iran for its "expansionism" in the Middle East, despite great efforts by Saudi Arabia.

The "Arab NATO" has a long way to go to become a strong player. Troops from Sunni Muslim states could become part of the equation in Syria if they contribute to multinational forces in control of the deescalation zones. The Sunni-populated areas would be the right places for them to be deployed. This would be a real contribution to regional stability.

In this case, they wouldn't have to oppose Iran but rather coordinate activities with it, carrying out the same peacekeeping mission. To do so, they will need an actor that does not take sides in the Sunni-Shia rift and can be a connecting link and a mediator, if need be. With the US taking an overtly hostile stance on Iran, hardly anybody but Moscow is fit for the role.

In Astana, Russia not only offered to mediate between Saudi Arabia and Iran, but it even hosted some discussions between them. It could be the latest diplomatic player looking to end the two-year war in Yemen. It's already mediating to end the conflict in Libya. Moscow is the most suitable Middle East mediator, as it talks to all sides except the jihadists. It can help Riyadh and Tehran agree to delineate and respect each other's spheres of influence in the Middle East region. The US, by contrast, is not on speaking terms with a number of Middle Eastern actors, like Iran, Hezbollah, the Houthis in Yemen, etc.

If the goal is to put an end to regional conflicts, the mediated diplomatic efforts will be much more effective than attempts to create an Arab NATO—a loose association of states dominated by the US with its long history of failed involvement in Middle Eastern affairs.

Trump Appears in the East

By Anzhelika Basisini. *RBC Daily*, May 24, 2017, p. 7.

US President Donald Trump has completed the Middle Eastern segment of his first trip abroad [as president]. In Saudi Arabia and Israel, the US president called for standing up to Iran, and did not clarify his approach to a Palestinian-Israeli settlement.

On Tuesday, May 23, US President Donald Trump flew from Israel to Italy, ending a four-day stay in the Middle East. Trump's first foreign trip as head of the White House had begun May 20 with a two-day visit to Saudi Arabia, after which he visited Israel.

Trump's speeches in both countries focused on threats coming from Iran. At a meeting of the Arab Islamic American Summit in Riyadh on May 21, the US president called for strengthening the international isolation of Iran after accusing Tehran of financing terrorism, supporting the regime of Bashar Assad in Syria and publicly calling for the destruction of Israel. According to Trump, "Iran has fueled the fires of sectarian conflict and terror" in the Middle East for decades. The US president called on the leaders of Arab and Muslim countries to unite their efforts and shoulder part of the burden of fighting extremism and terrorism.

In a statement adopted at the conclusion of the summit, leaders of the Islamic world expressed readiness to form a reserve contingent of 34,000 soldiers to conduct antiterrorist operations in Iraq and Syria. However, the leaders did not say when this contingent—dubbed an "Arab NATO" by the media—would be formed and what its mandate would be.

At a meeting on May 22 with Israeli President Reuven Rivlin, Trump again lashed out at Iran. "Most importantly, the United States and Israel can declare with one voice that Iran must never be allowed to possess a nuclear weapon—never, ever," Trump said (quoted by Reuters). Trump advised the Israeli president to take advantage of the fact that at the moment, many Middle Eastern countries have sided with Israel because of what is happening in Iran: He said Israel could take advantage of the benefits presented by the situation. Trump's declared position coincides with the approach to Iran of most Middle Eastern countries, including Israel and Saudi Arabia, and contradicts the position Trump took during his election campaign. During the campaign, Trump called Saudi Arabia, not Iran, the chief sponsor of terrorism, although he criticized Tehran for hypothetical noncompliance with the nuclear deal.

During his trip, Trump criticized not only Iran, but also the forces that Tehran supports in the region: the Palestinian movement Hamas and the Lebanese Shiite group Hezbollah.

Iranian President Hassan Rouhani, who was reelected on May 19, reacted to the statements. He called the summit a "show devoid of political and practical usefulness." Washington should stop [pursuing] militaristic policies, intervening in the domestic affairs of other states, spreading Iranophobia, and selling dangerous and useless weapons to the chief sponsors of terrorism, Iranian Foreign Ministry spokesman Bahram Ghassemi said in response to the May 22 statements of the American president. According to him, the American president's main purpose was to sell American weapons to countries in the region. The main commercial result of Trump's visit to Riyadh was a nearly $110 billion arms deal.

"Trump's anti-Iran rhetoric demonstrates the behavior that his Middle Eastern allies expect of him," Leonid Isayev, a senior lecturer at the Higher School of Economics, told RBC. According to the expert, Middle Eastern leaders are demonstrating their loyalty to Washington, and in exchange they are counting on guarantees of stability and protection, as was the case before the administration of the previous US president, Barack Obama. Obama pursued a different strategy. He believed the main threat to be ISIS (banned in Russia), not Iran, so he was willing to cooperate with Tehran on fighting terrorism, Isayev explains.

With his visit and exchange of courtesies, Trump showed the rulers of Saudi Arabia that the [US-Saudi] relationship will evolve differently under his administration, but this does not mean that a real coalition against Iran will be formed, since nobody needs a war, Isayev said.

Trump's "historic"—as Israeli Prime Minister Benjamin Netanyahu put it—two-day visit to Israel did not clarify the new American administration's approach to settling the Palestinian-Israeli conflict. At the beginning of his time in Israel, Trump confirmed the inviolability of the union between the US and the state of Israel. He said this about it before leaving: "My administration will always stand with Israel" (quoted by Reuters)....

During his visit to Israel, Trump met not only with leaders of the Jewish state, but also with Palestinian President Mahmoud Abbas. The meeting in Bethlehem was their second of late (Abbas visited Washington on May 3). However, the participants did not mention specific agreements.

Speaking about a possible solution to the problem, Trump said that it should be reached in an environment free of violence. Abbas did not comment on Trump's words about violence. According to the Palestinian leader, the conflict with Israel is not religious in nature, but the main problem is the continuing settlement activity by Israel in the disputed territories (the West Bank) and the non-recognition of the Palestinian state. Abbas repeated his position that a peaceful solution should be based on creating two separate states within the 1967 boundaries.

Trump did not talk about the two-state principle on this trip. He had previously indicated that he is fine with any solution that satisfies the parties. Netanyahu also did not address the possibility of a Palestinian state and the issue of [control over] Jerusalem. The Israeli prime minister said on Monday that a peace agreement with the Palestinians must be real and lasting, and [must] recognize the Jewish state.

The American president's Middle Eastern strategy did not become any clearer as a result of the visit, because he does not have a clear understanding of the situation in the region—largely due to a shortage of experts at the State Department, Isayev explained. Trump has an overall approach to addressing problems in the Middle East; he doesn't have specifics, but is demonstrating his intentions and indicating which parties he is prepared to negotiate with in the future, the expert says....

Top Salesman

By Fyodor Lukyanov, research professor at the National Research University Higher School of Economics. *Rossiiskaya gazeta*, July 10, 2017, p. 2.

America is against everyone on all the major talking points—from climate to global trade. All the attention is on Putin and Trump. China is keeping a low profile, preferring to stay in the shadows. Super-active France is trying to make up the ground it has lost in international leadership over the past few years. And radical antiglobalization protesters, whom we had already forgotten about, are making a comeback. These are the main results of the G-20 summit in Hamburg, the club's most interesting high-level meeting since its inception in 2008.

The summit clearly demonstrated how everything in the global economy and international politics is intertwined and interconnected, and how changing one significant factor entails a wide variety of consequences. . . .

A remarkable situation is unfolding with regard to Syria and Ukraine. Six months ago, many speculated—some with hope, some with horror—that Trump and Putin could barter Ukraine for Syria. There was talk that Russia might pull back in the Middle East, allowing the US to restore its former influence there, and in exchange the Americans would reduce support for Kiev, giving Moscow more opportunities. In my opinion, this sort of simplification—reducing complicated circumstances to a primitive conceptualization—is always futile, but the discussion reflected [such] expectations. In fact, to take the simplification even further, now almost the reverse is on the table: giving Syria to Russia and Ukraine to America.

It seems the US actually does want to enhance its influence in this crucial area for Russia. Washington would not mind walking away from Syria, leaving Moscow to deal with that issue—more specifically, maintaining some leverage [there] but not assuming any long-term responsibility. Trump's interest in Ukraine can be presumed from his triumphal visit to Poland on the way to Hamburg. Trump acted like a salesman there, not only securing an order for Patriot missiles, but also strongly pushing American [natural] gas as an alternative to Russian gas. Polish President Andrzej Duda enthusiastically jumped on the idea, proposing his country as a hub for distributing American gas across Eastern Europe, including Ukraine.

To what extent that is feasible and economically viable is an open question. But it illustrates very well the approach and hierarchy of views. The emergence of a "wheeling and dealing" US president is flustering everyone else beyond measure. But he is the guy they have to deal with. So, starting with this G-20 summit, we will be getting used to such peculiarities.

Trial Agreement

By Aleksei Khlebnikov, Middle East expert at the Russian International Affairs Council. *Vedomosti*, July 11, 2017, p. 6.

The first meeting between the Russian and US presidents took place on the sidelines of the G-20 summit in Hamburg. Instead of meeting for one hour as planned, Vladimir Putin and Donald Trump spent 2 hours 20 minutes with each other. Russian-American relations are in a sorry state; a lot of problems and issues have been piling up. Apparently, Moscow and Washington have decided to focus on issues where progress is possible. Despite all the differences, there are several problems that Russia and the US can and must tackle together—Syria being the most pressing.

Even before his election, Trump had emphasized that [the US] and Moscow must jointly fight ISIS and Al Qaeda ([both] banned in Russia). Russia, in turn, has been waiting for the US to change its approach. Even though the Trump administration still has no clear Syria strategy, it has an understanding of a range of things affecting American policy in the region.

First, Trump does not want to involve the US in another war in the Middle East. Second, he does not want to exacerbate the situation in Syria, especially by entering into direct confrontation with Russia, because that could lead to unpredictable consequences. Third, Trump plans to cooperate with Russia on fighting terrorism. Fourth, Trump wants to demonstrate an approach to Syria that is different from Obama's soft and indecisive policies, since that would allow him to score more political points at home.

All four principles create a solid platform for in-depth discussions between Moscow and Washington on Syria.

It is no coincidence that the fifth round of Syria negotiations in Astana took place ahead of the Putin-Trump meeting, and that talks in Geneva will resume immediately after the G-20 summit wraps up. In fact, a lot of preparatory work had been done before the US and Russian presidents met. Following telephone conversations between Putin and Trump, as well as Tillerson's visit to Moscow and Lavrov's visit to the US, a working group was established for a number of purposes, including working out issues to be discussed during the presidents' first meeting. The US participated in the Syria negotiations in Astana. And in the spring, it raised its level of participation, sending an assistant secretary of state instead of its ambassador to Kazakhstan. This allowed the US to join the discussion of deescalation zones, as well as to voice its concerns and disagreements. As a result, both sides came to the talks in Germany with specific preliminary agreements in hand.

At the end of the meeting between Putin and Trump, the parties agreed to a ceasefire in southwestern Syria (Jordan is also party to the agreement). This is a new area that is not part of the four [existing] deescalation zones that Russia, Turkey and Iran agreed on in May. Southern Syria had been a sticking point for achieving consensus between Russia and the US. First, Washington has its own deescalation zone near the city of al-Tanf (on the border of Syria, Jordan and Iraq), where it is training opposition troops and from which the US has launched attacks on progovernment forces in the past two months. Second, Jordan and Israel have repeatedly expressed concern about the growing influence of Iranian forces in southern Syria.

This agreement confirms the US's growing role in Syria and Washington's desire to protect its allies. It also confirms Moscow's desire to come to terms, creating a common platform for further action in Syria. It is important to note that Putin had a telephone conversation with Israeli Prime Minister Benjamin Netanyahu immediately after the Astana talks concluded. Moscow is choosing to show regard for Tel Aviv's concerns. So the understanding that emerged between Moscow, Washington and Amman is an entirely logical result of the negotiations on designating deescalation zones in southern Syria....

4.3

Loose Cannons: Nuclear Policy and North Korea

Introduction

Most of the coverage in this section is prompted by the Trump administration's aggressive early statements on military policy (nuclear weapons in particular) and by North Korea's spate of missile tests. According to CBS News, Pyongyang conducted at least 11 such tests during Trump's first six months in office, including two separate launches of ICBMs in July 2017.

On Trump's nuclear policy, Russian political analysts offer different interpretations of similar facts. For example, Fyodor Lukyanov writes that Trump has no intention of reducing nuclear arms, as previous US presidents have done; he quotes Trump as saying: "We're never going to fall behind any country even if it's a friendly country, we're never going to fall behind on nuclear power." Based on this and other statements, Lukyanov concludes: "Trump is harking back to the period that to him defines America's golden age: the 1950s, when it wielded global might and influence, but without excessive commitments—and, most importantly, without political correctness. A time when there were no nuclear arms control agreements."

Likewise, Vladimir Kozin cites the Trump administration's proposed increases to the military budget and quotes Trump as saying with respect to Russia: "Let it be an arms race. We will outmatch them at every pass and outlast them all." And yet Kozin also writes that when it comes to details, Trump has been indefinite about nuclear policy, sending mixed messages about building up nuclear forces but also being open to negotiation with Russia. From this evidence, the analyst holds out hope that Putin and Trump together can turn back the Doomsday Clock.

With regard to North Korea in particular, Russian commentators are leery of both Washington's and Moscow's motives. Aleksandr Zhebin, in anticipation of Chinese President Xi Jinping's April visit to Mar-a-Lago, surmises that Trump would try to pressure Xi economically to curb Pyongyang's nuclear ambitions: "Trump is apparently trying to convince China to implement UN Security Council sanctions against North Korea according to Washington's interpretation.... China's refusal would give Trump a glib excuse for imposing the anti-Chinese trade sanctions he talked so much about during the election campaign.... China will essentially be given a choice: Either it steps up pressure on North Korea, or it will have to respond somehow to US military action on its borders." Andrei Akulov paints a less convoluted picture of Trump's motivations: He needs a "short victorious war" to shore up his shaky status in Washington.

Meanwhile, Russian experts are critical of Moscow's motives as well. After Rex Tillerson announces in March (following Kim Jong-un's launch of Rodong missiles) that "the policy of strategic patience has ended," Foreign Minister Sergei Lavrov assures him that Russia and its Chinese counterparts had some ideas about how to "resolve this problem through peaceful means only." "Yet as far as we know," Vladimir Frolov writes in an April 21 article, "Russia has not done anything of note to that end, except to block a joint statement by the UN Security Council condemning North Korea for developing nuclear weapons and conducting missile tests." Alexander Gabuev confirms to *The Moscow Times* that Russia actually has very little economic or diplomatic leverage with North Korea: Russia controls only 5% of North Korea's trade. In a later article, Frolov argues that the North Korea crisis benefits Russia in several respects. For example, it distracts Trump from being proactive elsewhere (Europe, the Middle East and the post-Soviet space); complicates US-Chinese relations; and gives Putin a chance to step in as the "pragmatic sage," giving Moscow room to maneuver. "Escalating tensions, not to mention a real armed confrontation, ties the US's hands and, by the Kremlin's logic, strengthens Russia's security." However, Frolov warns, Russia's logic of abetting North Korea as it develops nuclear weapons and ballistic missiles could someday backfire: "Ukraine could also be included in this chain of associations."

As a potential way out of the North Korean nuclear impasse, both Zhebin and Frolov recommend that Russia help broker a North Korea nuclear accord similar to the one that the West worked out with Iran in 2015—i.e., that they use the positive incentive of eased sanctions to scale back the missile program.

Aleksei Arbatov takes a longer view of nuclear relations, pointing out the dangers of multipolar nuclear potential in today's world. According to him, the greatest threat is not North Korea's aggressive stance, but the fact that Russia and the US are not actively cooperating on nuclear policy. "For the first time in more than half a century of nuclear arms negotiations and agreements...the world faces the imminent prospect of losing treaty-based legal controls over the most destructive weapons in the history of humankind." The weakest link, Arbatov writes, is the 1987 USSR-US Treaty on the Elimination of Intermediate-Range and Shorter-Range Missiles (INF). In addition, Trump has shown no interest in extending the New START arms reduction treaty. Arbatov concludes that now is the time for Moscow to make "serious proposals" to save the arms control regime.

Second Nuclear Century?

By Fyodor Lukyanov, chairman of the presidium of the Council on Foreign and Defense Policy. *Rossiiskaya gazeta*, Feb. 27, 2017, p. 6.

Donald Trump is obsessed with nuclear weapons. During his one month in office, he brought up the subject of nuclear weapons and Russia at least three times, not to mention his statements about the importance of strengthening [America's] nuclear arsenal in general. In an interview with Reuters late last week, the American president was explicit: He intends not only to stop arms reductions, but also plans to build up the arsenal to make it "top of the pack." "We're never going to fall behind any country even if it's a friendly country, we're never going to fall behind on nuclear power." Trump's intention is apparently to refuse to extend the New START treaty between Russia and the US that is set to expire next year.

Whether a "top of the pack" [nuclear arsenal] also means the biggest remains to be seen. Donald Trump has only a rough understanding of the nuclear issue. But the president's persistence in bringing it up is telling, and it must be treated with all seriousness. For the first time in a long while, a leading world politician is raising the issue of building up—not reducing—nuclear arms. As [Federation Council member] Aleksei Pushkov rightly stated in commenting on Trump's remark, this brings the world back to the 20th century—in fact, to a time when relations in this sphere were not very clearly defined.

The nuclear issue is a reference point for Moscow and Washington. And nothing can be done about that, as long as the two countries have the potential to destroy one another. It is too important a factor to forget about, even if a nuclear war remains out of the question for any sober-minded politician. This explains why relations [between the two countries] have been in a loop since the mid-20th century, i.e., since the start of the nuclear deadlock—constantly up and down, occasionally on the brink, but without going over the edge. The end of the cold war erased the lines in the sand, and that edge supposedly disappeared because it was no longer relevant. However, the technical capabilities remained, which doomed the cycle to repeat itself.

The failure to establish a new global system of order after the cold war led to the revival of the nuclear agenda—first as a means of containment, and then as an expansionist ambition. At the crucial stage of Western expansion, when NATO was seriously considering accepting Georgia and Ukraine, Moscow deemed it acceptable not only to apply military leverage to prevent this, but also to remind [the world] of its nuclear capabilities. This made its interlocutors nervous, but it worked: Direct military confrontation—which started to loom as a concern during the Georgian conflict, and even more so during the Ukrainian one—has been avoided.

However, every action has an equal and opposite reaction, and those who see nuclear weapons as a means of containment are sometimes joined by people who see it as a way to achieve dominance. Which is basically where Trump comes in.

Don't expect a return to the 1980s, with rampant spending and a nuclear arms race just for the sake of competition. The military will, of course, always find a way to spend the funds it is given, but for now the level of insanity is luckily not high enough to justify excessive spending. More than likely, Trump is harking back to the period that to him defines America's golden age: the 1950s, when it wielded global might and influence, but without excessive commitments—and, most importantly, without political correctness. A time when there were no nuclear arms control agreements, which first appeared in the 1960s. Before the creation of an effective oversight and containment system, the world experienced a difficult period, culminating in the Cuban missile crisis in 1962.

As always, Trump is being grotesque, but the idea that the old model of arms control agreements has exhausted itself has been said before. Back in the day, the George W. Bush administration doubted the expediency of maintaining the existing system of restrictions, instead advocating for the idea of reasonable sufficiency. In other words, each party creates its own list of threats and determines what it needs to prevent them. As Andrew Krepinevich, a prominent specialist on military policy, wrote recently, "The First Nuclear Age was characterized by the cold war-era bipolar international system and a corresponding bipolar nuclear competition between the United States and the Soviet Union." This makes creating a new model difficult, since it's unclear how to define various threats—from the ongoing [threat of] "mutually assured destruction" of Russia and the US, to the presence of nuclear states that either refuse to participate in any sort of oversight processes (China) or continue to improve their capabilities in order to address their own regional tasks (North Korea).

Statements like Trump's are risky, because they are not backed by any thought-out idea on how to change the system, but are driven by a desire to get rid of any restrictions in order to negotiate with one's hands untied. But abandoning an existing model does not necessarily result in a new one. And if the "second nuclear century" really is upon us, we need a serious discussion on how to maintain control. Russia should be the one to show initiative here. If we continue to simply react to everything Washington does, as has been our habit for the last few decades, we could find ourselves in a situation where we are playing by someone else's rules.

Donald Trump's Nuclear Policy: First Outlines

By Prof. Vladimir Kozin, chief adviser to the director of the Russian Institute for Strategic Studies. *International Affairs*, No. 3, 2017, pp. 111–120.

US President Donald Trump has inherited large strategic and tactical nuclear arsenals from his predecessor, Barack Obama, and a strategy of "unconditional offensive nuclear deterrence," which allows for the possibility of a preemptive nuclear strike against practically any country that is not an ally, friend or partner of the United States.

The rich legacy.

In January 2017, outgoing vice-president Joe Biden announced that, as of Sept. 30, 2016, the US possessed a total of 4,018 deployed and undeployed strategic and tactical warheads that were in service....

Obama left behind an extensive negative nuclear policy record. The 44th president left Trump with more than 15 unsolved problems to deal with, primarily the nuclear deterrence doctrine, the increased American military presence in Europe and Asia, initial stages in the deployment of the planned global layered missile defense, and modernization programs for the strategic and tactical nuclear missile forces. Had Hillary Clinton won the presidential election, solutions would have been put off indefinitely. She would even have gone further than Obama in nuclear rearmament, according to an article that appeared on Oct. 28, 2016 in *The New York Times*, an openly pro-Democratic daily.

While verbally championing a nuclear-free world, Obama carried out much smaller reductions of the US's stockpiles of nuclear warheads than his three immediate predecessors. He cut them by 10%, while George Bush Sr. slashed them by 41%, Bill Clinton by 22%, and George Bush Jr. by 50%....

Obama urged his successor not to adopt a minimal nuclear deterrence strategy. He never replaced the doctrine of mutual assured destruction with a more constructive mutual assured security doctrine. He also refused to adopt a no-first-use strategy....

Will Trump stick to the nuclear legacy of his predecessor or take another route? There is no clear answer yet to this fundamental and multifaceted question. Why?

Trump's military policy: first outlines.

Until now, Trump has made rather few statements about the US's future nuclear policy. He made most of them before the presidential election, mainly in Republican Platform 2016, the Republican election manifesto, of which he was one of the authors, and in some of his interviews. Republican Platform 2016 is so far the only detailed document setting out what appear to have become the priorities of Trump's military policy and strategy.

The platform criticizes the state of the US strategic nuclear forces and insists on the modernization of the country's traditional classic strategic nuclear triad. It attacks New START (Strategic Arms Reduction Treaty), a Russian-American agreement of 2010 that "has allowed Russia to build up its nuclear arsenal while reducing ours" and is "so weak in verification and definitions that it is virtually impossible to prove a violation." Trump launched a new attack on New START in an interview with Reuters on Feb. 23, 2017, branding it as "a one-sided deal" advantageous to Russia. Like Obama, Trump accused Russia of departing from the 1987 Intermediate-Range Nuclear Forces Treaty by allegedly developing a new cruise missile. But, like his predecessor, he provided no evidence of this.

Trump and Defense Secretary Jim Mattis have called for the modernization of the US strategic nuclear forces. Trump said on Twitter on Dec. 22, 2016: "The United States must greatly strengthen and expand its nuclear capability until such time as the world comes to its senses regarding nukes." Mika Brzezinski, a host on the MSNBC news television network, quoted Trump as saying the same month: "Let it be an arms race. We will outmatch them at every pass and outlast them all." Soon after that, Trump's press secretary, Sean Spicer, interpreted this statement as a warning to other nations not to seek to undermine US sovereignty.

At the same time, in one of his pre-election interviews, Trump said that his administration would be prepared to sign a legally binding agreement with Russia under which each country would pledge not to be the first to use a nuclear weapon against the other. During a hearing in Congress in January, Mattis said that the administration would like to hammer out a policy that would rule out the possibility of the United States ever using nuclear weapons. He questioned an initiative by the Obama administration to make a new air-launched nuclear cruise missile....

Trump's military policy is under heavy pressure from the Democratic Party. Two days before Trump's inauguration, two Democratic lawmakers, Sen. Edward Markey and Rep. Ted Lieu, introduced a bill to prohibit the new president from ordering a preemptive nuclear strike against anyone before the declaration of war by Congress. Markey and Lieu claimed that, during his election campaign, Trump had made contradictory statements on proliferation and on the first-strike issue. Before taking office, Trump did say that he would never order a preemptive nuclear strike, but added that he would be prepared to use any of the resources offered by the US's nuclear status. In October 2016, 10 former nuclear launch control officers wrote an open letter asking for Trump to be denied access to the country's nuclear launch codes because of his alleged incompetence.

As of March 1, 2017, there remained a whole range of aspects of the US's extensive and multifaceted nuclear policy that Trump still had not gotten around to, despite North Korean nuclear missile tests in 2016 and the political and military antagonism of India and Pakistan, both of which are nuclear powers. (Obama had spoken on those issues frequently.)

For this reason, on Jan. 26, 2017, the Science and Security Board of the Bulletin of the Atomic Scientists set the symbolic Doomsday Clock on the homepage of the magazine's Web site at two and a half minutes to the "catastrophic" midnight, instead of three minutes as had been the case before Trump was sworn in as president.

Trump has neither expressed support for nor modified Obama's proposal for an agreement with Moscow to further reduce the American and Russian strategic nuclear arsenals by about one-third from levels set by New START, which was signed in Prague in April 2010. Under New START, each country was to bring its number of nuclear warheads to 1,550 and its number of deployed delivery vehicles to 700 by 2018. Trump has proposed no other reduction options yet. After taking office, he has just said that he is open to an agreement with Moscow to substantially reduce nuclear stockpiles in exchange for lifting some of the economic sanctions against Russia. Moscow has turned down the idea at the official and expert levels, because of the unequal terms suggested by Trump....

Trump is avoiding withdrawing American tactical nuclear warheads deployed in four European countries and the Asian part of Turkey to the continental US, something that Russia has insisted on for a long time. Moscow pulled all former Soviet tactical nuclear weapons from Belarus, Kazakhstan and Ukraine to Russian territory by the mid-1990s. Gen. Mattis advocates sales of Lockheed Martin F-35C fighter-bombers, which can carry nuclear bombs, to European member states of NATO. The Pentagon is sticking to an "extended nuclear deterrence" strategy, which involves bringing 32 countries that are US allies under an American nuclear umbrella. Some of these countries are members of NATO and some are not. Trump has pledged to comply with "nuclear sharing" arrangements (agreements on joint nuclear missions) with NATO member countries that have no nuclear weapons of their own.

The 45th president has not stated his position on the Comprehensive Nuclear Test Ban Treaty (CTBT), a document the Senate refused to ratify in 1999.... Russia ratified it back in 2000.

Will the US resume full-scale compliance with the plutonium agreement of 2000 during Trump's presidency? His position on this accord will be a litmus test: Will his administration accumulate excess weapons-grade plutonium in a bid to make nuclear warheads?

Trump has not announced whether he will stick to the "Chicago triad," a war mechanism created at a NATO summit in Chicago in May 2012—a transatlantic group of nuclear, missile defense and conventional forces to be deployed near Russian borders....

Trump has repeatedly slammed the 2015 Iran nuclear deal, often calling it the "worst deal ever negotiated," but has shown no intention to seek its renegotiation.

Neither has he shown any desire to end the policy of blocking a proposal by some Arab and other states for creating a zone in the Middle East free from all three classical types of weapons of mass destruction—nuclear, chemical and biological. Previous US administrations constantly torpedoed the proposal.

Summing up, the new president's nuclear creed needs clarification. Sooner or later, he will have to make clear whether he wants his country's nuclear stockpiles to be enlarged or reduced. Most likely, at some point he will initiate some changes to two documents underlying US nuclear policy: the Nuclear Posture Review and US Nuclear Employment Strategy.

In an executive order of Jan. 27, Trump directed Mattis to "initiate a new Nuclear Posture Review to ensure that the United States nuclear deterrent is modern, robust, flexible, resilient, ready, and appropriately tailored to deter 21st-century threats and reassure our allies." This effectively means a task to modernize the nuclear forces and make them more efficient.

Will Trump agree?

Russia should come up with some practical armaments control proposals without waiting for Trump to clarify his position. Moscow should seek no-first-use treaties with the US and other nuclear member countries of NATO, or treaties completely banning the use of nuclear weapons. These should be legally binding documents with no expiration dates. It would, however, be the wrong decision for Russia to agree to the extension of New START or to signing an updated bilateral START because of the uncontrolled deployment of global missile defense and the modernization of US tactical nuclear weapons deployed near Russian borders. New START is the last bilateral deal that it made sense for Russia to enter. All nuclear countries, especially Britain and France as allies of the US with mutual commitments concerning strategic nuclear forces, should become involved in nuclear arms control negotiations. Russia should by no means cut its strategic nuclear forces any further. Some of these forces have been designed to overcome the American missile defense system, which is expanding uncontrollably; this expansion is dangerous and may set off a missile defense arms race....

Russia should propose a restrictive multilateral treaty on missile defenses, an agreement that would set range limits for missile interceptors and delineate deployment areas for them outside the territory of the state they belong to. Moscow should reiterate its demands that the US and its allies withdraw all their forces, especially heavy armaments, and new command facilities from European countries where they were deployed after April 1, 2014.

In putting forward such proposals, Moscow should stress that it is against nuclear war on any scale—limited, regional or global. At a meeting in Sochi in October 2016 of the Valdai Discussion Club, Russian President Vladimir Putin made a firm promise that Russia would always take its nuclear status very responsibly. He said that nuclear saber-rattling was "a despicable thing to do," and that the use of nuclear weapons would mean an end to world civilization.

In a telephone call on Jan. 28, Putin and Trump spoke about strategic stability and nonproliferation among various bilateral and international issues, and agreed to organize cooperation on these and other problems. This cooperation would be very important from the viewpoint of global peace and security. The Doomsday Clock of the Bulletin of the Atomic Scientists, which has gotten so close to a critical point since it was designed 70 years ago, must be turned back.

We Need an Iran Deal With North Korea

By Aleksandr Zhebin. *Nezavisimaya gazeta*, April 6, 2017, p. 3.

US President Donald Trump is to meet Chinese leader Xi Jinping for the first time since his election, today in Florida. Almost all observers believe that one of the main topics (if not the main topic) of the talks will be the US's attempt to convince China to join American efforts to compel Pyongyang to halt its nuclear missile program.

North Korean advancements last year raised serious concern in Washington. The main concern is what is regarded as the distinct possibility that North Korea could develop an intercontinental ballistic missile (ICBM) by 2020 that could deliver nuclear and perhaps thermonuclear warheads to the continental US.

During the run-up to the meeting, in an interview with *The Financial Times*, Trump actually threatened Beijing: If the Chinese refuse to help the US solve the North Korean nuclear problem, the Americans will do it themselves, although, as the president said, "it won't be good for anyone."

As with a tweet Trump wrote in response to North Korean leader Kim Jong-un's statement about an upcoming ICBM launch ("It won't happen!"), the interview prompted a wave of speculation about what the deliberately ambiguous phrases mean and what Washington's new policy will be toward Beijing and Pyongyang.

It is no secret that lately the US has been actively discussing the idea of preemptive strikes on North Korea's nuclear program sites. It was announced at the official level for the first time during US Secretary of State Rex Tillerson's recent visit to Asia, albeit cloaked in the diplomatic phrase that the US is considering "all options" with respect to North Korea. These options are being intensively rehearsed during joint US-South Korean military exercises taking place near North Korean borders.

This context draws attention to recent comments by the Russian Foreign Ministry's information and press department that both sides are responsible for the situation on the Korean peninsula, which is growing more tense "as a result of a new missile launch by North Korea on March 6 and the commencement of large-scale joint US and South Korean military exercises to rehearse offensive operations against North Korea."

It is hardly surprising that in such a situation, North Korea has accelerated its nuclear missile program. It appears Pyongyang intended to quickly achieve results that would convince the US and its allies that damage from choosing a military option would be unacceptably high for them.

Given that Tillerson has said that negotiations with North Korea are still premature, it is very likely that the situation will follow an already well-known scenario: rejection of dialogue, North Korean missile launches and nuclear tests, and new UN Security

Council sanctions on North Korea, plus additional sanctions from the US and its allies. A logical outcome of this scenario could be a large-scale armed conflict with a high likelihood of weapons of mass destruction being used right near our borders in the [Russian] Far East.

In the meantime, Trump is apparently trying to convince China to implement UN Security Council sanctions against North Korea according to Washington's interpretation. By doing so, Washington is hoping it will be able to destabilize the DPRK, cause its collapse and thus pave the way to the land borders of China and Russia in Asia for American troops.

China's refusal would give Trump a glib excuse for imposing the anti-Chinese trade sanctions he talked so much about during the election campaign but has still not dared to impose. China will essentially be given a choice: Either it steps up pressure on North Korea, or it will have to respond somehow to US military action on its borders.

The Korean peninsula has by all indications assumed an increasingly important role in implementing the US's Asia-Pacific strategy, the main objectives of which are containing China and Russia, continuing US military domination, and controlling regional allies. For almost 70 years, Washington has been using the unsettled Korean problem as a pretext for the continued deployment of American forward-based forces along Russian and Chinese borders, and now for the deployment of elements of a US global missile defense system. The emergence of the Korean issue as a leading topic in American-Chinese dialogue confirms that the peninsula has become one of the most complex knots in Chinese-US discord and could conceivably become an arena for the US and China to test their strength.

Meanwhile, it is already clear that merely talking about the need to implement UN Security Council resolutions and halt North Korea's missile launches and nuclear tests will not solve the problem. And although a compromise solution now appears virtually nonexistent, there is still time to achieve one.

Realistic approaches to resolving the situation could include the following:

- All parties recognize the desirability of a temporary moratorium on the actions that are causing the greatest concern for the other party, as a necessary intermediate step to stop the situation from deteriorating.

- [All parties] recognize the rationality of addressing the missile and nuclear issues separately. Due to their different natures and the fact that national-level resources for monitoring compliance with future accords on each of them have different capabilities, it would be easier to address them in isolation from one another.

- The US and its allies recognize that North Korea has legitimate security concerns, and consent to discuss and address related issues on a step-by-step basis.

In the big picture, what is needed to resolve the Korean problem is a deal as elaborately and chronologically structured as the one struck with Iran. For all the differences between the Korean and Iranian cases, the main lesson of the Iranian deal for Korea is that compromise—which initially seemed unattainable due to the virtually polar opposite positions of the US and Iran—was ultimately possible with political will, patient diplomacy and, at times, arm-twisting of the main disputants by the other negotiators.

False Calm: Why Russia Prefers Not to Notice the Nuclear Crisis at Its Borders

By international relations expert Vladimir Frolov. *Republic.ru*, April 21, 2017, https://republic.ru/posts/82098.

Ever since North Korea launched four Rodong medium-range missiles in early March as part of a simulated preventive nuclear strike on South Korean airports, seaports and US military bases in Japan, Washington and Pyongyang have been balancing on the brink of war—possibly a nuclear one.

The Trump administration abandoned the strategic patience policy that failed to prevent North Korea from acquiring nuclear weapons and long-range missiles. During his visit to Seoul on March 17, Secretary of State Rex Tillerson said all options were on the table, including military action "if they [North Korea] elevate the threat of their weapons program." By "threat," the US probably means North Korea preparing to test its intercontinental ballistic missile capable of reaching the US and conducting final tests of a thermonuclear warhead for such a missile. Right after he was elected, President Trump tweeted that "it won't happen," drawing a red line for himself worse than the one Obama drew with chemical weapons in Syria.

In stark contrast to this worrying situation, the Russian leadership and Foreign Ministry are treating a potential nuclear conflict near Russian borders (the North Korean nuclear test site is only 150 kilometers away) with Olympian detachment and even some indifference.

Russian TV news is still dominated by Syria.... Coverage of North Korea has been limited to simply restatements of Pyongyang's position, upbeat segments about fully stocked North Korean supermarkets (though the customers were leaving empty-handed), and home-grown PR about the life of the Great Leader and his progeny.

Vladimir Putin said nothing about the potential conflict around North Korea, and Foreign Minister Sergei Lavrov decided to play peacemaker after talks with Secretary Tillerson in Moscow: "We are all seeking to resolve this problem by peaceful political means and to denuclearize the Korean Peninsula through negotiations. We and our Chinese counterparts have some ideas about how to achieve that. We need to unite over our shared commitment to resolve this problem through peaceful means only." Yet as far as we know, Russia has not done anything of note to that end, except to block a joint statement by the UN Security Council condemning North Korea for developing nuclear weapons and conducting missile tests, saying it did not highlight the necessity of resolving the crisis through dialogue only....

Now it turns out that Moscow is helpless and prefers to keep quiet when there is a risk of a nuclear explosion (or several) 100 km from the Russian border that would bring a flood of refugees to Russia and bury any hope of "priority development" for priority development territories in the [Russian] Far East under radioactive dust. Not a word has been uttered by the government about plans to evacuate the people living in the border areas if a nuclear war does break out—it's as if the issue does not even exist. The silence seems odd next to all the chatter about a strategic pivot to the East and teaming up with China to form a Greater Eurasia. And it is particularly frustrating to see China engaged in dealing with the North Korean problem on par with the US while Russia remains on the sidelines. Chinese leader Xi Jinping visited Trump in Florida, which set Moscow's teeth on edge; the talks focused on the North Korean problem. China apparently promised to exert more pressure on Pyongyang and even discussed scenarios that would safeguard Chinese interests should a war break out and the North Korean regime collapse.

Moscow had been dreaming of a "New Yalta" where Russia, the US and China would rule the world together, but now it seems like three could be a crowd at this party. So the only thing left for Russia to do is to play the spoiler, as usual. This means supporting and defending Pyongyang in order to gain some influence with North Korea and then selling that influence to the US president....

Of course, the Foreign Ministry is working on how to push the US and North Korea to engage in direct talks and deescalate the situation, and these plans are being discussed with the Americans and the Chinese, but the US will not take Moscow's proposals seriously unless Russia strengthens its position.

However, blocking US proposals in the Security Council only weakens Russia's position, thus marginalizing the Council, which is the primary platform for Russian diplomacy. So far, limited use of military force has been Russia's preferred way of boosting its influence, securing leverage and creating favorable conditions for resolving a given crisis. But this has only worked in situations where Russia knew there would be no effective military response (e.g., Syria). When met with significant resistance (e.g., the Donetsk Basin), this strategy has resulted in a stalemate. With the North

Korean crisis, Russia thankfully does not have a limited military intervention option, so the lack of other effective foreign policy instruments is glaringly obvious. Thus, it is easier to save Assad in Syria and let the Chinese and the US save the Russian people from a nuclear war in North Korea. This kind of geopolitical outsourcing has been working for now, but it does not score the Russian leadership any reputational points.

Short Victorious War: US President's Magic Wand to Wave in a Pinch

By Andrei Akulov. *Strategic Culture Foundation Online Journal*, May 29, 2017, https://www.strategic-culture.org/news/2017/05/29/short-victorious-war-us-president-magic-wand-wave-pinch.html.

Putting together the bits of information coming from various sources leads one to the conclusion that a US preemptive strike against North Korea is a possibility that may turn into reality pretty soon. Everyone knows it's fraught with implications and nobody wants it but there is a good reason to believe it's coming.

North Korean leader Kim Jong-un has supervised the test of a new antiaircraft weapon system, and ordered its mass production and deployment throughout the country. It took place after Pyongyang conducted a second missile test within a week, sending a medium-range ballistic missile into the waters off its east coast on May 21. North Korea said the test was a success and the weapon could now be mass-produced. If a strike to knock out [North Korea's] nuclear and ballistic missile program infrastructure is planned, it needs to be delivered before the air defense systems are in place.

North Korea's missile program is progressing faster than expected, South Korea's defense minister said on May 16, after the UN Security Council condemned the launch of a new long-range missile and demanded Pyongyang halt weapons tests. North Korea has defied all calls to rein in its nuclear and missile programs, including from Russia and China. The country's leadership openly states that it has been working to develop a nuclear-tipped missile capable of striking the US mainland, and the recent tests are steps toward that goal. North Korea has conducted five nuclear tests so far, including two last year.

During the US-China summit at the Mar-a-Lago estate in Florida in early April, Chinese President Xi Jinping asked US President Donald Trump for a 100-day grace period to deal with North Korea's military provocations. The May 21 launch cast doubts on the efficacy of the measures taken. The 100-day period would end around the time the G-20 summit is held in Germany on July 7–8, with the problem of North Korea high on the agenda. US and Chinese leaders will tackle the burning issue on the sidelines of the event.

Meanwhile, Washington will deploy a third US aircraft carrier, the USS Nimitz, in the Western Pacific Ocean so it can join two US warships stationed near the shores of the Korean Peninsula in light of the crisis. The USS Nimitz will join the USS Carl Vinson and the USS Ronald Reagan in the area. Three carrier groups out of 11 is a huge force to be deployed, which would only be used for an impending large-scale operation.

The US is set to conduct another test of its Ground-based Midcourse Defense (GMD) system to shoot down an ICBM that would simulate a North Korean ICBM aimed at the US. The military has used the GMD system to intercept other types of missiles, but never an ICBM.

Finally, it has been recently revealed that the US military has moved two nuclear submarines near North Korea. President Trump was likely referring to an Ohio-class guided missile submarine (SSGN), the USS Michigan, which made an official port call in Busan, South Korea, on April 25, and the Los Angeles-class attack submarine (SSN) USS Cheyenne, which visited Sasebo, Japan, on May 2 as part of its regional deployment. The US Navy on average is deploying up to 10 Los Angeles-, Seawolf-, and Virginia-class attack submarines worldwide on any given day.

The USS Michigan is used for first strike missions. It is one of four Ohio-class strategic subs (SSBNs) converted to only fire conventional Tomahawks instead of nuclear ballistic missiles. The boat carries a massive load of 154 land attack cruise missiles. On top of that, the USS Michigan carries a dry deck shelter, which allows it to deploy special operations forces and their swimmer delivery vehicle mini subs. The USS Cheyenne is a Los Angeles-class attack submarine, which routinely accompanies carrier groups. It can fire Tomahawks.

Trump has said "a major, major conflict" with North Korea is possible because of its nuclear and missile programs, and that all options are on the table. On May 19, US Defense Secretary Jim Mattis expressed a cautious stance toward immediate military action against North Korea.

The US president is under assault from all sides. The possibility of his impeachment is being openly discussed in the media and in Congress. According to *Politico*, conservatives are starting to whisper "President Pence."

Donald Trump knows that military actions are an effective tool to hike ratings. The president saw a bump in his own poll numbers after the cruise missile strike in Syria he ordered on April 7. His approval rating jumped from 34% up to 42%. It leaped from 42% to 50% after the "mother of all bombs" was used on April 13 against ISIS positions in Afghanistan. Public support has dropped dramatically to roughly 38% since then. The president is in a bind. Something needs to be done immediately to rectify the situation.

The trend is worrisome, and the best tried-and-true way to reverse it is a short victorious war. True, it's a great risk. But bombing one's way to popularity may be a temptation impossible to resist. A sixth North Korean nuclear test or test-fire of an intercontinental ballistic missile may prompt action even before the 100-day "grace period" is over. The forces are there and poised. They cannot be in high alert standby mode too long. While world attention is riveted on Syria, a large-scale military conflict with terrible consequences may begin at any time, and the probability is very high.

Mutually Assured Distraction

By Matthew Kupfer. *The Moscow Times,* June 29, 2017, p. 2.

... In March, North Korea test-fired four ballistic missiles into the Sea of Japan. In response, the US began to deploy THAAD antimissile systems to South Korea. A month later, during a visit to the South, US Vice-President Mike Pence declared that the "era of strategic patience" with Pyongyang was over.

"North Korea would do well not to test [US President Donald Trump's] resolve or the strength of the Armed Forces of the United States in this region," he said.

Since then, however, missile tests have continued.

Enter Moscow. On Tuesday [June 27], the Russian Foreign Ministry announced that it has worked out a "road map" for regulating the situation on the Korean Peninsula. The plan reportedly includes a step-by-step scenario for bringing all sides to dialogue. It also calls for everyone to exercise restraint, avoid provocation, and abandon threats of force, Deputy Foreign Minister Igor Morgulov told the RIA Novosti news agency.

Perhaps most importantly, the "road map" proposes providing Pyongyang with a security guarantee, thereby allowing it to halt its nuclear missile program. That may sound good on paper, but geopolitical analysts say it is unlikely to work in practice.

"It's North Korea's Christmas wish list," Vladimir Frolov, a Russian foreign affairs expert, told *The Moscow Times* in an e-mail. "And it's a PR move on Moscow's part to appear relevant in the crisis without doing any heavy lifting."

The plan is weak, lacking specific demands for Pyongyang to freeze—let alone dismantle—its nuclear and missile programs, Frolov said. It also does not articulate any sort of punitive measures in case North Korea violates [the agreement].

"It's a coordinated move with China to cast the Trump administration as a reckless warmonger," Frolov added.

The problem, he says, is that, despite perceptions to the contrary, the Kremlin lacks leverage over Pyongyang. After the Korean

War, Moscow and Pyongyang were Communist allies. Soviet financial and technological aid was key to building the North Korean economy. But that ended with the Soviet Union's collapse.

In recent years, economic ties have picked up again. In 2014, for example, President Vladimir Putin wrote off Pyongyang's $11 billion debt to the Soviet Union. And North Korean laborers now toil in Russia's Far East and even helped construct St. Petersburg's Zenit Arena. Their work—essentially slave labor—provides much-needed hard currency for Pyongyang, which confiscates up to half of their paychecks.

Beyond that, Russia controls only 5% of North Korea's trade—much less than China does, according to Alexander Gabuev, a senior fellow at the Carnegie Moscow Center. As a result, it cannot impose limits on Pyongyang by economic pressure alone.

Any efforts to rein in North Korea will have to address the country's fundamental concerns, Gabuev writes. While the US worries that Pyongyang's missiles could eventually hit its west coast, the North Korean government views nuclear weapons as its only insurance policy against the US. It looks with alarm at events such as the overthrow of Libyan leader Muammar Qaddafi. He had abandoned weapons of mass destruction and begun a rapprochement with the West, but was nevertheless killed amid NATO air strikes.

Short of finding a way to ensure security guarantees for both Pyongyang and Washington, no road map for the Korean Peninsula is likely to work.

"The lesson that North Korea learned is that you must have a deterrent," Gabuev says. "For them, that's the nuclear bomb."

Nuclear Deterrence: An Eternal Guarantee

By Aleksei Arbatov. *Nezavisimaya gazeta*, July 5, 2017, p. 1.

At their upcoming meeting in Hamburg, the Russian and American presidents may address nuclear arms problems. At any rate, that would be logical because nuclear deterrence plays an increasingly prominent role in relations between the two powers as the most obvious indication of their retreat to a cold war model.

The hiatus in nuclear arms negotiations has been going on for six years now—the longest during 50 years of strategic dialogue between Moscow and Washington. Granted, there is a popular theory in both countries that nuclear weapons and the doctrine of nuclear deterrence based on the threat of using these weapons was a "factor of ensuring peace and security"; that for 70 years, it served to prevent a global war and will continue to do so in the foreseeable future....

Because the future is at stake, complacency over nuclear deterrence is hardly justified. A number of new factors and problems are eroding it both globally and within the framework of Russian-US military-strategic relations. Without jointly resolving these problems, the threat of a nuclear war will steadily increase.

First, a new nuclear world order will not be bipolar but polycentric. It's important to note that today, all nine nuclear states, with some provisos or other, envision delivering the first nuclear strike. Until recently, China and India were the only countries that pledged not to use nuclear weapons first. However, a discussion on abandoning this principle is ongoing in China; and India has stated that this would apply only to nonnuclear states, which brings its doctrine closer to [those of] other nuclear powers. The US, Russia, Great Britain, France, Pakistan, Israel (which neither admits nor denies that it has nuclear weapons) and North Korea—all of them explicitly or implicitly plan to strike first.

Meanwhile, the existence of stable strategic deterrence is an exception, not the rule, in relations between the nuclear powers. Such relations, based on the parity that was achieved by the Soviet Union, evolved solely between the USSR/Russia and the US, although this relationship is also growing increasingly turbulent. However, there is no reason to expect the same sort of relations between other nuclear countries—for example, between India and Pakistan. This applies particularly to North Korea and possible future nuclear states, if nuclear proliferation continues.

All nuclear powers without exception declare their intention to use nuclear weapons first only in response to aggression involving the use of other weapons of mass destruction or conventional weapons. However, the Cuban missile crisis of October 1962 vividly demonstrated that nuclear war is possible when a situation spins out of control, and not as a result of planned aggression. Similar situations, albeit not so dangerous, have occurred since.

Furthermore, sooner or later nuclear weapons or weapons-grade materials and expertise will inevitably fall into terrorists' hands through new nuclear powers, which will put an end to the role of nuclear weapons as "a factor of peace and stability." In keeping with the eternal laws of Hegelian dialectics, nuclear deterrence will destroy itself.

Second, the threat of accidental armed clashes and the probability of their lightning-fast escalation to a global nuclear scale is aggravated by the ongoing military buildup on both sides of the new borders between Russia and NATO [and] their large-scale military exercises. At the same time, tactical nuclear weapons are being deployed together with general-purpose forces at Russian forward operating bases and US storage facilities on NATO countries' territory. This danger also exists in Syria, where for the first time in history, Russia and the US are conducting combat operations in the same country without being military allies and without any clear agreement regarding common opponents, let alone common allies.

The probability of an accidental conflict is heightened by the deployment of new US and Russian weapons that blur the traditional boundaries between nuclear and conventional systems, defensive and offensive [weapons], as well as regional (in terms of theater of operations) and global systems. They rely on increasingly sophisticated and automated information control systems [and] attack capabilities with artificial intelligence that, along with the possible development of antisatellite weapons and cyber warfare assets, are pushing the human factor to the sidelines of the decision-making mechanism.

There are also other strategic innovations: concepts of the selective use of strategic nuclear weapons. The US experimented with such concepts in the early 1960s, as well as in the 1970s and the 1980s, but all of them were scrapped due to the probability of massive nuclear retaliation by the USSR. That changed in 2003, when plans for "deescalating aggression * * * by delivering strikes on a different scale, using conventional and/or nuclear weapons," including the possibility of "targeted combat use of certain components of the Strategic Nuclear Forces," appeared in official Russian documents.

Amid the ongoing escalation of tensions, similar ideas began periodically to leak into the press, apparently reflecting secret strategic projects of the relevant agencies in the US, Russia and most likely China. Russia's official military doctrine provides for delivering the first nuclear strike: "The Russian Federation reserves the right to use nuclear weapons * * * in case of aggression against the Russian Federation with conventional weapons, when the very existence of the state is under threat." Although this formula looks like tough self-restraint, it does not clarify how nuclear weapons could be used or how "a threat to the existence of the state" is defined. The same goes for the [military] doctrines of other nuclear powers.

As before, US military policy allows for the use of nuclear weapons first—according to the 2010 US nuclear doctrine, in "a narrow range of contingencies." Regarding security guarantees for its allies in Europe and Asia, the US "is * * * not prepared at the present time to adopt a universal policy that deterring nuclear attack is the sole purpose of nuclear weapons." The Donald Trump administration may place a greater emphasis on concepts of limited strategic nuclear war in the form of "tailored nuclear options."

The underlying idea now gaining momentum is that after a major downsizing of nuclear arsenals over the past quarter of a century, nuclear war has once again become possible in furthering policies through the use of force and would not result in a global catastrophe.

If both superpowers adopt such concepts, the risk of nuclear war will increase exponentially. An acute international situation could result in a fateful decision, and the process of uncontrolled escalation toward a global catastrophe may be set in motion. This danger would increase if the sides deploy precision-guided offensive and defensive strategic conventional systems, which can create the illusion that it is possible to launch and repulse targeted selective missile strikes.

Therefore, even the classic bilateral nuclear deterrence in relations between the two superpowers is subject to erosion. It is hardly possible to rely on it as an unconditional "factor of ensuring peace and security" in the future.

Third, stable nuclear deterrence is realized solely within the framework of the arms control and nonproliferation regime. Before practical arms control began (starting with the 1963 Partial Nuclear Test Ban Treaty), the world had been on the brink of nuclear war a number of times—including the dangerous episode of the Cuban missile crisis. The last cold war crisis erupted in fall 1983, when Russia and the US deployed medium-range missiles and nuclear arms control negotiations collapsed.

In other words, international conflicts coupled with an uncontrolled nuclear arms race have periodically brought the world to the brink of nuclear war, but not when arms control processes and regimes were in force. Likewise, there is a clear link between the successes and failures of the great powers' dialogue on nuclear disarmament on the one hand, and the progress or regress of the nuclear nonproliferation regime on the other.

At present, an unprecedented crisis of the nuclear arms control system is unfolding. For the first time in more than half a century of nuclear arms negotiations and agreements (since the 1963 treaty), the world faces the imminent prospect of losing treaty-based legal controls over the most destructive weapons in the history of humankind. The weakest link in the nuclear arms control system is the 1987 INF Treaty between the USSR and the US. The Strategic Offensive Reductions Treaty (New START treaty) will expire in 2021, creating a vacuum in strategic arms control. Time for signing a new treaty is running out.

What's more, the new US administration is showing no interest in signing a new START treaty or extending the current one until 2026. In the mid-2020s, the US will move forward with a comprehensive program to modernize its strategic nuclear arsenal (worth over $1 trillion) and will probably also expand its missile defense program, to which Russia would have to respond.

Unlike the cold war period, this offensive nuclear arms race would be compounded by rivalry over offensive and defensive strategic conventional weapons, as well as the development of space weapons and cyber warfare. This lowers the "nuclear threshold" in a potential conflict situation and undermines arms control prospects. In addition, the arms race would become multilateral, involving not only the US and Russia, but also China, the NATO countries, India, Pakistan, North and South Korea, Japan and other states.

All of this leads to one conclusion: for all the importance of resolving the current conflicts between Russia and the US, top priority on their agenda should be given to saving the arms control regime. Even though the Trump administration is showing no interest in this topic yet, if Moscow puts forward serous proposals, Washington would not be able to ignore them. Furthermore, considering the difficulties in relations between the two nuclear superpowers in other areas (Ukraine, Syria, Iran and North Korea), this sphere could quickly become a platform for resuming collaboration. In the past, breakthroughs in this field were achieved despite the wars in Vietnam, Afghanistan and Yugoslavia, and always helped ease tension.

Saving the INF Treaty is a priority. That would be followed by signing a new START treaty beyond 2021, and in this context coordinating measures in the field of missile defense systems and new strategic conventional weapons. In this situation, it is essential to restore dialogue between military experts to ensure the mutual abandonment of dangerous and untenable strategic concepts. There is no doubt that, as was often the case in the past, progress along this track would facilitate cooperation in other areas of Russian-US relations, and stop the transition into a [new] cold war and unrestrained military-political rivalry.

North Korea Nuclear Crisis: Why Russia's Attempt to Get Involved in the Big Game Is a Bad Idea

By international relations expert Vladimir Frolov. *Republic.ru*, Sept. 18, 2017, https://republic.ru/posts/86458.

... The North Korea crisis benefits Russia in every respect. First, it diverts the US from being proactive in the post-Soviet space, in Europe and the Middle East, giving Moscow an important respite and room to maneuver. Escalating tensions, not to mention a real armed confrontation, ties the US's hands and, by the Kremlin's logic, strengthens Russia's security. At the same time, Moscow does not really care about North Korea's nuclear weapons and ballistic missiles per se: This capability is not directed against Russia (this also holds true for China, which has a mutual military assistance agreement with North Korea).

Second, North Korea's nuclear missile blackmail is objectively weakening the US's military alliances with Japan and South Korea. If the US is vulnerable to North Korea's nuclear strike, [its] allies have reason to doubt that the US would sacrifice San Francisco or Seattle for the sake of Tokyo or Seoul. Therefore, this prompts US allies to look for alternative solutions, for instance, in Russia. Actually, Moscow has identified weakening and even completely dismantling the Japanese-US military alliance as a key condition for "a compromise solution to the Southern Kurile [Islands] problem." So far, these are only dreams, but who knows how things will work out in the future.

Third, the North Korea crisis is complicating US-Chinese relations, prodding Beijing toward further rapprochement with Moscow. The Trump administration is putting intense pressure on China, including threats to review trade ties between the two countries, and introduce so-called secondary sanctions against Chinese banks and companies doing business with North Korea.

Some Russian analysts are even inclined to see this as the US's focused strategy to weaken North Korea, with Pyongyang's nuclear program serving as just a pretext, but that is an exaggeration. In any case, China is catching most of the US's flak, while Russia is avoiding the US's pressure. This is a beneficial situation.

Finally, North Korea's nuclear missile crisis ideally suits Russia for demonstrating its role as a great power with substantial diplomatic potential, capable of influencing conflict settlements all over the world. Coupled with Russia's actions in Syria, Libya and Afghanistan, [its] participation in a settlement process on the Korean Peninsula is forging Russia's image as a global power for both domestic and foreign audiences, even if so far there has been little practical payoff from these efforts. An extra bonus is an opportunity to demonstrate that in contrast to the US, which behaves like a bull in a china shop, Russia can find more effective solutions to complicated conflict situations in various parts of the world.

A useful opportunity is emerging for [Russia] to head up an informal coalition of states opposed to the US's policy of changing undesirable regimes and imposing economic sanctions, as well as for emphasizing Russia's role as a global counterweight to the US, which strengthens Moscow's claims to "geopolitical parity" with Washington within the framework of the two nuclear superpowers' "special responsibility." As for the clumsy, tough style of the Trump administration, which is resorting to direct military threats against Pyongyang and has recklessly drawn several "red lines" for itself (which were immediately crossed), it allows Moscow and personally Vladimir Putin to play the role of "pragmatic sage" whose words should be heeded.

Overall, this situation is creating attractive opportunities for Moscow to play on US interests and pursue a policy of geopolitical trade-offs....

This high-risk game of upping the ante without fully calculating the consequences has already been tested in Ukraine and Syria. Of course, Moscow will not really "stand up for Pyongyang" in the Soviet style, fight for the [North] Korean regime or supply it with weapons, but that is not necessary. It is enough to covertly torpedo the US sanctions policy, including through selective violation of the sanctions regime and some strange economic projects like trans-Korean gas pipelines and railway lines.

When Vladimir Putin and kowtowing "public activists" say that the Kim Jr. regime will never abandon its nuclear deterrence capability—after all, he knows what fate befell Qaddafi or Saddam Hussein, and only nuclear weapons and the ability to "burn Seattle" can prevent a US military invasion, "color revolution" and regime change—they promote a logic that is dangerous for Russia: When all is said and done, Ukraine could also be included in this chain of associations. It has also abandoned the nuclear weapons and missiles deployed on its territory with guarantees from all the nuclear powers, including Russia (the Budapest Memorandum). Just like North Korea, Ukraine has existential security threats, and it already has the scientific-technical and resource potential to create a nuclear missile deterrence capability. Of course, this is a bad solution, and Ukraine's present leadership will not go that route (the West is strongly against it). However, almost all nationalist forces in Ukraine are in favor, and in case of regime change in Kiev, purely hypothetically, nothing would prevent the Ukrainians—as Putin put it in justifying North Korea's passion for the nuclear bomb—from "eating grass" to guarantee the survival of their state. By the way, other countries that have voluntarily scaled back their nuclear programs and removed other countries' nuclear weapons deployed on their territory (South Africa, Argentina, Brazil, Belarus, Kazakhstan) have never faced any US invasions and are feeling just fine.

Instrumentalizing nuclear missile proliferation as a tool of deterring the US is a bad idea for Russia. Its superpower status is ensured almost solely by its exclusive position as one of the five recognized nuclear powers and one of two powers (along with China) that have the potential for direct nuclear deterrence against the US. Expanding this closed club would erode Russia's influence on Washington and devalue Russia's claims to a new bipolarity with the US. (During the cold war, blocking nuclear proliferation was one of the most productive lines of cooperation between the superpowers; in 1985, the USSR simply used threats to get North Korea to join the Nuclear Nonproliferation Treaty, while the US "curbed" South Korea's nuclear missile program.) This is not the kind of a "multipolar world" [Russia] should seek: After all, new nuclear deterrence works not only against the US, but also against Russia....

4.4

Can We Be Friends? Russian-American Relations

Introduction

The press coverage in this section begins just after Trump's inauguration, and is punctuated by several major events: Sergei Lavrov's trip to the White House, where he met Trump for the first time; Trump's first face-to-face meeting with Putin on the sidelines of the G-20 conference; the overwhelming approval by the US Congress of a new sanctions package against Russia; and the subsequent official response from the Russian Foreign Ministry stating that the number of US staff working at the American Embassy in Moscow would be reduced to 455, bringing it to "exact parity with the number of Russian diplomats and technical staff currently in the US."

We should note that both the sanctions and Moscow's response were the latest steps in a diplomatic war that predated the Trump presidency: One of the Obama administration's last decisions was to expel 35 Russian diplomats and seize diplomatic facilities in late December 2016—which itself was announced as retaliation for Moscow's alleged interference in the US electoral process (see Part Three, above).

Between Trump's inauguration and the Lavrov-Trump meeting, articles about Russian-American relations are mainly speculative. The first one has to do with economics, not politics: Yakov Mirkin of the Institute of World Economics and International Relations discusses how Trump's promises of American energy independence and increased employment would force Russia to revitalize its own economy.

Two other themes touched on during this time are anti-Russian sanctions and bilateral diplomatic relations. Experts interviewed by *The Moscow Times* surmise that even if Trump wanted to lift the sanctions, his leverage is limited by his own cabinet and Congress, as well as Western European governments. As for diplomatic ties, Lavrov expresses guarded optimism in a Feb. 10 *Izvestia* interview: After alluding to the tension caused by Obama's December démarche, Lavrov affirms: "For our part, we are willing to work with the Donald Trump administration on the entire agenda of Russian-US relations, based on the principles of equality, mutual respect and alignment of interests."

However, Lavrov's visit to Washington to meet with Trump personally was marred by Trump's recent firing of FBI head James Comey (Russian news outlets, like their American counterparts, make much of Lavrov's quip on that subject) and the fact that Lavrov's photographer posted photos of the Oval Office meeting on the TASS Web site, revealing that Russian Ambassador Sergei Kislyak had also attended. Unlike the American media, which went into an uproar over Kislyak's presence, TASS mentioned it merely as a matter of course in a daily briefing the following week. Another issue that alarmed the American press was that Trump had shared classified information about an ISIS plot—intelligence provided by a US ally (which turned out to be Israel). On the Russian side, Kremlin spokesman Dmitry Peskov firmly refused to comment. Despite Trump's apparent candor with the Russian representatives, commentator Nikolai Zlobin predicts that the White House conversation will not bring major changes because Trump has no political will to improve relations with Russia.

Coverage in this section continues with the long-awaited first meeting between Presidents Putin and Trump, a closed session during the G-20 summit in Hamburg on July 7. Although the meeting lasted nearly two hours—twice as long as expected—Russian commentators are hesitant to call the event successful, or even conclusive. One positive note is cooperation in Syria (see details in Section 4.2, above). However, the Russian press devotes more attention to the continuing debate around Russia's alleged role in the US electoral process—especially since Washington and Moscow are telling different stories after the fact: Did Trump tell the Russians to stay out of America's business, or did he accept Putin's statements that the Russian leadership did not interfere in the election?

The "personal chemistry" noted between the two presidents in Hamburg clearly did not extend to the US Congress, which voted overwhelmingly on renewed sanctions legislation in late July. In early August, Trump signed the bill. After the strong notes of optimism about Russian-US relations that had been sounding in the Russian press for months, there was great uproar about Trump having betrayed Moscow's hopes. Granted, some commentators either downplay the significance of the sanctions (as Leonid Radzikhovsky argues, continuing a long-running theme in official circles) or reaffirm the contention that Trump is working against a hostile system in Washington. For example, Kirill Rogov states in an Aug. 11 interview that "Trump is his own person": As a presidential candidate, he appealed directly to voters with his own voice, but is now working within a system with entrenched anti-Russian sentiment.

However, the majority of Russian responses fault both Trump and the "system" for escalating bilateral tension. A statement from the Russian Foreign Ministry contains the inference: "The adoption of the new sanctions law clearly demonstrates that relations with Russia have become hostage to an internal power struggle in the US." Vladimir Frolov writes that the Russian side now perceives Trump as a "weakling," and that the US side does not trust him to conduct dialogue with Putin.

Trumponomics

By Yakov Mirkin, head of the International Capital Markets section at the Russian Academy of Sciences' Institute of World Economics and International Relations. *Rossiiskaya gazeta*, Jan. 23, 2017, p. 6.

What new opportunities and challenges does Trump's victory bring Russia? for many years, America's actions around the world have been based primarily on noneconomic factors: expanding [US] power, ideas and influence; and responding to threats as perceived by politicians and the military, but not businesspeople or the middle class.

However, with conflicts emerging in more and more areas (the Middle East, Eastern Europe), the US economy, much to everyone's surprise, has been gradually losing its vigor. In the meantime, growth has picked up in China, India and some other developing countries in Asia. Corporations have eagerly moved jobs from the US to cheaper countries (Mexico, Asia). The US economy has been growing by 1.5% to 2.5% a year.

The election of businessman Trump to the presidency was largely a blue- and white-collar response to stagnating incomes and job cutbacks. The new president thinks his mission is to restructure the US, as one would restructure a corporation. But how? He should do what business owners do when their company starts losing its edge. Forget about ideology—be more practical. You want the US to protect you—how about if you contribute a little too?

You want help—how will that benefit the US economy? For Russia, this could mean a "reset" in relations with the US—in reality, not just in words. This is business, pure and simple. Are there any risks for us in this "economization" of US policies? Of course! The essence of Trump's domestic policies (we're no longer talking about foreign policy here) is very simple: America first—America's interests take precedence. Make America a booming economy. But how?

First, achieve energy independence. This means that the US would cease to be the world's biggest oil importer. The new president says he is "committed to achieving energy independence from the OPEC cartel and any nations hostile to [America's] interests." US oil imports amount to approximately 10% of global production. If such a major consumer withdraws from the market, that would be a shock, pushing oil and gas prices down.

But how does the US plan to achieve energy independence? The answer is by lifting restrictions on US oil production (of which there are many). The shale revolution, shelf oil, clean coal, immense oil reserves on federal lands, radical deregulation—all of this would be put into action to make energy cheap for domestic consumers, both households and businesses. What would happen if this works? Clearly, it would cause a major shock to the energy industry, and global oil prices would plunge. Who would suffer? Primarily

Russia (the world's No. 2 oil producer), Saudi Arabia, Iraq and all the OPEC countries. Venezuela would be a disaster. Mexico would hurt. The Islamic world would lose much of its financial leverage.

Of course, all of this [planned action] still needs to happen. There is a big difference between promising something and actually doing it. But Trump has another idea that could also cause a global economic upheaval. What is it? His slogan about reindustrializing America: bringing businesses back from Mexico, China and other developing countries; investing in domestic production, roads, bridges, American education and the American middle class. Taxes, customs tariffs, trade rules, pressure from regulators—everything should serve this purpose. Essentially, this is deglobalization, protectionism. But the US is not just a country; it's the core of the global economy. What about the consequences? Very simple: China would slow down, as would all the Asian economies; Latin America would face huge problems. A slowdown in China and Asia would create problems for Russia, since Russia is a major commodities exporter to that part of the world.

Third, what would the Federal Reserve, America's central bank, be doing all this time? This is another branch of government in the US, and it's relatively independent from the president (that's how it's set up). If the Fed raises the interest rate, the dollar would automatically get stronger versus the euro and other international currencies. And that would put strong pressure on international prices for oil, gas, metals and food. That's how financial markets work. The consequences for Russia? International prices for oil and other commodities we export would drop, and the ruble would weaken against the strengthening dollar.

Of course, anything can happen in real life. The global economy is a complex system. You can't keep track of everything, and you can never be 100% certain that things will go the way someone says they will.

But what we can say at this point is that the new US president's ideas, if implemented, would weaken developing countries—both commodities exporters and manufacturing hubs—and Russia's economy would suffer the most. Cheap oil and gas, falling prices for other commodities, a strong dollar, a slowdown in China and other Asian economies—all of these things are real, and the challenges they pose to Russia are nothing new: [We need] growth, modernization and higher quality of life. Basically, [we need] the same Trumponomics, only adjusted for Russian reality. And if we are frank with ourselves, we'll admit that these changes are long overdue.

No Golden Opportunity

By Matthew Bodner and Mikhail Fishman.
The Moscow Times, Jan. 26, 2017, p. 4.

No actor on the world stage was as publicly energized by the prospect of a Donald Trump presidency as Russia. At first glance, the support seemed entirely emotional. But there was also a rational interest: Trump was open to lifting sanctions, after all.

Sanctions have had a negative impact on the Russian economy, a fact that Russian President Vladimir Putin was eventually forced to admit. They have also diplomatically isolated Russia to an extent unseen since the cold war.

With Russian industries struggling to survive without the support of Western financial markets—arguably the biggest impact of the sanctions regime—Trump, a so-called "dealmaker" with a relatable worldview, seemed to provide a lifeline for the Kremlin. But as Trump settles into office, it is growing clearer that sanctions relief is unlikely to come in the near future. And there is little Moscow can do to hasten it.

Even if Trump himself may want to lift sanctions—or trade them [for something else that would serve] his own interests—he will first have to negotiate with his own Congress at home, and then with his nation's closest traditional allies across the Atlantic.

Neither will be easy.

Trump's desire to strike a deal with Putin is not new, and has apparently not changed since he took office. In recent interviews, he reaffirmed his willingness to trade sanctions relief for Russian support in combating ISIS. He also said he would trade sanctions for a nuclear deal—apparently unaware that Obama already secured one in 2010.

"He simply doesn't understand what to do with Russia yet," says Fyodor Lukyanov, a Russian foreign affairs expert.

Trump, it seems, only knows that he wants to make a deal with Russia. To those ends, a meeting with Putin is expected in the near future. The focus will likely remain on the Middle East, where Putin and Trump appear to see eye to eye.

Beyond that, nothing is guaranteed.

Regardless of the new administration's rhetoric, there are many signs Russia will not be a top policy priority for the Trump administration. First, the administration is divided on Putin. Most notably, the new defense secretary, Gen. James Mattis, takes a much more hard-line position on the Russian leader than Trump himself.

Second, the allegations that Russia somehow helped Trump win the election will likely compel him to avoid looking too eager to work with Putin. They also reduce the likelihood of sanctions being lifted in the near term.

Assuming Trump wants to lift sanctions immediately, to what extent can he act unilaterally? In short, that depends on the type of sanctions under discussion. Some can be lifted with the stroke of his presidential pen, while others are enshrined in laws passed by large margins in the US Congress.

In terms of unilateral action, Trump has the greatest room to maneuver when it comes to the sanctions levied against Moscow for its actions in Ukraine. These are based on four Obama-era executive orders.[23] Trump, as president, can annul them. He can also overturn sanctions imposed in December by executive order as a response to Russia's alleged election interference.[24]

But Trump might not have the political capital to afford such unilateral action. President Obama, when signing the orders in question, enjoyed broad bipartisan support in the US Congress for taking measures against Russia's intervention in Ukraine. Many at the time, especially in Trump's own Republican party, argued that Obama's response was not strong enough.

Already, a bipartisan effort is under way to pass a bill that requires any easing of sanctions against Russia to be approved by Congress. If recent congressional actions are any indication, the proposal has a good chance of being passed. A similar law, restricting Obama's ability to unilaterally lift Iran sanctions, passed in 2015 with bipartisan support.

The remainder of US sanctions against Russia are acts of Congress, which means only it can overturn them. Specifically, these are sanctions imposed on Russia for violations of arms control statutes and violations of human rights.

Broadly speaking, the US Congress has been historically tough on all questions pertaining to Russia.

The issue of sanctions against Russia is not simply an American one. Washington's allies in Europe have closely mirrored and worked with the previous US administration to impose their own sanctions on Russia. On the whole, it has been an allied effort. This makes it unlikely that Trump will lift sanctions unilaterally, says political expert Vladimir Frolov.

However, the situation in Europe is changing in Russia's favor. New winds are blowing across the continent, and the moods may be shifting. Populist movements are on the rise, and voices in favor of loosening sanctions on Russia are growing stronger.

Even the cornerstone Franco-German axis is under strain. François Fillon, the front-runner in this year's French presidential election, is known for his lobbying against sanctions. On Jan. 23, after meeting German Chancellor Angela Merkel, he told reporters that Europe must be prepared to lift sanctions if Trump tries to go over their heads—"which is not inconceivable."

The lifting of European Union sanctions against Russia is no less complicated than the lifting of American sanctions. It would require a broad, union-wide consensus. Moreover, European sanctions are tied to the implementation of the Minsk ceasefire agreements in Ukraine. That wouldn't necessarily be a deal-breaker, says Lukyanov: It could be overcome, should the major actors—Germany, in particular—support a U-turn on Russia.

However, while France under a prospective Fillon presidency may be open to lifting sanctions, Germany under Merkel is not. "Under Merkel, Germany now is taking all responsibility for maintaining global liberal values," says Alexander Rahr, research director of the German-Russian Forum. And Moscow's ability to undermine Merkel's stance is extremely limited.

The question is, then: How long can Merkel hold the line? Even she would be forced to change tack were Trump to ignore the concerns of his strongest ally on the European continent and unilaterally lift sanctions, argues Rahr.

Since that remains an unlikely scenario, Moscow's dreams of a future free of sanctions will, for the moment, have to wait.

Russian Matryoshka: How Many Demands for Trump Can Hide Inside Putin?

By Tatyana Stanovaya, head of the analysis department at the Center for Political Technologies. *Republic.ru*, Jan. 27, 2017, https://republic.ru/posts/79023.

The first telephone conversation between Vladimir Putin and new US President Donald Trump will take place Saturday [Jan. 28]. Moscow has been looking forward to this event with enormous anticipation. Under Putin's rule, the Russian ruling elite's position toward the US has been based on a fundamental assumption: As soon as Washington abandons confrontation, we will find common ground....

Over the past 25 years, relations between Russia and the US have racked up a list of problematic topics, which are well known. The most painful set of these for Russia is security problems: the US's exit from the ABM [Antiballistic Missile Treaty], the enlargement of NATO, and the development of American long-range precision weapons programs (what [Russian Defense Minister] Sergei Shoigu recently called the emergence of nonnuclear deterrence). Russia is obviously worried about all this. It's also obvious that Moscow can't afford to compete with the US and make symmetrical responses.

But then logical questions arise: What does Russia really want, and what are its strategic interests? If Trump puts a block on NATO enlargement policy (which is actually on the downswing already, due to a crisis within the organization itself), [and] if the US generally becomes less invested (diplomatically, politically and financially) in NATO, then how can Moscow use that long-awaited victory?

The Kremlin has a realistic plan and an idealistic one. The first involves dispelling tension and interacting with NATO within the framework of common interests (terrorism, cybersecurity, sea pirates, Afghanistan, etc.). The field of interaction would be very narrow, and the discord and mutual distrust between the alliance and Russia would not disappear, no matter how "friendly" and constructive the US suddenly becomes....

Behind all of the accusations and demands [that Moscow has] addressed to the US, there has always been a very abstract idealistic plan lurking. It envisions Moscow gaining the right to veto global decisions on strategic security, particularly with regard to missile defense. The Kremlin has already made hopeless efforts to achieve this: In 2009, it tried to make the US link the reduction of strategic offensive weapons with the issue of missile defense. It didn't work. As Russian journalists often put it, Washington refused to provide any legal guarantees that the American missile defense system was not targeted [at Russia]. (Of course, there was practically no way it could have.) . . .

Russia's interests are nested inside a giant matryoshka, where each demand has a new one hidden inside. The demand to stop NATO enlargement holds a hidden desire to create something alternative and large-scale: a new Helsinki [i.e., the Helsinki Accords of 1975, guaranteeing territorial sovereignty and noninterference—*Trans.*]. The abandonment of European missile defense would not be enough, either. Moscow wants to preclude any possibility of deploying defense elements capable of striking intercontinental missiles. Thus, in essence, Russia is demanding guarantees that [the US] will completely renounce phase four of the missile defense deployment plan, which was frozen by Barack Obama in 2013.

But even this would not be enough for the Kremlin: The man in charge wants the US not to build any "umbrellas" at all without taking Russia's interests into account. A concession on one point immediately leads to a new demand, which if not met leads the players back to square one. . . .

There is also a second set of problems: Russia cannot convince the global community that it has a legitimate zone of traditional influence—the territory of the post-Soviet states—where the Kremlin wants to have a geopolitical monopoly, or at least priority. Here, again, we see the proverbial matryoshka: The demand "Don't interfere in the internal affairs of other states" conceals [Russia's] desire for its own monopoly to do just that—via trade and gas wars, pressure, bribery with cheap and often nonrepayable loans, and other tools of Russian foreign policy in the post-Soviet space. And inside this matryoshka, we find yet another: the expansion of that zone of traditional interests to the borders of the former Eastern bloc. Moscow is playing its own game in Serbia and Montenegro, Bulgaria and the Czech Republic. As an added bonus, Moscow is going for Syria and even the entire Middle East, trying to reclaim its status there as a power player. The concept of Russia's zone of traditional interests is becoming more and more elastic.

As a former KGB man who loves special operations, Putin has always dreamed of negotiating with more powerful counterparts to "cut a square deal behind the scenes." It's impossible for him not to like Trump's "big deal" idea, and both sides are likely to put in a lot of work to find the right formula. However, their approaches are fundamentally different. Trump is thinking about how to "sell" Russia the removal of sanctions; how to get out of a [diplomatic] crisis while effectively boxing [Russia] in so it doesn't get in his way; and how to neutralize those destructive (even in Trump's opinion) actions of the Kremlin that have become so worrisome to the international community. "Let's protect ourselves from Putin by taking pressure off him": This is the tactic of the new resident of the White House. Russia, however, has absolutely no desire to sit this game out; on the contrary, it's trying to get in the thick of the game....

Russia's demands to divvy up "spheres of influence" with the US might become much more ambitious than they look right now amid sanctions and the crisis in relations. A possible relaxation of the sanctions regime and [anti-Russian] rhetoric; a show of readiness to turn a blind eye to Russia's actions in Ukraine or excesses in Syria—these are merely preconditions for Moscow to make a possible pivot toward the West. But they might just be a bait-and-switch tactic, after which [Moscow] would demand that Washington make further strategic concessions and show more flexibility on issues of global security—even to the point of forming an interdependent global tandem. [This] "big deal" may become too expensive even for the US, which has absolutely no plans to end up in any way dependent on Russia—even as Putin is de facto trying to make it so.

Sergei Lavrov: 'We Are Willing to Work With the Donald Trump Administration on the Entire Agenda'

By Tatyana Baikova. *Izvestia*, Feb. 10, 2017, p. 1.

Editors' Note—Today Russia observes Diplomat's Day. In an interview with *Izvestia* correspondent Tatyana Baikova, timed to coincide with this holiday, Russian Foreign Minister Sergei Lavrov speaks about the specifics of his work, problems in relations with the US and NATO, a resolution on Syria, and other important aspects of [Russian] foreign policy.

* * *

Question—Today is Diplomat's Day. Recent events—the expulsion of our diplomats from the US, the assassination of the Russian ambassador in Turkey [and] the attempt to recruit our diplomat in America—show that diplomacy is turning from armchair conversations among respectable people strictly adhering to protocol into a rather dangerous job, sometimes comparable to a game without rules. In your view, how has a diplomat's job changed? Is Russia going to tighten security measures for [its] diplomats abroad?

Answer—Diplomats have always risked their lives. Of course, today, amid the surging threat of international terrorism, it is not becoming any safer. A commemorative plaque was installed in the Foreign Ministry building with the names of those who were killed in the line of duty. In the past few years alone, the mournful list came to include Dmitry Vishernev, an officer at the Russian Embassy in Abkhazia, and his wife; Vadim Nazarov, who had worked at the UN Assistance Mission in Afghanistan; and Russian Ambassador to Turkey Andrei Karlov.

Our staff often has to work under rather difficult conditions, sometimes in an openly hostile environment. The large-scale expulsion from the US is a case in point. It was the anti-Russian death throes of Barack Obama's outgoing administration. However, such actions, as well as recruitment attempts, accompanied by blackmail and threats, happen in other countries, too—not only in the US....

Q—During the US presidential election, a split in the American establishment was obvious. The election of Barack Obama eight years ago or George W. Bush at the beginning of the 21st century passed relatively calmly. Then suddenly such a flare-up of passions in the 2016 election. Why such a reaction? Are there any underlying causes?

A—An in-depth analysis of the factors that predetermined such an emotional tone in the US election campaign is better left to specialists: Americanists, political analysts and historians. The level of applied analysis at our ministry is high, as always, but it is aimed primarily at addressing tasks related to the development of interstate relations.

In building dialogue with the US, we of course follow and take into account the main trends of US sociopolitical life, as well as their impact on the country's policy in the international arena. Clearly, there has recently been growing demand among American citizens for change both in domestic affairs and in terms of interaction with the outside world. That became an important factor in ensuring Republican Party candidate Donald Trump's victory in the presidential election. However, a certain part of the political elite from the losing camp (and others, as well) became so embittered in the course of the election campaign, given the incredibly high stakes, that it seems to have set out to completely obstruct the new president's actions. I believe that American society is mature enough to successfully resolve the problems it faces, and will be able to respond effectively to internal difficulties and challenges.

For our part, we are willing to work with the Donald Trump administration on the entire agenda of Russian-US relations, based on the principles of equality, mutual respect and alignment of interests. We proceed from the premise that the development of constructive, mutually beneficial bilateral ties would bring very real benefits to the peoples of Russia and the US, and positively affect the situation in the world....

Honeymoon

By political analyst Leonid Radzikhovsky.
Rossiiskaya gazeta, Feb. 21, 2017, p. 6.

It's traditional to discuss the first 100 days of a presidency. But Trump has gotten off to such a running start, and his opponents have reacted so harshly, that it's possible to sum up this honeymoon already.

Domestically for the US, stocks are at record highs, the president's ratings are at record lows, [Trump's] team is being cobbled together with great difficulty (the secretary of the Treasury barely managed to squeeze by, while the labor secretary withdrew his nomination). An executive order that's of principal importance for the president has been blocked in court, and he is now working on a new one. After visiting the US, [European Union High Representative for Foreign Affairs and Security Policy Federica] Mogherini said in dismay: If things go on like this, the country could lose its global leadership position. [American] society is deeply divided as a new War of the Roses rages.... In short, if this is the path to "making America great again," it's going to be a bumpy road—you might even call it dialectical. As Lenin once said: "In order to unite, we need to divide." for now, we are witnessing the first stage.

Of course, Trump has some really ambitious plans like reconfiguring the Middle East. However, we are naturally more interested in relations between Russia and Trump. This is also an interesting subject. Everyone remembers the [Kremlin's] "champagne toasts" [over Trump's victory]. After a month, the champagne has gone flat, and that is absolutely normal. What would be abnormal is going to the extreme, and having our disappointment in Trump (even though he never promised us anything) turn our "scorned love" to hate. Such a hurricane of emotions is interesting from a psychological point of view—call it a Pygmalion complex. After all, nothing has happened. No need to confuse our hopes and dreams, and the promises we gave ourselves in Trump's name with the actual Donald Trump, who existed for 70 years outside our definition of him. Trump's motto—including where Russia is concerned—is trite: "Nothing personal, it's just business."

An important part of business is defining your priorities. Relations with Russia are a part of the overall puzzle (and not even the main one) that is being put together by Trump and around Trump. Given the degree of confrontation inside the US, all foreign policy merely becomes an instrument for tackling strictly domestic problems. [Trump's opponents] are constantly trying to drive him into a corner, get him up against the ropes and give him a good pummeling. Driving him into the "Russian corner" is the most obvious such tactic. Accusations of "suspicious ties" with Russia haunted Trump during his entire election campaign, and did not end on Election Day.

One such powerful missed blow was the brouhaha over Flynn. For a logical person, the fact that Flynn discussed something over the phone with the Russian ambassador once again proves the obvious: that he did not and could not have had any sort of "secret relationship" with Russia. If he were mixed up in something like that, then the former director of the Defense Intelligence Agency would have managed to keep it under wraps. But given the cold civil war, Flynn made a misstep, then "lied" to boot, so he went down. This also tarnished Trump's reputation. His next moves are obvious: [Trump] needs to step up his defense and get out of the dangerous "Russian corner" by finding an alibi. Which is what he is doing—a reasonable and unavoidable step. Hence the renewed interest in the Crimea's geography, statements about a hard-line policy, etc. "Nothing personal, it's just business."

His earlier overtures to Russia could also be part of the above formula. Back then, he had to offer something different from Obama. Obama's relationship with the Russians was bad. Why? [According to Trump,] because he's a wimp, so they don't respect him. But they will respect me. That's [Trump's] main message, not "Let's be friends with Russia." That is merely an afterthought to the main message: "Yes, good relations are possible." We—the Russian media and politicians—were the ones who put our own spin on those words. But that's our own hearing problem.

Meanwhile, Trump neither likes nor dislikes Russia. It's a blank slate for him, and anything he writes on it will be intended to solve his tasks. In the current situation, Trump is not going to venture into the "Russian minefield." With childlike simplicity, he said that the media are preventing [him] from improving relations with Russia. Of course—enemies of the people, etc. But is it just the media that's to blame? After all, the "deal" that Trump talks about must be mutually beneficial. But how? Nuclear disarmament is out—it's not even a very pressing issue right now. After [Trump's] Crimea speeches, compromise on Ukraine looks impossible. Small, purely symbolic gestures such as "handing over [Edward] Snowden" (who is not really all that important to Russia or the US) are also unlikely—since they are, as I said, purely symbolic.

One important issue for the US is the Middle East.

But the "big plan" announced by Trump is essentially an anti-Iranian union that would be a blow to Assad, no matter how you spin it. So the idea that has been voiced several times by Russia—that the US will realize that Assad is the lesser of two evils, which will lead to the creation of a military and political alliance on Syria—looks all but impossible. Of course, Trump would be willing to pay a high price for Russia to end its military-technical cooperation with Iran. But given that relations with Iran are on shaky ground as it is, Russia would not go for that right now.

So there is no common denominator in sight for the US and Russia.

But if improving relations is not of principal importance to the US, the same thing could be said of Russia. Any country's real problems have nothing to do with international matters of image or prestige. They are always domestic.

Kremlin and White House Intent on Eliminating Negative Balance

By Igor Subbotin. *Nezavisimaya gazeta*, May 11, 2017, p. 1.

US President Donald Trump's talks with Foreign Minister Sergei Lavrov [in Washington] marked the first meeting between the head of the White House and a high-ranking representative of the Kremlin. The minister's visit has been described as significant for bilateral relations, especially considering the negative track record of diplomatic relations between Moscow and the previous American administration.

Lavrov's trip to the US will probably expedite preparations for a personal meeting between Trump and Putin....

Lavrov commented that the purpose of the two presidents' meeting is not to create an outward effect. "Both we and our American colleagues feel strongly that when leaders meet, it's important not just to shake hands and listen to each other's opinions about mutual relations and international issues," the minister said. "Russia and the US wield such strong influence on international stability and security that such a meeting will certainly be expected to produce concrete results. To make that happen, we must prepare for it well. That's what we are doing now."...

"I don't think Trump is going to rack his brains over a meeting with Putin," Nikolai Zlobin, head of the Center on Global Interests in Washington, told NG. "If they do meet, [it will happen] as a G-20 event—something small and not very official. It's not [going to be like] the Chinese leader's state visit to the US. There won't be a fundamental agenda. They'll probably discuss common approaches; they'll agree to discuss Syria, Ukraine, Iran. In this sense, Iran is a difficult partner for Russia, because Russia can't drop Iran, and yet that's what Trump is going to demand from Russia. I would not expect much from this meeting." The analyst foresees that the Putin-Trump meeting will be cordial, but no big changes will come of it.

"Trump is constrained by the overall atmosphere in the American mainstream; [their sentiments are] extremely anti-Russian," Zlobin added. "He has no arguments to put up against that attitude. I don't think he needs another war among his own elite—another front. He's working on a lot of fronts as it is—from Iran to Obamacare. I'm not sure he has the political forces, the need and, most important, the desire to open up another. Not one of Trump's objectives would be met by improving relations with Russia." The expert also believes that most foreign policy issues in the US are continuing to develop the same way they did under ex-president Obama.

Lavrov's visit came amid controversy around FBI director James Comey, who was suddenly removed from his post by Trump. "Comey lost the confidence of almost everyone in Washington, Republican and Democrat alike. When things calm down, they will be thanking me!" Trump wrote about the dismissal on Twitter. Trump reportedly made his decision on the advice of US Attorney General Jeff Sessions and Deputy [Attorney General] Rod Rosenstein....

'They Tricked Us': White House Didn't Expect TASS Photographer to Cover Trump-Lavrov Meeting

By Pavel Borisov. *Meduza*, May 11, 2017, https://meduza.io/feature/2017/05/11/oni-nas-obmanuli-belyy-dom-ne-ozhidal-chto-fotograf-tass-snimet-vstrechu-trampa-i-lavrova.

Editors' Note—On May 10, Russian Foreign Minister Sergei Lavrov met with US Secretary of State Rex Tillerson in Washington. Then the Russian diplomat was hosted in the Oval Office by US President Donald Trump; this was their first meeting. Also in attendance was Russian Ambassador to the US Sergei Kislyak—but that became known only through pictures taken by a TASS photographer who happened to be at the meeting. White House representatives feel tricked, because the event was supposed to be closed to the press. *Meduza* tells what happened—and why the White House is miffed.

* * *

Trump met with Sergei Lavrov for the first time. The meeting took place in the White House [Oval] Office behind closed doors; we don't know what was said. Lavrov reported only that sanctions against Russia were not discussed. [Upon arrival] in Washington, Lavrov had met with Secretary of State Rex Tillerson. [As he went into that meeting,] he even managed to crack a joke to reporters in response to a question about the firing of FBI director James

Comey. He pretended not to know anything about the dismissal: "Was he fired? You are kidding!"

The only member of the press at the Lavrov-Trump meeting was a photographer. Meetings in the Oval Office, especially behind closed doors, are rarely photographed—and a situation where a Russian [news] agency representative is present without any photographer from the American media is totally unprecedented. The TASS Washington bureau claims that the photographer in this case, Aleksandr Shcherbak, regularly works with Lavrov and flew with him to the US. It is worth noting that something similar has happened before—with Japanese Prime Minister Shinzo Abe, who met Trump in November 2016, right after the latter's victory [in the presidential election]: Photos from that meeting were published only by the Japanese Foreign Ministry. At the time, Trump was not yet a sitting president.

[In the current case,] the TASS photographer uploaded not only photos of Trump and Lavrov, but also a shot [of them] with Ambassador Kislyak. This photo was the only way the world found out that Trump had met with the Russian ambassador at all and posed for the camera. Technically, there is nothing illegal or questionable about this from an ethical point of view, but past meetings with Kislyak have caused problems for several Trump administration officials, who were [subsequently] accused of colluding with Russia. For one person from the Trump team—former national security adviser Michael Flynn—a conversation with Kislyak cost him his job: He resigned over the fact that he had lied to Vice-President Mike Pence about the content of his conversation with the diplomat.

The White House maintains that the Trump administration was misled. According to *The Washington Post*, Shcherbak was introduced as Lavrov's personal photographer. The White House did not know that he also worked for the TASS state news agency, and [Washington] apparently did not expect to see photos of Trump and the Russian ambassador right after the meeting, on both the TASS Web site and that of the Russian Foreign Ministry. CNN sources said that the White House was "furious" over the situation. "They tricked us. * * * They lie,"[25] a source in the US administration told a CNN correspondent.

Lavrov Briefed Putin on His Meeting With Trump

[No author indicated.] *Itar-Tass Daily*, May 16, 2017, http://tass.com/politics/946111.

Russian Foreign Minister Sergei Lavrov briefed President Vladimir Putin on his May 10 meeting with US President Donald Trump, as he usually does, presidential spokesman Dmitry Peskov said about media rumors the US leader had allegedly shared some classified information.

"He [the foreign minister] always briefs the president on his contacts [with foreign leaders]," Peskov said when asked by the media about the details of last week's Lavrov-Trump meeting. Peskov did not disclose any details....

The question about the meeting emerged after *The Washington Post* said Trump might have shared with Lavrov and Russian Ambassador to the US Sergei Kislyak some top secret information about the terrorist group Islamic State [aka ISIS] (banned in Russia).

Earlier on Tuesday [May 16], Peskov dismissed such publications as "utter nonsense" in which there was "nothing to either confirm or deny."

Russian Foreign Ministry spokeswoman Maria Zakharova said that such media speculations were part and parcel of the campaign that had been launched long before the US presidential election with the aim of putting political pressures on the new administration in the White House and for bargaining over various appointments and lobbying.

Trump said on Tuesday that in his capacity of the head of state, he had the right to share information with Russia. He added that the information concerned terrorism and flight safety. He hopes it will prove useful in the struggle against terrorism.

Opponents Shake Hands: Results of the First Meeting Between Putin and Trump

By international relations expert Vladimir Frolov. *Republic.ru*, July 8, 2017, https://republic.ru/posts/84723.

Talks between Vladimir Putin and Donald Trump on the sidelines of the G-20 summit in Hamburg lasted over two hours, instead of the scheduled 30 to 60 minutes. This goes to show that the parties managed to address practically the entire agenda of relations and that the discussion was intensive. Melania Trump had to stop the meeting. Sergei Lavrov characterized the atmosphere as "constructive"; Secretary of State Tillerson noted that "there was a very clear positive chemistry between the two [presidents]"; Putin addressed Trump as "Your Excellency [Mr. President]" and Trump said on camera that "It's an honor to be with you." However, this was little more than an exchange of courtesies. The parties have vastly different interpretations of the substance and results of the talks; no "big deals" were even discussed; and only modest progress was achieved on secondary topics—disagreements on the big issues are too great.

The sides spent quite a bit of time discussing the issue of Russian interference in the US [presidential] election. According to Tillerson, Trump decisively and robustly began the talks with this issue, and then revisited it several times. According to US sources, the US insisted and will continue to insist on clear guarantees that the Russian side has no more plans to meddle in elections and political processes in the US or European countries. This démarche by Trump was expected. The American president had to demonstrate that he can protect US security and resolutely respond to Russian "hostile actions." It was important for Trump to show his audience that he has issued a warning to the Kremlin and indicated the threat of escalation....

Next came the homework piece we had predicted (apparently prepared on both sides) about setting up a special working group on cyber threats and cyber interference in political processes that will in fact work on practical solutions (most likely, it will be the group headed by [Russian Deputy Foreign Minister Sergei] Ryabkov and [US Under Secretary of State Thomas] Shannon).

This is a sensible move that allows both sides to leave a sensitive issue out of the equation, isolate its negative impact on the rest of the agenda of relations and say that they are protecting national interests while saving face. Trump will be able to say that a tool was created for bringing claims against Russia and deterring its aggression, and Putin will get a mechanism for discussing "American interference" in Russian elections. Understandably, the sides will not manage to agree on anything, [because] they have differing interpretations of the tasks of such a group (Moscow traditionally wants to discuss national Internet sovereignty to protect against America's information influence, while the US [wants to discuss] hacking attacks on critical infrastructure that now includes voting systems in [individual] American states). However, a well-known approach is at work here: If you want to bury a problem, set up a commission. And this would be an important positive outcome of the meeting—isolation of the destructive component [in relations] and readiness to move forward—which would be quite beneficial for Russia.

Russian Foreign Minister Sergei Lavrov had to spoil everything. Speaking to reporters after the meeting, Lavrov offered a rather tough interpretation of the discussion on cyber interference, putting the Trump administration in an embarrassing, dubious position: "Of course, President Trump mentioned that certain circles in the US are still exaggerating, although they cannot prove this, the topic of Russia's interference with the US election," Lavrov said (as quoted by RBC). According to the Russian minister, "Trump said that this campaign has already taken on a rather strange character, because over the many months [that these accusations have been made], not a single fact has been presented. The American leader said that he has heard President Putin's clear statements that the Russian leadership did not interfere in the election, and that he accepts these statements."...

The Americans immediately dismissed this Russian interpretation of the crucial part of the discussion, and it is understandable why: It portrays Trump as a weakling doing the bidding of the Russian president. In this version, Trump fully accepts the Russian position, completely rejects the conclusions of his intelligence agencies and all but concedes that Russian meddling in the election benefited him. This is not the message that Trump and Tillerson wanted to send to the American audience, thus further blowing up the issue. The American media are guaranteed to ask Trump tough questions at his [G-20] wrap-up news conference back in the US. Even if Trump did say such things to Putin (there are doubts about that), Lavrov should not have brought it up during a news conference; after all, Moscow wants the topic of Russian interference to recede into the background, too, so why play it up deliberately? This was reminiscent of the absurd trick Russia pulled when it published without the Americans' consent photos of Trump's meeting with Lavrov and Ambassador Kislyak in May. It would be strange to think that "trolling" that humiliates your partner helps build trust....

What is amazing is that no agreement was announced to continue top-level dialogue. There was no question about a special summit from the get-go—there is simply no agenda for it yet—but failure to confirm a meeting at the Asia-Pacific Economic Cooperation summit in November is disturbing. [This conversation in Hamburg] was a meeting of two geopolitical rivals who found one issue where their interests allow them to work together—Syria. What remains is a conflicting agenda, and addressing it will require both leaders to make substantive concessions and curtail their ambitions. The time for that has not come yet.

Worse Than Under Obama: Why New US Sanctions Have Caused Panic in Moscow

By international relations expert Vladimir Frolov.
Republic.ru, July 28, 2017, https://republic.ru/posts/85367.

The Russian political elite responded with thinly veiled panic to the news that the US House of Representatives passed the Countering America's Adversaries Through Sanctions Act. Russian Deputy Foreign Minister Sergei Ryabkov, who oversees US policy, described it as "destruction of prospects for normalizing Russian-US relations," as a result of which the US would turn into "a source of danger" for Russia (a strong statement for the usually reserved deputy minister).

Comments by pro-Kremlin experts betray confusion: The new sanctions nullify the results of the meeting between Putin and Trump in Hamburg, dashing hopes for a compromise. Moscow has been railroaded on a path to confrontation; any compromise would be a one-sided game. Disappointment with "our Trump" is obvious: He has turned out to be a weak president who failed to block his political opponents and uphold his foreign policy line. He is becoming irrelevant to relations with Russia. What kind of response should be expected from Moscow?

The Kremlin has kept its cool so far: Russian presidential press secretary Dmitry Peskov described the news from Washington as "quite sad in terms of Russian-American relations and the prospect of their development," but reaction from the Russian side may follow only after the new US law finally enters into force....

Panic among the Russian elite is justified. The normalization of relations with the US under Trump that the Kremlin had been counting on and that was seen as the most important element of the "positive scenario" of Putin's [2018] presidential campaign ([based on the notion that] in the difficult struggle with Obama, Putin upheld Russia's interests, [and] the US acknowledged that we were right) has failed. "Détente with America" was a necessary condition for transitioning to "a peaceful domestic development agenda." Now it seems to have been postponed indefinitely. The advocates of further confrontation with the US and Russia's foreign policy based on the use of military force will get more support in the country. So it's the sense of a historical impasse that is driving the panic.

With the sanctions going into force, the Trump administration can no longer carry out an independent policy with regard to Russia, since it has been deprived of crucial leverage over Moscow—i.e., the ability to "reward" cooperation by lifting sanctions. This takes away any incentive for the Kremlin to seek a "big deal" with Trump: After all, "weakling Trump" will be unable to steer his part of the deal through Congress anyway.

The US president will have the flexibility to soften only those elements of the sanctions package that directly concern mutual diplomatic concessions to Russia (and even those still have to be approved by Congress). At the same time, practically everything is focused on bringing about a complete U-turn of Russia's policy on Ukraine and [Moscow's stance on] Russian interference in the US election—an unlikely prospect at this point. It is also important that unlike Obama's executive orders that imposed sanctions for a limited duration subject to periodic review, the new sanctions law has no time frame and does not envision a process of reviewing their effectiveness. This is a clear indication that the situation has worsened for Russia compared to 2016. All this was brought about solely by [Moscow's] irresponsible misadventure with its interference in the US election. Otherwise, things would have been dramatically different.

Just before and immediately after the presidents' meeting in Hamburg, there was still hope that Trump personally was seeking to normalize relations. Given Trump's intention to do so and his general incompetence on this issue, it could have been easy to manipulate him without any serious concessions from the Russian side by methodically pushing through approaches to the Ukraine [conflict] that are favorable to us in exchange for [Russia's] cooperation with the US on Syria. Putin's remarks that "Trump can listen," in contrast to his predecessors, who "tried to pull the wool over our eyes," indicate that [Putin] is confident he can manipulate the unsophisticated American president. However, the sanctions law makes this a moot point.

The passage of the bill reflects the surprising understanding among US lawmakers that Trump cannot be trusted in a dialogue with Putin and that the US president should be greatly restricted when it comes to making concessions to the Kremlin. This came as a shock to Moscow, since it has rendered useless a key Russian foreign policy tool—Putin's ability to leverage personal diplomacy in relations with the US....

Moscow has no good options for responding to the new US sanctions. Any counteraction would worsen the situation for Russia without actually solving the problem. This accounts for the confusion within the Russian leadership, which has limited itself to restrained statements to the effect that it is impossible to keep tolerating such "rude behavior," but let's wait and see what the final version of the law will look like....

Statement From the Russian Foreign Ministry

[No author indicated.] *Rossiiskaya gazeta*, July 31, 2017, p. 6.

On July 27, the US Congress voted on a new law tightening sanctions against Russia. This yet again confirms the US's extremely hostile position in international relations. Under the guise of its "exclusivity," the US is arrogantly ignoring the opinions and interests of other states.

It is well known that the Russian Federation has done and is doing everything possible to normalize bilateral relations, and develop ties and cooperation with the US on a number of key foreign policy issues: namely, combating terrorism, the proliferation of weapons of mass destruction, drug trafficking, illegal migration, cybercrime, etc. We continue to believe that global issues can be resolved only through cooperation. We are confident that most people on the planet share this view. Nevertheless, using the completely preposterous pretext that Russia was interfering in its domestic affairs, the US persists in introducing harsh anti-Russian actions one after the other. This [policy] contradicts international law, and violates the UN Charter, World Trade Organization norms and basic standards of civilized international relations.

The US is approving illegal sanctions against the Russian Federation, confiscating Russian diplomatic property that is secured in legally binding bilateral agreements, and expelling Russian diplomats from the country. These are clear violations of the Vienna Convention on Diplomatic Relations, a universally recognized diplomatic agreement. The adoption of the new sanctions law clearly demonstrates that relations with Russia have become hostage to an internal power struggle in the US. Moreover, the new law aims to use political instruments to create an unfair competitive advantage for the US in the global economy. Such extortion aimed at restricting the activities of Russia's foreign partners is a threat to many countries and to international business. Despite Washington's constant attacks, we have behaved responsibly and showed restraint, ignoring such blatant provocations. However, recent developments demonstrate that certain US circles are determined to pursue a course of Russophobia and open confrontation with our country.

In light of this, we propose to the American side to bring the number of its diplomatic and technical staff working at the US Embassy in Moscow, and the Consulates-General in St. Petersburg, Yekaterinburg and Vladivostok to exact parity with the number of Russian diplomats and technical staff currently in the US. This means that the total number of staff employed at US diplomatic and consular offices in the Russian Federation shall be reduced to 455 people. If the US authorities once again unilaterally reduce the number of our diplomats in the US, we will respond in kind.

The Russian side is suspending as of Aug. 1 the US Embassy's use of warehouse facilities on Dorozhnaya Street in Moscow and dachas in Serebryany Bor.

We reserve the right to take other response measures that may affect US interests.

How Putin Expelled Diplomats and Hinted at Cooperation With the US

By international relations expert Vladimir Frolov. *Republic.ru*, Aug. 1, 2017, https://republic.ru/posts/85470.

Vladimir Putin's statement on downsizing the US diplomatic staff in Russia by 755 people and the Foreign Ministry's statement demanding that the US reduce its diplomatic staff in Russia to parity with Russian diplomatic staff in the US at 455 people looks like not just a response to sanctions on Russia's part, but a significant escalation of the conflict in Russian-US relations.

A more detailed analysis of the measures taken by Moscow, however, shows that there are no grounds for such alarmism. On the contrary, the Russian response is sufficiently restrained and does not completely close the possibility for restoring relations with the US. It makes a show of toughness for propaganda purposes, rather than causing any actual damage to US interests. Both the political and purely technical aspects of the measures announced are important here.

Politically, reciprocal expulsions of diplomats are the simplest and the least painful way of expressing serious disagreement with your partner's policy without causing real damage to your own interests or future relations. It is easy to lift such measures and return to previous levels of cooperation. As for diplomats and intelligence officers, expulsion from the host country is part of the job. In early 2001, the US and Russia, in a tit-for-tat move, expelled 50 diplomats each. Then in October, they were all but allies in the war against Al Qaeda and the Taliban in Afghanistan. Such measures are just an unfortunate incident, not a threat to vital interests.

It is quite important that Moscow's response measures were portrayed as a reaction to the law that was adopted by both houses of the US Congress, codifying and substantially expanding the US sanctions against Russia. At the same time, Trump, who has not signed this [draft] law yet despite stating such an intention, is being removed from the equation. He thus saves face and still has the opportunity to continue dialogue with the Kremlin. The Foreign Ministry's statement draws a clear line between "Russophobes in Congress" and Trump, who is being sent "rays of hope" for cooperation on issues that are crucial to him: combating terrorism, the proliferation of weapons of mass destruction, drug trafficking and illegal migration. Vladimir Putin's rather restrained comment in an interview with the state-controlled Rossia 1 TV channel, aired especially for this purpose, is further evidence of that: He stated plainly that at the moment, he is against further restrictions on cooperation. There will be no sanitation checks of McDonald's, no ban on "US tomatoes" and [exports of] Russian rocket engines [to the US], no selloff of US Treasury bonds by the Central Bank or other plans to cut off one's nose to spite one's face that were proposed by certain "concerned members of the public."

So far, Putin is not ready to completely write off his personal investment in the relationship with Donald Trump. He still hopes for a change for the better at some point, but cannot wait forever on a return on his investment, so he is partially cutting his losses.

Moscow waited seven months: It could have (and apparently should have) responded to the US expulsions [of Russian diplomats] immediately in a reciprocal move, but Gen. Flynn, Trump's [then] national security adviser, told [then] Russian ambassador Sergei Kislyak in a [December 2016] cell phone conversation monitored by the FBI that the Trump administration would review Obama's decision, and asked Moscow to refrain from retaliatory steps. Putin agreed, hoping that Trump would review anti-Russian sanctions altogether. Trump welcomed that decision in a tweet, and Gen. Flynn lost his job two months later, since he had no right to conduct such negotiations with the Russian ambassador until the new US administration took office.

Moscow still hoped that recreational compounds [owned by the Russian Embassy in Washington and the permanent mission in New York] would be returned, but two rounds of talks between Ryabkov and Shannon produced no results. Nevertheless, the current response turns out to be well timed: From a propaganda perspective, everything is being cast as a response to an unfriendly act by the US Congress (even though it's not). [Moscow] simply realized that the Russian recreational compounds, which were seized in such an outrageous manner, could no longer be returned quietly (that would now require Congressional approval). Shrugging off the Americans' escapades had become politically uncomfortable. Anti-American hysteria was whipped up in the Russian media with a clearly coordinated signal to the US: Don't label us as enemies, because then all hell could break loose.

It seems that the White House has read this array of signals correctly. A *New York Times* source in the Trump administration drew attention to the restrained tone of Putin's TV interview, free from flag-waving patriotism. It was as if the Russian leader was not sure about finally choosing a further trajectory in relations with the US, and left the door open.

If you look carefully at the technical aspect of the measures that were announced, they do not involve the expulsion of 755 US diplomats. Unlike the 35 Russian personnel put on an expulsion list 72 hours before New Year's, Moscow has not declared anybody persona non grata. This is only about downsizing the overall number of personnel at all US diplomatic missions (in addition to the Embassy in Moscow, there are also US Consulates-General in St. Petersburg, Yekaterinburg and Vladivostok) to a total of 455 diplomatic and technical staff (just as many as Russia has in the US after all the expulsions), including Russian citizens who work there. The US is to make these cuts on its own and within a reasonable time frame—by Sept. 1.

Of course, the US does not have 755 diplomats here, since Russian citizens make up the bulk of personnel at US diplomatic missions in Russia. Although the US does not provide open data on the current number of its diplomatic mission in Russia, *The Washington Post* and the Diplopundit blog offer a detailed analysis of the US diplomatic presence in Russia based on the State Department Inspector General's 2013 report.... In 2013, there were 1,279 personnel working at US diplomatic missions in Russia, including only 301 US citizens in direct-hire positions (representing 35 US government agencies, including intelligence services); 867 were local hires, including 33 with US passports. To compare, in 2007, the [US] diplomatic corps's total personnel was 1,878 (1,300 local hires)....

Russian diplomatic missions in the US almost never use local hires: All technical personnel—from drivers to schoolteachers—come from Russia on assignment from the Russian Foreign Ministry. This is primarily due to security considerations: Intelligence services are supposed to treat all local hires as enemy counterintelligence agents. Therefore, there has always been a discrepancy between the aggregate personnel numbers at Russian and US diplomatic missions.

Cutting Russian technical personnel would complicate the work of diplomatic missions; US visa processing would be especially delayed and expenses would increase significantly, because specialists to perform a number of technical functions would have to be sent in from the US. However, that is merely an inconvenience; the Embassy and the Consulates-General would retain their main functions, including conducting intelligence operations on Russian territory, unless there are more expulsions.

The Americans have experience in making do without local personnel: In 1986, following mutual expulsions, the Soviet Union limited the size of the US diplomatic mission to 251 and imposed a ban on local hires. Ambassador [Arthur A.] Hartman had to drive his own limousine, his wife had to fix snacks for the diplomatic staff and the Marines guarding the Embassy had to wash dishes, but that's it....

Carefully weighing his resources and assets, Vladimir Putin is using a selective approach in responding to the US sanctions. Russia's response measures are targeted against US diplomacy and intelligence services—i.e., the part of the Washington establishment that is blocking Trump's desire to improve relations with Russia. So far, US businesses, which Moscow sees as its ally in fighting the sanctions, have been kept out of the line of fire. [Moscow] is still betting on creating and deepening divisions within the US elite, continuing the "game of thrones" in the "house of cards" by proxy. As for the Russian public, the cargo cult of the USSR should be good enough: If quotas are imposed and the Americans are banned from hiring local service personnel, as the USSR did in 1986, then [Russia] could once again feel like a superpower.

After Sanctions, There's No Way Back

By Igor Ivanov, Russian foreign minister (1998–2004), president of the Russian International Affairs Council. *The Moscow Times,* Aug. 3, 2017, https://themoscowtimes.com/articles/after-sanctions-us-and-russia-must-rebuild-trust-op-ed-58576.

The event that some politicians tried to prevent and others tried to hasten has arrived: US President Donald Trump has signed a law that expands the sanctions package against Russia.

The law was passed unanimously by both Houses of Congress, something that has not happened too often in recent years. Subsequently, Russia responded swiftly.

This has become the new normal in US-Russia relations, and it looks like we will all have to live and deal with it for a long time to come. We could, of course, talk endlessly about why this has all happened and what could have been done to prevent such a turn of events. But what good would that do?

As things stand, there is no going back for either side. This is why it is far more important to detach ourselves from our emotions—which in any case are never a good place to turn to for advice—and, having assessed the situation with a clear head, think about what to do next.

Sanctions, of course, have never done anyone any good. Still, there is no reason to fall into despair. Ultimately, globalism dictates the rules for everyone—both for those who impose the sanctions and for those who are affected by them. The world is full of problems that require extensive international cooperation, and their number is only growing.

This is why there are more than enough areas where Russia and the US can and should develop a system of cooperation based on their objective interests.

Right now, it is imperative that we identify these areas of cooperation quickly so that we do not miss opportunities that might present themselves, however limited they may be.

In today's world, all states—large and small, rich and poor—are preoccupied with security issues. Most likely, the remainder of the 21st century will continue to unfold under conditions of growing risks and challenges. And there will be fewer and fewer islands of stability, until barely any remain at all.

Every day, reports come in from all over the world of yet another terrorist attack that has claimed the lives of dozens, if not hundreds, of people. For the time being, suicide bombers are content to use conventional explosives to achieve their ends.

But that is only for the time being. There is no guarantee that they will not get their hands on far more deadly weapons. It is just a matter of time before they do, unless the international community recognizes this threat and comes together in order to put a reliable defensive screen in place.

Russia and the US are not simply the largest nuclear superpowers. Objective circumstances have aligned themselves in such a way that Russia and the US are, more than any other countries, capable of steering the world toward either confrontation or cooperation.

The fact that Washington continues to impose sanctions against Russia—and that Russia invariably takes retaliatory steps—gives cause to believe that the two countries have embarked upon a long separation, and will be content in the near future to plot against each other.

If we start down this path, then the chickens will come home to roost very quickly.

Paradoxical as it may sound amid the openly hostile and shortsighted actions on the American side, Russia and the US have no choice but to look for cooperation opportunities.

During their meeting in Hamburg, Vladimir Putin and Donald Trump spoke in favor of cooperation. They identified very specific areas in which cooperation could take place, namely Syria, Ukraine and the field of cybersecurity, which is of particular relevance right now.

The two sides need to expend a great amount of effort in order for these agreements to be implemented. Only then will trust gradually start to be restored, and only then will the sanctions fade away.

Sanctions

By political analyst Leonid Radzikhovsky.
Rossiiskaya gazeta, Aug. 8, 2017, p. 3.

Of course, the sanctions [adopted by the US Congress] are aimed not only against Russia, but also against the man who signed them: Trump. The law prohibits the president from reevaluating the sanctions without the consent of Congress—so these are sanctions against the president of the United States. This is entirely within the spirit of the "peaceful civil war" that has been going on since Trump entered the White House.

But that does not change the fact that these sanctions are also aimed against Russia. So what consequences could they have for Russia?

"Cold war," "relations on the brink"—I find such mantras very overblown. A cold war is a clash between two opposing social systems, where each one hopes to absorb the other. Such a situation is simply impossible today—the real cold war ended with the complete victory of capitalism; that much is a fact. Russia does not have a social system that poses an alternative to America's. We have a market economy and an open society. Unlike the USSR, Russia is not a leader of some global bloc that opposes the West. Therefore, any talk about a cold war is pointless.

I don't see a dangerous brink, either. The US and Russia are not a military threat to one another; we don't have any territorial disputes. Negotiations on nuclear arms reductions could continue or halt, but that is a diplomatic process that should not be confused with "the threat of war." That danger no longer exists, since neither country is willing to threaten the other with nuclear homicide/suicide, in turn being reduced to "radioactive dust." Quite the opposite: The US and Russia are working together on reducing the threat posed by North Korea's nuclear program, for one.

Then there's economics. There are two extreme points of view on this matter: The "irreconcilable opposition" is ecstatic, thinking that now the Russian economy will be knocked out and the system will collapse; optimistic bureaucrats say that new sanctions (along with those that already exist) will only boost [Russia's] economy. Both camps are indulging in wishful thinking.

The sanctions that were introduced against Russia in 2014 are hardly giving it a boost—the damage from them is getting varying assessments, but not a single serious expert believes they are an "invigorating boost" for the economy as a whole (even though the agriculture sector really has benefited [from sanctions]). But neither are the sanctions fatal—the Russian economy has been able to adapt not only to them, but to a much more difficult circumstance: a nearly 50% drop in oil prices. But that's not all—as we know, right now, the decline in gross domestic product we saw in 2014–2016 has been replaced by weak growth (about 1.5% to 2% of GDP in 2017). Perhaps the new sanctions package will put the brakes on that growth, but we are hardly in for an "economic catastrophe."

In addition, the sanctions look fierce in terms of PR, but have a very intricate legal framework. This leaves them open to interpretation depending on the given political and economic situation. Finally, European Union countries have already expressed their discontent with the new sanctions, namely regarding the Nord Stream 2 [gas pipeline project]. We will have to see how the EU responds to its American allies, but it cannot be ruled out that a compromise will be found. Of course, things are not exactly smooth within the EU: Because of the controversy over Siemens [supplying turbines to the Crimea], the EU is now expanding its set of sanctions against Russia.

There is another indicator: As if in response to the sanctions, the Russian stock market reacted with growth [following the US law's adoption]. According to experts, this was the result of foreign investment (however small). The reasons for this are clear: The sanctions have long been factored into stock prices on the Russian market, so market speculators have responded accordingly. This is not a very important factor, but it shows that the Russian economy is not in for a catastrophe, at least in the near future.

However, in the long term (and everyone understands that these sanctions will be around for years), they will definitely worsen the investment climate and hinder the development of modern technologies. However, the problem is that for a large European country, [Russia] had problems developing modern technologies even before the sanctions. So obviously there's a different issue here.

Finally, the sanctions are going to have zero effect on domestic policy in Russia. I'm not even expecting the "consolidation effect" that many people write about. Russian society is already 100% loyal to the regime, the political situation is fairly stable, and there is not going to be a repeat of "mass mobilization against enemy forces" as in 2014. The regime has no need for that, either, since everything is fine.

So has anything changed?

Only on a psychological level for the elite; they are no longer harboring hope that sanctions will be lifted or that relations with the West will improve. That's it. Trump's sensational electoral victory created such hope, hence all the exhilaration in late 2016. But those hopes were doomed to failure from the start. All the champagne toasts were in vain. This is not even about domestic power struggles within the US—there was simply no basis for a real "reset" with the US and a repeal of sanctions. Under different circumstances, Trump could have gladly agreed to a Big Deal with Russia—but what would have been the bargaining chip? Neither Russia nor the US is about to change its stance on Ukraine—after all, that's what the 2014 sanctions were about. An antifascist front, an entente to fight international terrorism—all that is just words. Both Russia and NATO are fighting in Syria, in very different ways, with different allies and different political goals.

So it would have been very difficult to come to an actual agreement there. Yes, there could have been closer cooperation in terms of PR, which is out of the question now. However, the overall framework of both Russian and American policy was formulated a long time ago, which in turn defined the two countries' relationship with each other. Little has changed here, and the sanctions are merely another indication of a psychological divide.

'Trump Is His Own Person'

By Georgy Asatryan. *Izvestia*, Aug. 11, 2017, p. 3.

Editors' Note—The Russian Academy of Sciences' US and Canada Institute, founded by Academician Georgy Arbatov in 1967, is considered one of the leading think tanks for American studies in Russia. Academician Sergei Rogov, an internationally recognized expert on the US, headed the institute for 20 years before moving to the position of academic director in 2015. *Izvestia* met with this researcher to discuss strained Russian-US relations and Donald Trump's policies.

* * *

Question—Are anti-Russian sanctions here to stay?

Answer—Unfortunately, in the US there is bipartisan consensus on Russia, as [there was] during the first cold war, and it won't go away any time soon. I remember the Jackson-Vanik amendment (a 1974 amendment to the Trade Act to limit US trade with countries that restrict emigration, including the Soviet Union—*Ed.*) being adopted when I was in graduate school. It took 40 years to repeal it. I'm afraid this story could repeat itself.

Q—Just a few months ago, many people in Russia, including politicians, hoped that Trump would improve [bilateral] relations and contacts....

A—Those were just illusions, though Trump did talk a lot on the campaign trail about normalizing relations with Russia. The thing is, the US establishment completely rejects his position. I've mentioned the bipartisan consensus, but there's also the media: major [TV] networks, *The New York Times* and *The Washington Post*. Even within the Trump administration, very few folks like the idea of normalizing ties with Russia. Vice-President Mike Pence especially opposes it.

Most appointees to key positions in the Department of Defense and the State Department are staunchly anti-Russian.

Trump's leverage with Congress is limited. The Senate recently refused to repeal Obamacare. Trump's tax reform has hit a dead end. Secretary of State Rex Tillerson urged senators not to impose new sanctions on Russia, but the Senate passed the bill overwhelmingly nonetheless. All this indicates Trump has no control over US politics or his own administration, for that matter.

The latest developments remind me of the TV show "Game of Thrones," where everyone kills everyone, and in the most brutal fashion (laughs).

Q—Will Russia get its diplomatic property back?

A—What the Americans did is a blatant violation of international law....

As for expelling diplomats, these things happen regularly, but the way they explained it this time was very strange. Last December, the State Department notified the Russian Foreign Ministry about the expulsion of Russian diplomats, not even bothering to provide a formal reason. I thought we would counter on the very same day, Dec. 29. But the authorities decided not to respond to this provocation, so as not to fall into the tit-for-tat pattern with the new administration straightaway.

Q—Russia's new ambassador, Anatoly Antonov, will soon go to the US. You wrote earlier that the Americans openly bullied our previous ambassador, Sergei Kislyak. How will they receive Antonov?

A—It'll be tough for him. Anti-Russian hysteria is now sky high. But Antonov is a very experienced diplomat; he headed the Russian delegation at the New START talks (Strategic Arms Reduction Treaty—*Ed*.). He's not an American studies expert, but military issues play an important role in Russia-US relations—especially since, in addition to sanctions, some in Congress are threatening to withdraw from the Intermediate-Range Nuclear Forces Treaty (INF Treaty). The 2018 [US] National Defense Authorization Act includes a provision stating that the US is to withdraw from the treaty in 15 months.

If that happens, who knows whether the New START could survive in a vacuum? There is no treaty on conventional armed forces in Europe, either. There are major problems with several other treaties as well. For example, the US has yet to ratify the Comprehensive Nuclear Test Ban Treaty. We might be facing the collapse of the entire system of arms control treaties concluded at the end of the cold war. This would mean that a new cold war would unfold in a dangerous environment where there are no rules. This is very serious. The Soviet Union and the US negotiated those treaties not because they wanted to disarm, but because a no-holds-barred situation is extremely dangerous. As an expert on these issues, Anatoly Antonov may play an important role here.

Q—How important is it for Vladimir Putin and Donald Trump to have a good personal relationship?

A—The meeting in Hamburg showed that the two presidents had good chemistry, but I wouldn't overestimate the importance of personal relationships. Of course, it's bad when people openly dislike each other. But let's not forget that great personal relations between "buddy Boris [Yeltsin]" and "buddy Bill [Clinton]" did not stop the US from launching NATO expansion or starting the Kosovo war. The same goes for George W. Bush, who had a good personal relationship with Putin and yet withdrew from the ABM Treaty, invaded Iraq and started another wave of NATO expansion. Personal relationships are important, but it's the strategic vision on both sides that plays the decisive role. Right now, the US does not have a clear strategy. Trump isn't making anti-Russian statements, but America's anti-Russian policy continues and is even getting harsher.

Q—And in Syria, is it possible for the two countries to bring their positions closer together?

A—It is, because ISIS (an organization banned in Russia—*Ed.*) is a common enemy for both Russia and the US. We haven't had an enemy like that since Hitler. It's the kind of enemy that makes countries join forces. That didn't happen in Syria because America's main objective was to overthrow the Assad regime. So cooperation between Russia and the US was extremely limited and did not go much beyond deconfliction. There's been some progress recently, though.

Q—How interested is Trump in the Donetsk Basin conflict?

A—So far, it's unclear. Unlike Obama, Trump hasn't been very tough on the Ukraine issue, although in recent weeks, his administration has made several strong statements. But, mind you, it wasn't Trump himself who made them. The State Department said that the sanctions will stay in place until the Crimea is returned to Ukraine, which will never happen, so the sanctions will remain in place forever. Although nothing is truly forever.

Kurt Volker's appointment as the US special envoy for Ukraine means that there could be new elements introduced into US policy. Volker is tough, but he's a realist and a pragmatist. It's possible that with him we'll see a shift in US policy, since so far Kiev has been enjoying unconditional endorsement from Washington.

Q—Many people from the "Bush clan" supported Trump. I mean statements by politicians like [Donald] Rumsfeld, [Dick] Cheney, [Condoleezza] Rice and [Robert] Gates.

A—That's natural, since there are pretty much no liberals left in the Republican Party. The only difference is the degree of conservatism. A former president never criticizes the new president from the same party; it's considered improper. Besides, Condoleezza Rice and Robert Gates played a certain role in Tillerson becoming secretary of state: Trump didn't know him, and they were the ones who recommended him for the post. Today they aren't bashing Trump, but they aren't sticking up for him, either.

Q—So we can say that the "Bush clan" more or less supports Trump?

A—No. There are no grounds for [assuming] that. Trump is his own person. He won by appealing to the voters directly, beating Jeb Bush among others. He went over the establishment's head to talk to the common folk, who then voted for him.

Q—Some Democrats would like to see Trump impeached. There have been a number of calls to that effect in Congress. Is impeachment a possibility?

A—The Democrats are still in shock over losing the presidential race. They thought Trump was a perfect punching bag, Hillary Clinton would become president and the Democrats would secure a majority in Congress. Defeat plunged the Democratic Party into hysteria, so instead of getting to the bottom of why they no longer connect with their voters, they found an easy explanation: It's all Russia's fault.

When I was in Washington in June, I heard from some prominent Democrats that Trump might voluntarily step down. In that case, Mike Pence would become president, and he is much tougher on Russia. He never publicly supported normalizing relations with Russia. As a former congressman, Pence wields significant influence among Republicans on Capitol Hill. In short, impeachment is possible, but unlikely.

EPILOGUE

Where Things Stand in Russian-American Relations

Introduction

In the wake of the dramatic negative shift that occurred in the Russian media's perceptions of Donald Trump in just a matter of months, we include several analyses that offer more recent perspectives on relations between Moscow and Washington in general.

Alexander Gabuev and Vladimir Frolov observe that "meddling" (real and perceived) is assuming a disproportionate role in diplomacy. According to Gabuev, propaganda itself has become the main reference point for Russian-American relations. "It doesn't really matter whether Russian intelligence services did meddle in the 2016 presidential campaign.... What matters is that to the new generation of the US foreign policy establishment, Russia is a foreign power that seriously interfered in the democratic process in their country." On the Russian side, too, Gabuev writes, "real knowledge of America is being replaced with our own propaganda clichés. The future clash of these two groups [of Russian and American diplomats], driven by emotion rather than knowledge and pragmatism, may turn out to be much more devastating than the current level of confrontation."

Frolov also sees the "meddling" issue as a pervasive roadblock to normalizing relations, pointing out a dissonance in perceptions on this issue. Moscow continues to blame the whole mess on Obama-era Democrats and their supporters, while Washington views this stance as an attempt to cover up Russia's efforts to expand its influence where it did not belong. Frolov faults the Russian side for underestimating the anger on the American side: "By refusing to discuss with the US what soured our relations and blaming it all on the long-gone Obama administration, Moscow is merely burying its head in the sand." In a later article, published just before special counsel Robert Mueller's first indictments, Frolov remarks that now both Democrats and Republicans are obsessed with "Russian meddling," turning the issue into a snowball that is destroying everything in its path.

Ivan Kurilla frames the "meddling" theme in the narrative of a long-running diplomatic tug-of-war between Moscow and Washington. Kurilla's analysis comes just after Trump's response to the Russian Foreign Ministry's reduction of diplomatic staff (see Section 4.4, above), in which Russia was given only 48 hours to close its consulate in San Francisco and two annexes, one in Washington and one in New York. While lamenting the seemingly endless rounds of retaliatory actions, Kurilla still believes that "the Kremlin hasn't lost hope for cooperating with Trump." He concludes that improving Russian-US relations should also be a goal in itself: "In this sense, it's important to see that these relations go beyond diplomacy" and extend to the broader context of civil society.

In a similar vein, Tatyana Stanovaya writes that Russians continue to view Trump as a separate entity from Washington as a whole: "Russians think that Trump has 'uncoupled' himself from the US elite, and 'Washington' is no longer a monolithic center but a chaotic, aggressive, anti-Russian environment, with Trump caught in the middle and unable to do anything. This means that Russia's US policy will follow the guiding principle of 'being friends with Trump and enemies with America.'"

However, this more complex outlook on Russian-US relations may lead to a kind of paralysis, as Andrei Kolesnikov writes with a mixture of humor and despair: Citing the fact that Trump and Putin failed to hold a bilateral meeting at the November 2017 APEC summit in Danang (for which the official explanation was that their schedules could not be coordinated), Kolesnikov posits that the two sides not only are at a loss for what to say to each other, but have no political will to move past their differences: "Today, the two countries are facing a new type of Vietnam syndrome: the inability to address crucial problems due to the lack of will to address them."

A Generation Raised on Meddling

By Alexander Gabuev, director of the Russia in the Asia-Pacific program at the Carnegie Moscow Center. *Vedomosti*, Aug. 8, 2017, p. 6.

President Donald Trump has signed the Countering America's Adversaries Through Sanctions Act,[26] which means confrontation between Russia and the US is now enshrined in a legal act and thus bound to continue for many years to come. Yet, as important as it is, this is not the only indication that Russian-US relations may get even worse. The White House at least made an attempt, albeit a clumsy one, to avoid imposing sanctions. But the next administration, be it Democratic or Republican, will be much more hostile toward Russia. There will be a new generation running US foreign policy. These people will genuinely believe that our country is a threat to America and will know much less about it than the politicians of the cold war era. This factor, a direct result of the Russian-US conflict of recent years, is even more important and more dangerous than the new sanctions.

The US foreign policy elite are currently in the midst of a generational shift. The professionals who grew up during the cold war are being replaced with new people who are mostly under 50. This new generation started filling mid-level bureaucratic positions (which are crucial to how the US government functions) back when George W. Bush and Barack Obama were in office. These people were poised to play an even more prominent role: for example, Jake Sullivan, who would have been the national security adviser in a Hillary Clinton administration, is only 40. Donald Trump's unexpected victory somewhat slowed down this process of generational change—both for the Democrats (Sullivan, for example, works at the Carnegie Endowment now instead of the White House) and for most of the Republicans who were part of the Never Trump movement—but did not stop it completely.

These people's formative years came at a time when Russia was no longer the US's top foreign policy priority. You had to be an expert on China, terrorism or cybersecurity to make a brilliant career in government service. Obama's description of Russia as a "regional power" is a cliché reflecting the consensus of this new generation, which no longer views Russia as the biggest threat to America's national security and generally is not that interested in Russia.

Meddling in the US election changed the situation dramatically. It doesn't really matter whether Russian intelligence services did meddle in the 2016 presidential campaign, whether it was their goal to put Donald Trump in the White House and whether their actions had a noticeable effect on the election results. What matters is that to the new generation of the US foreign policy establishment, Russia is a foreign power that seriously interfered in the democratic process in their country and helped bring to power a person who will destabilize the foundations of the country they love over the next few years. Considering that political appointees in the US plan their lives (including marriage and children) almost entirely based on election cycles, some of them now think that Russia has robbed them of the best part of their lives.

It is this generation that will soon be in charge of the National Security Council, the Pentagon, the State Department, the Treasury and the CIA. However, they will know and understand Russia much less than their cold war-era predecessors. They won't have the respect that the two superpowers had for each other at the peak of their confrontation. They will view Russia as a real threat, a cocky and bitter opponent bent on disrupting the liberal international order and damaging US interests all over the world—meaning that Moscow must be put in its place by whatever means are available: new sanctions, supplying arms to conflict zones where Russian troops are present, cyberspace operations, etc.

The problem is that in Russia, too, the outgoing cold war generation in the foreign policy elite (let alone intelligence services) is being replaced with people who genuinely think that the US is Russia's enemy, and that fighting America is an inevitable part of their job—even our country's mission. Just like their US counterparts, many of these people think that the enemy is in a long-term decline (which is why the US keeps trying to harm Russia), and real knowledge of America is being replaced with our own propaganda clichés. The future clash of these two groups, driven by emotion rather than knowledge and pragmatism, may turn out to be much more devastating than the current level of confrontation. This will be extremely dangerous for Russia. Even if nuclear deterrence prevents a large-scale military conflict with the US, armed and systemic confrontation with a country that is still the most powerful nation on the planet will consume a lot of resources our country needs to deal with serious domestic challenges.

The root of the problem is not rivalry between two systems, which was at the core of the confrontation during the cold war; it is a series of mistakes and miscalculations on both sides due to the carelessness of political leaders and their current level of knowledge about each other (which is extremely low and keeps getting lower). The latter includes knowledge of key players: At a critical time for bilateral relations, the Russian authorities and civil society have not had a lot of contacts on Capitol Hill and in the Beltway. There are only a handful of Russians with good access to Washington who are regarded as patriots of Russia with an independent opinion, rather than as SVR [Foreign Intelligence Service] agents. Since Russia has become a toxic issue, the quantity and quality of communication channels on both sides will inevitably diminish, and this will make the situation with Russia-US relations even more dangerous.

Sooner or later, Russia will have to address the problem of poor understanding of the US establishment and inadequate contact with it. The cost of emotional confrontation with the US is extremely high, regardless of whether Russia becomes more liberal in the future or remains authoritarian. It is impossible, of course, to make the US establishment develop warm feelings for Russia overnight: Without a transformation of Russia's regime, which is highly unlikely, even the all-powerful Russian hackers are hardly capable of effecting such a change. Russia should seek to develop a network of personal contacts with leading members of the US foreign policy establishment and civil society, as well as professional ties based on at least a modicum of trust and mutual respect. This would enable us to start developing communication channels with a broad segment of the American elite who oversee US foreign policy, and would also help us understand this policy better. Such contacts would also help US decision-makers understand Russia better....

How the New Cold War Is Getting Out of Control

By Ivan Kurilla, history professor at the European University in
St. Petersburg. *RBC Daily*, Sept. 5, 2017, p. 5.

Demands to close the Russian Consulate in San Francisco (which survived the détente and has been around since the mid-19th century) are a response to Moscow's demand to dismiss several hundred members of the [US] diplomatic staff. That, in turn, was a response to the [US] Congress adopting [a new set of anti-Russian] sanctions and the expulsion of [35 Russian] diplomats—which were themselves a response to Russia's meddling in the US election, which was a response to the sanctions adopted over Russia's actions in eastern Ukraine. The latter was a response to the US helping the Independence Square rallies, which came about due to [Russia] granting asylum to [Edward] Snowden and [passing] the Dima Yakovlev Law, which was a response to the Sergei Magnitsky Act, etc., etc. Each event leads to another, until your memory begins to fail you. The list is endless and extends not only into the past but also, alas, into the future.

The logic of a response step to each unfriendly step is clear—but what isn't clear is the end point, the goal of this downward spiral. The severing of diplomatic relations between two nuclear states that are also permanent members of the UN Security Council looks impossible only to those who have studied the lessons of the Cuban missile crisis. The current generation of politicians no longer remembers that vaccination. But is it really necessary to once again force people into bomb shelters in order to finally stop this dangerous game? What if we don't manage to [avert the crisis] this time?

The purpose of each of these [response] steps also remains unclear. If the sanctions are seen as an incentive to change policies (of course, the world has yet to see sanctions ever be successful against a major state), then shuttering diplomatic facilities strikes a blow to each side and makes cooperation at a nonpolitical level (cultural

EPILOGUE *Where Things Stand in Russian-American Relations*   **343**

and educational exchanges, personal contacts, travel) particularly difficult. And it is these ties that must be leveraged when interstate relations hit an impasse. The first steps toward exiting the cold war began with the signing of the Soviet-American Lacy-Zarubin agreement in 1958, which created opportunities for cultural exchange between the two countries. Now it seems bilateral relations are devolving to the model that existed before that agreement.

It's not that the question of "Who is to blame?" is irrelevant (I know plenty of people who believe that Russia is to blame for the sudden chill in Russian-American relations, and plenty who think that the US is at fault): The sanctions had specific causes, and the Kremlin is not concealing the fact that it took drastic steps in an attempt to change the vector of global development (which, in its opinion, was headed in a direction that did not suit its best interests). However, I'm not sure what purpose answering that question would serve. It's hardly possible to convince the decision-makers in the White House and the Kremlin that they are wrong. The parties can't even agree on whether the argument is about values or power.

Media outlets remind us that the last mutual mass expulsions of diplomats took place in 1986, at the height of "cold war, take two" and just before the start of perestroika.

However, today's war of rhetoric is reminiscent not so much of the 1980s or even the 1950s, but rather the 1930s, when the US accused the USSR of interfering in its domestic affairs. At the time, the Communist International really was quite active in America; the Soviet government declared [that organization] an independent international entity, but the Americans knew that it was financed and controlled by the Kremlin. Incidentally, there is another parallel to that time: American right-wingers were convinced that the Roosevelt-era State Department had been infiltrated by Soviet agents. The late 1940s saw the high-profile espionage case against prominent State Department agent Alger Hiss (apparently he had been spying for the Soviets since the 1930s). The Hiss case resulted in a defeat for Roosevelt-[era] Democrats and the meteoric rise of a young senator from California—Richard Nixon.

This episode at the start of the cold war coincided with a rise in anti-Soviet propaganda in the US and anti-American propaganda in the Soviet Union. Propaganda naturally had an effect on diplomatic exchanges: In 1962, George Kennan, the US ambassador in

Moscow, was declared persona non grata—an unprecedented event in the history of bilateral relations between the two countries. The reason for this was an interview with Kennan in which he complained about surveillance and the hostile atmosphere surrounding American diplomats in the USSR, comparing it to the situation Americans in Berlin faced at the start of World War II.

It is important to point out that even back then, foreign policy was used to settle domestic policy scores: The attack on Hiss resulted in the left wing of the US Democratic Party exiting the stage, while the Soviet threat—regardless of how real it was—became merely a pretext for that reshuffle. In the Soviet Union, anti-Americanism was accompanied by a war against "cosmopolitanism" and closed the door to social reforms.

However, as we look for analogies to the past in today's news headlines, we can also find cause for historical optimism. Deteriorating relations and diplomatic wars eventually give way to compromise and cooperation. Taking irreconcilable differences out of the equation allowed [the two sides] in the early 1970s to come up with the formula of "peaceful coexistence of two states with different social systems" and to begin a political rapprochement. The very same politicians began to behave differently in the changing situation. Twenty years after unmasking Hiss, Nixon became one of the architects of the détente, while Soviet "hawks" sat down at the negotiating table with their American partners.

As we examine Russian-American relations in the context of both states' domestic policy, we see that in today's Russia, the confrontation with the US is a shot in the arm for the "screw-tightening party." However, this scenario has run its course in the last five years, and who's to say that it would play well in the run-up to the [2018 Russian presidential] election. One still gets the sense that the Kremlin hasn't lost hope for cooperating with Trump. In the US, Trump's foes are still the most ardent supporters of confrontation, and apparently this scenario is doomed to last until the end of Trump's presidency. It's a shame that rapprochement between Russia and the US is once again hostage to the domestic situation in both countries, but this does not mean that [improving] Russian-American relations is not a goal in itself. In this sense, it's important to see that these relations go beyond diplomacy; [we must] not create obstacles to contacts at the level of civil society that are able to safeguard elements of trust. These elements are going to be very much in demand at the next stage. Here's hoping that we won't have to wait too long.

Head in the Sand

By international relations expert Vladimir Frolov.
Republic.ru, Oct. 10, 2017, https://republic.ru/posts/86905.

Moscow is sending mixed signals to Washington on the prospects of Russia-US relations. At the top level, Vladimir Putin and Foreign Minister Sergei Lavrov express their confidence that tensions will eventually dissipate, the US will deal with the "domestic crisis poisoning its relations with Russia," and "the world will breathe a sigh of relief" when Russia and the US finally engage in "open and fair cooperation." Speaking at the ceremony where the new US ambassador to Russia, Jon Huntsman, presented his credentials, Vladimir Putin said Russia welcomed "constructive, predictable and mutually beneficial cooperation based on the strict observance of the principles of equality, respect for other countries' national interests and noninterference in each other's domestic affairs." Russia has many friends among US businessmen, Putin said, and they should persuade Donald Trump to improve relations with Russia.

So far, Russia has avoided criticizing Trump directly, depicting him as a victim of the "Russophobic campaign" launched by the Democrats. It is the Democrats, Russia says, who keep pushing the "Russian meddling" narrative after they lost the 2016 presidential election. That is not true but it helps Moscow dodge unpleasant questions about its own actions. Lavrov always blames the souring of relations on the Obama administration which, he says, "planted a time bomb on its way out." It is safe, of course, for Lavrov to say that, because the Obama administration can no longer respond to Russia's top diplomat, and it is also smart, as Lavrov knows Trump hates anything to do with the previous president's legacy.

Moscow is keeping the door of cooperation open for Trump, waiting for the US president to defeat his domestic foes and remember his campaign promise to improve relations with Russia—except that Russia wants better relations on its own terms, not on America's.

War games.

At the lower level, however, Russia has been using much tougher rhetoric recently, and this has a marked negative effect on Russian-US relations. The Defense Ministry is openly accusing the US of supporting ISIS in its fight against [Syrian] government forces near Deir al-Zour and even of providing al-Nusra militants with aerial reconnaissance (that they used to attack Russian military police in Hama Province), and to shell a command post of the Syrian Army, killing Russian Marine Col. Valery Fedyanin and [Lt.] Gen. Valery Asapov.

The Pentagon refuted the accusations of assisting terrorists. Outgoing US Ambassador to Russia John Tefft lashed out at the charges, telling *Kommersant* that they had "nothing to do with reality" and that they made the US "doubt whether Russia is really interested in working with us in Syria." Yet even after direct talks between General Staff Chief Valery Gerasimov and Joint Chiefs of Staff chairman Joseph Dunford, the Russian military continued complaining that mobile groups of ISIS fighters keep "popping up like a jack-in-the-box" from the security zone around the US military base at al Tanf.

It is puzzling that the Defense Ministry pursues its own line in dealing with the US, especially since the Russian leadership insists that Syria is practically the only area where our two countries can work together and, in fact, that such cooperation can help improve relations. The Defense Ministry's claims to the effect that "the US remains the biggest obstacle to a complete elimination of terrorists in Syria" hardly contribute toward this goal and certainly don't help create an atmosphere of trust between the parties. If there is an accident and US troops are killed in a Russian air strike, a bitter conflict will ensue between Russia and the US in Syria. In that case, the US will immediately impose new sanctions on Russia, former under secretary of defense Dov Zakheim told a group of Russian experts at a meeting at the Moscow State Institute of International Relations (MGIMO) a few days ago.

Foreign policy choir.

Sergei Lavrov has also been quite critical of US actions in Syria recently, only without such radical statements. So perhaps it's not that the Russian military has gone rogue; perhaps different players in Russia have been assigned different roles in this [good cop/bad cop] game. But that would only invite further questions as to what strategic goals this game is pursuing. There is also another possibility: Having received no clear instructions from Putin, various Russian agencies are pursuing their own uncoordinated goals with respect to the US. As a result, we are hearing several different voices more or less in line with one strategic policy and with clear red lines they are not allowed to cross. Also, the Foreign Ministry has clearly lost its coordinating role in foreign policy. Today, it is merely one of the many players on the stage, as a delegation from the Washington-based Center for the National Interest (CFTNI) pointed out in its report after a recent visit to Moscow.

Tougher rhetoric is now being used in Russia-US contacts over Ukraine. In the run-up to a meeting between special envoys for Donetsk Basin settlement Vladislav Surkov and Kurt Volker in Belgrade on Oct. 7, Moscow publicly threatened to withdraw from the talks unless Washington got Kiev to show more flexibility in discussing political aspects of the settlement. For example, Moscow wants Ukraine to extend the law on the special status of certain areas of the Donetsk Basin (on Oct. 6, the Supreme Rada approved on first reading the extension of the special status for another year). "Unless security measures and political steps are synchronized, there is no need for Surkov and Volker to discuss the UN mission, or for the Normandy Four [Russia, Ukraine, Germany and France] to discuss the road map. The talks will have to be suspended," Aleksei Chesnakov, a political analyst close to Surkov, told *Gazeta.ru*. This rhetoric comes, in part, in response to a series of tough public statements by Volker, who said, among other things, "We can guarantee that you will find yourself in an even worse situation."

The meeting between Surkov and Volker eventually did take place, and the parties showed moderate progress, but the very fact that Moscow threatens to walk out of the Ukraine dialogue indicates that the Kremlin does not really expect its relations with the US to improve and is even ready to escalate tensions, thinking that escalation and tough rhetoric are much more effective in dealing with the US than flexibility and tactical concessions. This flies in the face of what US Ambassador Jon Huntsman said recently—namely, that restoring Ukraine's sovereignty over its entire territory will be a central issue in his dealings with Moscow.

We are hearing tougher rhetoric concerning the Russian media in the US. The RT television channel and Sputnik news agency may be forced to register as foreign agents. The US government is yet to do so (though it well may), but Moscow has already launched a media campaign threatening US media and journalists in Russia with similar restrictions. This counterproductive reaction only further antagonizes the US. Besides, Moscow should remember that, apart from RT and Sputnik, there are other Russian media organizations working in the US, and almost all of them are government-controlled (Itar-Tass, Channel 1, VGTRK [All-Russia State Television and Radio Company]), and the Americans can hit them with mirror sanctions. Again, instead of a coordinated strategy pursuing long-term goals, what we have is a mishmash of knee-jerk reactions by different agencies who haven't thought through the consequences of their actions.

Question of meddling.

There is one problem in Russia-US relations, the negative effect of which Moscow either doesn't understand or grossly underestimates. Unless a diplomatic solution is found to this problem, it won't be possible to normalize Russian-US relations, let alone take them to a new level. I am referring to Russia's alleged meddling in the 2016 US presidential election.

As CFTNI representatives wrote in their report, Russia does not fully appreciate the extent of anger and irritation within the US political establishment (both Democrats and Republicans) caused by reports of Russia's meddling from US intelligence services and congressional inquiries. Moscow refuses to see that this indignation was the chief obstacle to the Kremlin's hopes of improving relations with the Trump administration. As head of the US delegation, CFTNI president Dimitri Simes said at the MGIMO round-table discussion that Russian-US relations cannot be improved without a diplomatic solution that would put this matter to rest. That means Russia must acknowledge its meddling and offer firm guarantees that nothing like that will ever happen again.

Washington views Moscow's attempts to deny its involvement as a cover-up, Simes said, and this further fuels anti-Russian sentiment. The US is equally irritated by Moscow's strange refusal to discuss US sanctions and what needs to be done to get them lifted. [Moscow's line of thinking is as follows:] "It wasn't our decision to impose those sanctions, and it is beneath us to discuss how to get them lifted." This eliminates all possibility of a reasonable dialogue, which Moscow believes can only start after unilateral concessions by the US—something that Trump would never call a "good deal."

Probes into Russian meddling by special counsel Robert Mueller and congressional intelligence committees are ongoing, bringing to light more and more unpleasant facts. Reports of Russian operatives launching massive ad campaigns on Facebook and Google, targeting the US audience and clearly aiming to help Trump, discredit Hillary Clinton and emphasize polarizing issues that divide the American people, make Russia look very bad. It doesn't really matter that the actual effect of the Russian "ad campaign" was negligible compared to the amount of collaboration between Facebook and the campaigns of Trump and Clinton, the reach of US Web sites like Breitbart News, or the mainstream media frenzy over Democratic National Committee documents and Clinton campaign chairman John Podesta's e-mails that were leaked by hackers. CNN reports that Russia's campaign on Facebook specifically targeted voters in Michigan and Wisconsin, key states where Trump won by a slim margin of just a few thousand votes. This makes the situation look even worse, implying that the Trump campaign and Russian operatives worked together on those targeted campaigns.

The infamous Trump dossier put together by former British spy Christopher Steele has come to play a prominent role in the probes by special counsel Mueller and congressional committees. This is bad news. A year ago, the dossier seemed like a product of someone's sick imagination. Today, a number of episodes described in it have been corroborated (Steele has been questioned by Mueller).

Given the circumstances, it is hard to imagine a solution that would suit both parties. The CFTNI delegation did not see any interest to cooperate from Moscow. As always, Russian officials merely joked about it and denied everything. The scenario proposed by former under secretary of defense Dov Zakheim (Vladimir Putin admits that Russia did meddle, yet denies personal knowledge of the plot and promises to find and punish the perpetrators) looks naïve, of course, and shows how clueless the Americans are about the actual state of affairs in Russia.

Perhaps Putin and Trump missed their best chance to have a heart-to-heart and put the meddling incident to bed, promising each other they would never do anything like that again when they first met in person in Hamburg in July. Russia's initiative to set up a joint working group on cyber threats was probably intended for this very purpose, among other things. But it was formulated very poorly, without considering the response it would likely elicit in the US. Besides, Russia jumped the gun by touting the initiative as a great achievement, thus sealing its fate.

It seems like the Russian leadership, being unable to promptly put this entire matter to bed, is reluctant to take any proactive steps to mend fences with the Trump administration. Moscow thinks that these initiatives won't be appreciated anyway and won't quell anti-Russian hysteria in the US. Meanwhile, by creating problems for the Americans, the Kremlin may force the Americans to budge. But this is flawed logic. It doesn't take into account how the US might interpret such countermeasures given the current situation of chaos and severe crisis in Trump's foreign policy team, which may soon lose Secretary of State Rex Tillerson, once regarded as "Russia's friend." By refusing to discuss with the US what soured our relations and blaming it all on the long-gone Obama administration, Moscow is merely burying its head in the sand.

The 'Russian Trail' Saga: How Trump's Hopes Were Lifted and Then Dashed Again

By Vladimir Frolov. *Republic.ru*, Oct. 29, 2017,
https://republic.ru/posts/87324.

Special prosecutor Robert Mueller, who is investigating Russian intervention in the 2016 US presidential election, filed the first formal charges on Friday, Oct. 27. The names of the defendants were not disclosed, but the first arrests are expected to be made Monday. Those at greatest risk are former Trump campaign manager Paul Manafort, former national security adviser Michael Flynn and former foreign policy adviser to the Trump campaign Carter Page.

This fact brings the "Russian trail" investigation to a whole new level: The media will be actively discussing the substance of the charges, shedding light on the investigation team's leading theories. This will inevitably exacerbate the domestic political crisis in the US....

The irony is that all last week, it seemed that the "Russian meddling" story was about to turn in the president's favor.

New hope.

...A real gift for Trump was an article in *The Washington Post* reporting that Hillary Clinton's campaign staff and the Democratic National Committee (DNC), working through law firm Perkins Coie (which has close ties to [certain] Democrats), had hired private research firm Fusion GPS in April 2016 to collect damaging information on Donald Trump (so-called "opposition research").[27] There is nothing illegal about this; all candidates in all campaigns conduct such research on their opponents. The nasty nuance was that Fusion GPS subcontracted with British firm Orbis Business Intelligence to study Trump's ties, and the one who did that work was former British intelligence officer Christopher Steele, who had worked in Moscow under diplomatic cover until 1994 (he later headed the Russian division of MI-6). Steele gained broad notoriety as the author of a controversial dossier on Donald Trump, describing scurrilous episodes during his stay in the Russian capital in 2013, and painting a sweeping picture of the Trump campaign team's allegedly close cooperation with the Russian secret service to discredit Hillary Clinton and suppress the Ukraine topic during the presidential campaign....

The Washington Post article enabled Trump and his allies to launch a massive attack against the Democrats, and Hillary Clinton in particular, accusing them of collusion with Moscow to meddle in the American election by fabricating and distributing damaging material on Trump....

Hope dashed.

The theory about Clinton collaborating with Moscow against Trump is belied by the fact that the Democrats never used the Steele dossier during the campaign....

American intelligence agencies have not worked closely with the Steele dossier [either]....

Just look at Steele's description of the Russian operations management process: Dmitry Peskov was in charge of the file containing dirt on Trump; the interference operation was controlled first by the [Russian] Foreign Ministry, then the FSB, then the Kremlin administration; Igor Sechin [CEO of state-run oil giant Rosneft] met with Carter Page (a nobody), promising Trump 19% of Rosneft if he lifted the sanctions; [Igor] Diveikin, an assistant to [Putin's deputy chief of staff Vyacheslav] Volodin, managed the collection of intelligence on the US election and also met with Page; Trump's legal adviser Michael Cohen met in Prague with [Federation Council] Sen. [Konstantin] Kosachov and arranged to transfer money from Trump to Russian hackers under the guise of pensions to Russian citizens in the US and Europe—the list goes on. Obviously, this is all poppycock, but it was not provided by intelligence agencies (some people who work there do have a sense of humor, of course, but in such cases, they still try to maintain a semblance of plausibility). It was cooked up by a man whose knowledge of how things work in Russia is either lacking or seriously outdated (Steele was expelled from Russia in 1994)....

Trump and his associates failed to turn the "Russian meddling" debate to their advantage. By the end of last week, the media had already unveiled new negative material on him. First, *The New York Times* confirmed that during the July [sic; June] 2016 meeting with Trump's son and son-in-law, Russian lawyer Natalia Veselnitskaya gave them a memorandum from Russian Prosecutor General [Yury] Chaika about alleged illegal donations to the Clinton campaign from the American investment firm Ziff Brothers and Hermitage Capital hedge fund founder William Browder.[28] Then *The Wall Street Journal* reported that Rebekah Mercer, a key donor of the Trump campaign, had asked data analytics firm Cambridge Analytica (which was promoting Trump on social media) to contact Julian Assange of Wikileaks to offer him more accurate and efficient analysis of the email correspondence stolen from the Democrats (Assange allegedly refused).[29] This borders on violation of a ban on foreign funding of election campaigns ([investigators] have established the campaign team's intention to procure "a thing of value" from a foreign citizen). The media and Mueller are paying increased attention to the Trump campaign staff's Internet work—and the one in charge of that activity was Trump's son-in-law, Jared Kushner.

The unpleasant part for Moscow is that while "Russian meddling" in the election used to be the hobbyhorse of Democrats (who could have been dismissed as sore losers), now Republicans are talking about the same thing—and not in a good way. Now even Trump believes that Russia was trying to hurt him in the election. "Russian meddling" has become a snowball in the US: Now that it's been released, it's rolling downhill, destroying everything in its path, including Russia's foreign policy interests. Whoever started this unobtrusive trolling could hardly have counted on such a devastating effect.

Cold Peace and Hybrid War: How Russia Will Respond to New Sanctions

By Tatyana Stanovaya, head of the analysis department at the Center for Political Technologies. *Republic.ru*, Oct. 27, 2017, https://republic.ru/posts/87302.

The US State Department has put together a list of 39 Russian entities to be hit with sanctions under a law Donald Trump signed in August. This does not mean, though, that these entities are already under restrictions, the State Department stressed; this is just a list of entities that the administration believes have close ties to the Russian government. Working with these entities will be prohibited under sanctions after Jan. 29, 2018. Moscow's response to this new anti-Russian measure by the Trump administration was reserved and disinterested. Yet the actual consequences will be much more serious, if latent.

The new wave of sanctions caught Russia unawares. Since the euphoria from "our guy" Trump winning the election died down, Russia has been watching all the discussions in the US about sanctions with a weary eye, dismissing them as a by-product of domestic political strife. It seems that Russian officials have to improvise whenever they face media outlets looking for a sensation. For example, some Russian parliamentarians came up with an idea of a "sanctions-for-sanctions" bill, but at this point no one has the slightest idea of what this law might look like. The idea is out there, but it is so vague that it will be a while before it can be translated into something practical. And even then, it will be more of a symbolic gesture. Deputy Foreign Minister Sergei Ryabkov is appealing to the Europeans, urging them not to kiss up to the Americans who want to solve their domestic political problems at the expense of European companies: "The only way to describe this is to say that the US is holding international businesses and foreign companies hostage," he said. . . .

Presidential spokesman Dmitry Peskov... was reserved in his comments. While he did refer to the black list as an "alarming" development, he suggested waiting for an official decision. On the whole, Russia's rhetoric is getting less geopolitical and more corporate: Sanctions are increasingly viewed as part of a complex system of measures intended to undermine Russia's positions on various markets (energy, arms exports, etc.) rather than as part of Washington's strategic policy. This enables Moscow to keep the door open for Trump while demonstrating resolve in responding with countersanctions.

This brings us to the most interesting part: The primary consequence of US sanctions will be not just that anti-American sentiment will drive the Russian elite to rally around Putin; more importantly, it will help Russia develop its hybrid warfare tools, including propaganda, trade and political instruments.

Apparently, the Kremlin has made a political decision not to attack the Trump administration or Donald Trump personally no matter what. At the same time, however, Russia will commit substantial intellectual, administrative and financial resources to wage a hybrid war against the sources of external threats (i.e., anybody who advocates or pursues anti-Russian policies). The Kremlin no longer thinks there is a united anti-Russian front coordinated from headquarters (Washington). Instead of demonizing the State Department, Moscow now thinks there is a fragmented array of proglobalist, anti-Russian forces. In the context of the sanctions war, such a shift in Russia's perception of the US will have practical implications.

First, the security clan segment of the Russian elite will view the new black list as additional proof that the US is waging a propaganda war against Russia. In response, Russian security agencies, especially the General Staff, will develop more sophisticated cyber tactics against other countries. Now that the General Staff has been blacklisted by the State Department, it can demand more political and financial support from the Kremlin to develop a more comprehensive and aggressive cyber policy with respect to external threats. The Russian leadership thinks this is particularly important today, given the growing chaos in international affairs. A more chaotic world means that rules and values no longer apply, and key international principles are no longer enforced, which makes it permissible to pursue a more aggressive policy outside the bounds of the law.

Second, given that the Kremlin thinks everything boils down to unfair market advantages (as Putin said repeatedly, including in his latest speech at the Valdai Forum), Russian companies will get the green light to be more aggressive in pursuing their international interests. Competition will get tougher and less civilized, inevitably resulting in further damage to the reputation of Russian businesses affiliated with the government. The recent incident with Siemens turbines for the Crimea is a vivid example of that.

Third, anti-American mobilization within the Russian elite will continue, but in a different way. Before Trump, Russians thought of the collective "Washington" as a relatively monolithic geopolitical entity coordinating anti-Russian policies around the world (Europe, NATO, the UN, former Soviet republics, etc.). Today, their view of the US is more ambivalent. For example, during the "reset period," improved relations between Russia and the US brought down the degree of hostility in anti-American rhetoric in Russia. Today, however, there is no direct correlation between these two things. Russians think that Trump has "uncoupled" himself from the US elite, and "Washington" is no longer a monolithic center but a chaotic, aggressive, anti-Russian environment, with Trump caught in the middle and unable to do anything.

This means that Russia's US policy will follow the guiding principle of "being friends with Trump and enemies with America." At the political level, the anti-Western (not just anti-American) trend will continue and will probably become even more pronounced, especially in the context of the upcoming [Russian] presidential election....

When a country gets ready for a digital hybrid war (or is already waging one), it is important to have your own digital fronts well protected. A quirk of the current stage in this standoff with external threats, though, is that it is increasingly less about geopolitics, and more about business and corporate interests. In a way, this is because the Russian government is more technocratic now; it is adapting to new challenges, seeking greater flexibility and shedding ideological constraints. However, this doesn't mean that Russia's policies will become more balanced. Even if Russia abandons aggressive and emotional rhetoric and adopts a more level-headed and pragmatic approach, its position will remain as conservative as ever or perhaps even more isolationist.

Why Trump, Putin Only Chatted on the Sidelines

By Andrei Kolesnikov, head of the Carnegie Moscow Center.
RBC Daily, Nov. 13, 2017, p. 5.

Public officials sometimes have nothing to say to each other, so they simulate filling the pause with something ostensibly substantive. Aleksei Bukalov, the legendary TASS correspondent in Rome and the Vatican, told me how in Soviet times he was once recruited to interpret for chairman of the Presidium of the USSR Supreme Soviet Nikolai Podgorny on a trip to Somalia. In the Mogadishu airport, the interpreter hinted to his client that it would be good to say something to the host—at least chat about the weather. Podgorny thought hard and then a light bulb went off. He asked the local leader: "Do you have Jews here?" "Yes, but only a few," the leader said, taken aback. "Good," Nikolai Vikstorovich [Podgorny] said approvingly.

When it came time for Russia and the US to "chat about the weather" at the APEC summit, their light-bulb moment was a joint statement that "the conflict in Syria has no military solution." (Who knew? The only things we've seen so far that even look like solutions have been military.) The statement was coordinated by the Russian Foreign Ministry and the US State Department, and it was shown to the public precisely to throw a diplomatic veil over the diplomatic failure of both sides: the full-fledged talks between Vladimir Putin and Donald Trump that didn't happen. The [two leaders'] conversation was characterized as communication "on the margins," while Rex Tillerson and Sergei Lavrov conversed "on the sidelines" of the summit. So this was the news we got from the sidelines and margins, along with friendly handshakes.

You can talk about behind-the-scenes discord (who meets on whose territory), but if the two leaders really had something important to say to each other, something affecting the fate of the world, they would have disregarded the war between [Russian and US] protocol services and just met and talked—for example, about North Korea, as stated at the outset. There is essentially no conversation more important, since the threat of nuclear war is at stake. Instead, the world learned that Putin is offended about suspicions of interference in the US presidential election and that Trump is very polite.

If everything is so hunky-dory, why not get right down to the nitty-gritty? In this case, unlike in many other "domestic" situations in the US, the cursed checks and balances [in the American government—*Trans.*] that our elite are convinced are impeding Trump should not impair meaningful conversation between the two presidents. However, it seems Trump fears taking any step—even a purely routine one—that could be seen as a concession and thus a sign of weakness. Putin's Russia is now so "toxic" to the Western establishment and public opinion that the US president is no longer allowed to make a mistake even in tone, style and format when communicating with his Russian counterpart. Prior to that, as Bulgarian analyst Ivan Krastev once commented, "with the advent of Trump, Putin has lost the monopoly on unpredictability."

However, the basic problem is not this, but rather that neither side has a foreign policy strategy (in the true sense of the word), [instead] making moves that could be called tactical—except that they don't even exhibit any tactics. They are more aptly described in the psychological terms of action and reaction. Someone said or did something, and the opposite side responded "reciprocally" or "symmetrically," and vice versa.

And this is a trait inherited from Soviet/Russian-American relations. There was no actual strategy even during the détente of the early 1970s, when there was in fact a desire to reduce tensions and negotiate—and that was why détente was so short-lived. In his memoirs, Henry Kissinger wrote that he spent dozens of hours in conversations with Brezhnev, but found nothing that even resembled a long-term political plan. Likewise, if the sides lack not only a strategy, but also a mutual desire to improve relations, which is what we are seeing today, we will never get beyond joint declarations. And the new ambassadors, Jon Huntsman and Anatoly Antonov, are doomed to the torment of Tantalus. Our ambassador has already complained that he has been unable to arrange a meeting with anyone in Congress.

Russia's "toxicity" in the eyes of Americans and the US's intractability in the eyes of the Russian elite are leading to a stalemate. Anti-Western hysteria, which is hurtling toward a "campaign against cosmopolitanism," in principle prevents a sober assessment of the situation. Kissinger, describing the upper echelons of the Soviet administration, wrote that these were people who had lived through World War II and did not want it repeated, because they knew what it had cost and what [another such war] would cost. Our current "elite" are capable of only stirring up the masses with "We can repeat it!" And this is dangerously irresponsible. Against this backdrop, the nuclear parity of the cold war could paradoxically serve as a paragon of rational equilibrium.

Vietnam, where this diplomatic failure occurred, is a very symbolic place for such a fiasco. The proxy war the US and the Soviet Union waged for years in Vietnam in the 1960s and early 1970s was ended through gargantuan political and diplomatic efforts. And this lamentable history ended precisely because there was clear political will to end the war, the sides' pride notwithstanding. Today, the two countries are facing a new type of Vietnam syndrome: the inability to address crucial problems due to the lack of will to address them.

Honor and protocol are more important.

Timeline of Relevant Events During Trump's Candidacy and Presidency

- **June 16, 2015**—Donald Trump announces his presidential candidacy.
- **Oct. 28, 2015**—Trump signs letter of intent to build a Trump-branded building in Moscow.[30]
- **May 2016**—CrowdStrike says Cozy Bear and Fancy Bear, suspected of being affiliated with Russia's GRU, are responsible for DNC server hacks that occurred during the summer of 2015.
- **June 3, 2016**—Publicist Ron Goldstone contacts Donald Trump Jr. on behalf of Emin Agalarov about meeting with a Russian official who allegedly has incriminating information about Hillary Clinton's dealings with Russia. *The New York Times* reports the story on July 11, 2017.[31]
- **June 9, 2016**—Jared Kushner, Paul Manafort and Donald Trump Jr. meet in Trump Tower with Ron Goldstone and Natalya Veselnitskaya, Rinat Akhmetshin and Ike Kave-

---

Above: Russian Foreign Minister Sergei Lavrov, Donald Trump and Russian Ambassador Sergei Kislyak in the White House Oval Office, May 2017. Photo: Aleksandr Shcherbak. Reprinted with permission from TASS.

ladze. *The New York Times* reports the meeting on July 9, 2017.³²

- **June 13, 2016**—Guccifer 2.0 releases batch of hacked DNC documents.
- **June 20, 2016**—Paul Manafort named Trump's campaign manager, replacing Corey Lewandowski.
- **July 18, 2016**—Sergei Kislyak meets with Carter Page at Republican National Convention. Jeff Sessions speaks with Kislyak at a Heritage Foundation event.
- **July 21, 2016**—Trump wins Republican presidential primary.
- **July 22, 2016**—WikiLeaks releases 19,252 e-mails and 8,034 attachments from the DNC.³³
- **July 25, 2016**—DNC and Clinton campaign accuse Russian intelligence of hacking their e-mails and giving them to WikiLeaks.
- **July 27, 2016**—Trump says at a news conference that he hopes Russia can find Clinton's missing e-mails.
- **Aug. 2016**—Rebekah Mercer asks Cambridge Analytica if the company could organize the Clinton e-mails released by WikiLeaks.³⁴
- **Aug. 19, 2016**—Manafort leaves Trump campaign over reports about his activities as adviser to former Ukrainian president Viktor Yanukovich.
- **Sept. 8, 2016**—Kislyak meets with Sessions in Washington.
- **Oct. 7, 2016**—The Department of Homeland Security and the Office of the Director of National Intelligence issue a joint statement accusing Russian government of hacking computer systems of US political organizations and releasing hacked information through DCLeaks, WikiLeaks and Guccifer 2.0 in order to interfere with the US presidential election.
- **Oct. 24, 2016**—Trump denies any connections with Russia.

- **Nov. 8, 2016**—Trump elected president.
- **Nov. 18, 2016**—Trump announces Michael Flynn as his pick for national security adviser and Jeff Sessions as his choice for attorney general.
- **Dec. 1, 2016**—At a Trump Tower meeting, Jared Kushner asks Sergei Kislyak about establishing a back channel for direct communication with Russia. The details of the meeting are reported in late May 2017.[35]
- **Dec. 9, 2016**—John McCain delivers the "Steele dossier" to FBI Director James Comey. The dossier, a private intelligence report written by former MI-6 officer Christopher Steele, alleges secret contacts between the Trump campaign and Russia, and that Russia has compromising material on Trump. The contents of the dossier are published by BuzzFeed on Jan. 10, 2017. Perkins Coie law firm hires the research firm Fusion GPS to do opposition research on Trump on behalf of the DNC. Fusion GPS subsequently contracts Steele to compile the dossier.[36]
- **Dec. 13, 2016**—Jared Kushner meets with Sergei Gorkov, head of the Russian state-owned Vnesheconombank.
- **Dec. 22, 2016**—Michael Flynn asks Sergei Kislyak to delay or veto UN Security Council Resolution No. 2334 on condemning Israeli settlements. Flynn later admits to lying to the FBI about this contact with Kislyak.[37]
- **Dec. 29, 2016**—President Barack Obama expels 35 Russian diplomats, shuts down two Russian diplomatic compounds in the US and expands sanctions against Russia after signing Executive Order 13757 to punish Russia for meddling in the presidential election. The same day, Flynn calls Kislyak, requesting that Russia not escalate the situation. The next day, Putin announces he will not take countermeasures against the US in response to Obama's actions.[38]
- **Jan. 6, 2017**—Office of the Director of National Intelligence releases unclassified version of a report stating that

Putin had ordered a campaign to influence the US presidential election.

- **Jan. 10, 2017**—In a Senate confirmation hearing, Sessions denies communicating with Russian government during Trump election campaign. BuzzFeed publishes Steele dossier.
- **Jan. 11, 2017**—Trump tweets that he has nothing to do with Russia.
- **Jan. 19, 2017**—*The New York Times* reports that Paul Manafort, Carter Page and Roger Stone are under investigation by the FBI, NSA and CIA.[39]
- **Jan. 20, 2017**—Trump sworn in as US president.
- **Jan. 21, 2017**—Flynn appointed national security adviser.
- **Jan. 24, 2017**—Flynn interviewed by FBI about contacts with Kislyak. Flynn would on Dec. 1, 2017, plead guilty to lying to FBI during this interview.
- **Jan. 26, 2017**—Acting Attorney General Sally Yates tells Trump administration that Flynn was not truthful to FBI about Russia contacts and may be vulnerable to Russian intelligence.[40]
- **Jan. 24, 2017**—NBC reports that FBI had been eavesdropping on Flynn's conversations in December with Kislyak but found nothing improper.
- **Jan. 27, 2017**—Comey has private dinner with Trump during which Comey would later state Trump requested loyalty from him.[41] On the same day, Ukrainian parliamentary deputy Andrei Artemenko meets with Trump lawyer Michael Cohen and Felix Sater to discuss Artemenko's proposed Ukrainian conflict settlement plan that envisaged lifting sanctions on Russia and allowing Moscow to lease the Crimea for either 50 or 100 years. Cohen said he gave the plan to Michael Flynn. *The New York Times* makes the revelation on Feb. 19.
- **Jan. 31, 2017**—Trump fires Yates.
- **Feb. 9, 2017**—Sessions sworn in as attorney general.

- **Feb. 13, 2017**—Flynn dismissed as national security adviser.
- **Feb. 14, 2017**—Trump asks Comey to drop any investigation of Flynn, Comey says in testimony to Congress on June 8, 2017.[42]
- **Feb. 17-19, 2017**—Munich Security Conference.
- **Feb. 28, 2017**—Trump addresses joint session of Congress.
- **March 2, 2017**—Sessions recuses himself from any investigations related to Russian interference in 2016 election after reports emerge that he had undisclosed contact with Russian officials during the campaign.
- **March 6, 2017**—North Korea launches four Rodong medium-range missiles.
- **March 17, 2017**—Trump meets with German Chancellor Angela Merkel. Rex Tillerson visits Seoul, South Korea.
- **March 20, 2017**—House Intelligence Committee holds first public hearing during which Comey says there is an FBI investigation into possible links and coordination between persons affiliated with the Russian government and Trump campaign staff.[43]
- **March 30, 2017**—Flynn tells FBI he will testify in exchange for immunity from prosecution.[44]
- **April 4, 2017**—Chemical weapon attack in Khan Sheikhoun, Syria. North Korea test-fires ballistic missile.
- **April 6-7, 2017**—Trump meets with Chinese leader Xi Jinping at his Mar-a-Lago estate in Florida.
- **April 7, 2017**—US launches cruise missile strikes against Syria's Shayrat air base.
- **May 9, 2017**—Trump fires Comey.
- **May 10, 2017**—Trump tells Sergei Lavrov and Kislyak at White House meeting that he fired Comey to relieve pressure from the investigation and shares classified intelligence with them about ISIS.[45]

- **May 11, 2017**—Trump says in NBC interview that FBI's Russia investigation was a consideration for him when he fired Comey.
- **May 14, 2017**—North Korea test-fires ballistic missile.
- **May 17, 2017**—Deputy Attorney General Rod Rosenstein appoints former FBI director Robert Mueller as special counsel to oversee investigation into Russian election interference and related matters.
- **May 20, 2017**—Trump embarks on an eight-day, five-country trip that starts in Saudi Arabia.
- **May 21, 2017**—North Korea test-fires medium range ballistic missile.
- **May 22, 2017**—Trump arrives in Israel.
- **May 23, 2017**—Former CIA director John Brennan testifies before House Intelligence Committee about contacts between Trump campaign staff and Russian officials but could not say they constituted collusion or collaboration.[46]
- **May 24, 2017**—Trump travels to the Vatican.
- **May 25, 2017**—NATO Summit in Brussels.
- **May 26, 2017**—Trump attends Group of Seven meeting on Sicily.
- **June 5, 2017**—Putin gives interview to NBC's Megyn Kelly.
- **June 8, 2017**—Comey testifies before Senate Intelligence Committee.
- **June 14, 2017**—*The Washington Post* confirms Mueller is investigating Trump for obstruction of justice relating to his firing of Comey.[47]
- **July 4, 2017**—North Korea test-fires ballistic missile.
- **July 7, 2017**—Trump meets with Putin at G-20 Summit in Hamburg.
- **July 9, 2017**—*The New York Times* reports June 9, 2016, Trump Tower meeting with Veselnitskaya.[48]

- **July 14, 2017**—Trump celebrates Bastille Day in France with French President Emmanuel Macron.
- **July 21, 2017**—*The Washington Post* reports Sessions talked with Kislyak about Trump campaign matters.[49]
- **July 26, 2017**—FBI raids Paul Manafort's home, which is reported in the press on Aug. 9.[50]
- **July 27, 2017**—Congress passes Countering America's Adversaries Through Sanctions Act, expanding sanctions against Russia and putting presidential action with respect to existing sanctions under Congressional oversight. Former Trump campaign associate George Papadopoulos is arrested.
- **July 28, 2017**—North Korea test-fires ballistic missile.
- **July 30, 2017**—Putin orders US to cut its diplomatic staff in Russia by 755 people in response to new sanctions.
- **Aug. 2, 2017**—Trump signs the Countering America's Adversaries Through Sanctions Act.
- **Aug. 3, 2017**—Special Counsel Robert Mueller impanels grand jury in Russia probe.
- **Aug. 29, 2017**—North Korea test-fires ballistic missile.
- **Aug. 31, 2017**—Trump administration orders Russia to close its consulate in San Francisco and two annexes, one in Washington and the other in New York.
- **Sept. 6, 2017**—Facebook says it sold advertising to Russian companies seeking to sway voters during 2016 election.[51]
- **Sept. 7, 2017**—Trump Jr. confirms he met with Russians in June 2016 at Trump Tower to obtain damaging information on Clinton.
- **Sept. 13, 2017**—Justice Department asks RT America supplier to register as a foreign agent.
- **Sept. 15, 2017**—North Korea test-fires ballistic missile.
- **Sept. 18, 2017**—Mueller tells Manafort he will be indicted.

- **Sept. 22, 2017**—The Kremlin, White House both deny that Russia purchased advertising on Facebook.[52]
- **Oct. 26, 2017**—Twitter says it will refuse to accept advertising from accounts affiliated with RT and Sputnik.
- **Oct. 29, 2017**—Mueller files first charges in Russia probe.
- **Oct. 30, 2017**—Manafort and Rick Gates surrender themselves to FBI custody on charges that include conspiracy against the US. Mueller says Trump campaign staffer George Papadopoulos has admitted to lying to the FBI.

Endnotes

1. Adam Davidson, "Trump's Business of Corruption," *The New Yorker*, Aug. 21, 2017, https://www.newyorker.com/magazine/2017/08/21/trumps-business-of-corruption.

2. Adam Szubin, serving as acting Treasury secretary for terrorism and financial crimes, said in a late January 2016 interview that the US government knows Putin is corrupt. The interview came just days after a British government inquiry found that Putin very likely had ordered the 2006 assassination of ex-KGB agent Aleksandr Litvinenko. " 'Putin is Corrupt' Says US Treasury," BBC News, Jan. 25, 2016, http://www.bbc.com/news/world-europe-35385445. On Jan. 28, White House Press Secretary Josh Earnest said that Szubin's assessment "best reflects the administration's view."

3. On Oct. 7, 2016, the Obama administration accused Russia of stealing e-mails from the Democratic National Committee's servers and giving them to WikiLeaks. "Joint Statement from the Department of Homeland Security and Office of the Director of National Intelligence on Election Security," US Department of Homeland Security, Oct. 7, 2016, https://www.dhs.gov/news/2016/10/07/joint-statement-department-homeland-security-and-office-director-national.

4. Reference to protests on Moscow's Bolotnaya Square, among other places, following the 2011 State Duma elections and the 2012 presidential election.

5. Reference to a scene in O. Henry's short story "The Roads We Take," where a train robber in the Wild West shoots his partner, claiming that the one horse they have left, named Bolivar, is too tired to carry both of them.

6. According to *The Washington Post*, Republican platform committee member Diana Denman proposed inserting new language that voiced stronger support for Ukraine; Trump staffers changed the suggested phrase "lethal defensive weapons" to "appropriate assistance." Josh Rogin, "The Trump

Campaign Denies Its Own Ukraine Policy," *The Washington Post*, Aug. 1, 2016, https://www.washingtonpost.com/news/josh-rogin/wp/2016/08/01/the-trump-campaign-denies-its-own-ukraine-policy/?utm_term=.dfac5a9115c5. The full text of the Republican Party's 2016 platform can be found here: https://www.gop.com/the-2016-republican-party-platform/.

7. In October 2011, under Yanukovich's presidency, Timoshenko was sentenced to seven years in prison for abuse of office. Shortly after Yanukovich was ousted by a massive Ukrainian protest movement and fled to Russia in February 2014, she was freed by the new Kiev government.

8. David E. Sanger and Maggie Haberman, "Transcript: Donald Trump on NATO, Turkey's Coup Attempt and the World," *The New York Times*, July 21, 2016, https://www.nytimes.com/2016/07/22/us/politics/donald-trump-foreign-policy-interview.html.

9. Megan Twohey and Scott Shane, "A Back-Channel Plan for Ukraine and Russia, Courtesy of Trump Associates," *The New York Times*, Feb. 19, 2017, https://www.nytimes.com/2017/02/19/us/politics/donald-trump-ukraine-russia.html.

10. See, for example: "Trump Jr. Scandal: Russian Lawyer Veselnitskaya Ready 'to Share Everything' With Senate," RT.com, July 18, 2017, https://www.rt.com/news/396728-russian-lawyer-scandal-america/.

11. Del Quentin Wilber and Byron Tau, "Special Counsel Robert Mueller Impanels Washington Grand Jury in Russia Probe," *The Wall Street Journal*, Aug. 3, 2017, https://www.wsj.com/articles/special-counsel-mueller-impanels-washington-grand-jury-in-russia-probe-1501788287.

12. Ken Dilanian, "FBI Finds Nothing Amiss in Flynn-Russia Eavesdrop: Official," NBC News, Jan. 24, 2017, https://www.nbcnews.com/politics/politics-news/fbi-finds-nothing-amiss-flynn-russia-eavesdrop-official-n711226.

13. Greg Miller, Adam Entous and Ellen Nakashima, "National Security Adviser Flynn Discussed Sanctions With Russian Ambassador, Despite Denials, Officials Say," *The Washington Post*, Feb. 9, 2017, https://www.washingtonpost.com/world/national-security/national-security-adviser-flynn-discussed-sanctions-with-russian-ambassador-despite-denials-officials-say/2017/02/09/f85b29d6-ee11-11e6-b4ff-ac2cf509efe5_story.html?utm_term=.b5e2ae621270.

14. Alexandra King, "Kremlin Spokesman: 'Russia Is Being Demonized,' " CNN, March 14, 2017, http://www.cnn.com/2017/03/12/politics/peskov-on-gps-cnntv/index.html.

15. "Interview to NBC," Kremlin.ru, June 5, 2017, http://en.kremlin.ru/events/president/news/54688.

16. Adam Entous, Devlin Barrett and Rosalind S. Helderman, "Clinton Campaign, DNC Paid for Research That Led to Russia Dossier," *The Washington Post*, Oct. 24, 2017, https://www.washingtonpost.com/world/national-security/clinton-campaign-dnc-paid-for-research-that-led-to-russia-dossier/2017/10/24/226fabf0-b8e4-11e7-a908-a3470754bbb9_story.html?utm_term=.aafc3650b30c.

17. Damian Paletta, "U.S. Blames Russia for Recent Hacks," *The Wall Street Journal*, Oct. 7, 2016, https://www.wsj.com/articles/u-s-blames-russia-for-recent-hacks-1475870371.

18. Rebecca Ballhaus, "Trump Donor Asked Data Firm If It Could Better Organize Hacked Emails," *The Wall Street Journal*, Oct. 27, 2017, https://www.wsj.com/articles/trump-donor-asked-data-firm-if-it-could-better-organize-hacked-emails-1509133587.

19. David A. Fahrenthold, "Trump Recorded Having Extremely Lewd Conversation About Women in 2005," *The Washington Post*, Oct. 8, 2016, https://www.washingtonpost.com/politics/trump-recorded-having-extremely-lewd-conversation-about-women-in-2005/2016/10/07/3b9ce776-8cb4-11e6-bf8a-3d26847eeed4_story.html?utm_term=.1e19aea0d542.

20. A PDF file of the public version of the DNI report released on Jan. 6 can be found here: https://www.dni.gov/files/documents/ICA_2017_01.pdf.

21. With regard to confidence ratings, the concluding sentences from this paragraph in the report read: "All three agencies agree with this judgment. CIA and FBI have high confidence in this judgment; NSA has moderate confidence."

22. A full text of the Astana memorandum, which was executed in English, can be found on the Web site of the Russian Ministry of Foreign Affairs, among others. The MFA copy was posted on May 6, 2017. "Memorandum on the Creation of De-escalation Areas in the Syrian Arab Republic." http://www.mid.ru/en/foreign_policy/news/-/asset_publisher/cKNonkJE02Bw/content/id/2746041.

23. These refer to Executive Order 13660 (March 6, 2014) "Blocking Property of Certain Persons Contributing to the Situation in Ukraine"; Executive Order 13661 (March 16, 2014) "Blocking Property of Additional Persons Contributing to the Situation in Ukraine"; Executive Order 13662 (March 20, 2014) "Blocking Property of Additional Persons Contributing to the Situation in Ukraine"; and Executive Order 13685 (Dec. 19, 2014) "Blocking Property of Certain Persons and Prohibiting Certain Transactions With Respect to the Crimea Region of Ukraine."

24. This refers to Executive Order 13757 (Dec. 29, 2016) "Taking Additional Steps to Address the National Emergency with Respect to Significant Malicious Cyber-Enabled Activities." The sanctions stemming from that executive order are outlined in a White House statement dated Dec. 29, 2016, https://obamawhitehouse.archives.gov/the-press-office/2016/12/29/statement-president-actions-response-russian-malicious-cyber-activity. The sanctions include declaring 35 Russian intelligence operatives persona non grata and shutting down two Russian diplomatic compounds, one in Maryland and the other in New York.

25. The Russian publication cut out part of the last sentence from the CNN source. The full sentence quoted by Jim Acosta of CNN (May 12, 2017) read: "That's the problem with the Russians—they lie." http://www.cnn.com/2017/05/11/politics/oval-office-photos-donald-trump-russians/index.html.

26. A PDF of the act, which became law on Aug. 2, 2017, can be found here: https://www.congress.gov/115/plaws/publ44/PLAW-115publ44.pdf.

27. David E. Sanger and Eric Schmitt, "Spy Agency Consensus Grows That Russia Hacked DNC," *The New York Times*, July 26, 2016, https://www.nytimes.com/2016/07/27/us/politics/spy-agency-consensus-grows-that-russia-hacked-dnc.html.

28. Sharon LaFraniere and Andrew E. Kramer, "Talking Points Brought to Trump Tower Meeting Were Shared With Kremlin," *The New York Times*, Oct. 27, 2017, https://www.nytimes.com/2017/10/27/us/politics/trump-tower-veselnitskaya-russia.html.

29. Jack Stubbs, "Putin Says He Doesn't Know Who Hacked US Democratic Party: Bloomberg," Reuters, Sept. 2, 2016, https://www.reuters.com/article/us-russia-usa-putin/putin-says-he-doesnt-know-who-hacked-u-s-democratic-party-bloomberg-idUSKCN1180NV.

30. "Trump's Business Sought Deal on a Trump Tower in Moscow While He Ran for President," *The Washington Post*, Aug. 27, 2017, https://www.washingtonpost.com/politics/trumps-business-sought-deal-on-a-trump-tower-in-moscow-while-he-ran-for-president/2017/08/27/d6e95114-8b65-11e7-91d5-ab4e4bb76a3a_story.html.

31. Jo Becker, Adam Goldman and Matt Apuzzo, "Russian Dirt on Clinton? 'I Love It.' Donald Trump Jr. Said," *The New York Times*, July 11, 2017, https://www.nytimes.com/2017/07/11/us/politics/trump-russia-email-clinton.html.

32. Matt Apuzzo, Jo Becker and Adam Goldman, "Trump's Son Met With Russian Lawyer After Being Promised Damaging Information on Clinton," *The New York Times*, July 9, 2017, https://www.nytimes.com/2017/07/09/us/politics/trump-russia-kushner-manafort.html.

33. Karen Tumulty and Tom Hamburger, "WikiLeaks Releases Thousands of Documents about Clinton and Internal Deliberations," *The Washington Post*, July 22, 2016, https://www.washingtonpost.com/news/post-politics/wp/2016/07/22/on-eve-of-democratic-convention-wikileaks-releases-thousands-of-documents-about-clinton-the-campaign-and-internal-deliberations/.

34. Rebecca Ballhaus, "Trump Donor Asked Data Firm if It Could Better Organize Hacked Emails," *The Wall Street Journal*, Oct. 27, 2017, https://www.wsj.com/articles/trump-donor-asked-data-firm-if-it-could-better-organize-hacked-emails-1509133587.

35. Ellen Nakashima, Adam Entous and Greg Miller, "Russian Ambassador Told Moscow That Kushner Wanted Secret Communications Channel With Kremlin," *The Washington Post*, May 26, 2017, https://www.washingtonpost.com/world/national-security/russian-ambassador-told-moscow-that-kushner-wanted-secret-communications-channel-with-kremlin/2017/05/26/520a14b4-422d-11e7-9869-ba8b446820a_story.html.

36. Adam Entous, Devlin Barret and Rosalind Helderman, "Clinton Campaign, DNC Paid for Research That Led to Russia Dossier," *The Washington Post*, Oct. 24, 2017. https://www.washingtonpost.com/world/national-security/clinton-campaign-dnc-paid-for-research-that-led-to-russia-dossier/2017/10/24/226fabf0-b8e4-11e7-a908-a3470754bbb9_story.html.

37. "Michael Flynn's Guilty Plea: 10 Key Takeaways," *The New York Times*, Dec. 1, 2017, https://www.nytimes.com/2017/12/01/opinion/michael-flynn-guilty-plea-takeaways.html?

action=click&pgtype=Homepage&clickSource=story-heading &module=opinion-c-col-left-region&region=opinion-c-col-left-region&WT.nav=opinion-c-col-left-region.

38. Michael S. Schmidt, "Documents Reveal New Details on What Trump Team Knew About Flynn's Calls With Russia's Ambassador," *The New York Times*, Dec. 1, 2017, https://www.nytimes.com/2017/12/01/us/politics/flynn-russia-sanctions.html.

39. Michael S. Schmidt, Matthew Rosenberg and Adam Apuzzo, "Intercepted Russian Communication Part of Inquiry Into Trump Associates," *The New York Times*, https://www.nytimes.com/2017/01/19/us/politics/trump-russia-associates-investigation.html.

40. "Yates: I warned Warned White House That Flynn Could Be Blackmailed," AP, May 8, 2017, https://nypost.com/2017/05/08/yates-i-warned-white-house-that-flynn-could-be-blackmailed/.

41. Michael S. Schmidt, "In a Private Dinner, Trump Demanded Loyalty. Comey Demurred," *The New York Times*, May 11, 2017, https://www.nytimes.com/2017/05/11/us/politics/trump-comey-firing.html.

42. "READ: James Comey's Prepared Testimony," CNN.com, June 8, 2017, http://www.cnn.com/2017/06/07/politics/james-comey-memos-testimony/index.html.

43. Matt Apuzzo, Matthew Rosenberg and Emmarie Huetteman, "FBI Is Investigating Trump's Russia Ties, Comey Confirms," *The New York Times*, March 20, 2017, https://www.nytimes.com/2017/03/20/us/politics/fbi-investigation-trump-russia-comey.html.

44. Shane Harris, Carol E. Lee and Julian E. Barnes, "Mike Flynn Offers to Testify in Exchange for Immunity," *The Wall Street Journal*, March 31, 2017, https://www.wsj.com/articles/mike-flynn-offers-to-testify-in-exchange-for-immunity-1490912959.

45. Jessica Taylor, "Report: Trump Told Russians He Fired 'Nut Job' Comey Because of Investigation," NPR.org, May 19, 2017, https://www.npr.org/2017/05/19/529171249/report-trump-told-russians-he-fired-nut-job-comey-because-of-investigation.

46. Brian Naylor, "Former CIA Director Tells Lawmakers About 'Very Aggressive' Russian Election Meddling," NPR.org, May 23, 2017, https://www.npr.org/2017/05/23/529598301/former-cia-director-tells-lawmakers-about-very-aggressive-russian-election-meddl.

47. Devlin Barrett, Adam Entous, Ellen Nakashima and Sari Horwitz, "Special Counsel Is Investigating Trump for Possible Obstruction of Justice, Officials Say," *The Washington Post*, June 14, 2017, https://www.washingtonpost.com/world/national-security/special-counsel-is-investigating-trump-for-possible-obstruction-of-justice/2017/06/14/9ce02506-5131-11e7-b064-828ba60fbb98_story.html?utm_term=.1129f80f59c3.

48. Matt Apuzzo, Jo Becker and Adam Goldman, "Trump's Son Met With Russian Lawyer After Being Promised Damaging Information on Clinton," *The New York Times*, July 9, 2017, https://www.nytimes.com/2017/07/09/us/politics/trump-russia-kushner-manafort.html.

49. Ellen Nakashima and Greg Miller, "Sessions Discussed Trump Campaign-Related Matters With Russian Ambassador, US Intelligence Intercepts Show," *The Washington Post*, July 21, 2017, https://www.washingtonpost.com/world/national-security/sessions-discussed-trump-campaign-related-matters-with-russian-ambassador-us-intelligence-intercepts-show/2017/07/21/3e704692-6e44-11e7-9c15-177740635e83_story.html.

50. Carol D. Leonnig, Tom Hamburger and Rosalind S. Helderman, "FBI Conducted Predawn Raid of Former Trump Campaign Chairman Manafort's Home," *The Washington Post*, Aug. 9, 2017, https://www.washingtonpost.com/politics/

fbi-conducted-predawn-raid-of-former-trump-campaign-chairman-manaforts-home/2017/08/09/5879fa9c-7c45-11e7-9d08-b79f191668ed_story.html.

51. Carol D. Leonnig, Tome Hamburger and Rosalind S. Helderman, "Russian firm tied to pro-Kremlin propaganda advertised on Facebook during election," *The Washington Post*, Sept. 6, 2017, https://www.washingtonpost.com/politics/facebook-says-it-sold-political-ads-to-russian-company-during-2016-election/2017/09/06/32f01fd2-931e-11e7-89fa-bb822a46da5b_story.html.

52. Eileen Sullivan, "Trump Dismisses 'Russia Hoax' as Facebook Turns Over Ads Tied to Campaign," *The New York Times*, Sept. 22, 2017, https://www.nytimes.com/2017/09/22/us/politics/trump-russia-hoax-facebook-ads.html.

Subject Index

A

Adelson, Sheldon
Palestinian-Israeli settlement role, 135

Afghanistan
NATO withdrawal from, 217
US global policeman attempts, 76

Agalarov, Aras
Emin video promoting Miss Universe pageant, 18
Trump campaign funding charges, 154
Trump contacts, 1
Trump Tin Russia proposed, 17

Antonov, Anatoly
Appointment, 334
Toxic Russian-American relations atmosphere impacting future talks, 359

APEC summit
Trump-Putin chat, 357

APT 29
Hacking, 178

arms control
START Treaties (see entry below)
Trump administration prospects, 113
Trump as negotiator (see entry below)

Artemenko, Andrei
Ukraine peace plan proposal, 160

Assange, Julian
Intentional release of DNC e-mails, 176

B

Baltics
Trump's NATO criticisms, concerns re, 112

bankruptcy
Trump's problems with, 7, 90

Bannon, Steve
Palestinian-Israeli settlement role, 135

branding
Generally, 90
Trump Tower Batumi, 13
Trump trademark registered in Russia, 11

Brennan, John
House Intelligence Committee testimony, 168

Brexit
Conservative renaissance movement, 99
EU impact, 218
Trump approval, 209, 216
Trump victory compared, 91

Browder, William
Magnitsky Act lobbying, 163

Buchanan, Patrick
2000 Presidential campaign vs. Trump, 1, 4

Bulgaria
Russian zone of interests as including, 307

Bush, George H. W.
Cold war victory claim, 137
Nuclear disarmament policy, 273
Trump foreign policy compared, 79

Bush, George W.
Gore contest, 2000, 74
Iraq war, Trump criticism, 9
Nuclear disarmament policy, 273
Obama policies contrasted, 77
Prosperity, Obama administration compared, 118
Putin view, 32

Bush, Jeb
Trump primary battles, 31

C

Cambridge Analytica
Election meddling, 353

checks and balances
Russian-US negotiations impacted by, 358
Threats to US political system, 29

China
Import duties in a Trump administration, 91
North Korea relations
  As complicating US-Chinese relations, 268
  Assistance, US trade threats, 293
  Russian and Chinese involvements compared, 282
  Trump call for pressure on, 268
  Trump demand for China involvement, 278
Trump job-stealing claims, 57
Trump policies, Sino-Russian effects, 27
Trump promise to bring back jobs from, 301

CIA
Brennan's House Intelligence Committee testimony, 168
Pompeo appointment, 129

climate agreement
Consequences of America exiting, 227
Macron appeal to American people, 229
Macron reaction to US withdrawal, 235
Trump criticisms, 90
Trump promise to revisit issue, 236
US withdrawal announcement, 205, 229

Clinton, Bill
Dole contest, 1996, 74
E-mail hacks of Clinton Foundation, 176
Nuclear disarmament policy, 273
Yeltsin relationship, 335

Clinton, Hillary
Campaign hacks, possible motives, 179
Classified information, mishandling problem, 32
Democratic nomination, 33
DNC's Sanders e-mails, release of, 157
E-mails, FBI investigation, 51
Exceptionalism, 24, 43, 52
Hawkish Russian policy, 60
Latent distrust of women leaders as election factor, 96
Negative views of, 98
Obama presidential contest, 34
Obama's Russia strategy compared, 32
Presidential dynasties concern, 51
Primary battles, 29
Putin relationship strategies, 24
Putin understanding difficulties, 65
Russian policy predictions, 34
Russophobism charges, 47
"Send her to jail" slogan, 100
Traditional American foreign policy consensus, 77
Ukraine policy, 110

CNN
Fake news, Trump criticism, 140

Coats, Daniel
Russian travel ban, 188

Cohen, Mike
Russia contacts, 160

Comey, James
Firing, 298, 314

counterterrorism
See ISIS and Terrorism

Cozy Bear
Hacking, 178, 179, 193

Crimea
NATO response to Russian annexation, 210
Russian lease proposal, 161

Sanctions, lifting, 161
Trump recognition of Crimea as
  Russian, 111, 210
Trump views of annexation, 37

CrowdStrike
Hacking, Russian espionage
  groups charges, 175, 178

Cruz, Ted
Trump primary battles, 28, 31

cyberattacks
See Hacking and Spying

Czech Republic
EU proposals for NATO
  successor military force, 115
Russian zone of interests as
  including, 307
Trump appeal to "second-rate"
  EU members, 233

D

DCLeaks.com
Hacking, 178

Democrats
Fusion GPS, DNC hiring, 351
Hacking of Democratic Party
  servers, 193
Putin-Trump bromance
  suggestion, 151
Russian press coverage of DNC
  hacks, 47
"Russophobic campaign" of, 345
Trump impeachment
  sentiments, 336
WikiLeaks (see entry below)

Dole, Bob
1996 campaign, 74

dossier
See Trump Dossier

Dugin, Aleksandr
Trump support, 34

E

election meddling
See also Hacking and Spying
Cambridge Analytica, 353

Electronic voting systems, fraud
  concerns, 72
Formal charges filing, 351
Graham comments, 187
McCain comments, 187
Mook charges, 158
Moscow underestimation of
  problem, 348
Mueller investigation, 349
Putin interview responses, 168
Putin knowledge denial, 350
Republican concerns, 353
Rigged election charges, 72
Russian public opinion, 38, 48
Ryabkov on Russian observers
  in US election voting, 71
Trump rigged election
  charges, 72
Trump post election press
  conference, 140, 141

election predictions
Zhirinovsky effect, 97

elitism
See also Globalism, Populism
  and Nationalism
American elite as unprepared for
  Trump election, 121
Angry electorate reaction, 77
Anti-elite revolt in American
  society, 52
Bush-Clinton criticism, 56
Russian sanctions, elites
  impacted, 332
Trump conspiracy charges, 42
Trump criticisms, 32
US-Russia relationships,
  political elites as driving, 25

Europe and European Union
Generally, 132
Brexit, EU impact, 218
Crumbling foundation of
  American leadership, 219
External stabilizer role in US-
  Russian relations, 223
Macron vs. Merkel leadership
  tensions, Trump
  influences, 235
Mounting anti-American
  sentiments, 219
NATO (see entry below)

North-South internal divisions, 225
Old Europe and New Europe, 231
Pence praise of common market, 211
Populist and nationalist forces, strengthening of, 221
Russian relations, 132
Russian sanctions
  EU policy, 304
  EU responses, 331
  Trump administration concerns, 207
Trump administration effect on balance of power, 224
Trump administration play-ing of European card, 222
Trump administration references to new challenges, 208
Trump appeal to "second-rate" EU members, 233
Trump approval of Brexit, 209, 216
Trump desire to pit Eastern Europe against Western Europe, 235
Trump influences in Eastern Europe, 230
Trump view of foreign policy issues, 78
US military protection, continuing need for, 214
Visegrad group, 225
Washington's firmer position in Europe, EU effects, 223

exceptionalism
Clinton praise of, 52
Clinton view, 24, 43
Globalism tensions, 45
Russian Constitution, 44
Russian criticized, 50

F

fake news
Pence criticism, 139
Politico Magazine study, 49
Russian hacking involvement, fake premises for, 190

Fancy Bear
Hacking activities, 178, 193, 194

FBI
Clinton e-mail investigation, 51
Comey firing, 298, 314
Kislyak eavesdropping, 165
Kushner's campaign role, investigation, 169
Manafort's Ukraine activities, investigation, 150
Republican Party arms sales campaign plank, investigation of removal of, 157

Fillon, François
Russian relations, 133
Russian sanctions policy, 108, 304

Finland
EU proposals for NATO successor military force, 116

Flynn, Michael
Activities in Russia, 157
Appointment, 125
Firing, 166, 243, 311
ISIS threat, prioritizing, 129
Kislyak contacts
  Incomplete information to Pence re, 166
  Kislyak's comments on, 170
Radical Islam views, 126
Russian sanctions, Flynn-Kislyak negotiations, 325
Ukraine peace plan proposal, 160

foreign trade
Dollar strength issues, 301
Globalization as paving way for future agreements, 212
NAFTA's fate in a Trump administration, 91
North Korea
  Generally, 268
  China's assistance, US trade threats, 293
  Russia, 287
Pence praise of EU common market, 211
Russian sanctions

Market advantage motive
claims, 356
Trade implications, 323
Trans-Pacific and Transatlantic
Partnerships (see entry below)
Trump energy independence
commitment, 300
Trump import duties threats, 57
Trump tariffs promise, 301
Trump view of trade as foreign
policy tool, 124
World Trade Organiation, 91

Fox News
Anti-immigrant agenda, 41
Negative views on Russia and
Putin, 43
Pro-Trump slant, 40

framing
Populist rhetoric, 42

France
EU proposals for NATO
successor military force, 115

Friedman, David
Palestinian-Israeli peace
process view, 135

Fusion GPS
DNC hiring, 351

G

G-20 meeting
See Hamburg G-20 Summit

Gates, Rick
Ukrainian lobbying
activities, 152

Gatov, Vasily
Hacking charges, comments, 177

Georgia
Nuclear policy and Georgian
conflict, 270
Trump Tower Batumi, 1, 13

Germany
EU proposals for NATO
successor military force, 115
NATO financial support, 210

Glazyev, Sergei
Reaction to Trump victory, 104

globalism
See also Elitism; Populism and
Nationalism,
Collapse of fundamental
principles constituting
globalization, 121
Dark side of globalization, 75
Exceptionalism tensions, 45
Future trade agreements,
globalization as paving
way, 212
Hamburg G-20 Summit
protesters, 263
Isolationist Trump and globalist
Macron meet, 235
New era of slowing
globalization, 119
Reaction of globalized world to
Trump victory, 120
Trump capitalism and globalist
capitalism distinguished, 117
Trump opposition to
globalization, 37, 77
Trump views, 36
Uncontrollable forces of
globalization, 76
US-led liberal international
order, fate of in Trump
administration, 30
"Who's Afraid of Donald
Trump?", 36

Gore, Al
Bush contest, 1996, 74

Gorkov, Sergei
Kushner's meetings with, 169

Graham, Lindsey
Iran criticisms, 241
Moscow election interference
comments, 187

GRU
Manafort connection, 153

H

hacking and spying
Generally, 173 et seq.
APT 29, 178
Blackmail of Western politicians, 199
Clinton campaign hacks, possible motives, 179
Clinton Foundation hacks, 176
Cozy Bear, 178, 179, 193
CrowdStrike, Russian espionage groups charges, 175, 178
DCLeaks.com, 178
Democratic Party as victim, 193
Did the US Believe in Russian Hackers?, 181
Digital hybrid war, preparation for, 356
DNC e-mails
  Generally, 157
  Russian media comments, 47, 175
Election meddling (see entry above)
Fake premises for Russian involvement, 190
Fancy Bear, 178, 193, 194
Gatov comments, 177
Graham comments on Moscow election interference charges, 187
Kerry-Lavrov Syria discussions, disruption of, 180
KGB, 180
Kislyak, FBI eavesdropping, 165
Klimenko dismissal of charges, 176
Legitimate targets for Russian HUMINT and SIGINT, 179
McCain comments on Moscow election interference charges, 187
Mook's Russian election meddling charges, 158
Moscow underestimation of election meddling problem, 348
Motives for Moscow's interference, 181
National Intelligence Report
  Generally, 143
  Kremlin reponsibility finding, 193
  Obama reaction, 186
  Priebus reaction, 189
NATO cyber security role, call for, 222
NATO officer victim, 179
NSA view, 190
Nuclear secrets implications, 183
Obama diplomat expulsion order, 297, 308
Obama reaction to National Intelligence Report, 186
Obama sanction retaliations, 180
Paranoia charges by Russian commentators, 174
Phishing activities by unknown persons, 194
Podesta e-mails, 180
Priebus approval of intelligence services findings, 189
Putin denial of government participation, 317
Putin personal responsibility, intelligence agencies report, 193
Snowden publication of NSA secrets, 183
Sources, speculations, 195
Tillerson confirmation hearings testimony, 198
Trump administration response predictions, 185
Trump criticism of Russia, 109
Trump post election press conference, 140
Trump suggestion of idle 400-pound hacker, 184
Trump support reactions to "Russian trail" charges, 184
Trump team members' Russian contacts, 145
US intelligence agencies report, 175, 178
WikiLeaks (see entry below)
Working group on cyber threats in political processes creation, 318

Hamburg G-20 Summit
Antiglobalization protesters, 263
Leaders' photo shoot, Trump at far right, 234
Russia-US nuclear arms discussion possibilities, 288
Syria tensions, 263
Trump administration speakers' remarks, 209
Trump as salesman, 263
Trump policies statements, 205
Trump-Putin sideline meeting
  Generally, 233, 264
  Lavrov characterization, 317
Ukraine tensions, 263

Hungary
Trump appeal to "second-rate" EU members, 233

Huntsman, Jon
Toxic Russian-American relations atmosphere impacting future talks, 359

I

immigration
Deportation of undocumented immigrants, 100
Mexico (see entry below)
Trump anti-immigrant agenda, 41
Trump "rapists" accusation, 148

international trade
  See Foreign Trade

Iran
Graham criticisms, 241
Hamas and Hezbollah support, Trump criticism, 261
Hezbollah support issue, 127
ISIS fight, Trump praise for Iranian assistance, 122
Moscow Proposes Trump Take a Different View of Iran, 239
Munich Security Conference discussions, 241
Nuclear policy agreement, Trump criticism, 275
Russian-American relations, Iran tensions affecting, 312
Saudi Arabia conflict, Russian mediation proposals, 259
Syria, Iranian forces in, 240, 265
Trump proposed abandonment of nuclear program agreement, 122, 240
Trump terrorist financing charges, 260
Trump's aggressively anti-Iranian stance, 242

Iraq war
Trump criticism, 9
Trump opposition, 57
US global policemen attempts, 76

IRS
Trump problems with, 90

ISIS and terrorism
Generally, 237 et seq.
Classified information shared during Lavrov-Trump meeting, 316
G-20 Summit, Trump-Putin sideline meeting, 264
Iranian help in war on terror, Obama vs. Trump strategies, 261
Iranian terrorist financing, Trump charges, 260
Lavrov thoughts on diplomacy challenges in the modern world, 308
Lavrov-Trump meeting, classified information shared during, 316
Nuclear weapons, growing threat of terrorist acquisition, 289
Pence call for NATO counterterrorism role, 221
Saudi Arabian Trump visit, 256
Syria, ISIS role in, 250
Syrian conflict impacting war on terrorism, 253
Trump call for Saudi Arabia support, 122
Trump plan for defeating, 110
Trump policies, US-Russian effects, 27
Trump praise for Iranian assistance in fighting, 122

Trump to halt plan to fight ISIS
state with Russia, 243
US-Russia cooperation calls, 264
US-Russia joint
counterterrorism
activities, 112

Islamophobia
Trump campaign rhetoric, 111

Israel
Classified information shared
during Lavrov-Trump
meeting, 316
Embassy relocation issue, 136
Trump presidential trip, 260
Trump support pledge, 262
Trump view on Jerusalem as
capital, 135
Trump view on two-state
principle, 262
Trump view on US military
support, 123

J

Jinping, Xi
Mar-a-Lago visit, 268, 282

K

Kaczynski, Jaroslaw
Trump handshake, 231

Kerry, John
Lavrov Syria discussions
Generally, 110
Hacking disruption of, 180

KGB
Hacking and spying
activities, 180
Putin's KGB background,
implications, 307

Khalilzad, Zalmay
Trump's foreign policy
compared to Roosevelt's, 78

Kilimnik, Konstantin
Manafort connection, 153
Ukraine settlement
proposal, 162

Kislyak, Sergei
Collusion charges
surrounding, 170
FBI eavesdropping, 165
Flynn contacts
Incomplete information to
Pence re, 166
Kislyak comments on, 170
Kushner meetings, 168
Oval Office meeting, TASS
photographer affair, 314
Russian sanctions, Flynn-
Kislyak negotiations, 325
Trump administration contacts,
collusion charges, 168
Trump staffer meetings and
collusion accusations, 315

Kissinger, Henry
Brezhnev discussion
frustrations, 358
Trump's foreign policy
compared, 79

Klimenko, German
Hacking charges, dismissal, 176

Kosachov, Konstantin
Flynn resignation
comments, 166
Russian relations view, 139

Kushner, Jared
FBI investigation of
activities, 169
Gorkov meetings, 169
Internet activities, 353
Kislyak meetings, 168
Manafort resignation
proposal, 150
Moscow back channel
Discrediting, 232
Request for, 169
Palestinian-Israeli settlement
role, 135
Veselnitskaya Trump Tower
meeting
Generally, 2, 163
Illegal donations to Clinton
campaign, information
re, 353

L

Latvia
EU proposals for NATO successor military force, 115

Lavrov, Sergei
Classified information shared during Trump meeting, 316
Diplomacy challenges in the modern world, 308
Kerry Syria discussions
  Generally, 110
  Hacking disruption of, 180
North Korea policy, 281
Oval Office meeting, TASS photographer affair, 314
Putin briefed on Trump meeting, 316
Tillerson meeting on Russian-American relations, 254
Trump talks with, 312
Willingness to work with Trump administration, 308

Le Pen, Marine
Conservative renaissance movement, 99
Russian relations, 133

Lebed, Aleksandr
Political ambitions, 1
Trump meeting, 2

Lewandowski, Corey
Firing from Trump campaign, 147
Manafort picked to replace, 148

Liberal Democratic Party of Russia
1993 Duma elections, 103

Libya
US global policemen attempts, 76

M

Macron, Emmanuel
Appeal to American people re climate agreement, 229
Bastille Day invitation to Trump, 231, 235
Climate agreement, Macron reaction to US withdrawal, 235
Isolationist Trump and globalist Macron meet, 235
Merkel tensions, Trump influences, 235

Magnitsky, Sergei
Katsyv, Magnitsky Act charges against, 163

Make America Great Again
Efficacy, 99
Putin slogans compared, 25, 49
Russian resonance, 34
Trump isolationism tensions, 117

Manafort, Paul
Appointment to Trump campaign, 147
GRU connection, 153
Indictment, 145
Lewandowski replaced by, 148
Moscow's influence charges, 156
Resignation proposal, 150
Savimbi and Yanukovich lobbying activities, 151
Ukraine activities investigated, 149
Yanukovich employment of, 147

markets
Reaction to Trump victory, 91

Mattis, James
NATO Brussels summit meeting remarks, 207
Nuclear Posture Review, 276
Russian-American relations, Trump vs. Mattis positions, 303
Strategic nuclear forces, call for modernization of, 273
Syria deescalation areas agreement, 254

McCain, John
Hostility toward Russia, 106
Moscow election interference comments, 187
Obama contest, 2008, 74

Merkel, Angela
Anti-Russia line, 198
Criticism of America's
   isolationist policy, 234
Macron tensions, Trump's
   influences, 235
NATO funding level discussion
   with Trump, 221
Need for US military power, 208
Putin relationship, 32
Russian sanctions policy, 304
Trump administration effect on
   balance of power, 224
Ukraine, US-Germany dual
   leadership, 111

Mexico
Great wall promises, 57
Trump promise to bring back
   jobs from, 301
Trump's "rotten"
   characterization, 36

Middle East
Generally, 237 et seq.
Arab NATO plan
   Arab Islamic American
      Summit discussion, 260
   Saudi Arabia and Egypt
      discussions, 258
   Trump's advocacy, 256
   Washington's attempts to
      forge, 238
Contradictions in Trump
   approach, 111
Major international interests
   colliding, 242
Moscow Proposes Trump Take a
   Different View of Iran, 239
Russian-American relations
   common ground, 303
State Department experts
   advising Trump, 262
Trump administration policy
   predictions, 110, 128
Trump ambitious plans, 310
Trump commitment to Sunni
   Arab nations, 257
Trump criticisms of Hamas and
   Hezbollah, 261
Trump presidential trip, 260
US global policemen
   attempts, 76

Miss Universe pageant
Broadcasting rights
   negotiation, 14
Emin video promoting, 18
Trump-Agalarov contacts, 1, 14

Montenegro
Russian zone of interests as
   including, 307

Mook, Robby
Russian election meddling
   charges, 158

Mueller, Robert
Election meddling
   investigation, 349
Formal charges filing, 351
Grand jury call, 164
Kushner internet activities
   investigation, 353
Manafort indictment, 145
Trump dossier investigation, 349
Trump Russian contacts
   investigation, 143

Munich Security Conference
Iran tensions aired at, 241
US signals at, 206
Western Elite's Total
   Discombobulation, 213

Murdoch, Rupert
Politics of, 40

Mussolini
Trump policy compared, 35

N

NAFTA
Fate in a Trump
   administration, 91

nationalism
See Populism and Nationalism

NATO
Brussels summit meeting
   Generally, 205
   Mattis remarks, 207
   Pence remarks, 207, 220
Chicago triad agreement,
   nuclear policy, 275
Crimea annexation, NATO
   response, 210

Cyber security role, call for, 222
EU proposals for successor
  military force, 115
Fate in a Trump
  administration, 91
Funding imbalances, 210
Germany, financial support, 210
Hacking of NATO officer's
  e-mail, 179
Nuclear policy, Chicago triad
  agreement, 275
Open door policy, 125
Pence call for counterterrorism
  role, 221
Post-Soviet states membership
  issues, 125
Russia common interests, 306
Spending benchmarks, 208
Trump abolition threats during
  campaign, 114
Trump administration funding
  demands, 207
Trump administration
  references to new
  challenges, 208
Trump call for audit, 155
Trump criticism of US security
  commitments to, 78, 154
Trump criticisms and
  contribution demands, 90,
  112
Trump fair share demand, 215
Trump Merkel funding level
  discussion, 221
Trump view as obsolete, 210,
  215, 220
Withdrawal from
  Afghanistan, 217

NBC
Kislyak, FBI eavesdropping
  report, 165

negotiation
See Trump as Negotiator

Netanyahu, Benjamin
Trump support for, 134

North Korea
Generally, 267 et seq.
  See also Nuclear Policy
China involvement, Trump's
  demand for, 278

China's assistance, US trade
  threats, 293
Chinese and Russian
  involvements compared, 282
Foreign trade, 268
ICBM capability concerns, 267,
  278
Iran deal for North Korea,
  proposal, 277
Kim Jong-un tweets, 278
Missile tests, 274, 283
Mutually Assured
  Distraction, 286
Preemptive strikes on nuclear
  sites, 278
Putin policy, 281
Russia's road map proposal, 286
Russia-North Korea foreign
  trade, 287
Russian and Chinese
  involvements compared, 282
Russian diplomatic potential
  presented by, 294
Russian policy tensions, 268
Security Council condemnation
  of weapons test, 283
Strategic patience policy, ending
  of, 268, 281
THAAD antimissile system
  deployment to South
  Korea, 286
Tillerson statement on
  negotiations, 278
Trump administration
  references to new
  challenges, 208
Trump call for China
  pressure, 268
Trump demand for China
  involvement, 278
Trump popularity and
  attractiveness of a
  short victorious war, 285
Trump reaction to missile
  tests, 267
US Chinese relations
  complications, 268
US forces deployment in South
  Korea, 279
US Japan relations impacted
  by, 293

US naval forces
  deployments, 284
US preemptive strike
  possibilities, 283
Washington's and Moscow's
  motives criticized, 268

NSA
Hacking and spying view, 190
Snowden publication of secret
  data, 183

nuclear policy
Generally, 267 et seq.
  See also START Treaties
Budapest Memorandum, 295
Chicago triad agreement, 275
Clarification of Trump strategy,
  call for, 276
Cold war deadlock, persistence
  of, 270
Comprehensive Nuclear Test
  Ban Treaty, 275
Cuban missile crisis and
  accidental use of nuclear
  weapons, 289
Doomsday Clock
  settings, 268, 274
First use policies, 290
G-20 summit, Russia-US
  nuclear arms discussion
  possibilities, 288
Georgian conflict, 270
Growing threat of terrorist
  acquisition, 289
Hacking and spying, nuclear
  secrets implications, 183
Hiatus in US-Russia arms
  negotiations, 288
Iran agreement
  Trump criticism, 275
  Trump's proposed
    abandonment, 122
  Washington withdrawal, 240
Iran deal for North Korea,
  proposal, 277
Kim Jong-un tweets, 278
Mattis call for modernization of
  strategic nuclear forces, 273
Moscow Proposes Trump Take a
  Different View of Iran, 239
Mutual assured destruction,
  persistence of, 273

New START agreement,
  implementation, 275, 276
New START treaty, 291
North Korea (see entry above
Nuclear Posture Review, 276
Obama's negative nuclear policy
  record, 272
Pentagon's extended nuclear
  deterrence strategy, 275
Plutonium agreement of 2000,
  275
Polycentric vs. bipolar nature of
  new nuclear world order, 288
Post cold war approaches to
  arms control, 271
Preemptive strikes on North
  Korea's nuclear sites, 278
Putin pledge, 277
Putin-Trump telephone
  conversation, 277
Republican Platform 2016, 273
Russia involvement
  concerns, 293
Russia diplomatic potential
  presented by North Korean
  problems, 294
Russia-US arms discussion
  possibilities, 288
Russia-US policy coordination
  calls, 269
Self-defense first use
  policies, 290
Terrorist acquisitions, growing
  threat of, 289
Trump arms race remarks, 203,
  267, 273
Trump obsession with nuclear
  weapons, 269
Trump policy, predictions, 273
Trump policy, Russian
  analyses, 267
Trump risky statements, 271
Ukrainian conflict, 270
Ukrainian nuclear club
  membership, 295
US and South Korean military
  exercises, 278
US arsenal as Trump
  administration takes over, 272
US guarantees to NATO, Trump
  criticism, 154

US historical disarmament
   policies, 273
US offshore deployments, 275

O

Obama, Barack
Anti-Israel resolutions, UN
   Security Council, 134
Democrat e-mail hack,
   response to, 158
Diplomat expulsion
   order, 297, 308
George W. Bush policies
   contrasted, 77
Hacking, Obama sanction
   retaliations, 180
Hillary Clinton presidential
   contest, 34
Intelligence agencies joint report,
   Obama reaction, 186
Iranian help in war on
   terror, Obama vs. Trump
   strategies, 261
Leadership Trump compares to
   Putin, 27
McCain contest, 2008, 74
Neocons' activities in Obama
   administration, 105
Nuclear policy, Obama's
   negative record, 272
Patient foreign policy, 34
Prosperity, Bush administration
   compared, 118
Putin relationship, 32
Putin vs., Trump analysis, 34
"Regional power" remark, 340
Russian relations
   reset, 26, 60, 125
Saudi Arabia,
   Obama vs. Trump
   policies, 256
Soft on Russia criticisms, 60
Syria, Trump distancing from
   Obama policies, 265
Trump comparison of Putin
   to, 27, 50
Trump foreign policy approach
   contrasted, 30
Ukraine, compartmentalization
   strategy, 111

UN Security Council anti-Israel
   resolutions, 134

Obamacare
Repeal movement, 100
Trump opposition, 40

Orban, Viktor
Old Europe and New
   Europe, 231

P

Page, Carter
Russian interest charges, 156

Palestine
Trump support of two-state
   solution, 123
Trump view on two-state
   principle, 262

Pence, Mike
CNN and fake news
   criticism, 139
EU common market, praise
   of, 211
Future of Russia-US relations,
   remarks, 207
Kislyak contacts,
   Flynn's incomplete
   information re, 166
NATO Brussels summit meeting
   remarks, 207, 220
NATO counterterrorism role,
   call for, 221
Orthodox foreign policy
   views of, 79
"President Pence" and
   conservative mutterings, 285
Putin criticized, 50
Russian-American relations,
   Pence vs. Trump policies, 336
Ukraine conflict remarks, 208

Peskov, Dmitry
Comments about Kislyak
   meeting with Trump, 167
Dossier preparation, 352
Sanctions, official
   response, 320, 355

Podesta, John
E-mail hacks, motive, 180

Phishing activities
victimization, 194
Ukrainian lobbying
activities, 152

Poland
Patriot missile sales, 263
Trump influences in Eastern
Europe, 231
Trump NATO criticisms,
concerns re, 112
Trump reception
expectations, 233
Ukraine, Polish views, 232

Politico Magazine
Fake news study, 49

Pompeo, Mike
CIA appointment, 129
ISIS threat, prioritizing, 129

populism and nationalism
See also Elitism; Globalism
America first as Trump
policy, 137, 138
Conservative renaissance
movement sweeping globe, 99
Demagogues and populists
distinguished, 92
Europe, strengthening populist
and nationalist forces in, 221
Framing rhetoric, 42
Isolationist Trump and globalist
Macron meet, 235
Isolationist-internationalist
tensions in US, 56, 74, 138
Merkel criticism of America's
isolationist policy, 234
Trump appeal to, 58
Trump popularity in Poland, 231
Trump transactional neo-
isolationist populism, 62
Two Faces of American
Capitalism, 117
Uglier aspects, 61
US vs. European politics, 61

Priebus, Reince
Hacking, approval of
intelligence services
findings, 189

Pushkov, Aleksei
Trump dealings with American
political elite, 140

Putin, Vladimir
Advantages realized by Trump
election, 101
Clinton strategies for
relationship with, 24
Clinton understanding
difficulties, 65
Democrat's Trump bromance
suggestion, 151
Election meddling knowledge
denial, 350
"Genius" analysis of Trump
claimed, 23
George W. Bush, Putin view, 32
Hamburg G-20 Summit (see
entry above)
KGB background,
implications, 307
Lavrov brief on Trump
meeting, 316
Leadership Trump compares to
Obama, 27
"Make America Great
Again,"Putin slogans
compared, 49
Meddling in US presidential
election, interview
responses, 168
North Korea policy, 281
Nuclear policy pledge, 277
Obama vs., Trump analysis, 34
Pence criticism of, 50
Praise of Trump, effects, 34
Russian Trump
characterization, 102
Sanctions, response options, 327
Syria cruise missile strike
reaction, 250
Syria policy, Trump support, 28
Tillerson meeting, Syria
issues, 246, 252
Traits shared with Trump, 25
Trump admiration of leadership
style, 43
Trump as doubtlessly
talented, 31
Trump as puppet charges, 129,
145, 154

Trump claims they could be pals, 24
Trump endorsement in Republican primaries, 31
Trump friend-of-Putin claim, 23
Trump "great relationship" claims, 57
Trump meeting. See Hamburg G-20 Summit (see entry above)
Trump-Obama comparison, 27, 50
Trump praise for, 26
Trump presidency, reasons for favoring, 32
Trump support as myth, 105
Trump telephone discussion of Syria deescalation areas agreement, 254
US relationship, Trump "position of strength" claim, 60
Zones of interest politics negotiations, 36

R

Reagan, Ronald
Fox News support, 41
Robert Murdoch support, 40
Trump emulating, 99

real estate sales to Russians
Florida condos, 9
Manhattan apartments, 5

Republicans
Nuclear policy campaign plank, 273
"President Pence", conservative mutterings, 285
Trump marginalization, 56
Ukrainian arms sales campaign plank, removal of, 150
Generally, 150
FBI investigation, 157

Rinehart, Billy
Phishing activities victimization, 194

Rodina party
Reaction to Trump victory, 85

Rogov, Sergei
Observations on Russian sanctions, 333

Romney, Mitt
Consideration for secretary of state, 126
US-Russian relationship view, 26

Rubio, Marco
Trump primary battles, 28, 31, 33

Russian Constitution
Exceptionalism, 44

Russian media
Coverage, North Korea vs. Syria, 281
DNC e-mails hack comments, 47, 175
Reaction to Trump victory, 83 et seq.
Sanction responses, 326
Trump support vs. Clinton, 158
US activities, tougher rhetoric concerning, 348
US election coverage, 46
US voter fraud charges, coverage, 47

Russian public opinion
Sanction responses, 325
Ukrainian elections of 2004 and 2010, 39
US election interest
  Generally, 38, 48
  Russian public debate parallels, 102

Russian sanctions
Blame assessments, 343
Cold war era sanction wars, 327
Comintern era, 343
Congress-Trump tensions over sanctions, 330
Congressional authority re lifting, 303
Congressional vs. executive control, 322
Countering America's Adversaries Through Sanctions Act
  Generally, 320

Congress-Trump tensions
over sanctions, 330
Russian response
predictions, 354
Tillerson opposition, 334
Trump signing, 328, 339
Economic impacts, 330
Election meddling (see entry
above)
Elites impacted, 332
Entities subject to new
sanctions, 354
EU policy, 304
EU responses, 331
European mandates as separate
problem, 304
Executive orders vs.
Congressional legislation, 303
Flynn-Kislyak negotiations, 325
Foreign ministry response, 322
Foreign trade implications, 323
French policy, 304
German policy, 304
Investment impacts, 331
Market advantage motive
claims, 356
Moscow options for
responding, 322
New cold war, tit-tat-sanctions
as, 342
Panic among the Russian
elite, 320
Peskov response, 320, 355
Putin response options, 327
Reciprocal expulsions, 324
Response choices, 328
Retaliatory expulsions, 323
Rogov observations, 333
Russian media responses, 326
"Russophobes in Congress"
charge, 325
START negotiations
impacts, 334
Stock market impacts, 331
Tillerson opposition to
legislation, 334
Tit-for-tat expulsions
Generally, 326
As new cold war, 342
Toxic atmosphere impacting
future talks, 358

Trump ability to act
unilaterally, 303
Trump administration ability to
relax, 321
Trump administration
lightening hints, 216
Trump administration lifting
hints, 302
Trump promise to review
Obama actions, 325
US businesses, retaliations
impacting, 325, 327
Vienna Convention on
Diplomatic Relations, 323
Visa processing impacts, 327

Russian-American relations
Generally, 297 et seq.
ABM Treaty issues affecting, 305
Big business
circumventions, 199
Bulgaria as within Russian zone
of interests, 307
Bureaucratic obstacles to Putin-
Trump accord, 129
Checks and balances of
US system impacting
negotiations, 358
Classified information shared
during Lavrov-Trump
meeting, 316
Costs of emotional
confrontations, 341
Crimea annexation, Trump
views, 37
Crimea and Donetsk Basin, 161
Czech Republic as within
Russian zone of interests, 307
Domestic crises poisoning, 345
Emotional confrontations,
costs, 341
Europe external stabilizer
role, 223
European Union, 132
Fillon, Russian sanctions
policy, 108
Forecasts of a New World
Order, 107 et seq.
Foreign Ministry coordinating
role, 347
Hacking, Obama
retaliations, 180

Honeymoon for Trump administration, 310
Iran tensions affecting, 312
Kosachov view, 139
Lavrov-Trump meeting, classified information shared during, 316
Lavtrov willing to work with Trump Administration, 308
Law-enforcement, security and military agencies cooperation problems, 126
Legitimate zone of traditional influence assertion, 306
Matryoshka doll, Russia's interests as nested as, 306
Negotiations on, 126
Middle East common ground, 303
Montenegro as within Russian zone of interests, 307
NATO issues affecting, 305
NATO-Russia common interests, 306
Negative balance, 312
New foreign policy actors in post cold war era, 339
North Korea policy tensions, 268
Obama reset, 26, 60, 125
Obama vs. Clinton strategies, 32
Oval Office meeting, TASS photographer affair, 314
Pence remarks, 207
Pence vs. Trump policies, 336
Political obstacles to Putin-Trump accord, 129
Political elites as driving, 25
Results of first meeting between Putin and Trump, 317
Sanction retaliations impacting, 324
Sea-change predicted for Trump presidency, 109
Serbia as within Russian zone of interests, 307
Snowden affair, 26, 312
Syrian military conflicts impacting, 346
Tillerson confirmation hearings testimony, 198
Tillerson-Lavrov meeting, 254
Toxic atmosphere impacting future talks, 358
Trump administration ability to relax sanctions, 321
Trump administration rush to lift, 169
Trump call for normalization, 122
Trump campaign promise, 346
Trump desire to lift, 105
Trump friend-of-Putin claim, 23
Trump intention to normalize, 105
Trump post-election press conference, 139
Trump presidency as energizing Russia, 302
Trump reset considerations, 300
Trump "superpower" characterization, 155
Trump view of Obama mistakes, 311
Trump vs. Mattis positions, 303
Ukraine, Minsk agreement implementation, 111
Ukraine tensions impacting, 347
Vietnam syndrome, 359
War on terrorism, US-Russia cooperation calls, 264
Working group on cyber threats in political processes creation, 265, 318

Ryabkov, Sergei
Russian observers in US election voting, 71
US election prediction, 67
Working group on cyber threats in political processes creation, 318

S

sanctions
See Russian Sanctions

Sanders, Bernie
Democratic National Committee negative e-mails, release of, 157
Primary battles, 29, 33
Russian media coverage, 47

Saudi Arabia
Fighting ISIS, Trump's call for Saudi support, 122
Iran conflict, Russian mediation proposals, 259
Obama vs. Trump policies, 256
Trump's presidential trip, 260
Trump's visit, 256
US arms sales to, 258

Savimbi, Jonas
Manafort lobbying activities, 151

Sechin, Igor
Russian Trump characterization, 102

Serbia
Russian zone of interests as including, 307

Sessions, Jeff
Target of Russian agent hunters, 167

Shankov, Pavel
US election prediction, 63

Shannon, Thomas
Working group on cyber threats in political processes creation, 318

Slovakia
Trump's appeal to "second-rate" EU members, 233

Snowden, Edward
Generally, 26, 312
Publication of NSA secrets, 183

Spicer, Sean
Trump's arm race policy, 274

spies
See Hacking and Spying

START Treaties
New START agreement
Generally, 291
Implementation, 275, 276
Russian sanctions, START negotiations impacts, 334
Trump as negotiator (see entry below)
USSR era, 269

Steele, Christopher
Credibility questioned, 352
Trump dossier, 349

Stein, Jill
Russian media coverage, 47

Surkov, Vladislav
Ukraine, Surkov-Volker meeting, 347

Sushentsov, Andrei
US election prediction, 63

Suslov, Dmitry
US election prediction, 62

swamp draining
Trump campaign promises, 42

Sweden
EU proposals for NATO successor military force, 116

Syria
Astana plan
  Iranian involvement, 242
  Putin-Trump meeting effects, 265
  Russian involvement, 259
  White House reaction, 255
Cruise missile strike, Putin reaction, 250
Deescalation areas agreement, 254
G-20 Summit, Trump-Putin sideline meeting, 264
Hamburg G-20 Summit, Syria tensions, 263
Hillary Clinton policy, 32
Iranian activities in, 240, 265
ISIS role in, 250
Kerry vs. Lavrov tensions re, 110
Khan Sheikhoun case, 248
Moscow-US tensions, 129, 244, 247
Putin-Trump ceasefire agreement, 265
Russian support for Assad, Trump vs. Obama views, 110
Russian-American relations, Syrian military conflicts impacting, 346
Sarin use, responsibility for, 248
Tillerson-Putin meeting on Syrian issues, 246, 252

Trump distancing from Obama
   policies, 265
Trump policy re deposing
   Assad, 122
Trump support for Putin
   policy, 28
Trump views on Assad regime
   change, 245, 248
Trump warning re US
   intervention, 110
US cruise missile strike, 245, 247
West's failures, 200

T

Taruta, Sergei
Ukraine settlement
   proposal, 162

television
Miss Universe pageant,
   broadcasting rights
   negotiation, 14
"The Apprentice," 7
Trump skills, 40

terrorism
See ISIS and Terrorism

Thatcher, Margaret
Murdoch support, 40

Tillerson, Rex
Confirmation delay, 239
Confirmation hearings
   testimony, 198
Lavrov meeting on Russian-
   American relations, 254
Motives for secretary of state
   nomination, 182
North Korea negotiations
   statement, 278
North Korea strategic patience
   policy, ending of, 268, 281
Putin meeting, Syria
   issues, 246, 252
Sanctions legislation
   opposition, 334

trade
See Foreign Trade

**Trans-Pacific and Transatlantic
Partnerships**
See also Foreign Trade,
Fate in Trump
   administration, 120
Russian opposition, 155
Trump views, 37
Trump withdrawal, 215

Troitsky, Mikhail
Reaction to Trump
   victory, 124
US election prediction, 62

Trump as negotiator
Arms control
   Generally, 125
   Trump administration
      prospects, 113
   Trump proposal, 114
Business negotiations with
   Russian companies and
   individuals, 1
"Good deal" claims, 56
Reputation, 129
Sanctions negotiations, 126
Skills claims, 32, 35, 58

Trump dossier
Fusion GPS, DNC hiring, 352
Mueller investigation, 349
Peskov activities, 352
Steele credibility questioned, 352

Trump, Donald
Business activities in
   Russia, 1 et seq.
First 200 days of foreign
   policy, 203 et seq.
Forecasts of a New World
   Order, 107 et seq.
Nuclear policy and North
   Korea, 267 et seq.
Presidential campaign
   Generally, 21 et seq.
   Forecasts and
      analyses, 55 et seq.
   Responses to victory, 81 et seq.
"Russia ties"
   controversy, 143 et seq.
Russian-American
   relations, 297 et seq.

Trump, Donald Jr.
Veselnitskaya Trump Tower meeting
　Generally, 2, 163
　Illegal donations to Clinton campaign, information re, 353

Trump, Eric
Manafort resignation proposal, 150

U

Ukraine
Arming, Trump administration policy, 111
Clinton policy, 110
Hamburg G-20 Summit, Ukraine tensions, 263
Manafort activities investigated, 149
Merkel-US dual leadership, 111
Minsk ceasefire agreements, 304
Nuclear club membership, 295
Nuclear policy and Ukrainian conflict, 270
Obama compartmentalization strategy, 111
Obama sanctions, Minsk agreement implementation, 111
Pence remarks, 208
Polish views, 232
Republican Party arms sales campaign plank, removal of, 150
FBI investigation, 157
Russian-American relations, Ukraine tensions impacting, 347
Settlement proposals, 160
Surkov-Volker meeting, 347
US global policemen attempts, 76
US Russia joint counterterrorism activities, disruption, 112
Volker appointment as US special envoy, 336

United Kingdom
Brexit
EU proposals for NATO successor military force, 115
Trump visit postponments, 236

United Nations
Trump tweets re, 134

USSR
START treaty negotiations, 269
US cold war policy, 33

V

Veselnitskaya, Natalya
Trump Tower meeting
　Generally, 2, 163
　Illegal donations to Clinton campaign, information re, 353

Vietnam syndrome
Russian-American relations, 359

Volker, Kurt
Appointment as US special envoy for Ukraine, 336
Ukraine, Surkov-Volker meeting, 347

W

Wikileaks
DNC e-mails release
　Generally, 157
　Russian media comments, 175
Hacking motives
　Generally, 178, 182
Podesta e-mails, 180

World Trade Organization
Fate in a Trump administration, 91

Y

Yanukovich, Victor
Manafort lobbying activities, 147, 151
Moscow distrust of, 156
Ukraine settlement proposal, 160, 162

Yeltsin, Boris
Clinton relationship, 335

you're fired!
Emin video stunt, 18
"The Apprentice", 7

Z

Zhirinovsky, Vladimir
Election predictions,
 Zhirinovsky effect, 97
Nationalist politics, 61

Zlobin, Nikolai
Trump post election press
 conference, 141

zones of influence
Generally, 36
Baltic states as within Russian
 zone, 307
Belarus and Bulgaria as within
 Russian zone, 307
Central Asia, the Caucasus,
 Moldova, and Ukraine as
 within Russian zone, 307
Crimea as within Russian
 zone of interest, Gingrich
 acknowledgement, 307
Czech Republic as within
 Russian zone, 307
Estonia as within Russian
 zone, Gingrich
 acknowledgment, 307
Hungary as within Russian
 zone, 307
Legitimate zone of traditional
 influence assertion, 306
Moldova, Ukraine and Belarus
 as within Russian zone, 307
Montenegro as within Russian
 zone, 307
Poland as within Russian
 zone, 206, 307
Post-Soviet states, traditional
 Russian interests, 306
Putin desire for, 36
Putin, politics negotiations, 36
Russian traditional zone, going
 outside of, 307
Serbia as within Russian
 zone, 307
Syria tensions, 256
Traditional Russian interests,
 post-Soviet states, 306
Ukraine and Belarus as within
 Russian zone of interest, 307

Publication and Author Index

Ekspert
Yevstafyev, Dmitry 117
Mirzayan, Gevorg 247

Itar-Tass Daily 17, 165, 166, 316

International Affairs
Danilov, Dmitry 215
Kozin, Vladimir 272
Oganesyan, Armen 56
Ryabkov, Sergei 66

Izvestia
Asatryan, Georgy 333
Baikova, Tatyana 308
Bruter, Vladimir 189
Kosachov, Konstantin 43
Nadein, Vladimir 2
Ontikov, Andrei 239
Sinebryukhov, Lev 7
Vedrussov, Aleksandr 36
Zabrodin, Aleksei 139

Kommersant
Aminov, Khalil 11, 15
Khvostik, Yevgeny 11
Ryabova, Anna 11
Sichkar, Olga 11
Strokan, Sergei 185

The Moscow Times
Berkman, Hannah 175
Bodner, Matthew 62, 109, 302

Cichowlas, Ola 85
Fishman, Mikhail 100, 302
Frolov, Vladimir 31, 168, 178
Golubock, D. Garrison 18
Ivanov, Igor 328
Kovalyov, Aleksei 46
Kupfer, Matthew 85
Lipman, Maria 51, 59
Medetsky, Anatoly 9
Nechepurenko, Ivan 25
Ostrovsky, Simon 5

Nezavisimaya gazeta
Arbatov, Aleksei 288
Dunayev, Vladislav 4
Mukhin, Vladimir 114
Subbotin, Igor 167, 213, 312
Zhebin, Aleksandr 277

Novaya gazeta
Latynina, Yulia 192
Martynov, Kirill 94
Mineyev, Aleksandr 209
Oreshkin, Dmitry 97
Panov, Aleksandr 149

RBC Daily
Basisini, Anzhelika 260
Kolesnikov, Andrei 230, 357
Kurilla, Ivan 342
Troitsky, Mikhail 124

Rossiiskaya Gazeta
Dunayevsky, Igor 147
Lukyanov, Fyodor 28, 137, 241, 263, 269
Makarychev, Maksim 235
Mirkin, Yakov 299
Radzikhovsky, Leonid 310, 330
Samozhnev, Aleksandr 147
Shestakov, Yevgeny 206, 254
Yegorov, Ivan 195

Russia in Global Affairs
Suslov, Dmitry 74

Slon.ru (Republic.ru)
Baier, Aleksei 33
Frolov, Vladimir 134, 154, 160, 280, 293, 317, 320, 324, 345, 351
Gatov, Vasily 40
Kashin, Oleg 102
Kuvaldin, Stanislav 227
Movchan, Andrei 89
Stanovaya, Tatyana 198, 305, 354
Suchkov, Maksim 128, 181

Sovetskaya Rossia
Frolov, Aleksandr 48

Strategic Culture Foundation Online Journal
Akulov, Andrei 224, 256, 283
Bobkin, Nikolai 122
Gorka, Alex 71
Korzun, Peter 132, 243, 245

Vedomosti
Gabuev, Alexander 339
Khlebnikov, Aleksei 264
Rozhkov, Aleksei 14
Zheleznova, Maria 38

Zavtra
Nagorny, Aleksandr 104
Prokhanov, Aleksandr 87

www.ingramcontent.com/pod-product-compliance
Lightning Source LLC
Chambersburg PA
CBHW060448170426
43199CB00011B/1136